ADVANCE PRAISE FOR

Stewardship as Teacher Leadership:

Portraits from the Profession

"The global educational landscape is shifting dramatically, and teacher leadership has never been so critical, so essential, so important. *In Stewardship as Teacher Leadership*, Carrie Rogers makes a compelling, grounded and personal case for teacher agency and teacher leadership. This book breaks new ground—it is a must read for educators everywhere."

—Dr. Alma Harris
Swansea University School of Education

"Carrie Rogers argues that teachers are moral stewards when they do the challenging work of preparing children to become citizens in our democracy. And in order to accomplish such essential work, schools need effective teacher leaders who know how to use power, build relationships and change school culture for the benefit of all of their students and communities. Educators and those who want to support schools as learning organizations need to read this book."

—Marya Levenson, Professor Emerita
and Co-Director of the Brandeis Teacher Leadership Program

"Through her argument that teacher leadership is stewardship, Carrie Rogers provides a unique illustration of teaching driven by self-accountability and trust. She broadens our thinking beyond roles and responsibilities toward those core beliefs that motivate teachers to continue their work with and for their students."

—Dr. Jill Bradley-Levine, Department of Educational Studies
Teachers College, Ball State University

I0809497

Critical Studies in Teacher Leadership series

Eleanor J. Blair, *Editor*

Teacher leadership as a term is used broadly to describe the many roles and responsibilities of good teachers working in 21st-century schools. Teacher leaders, acting in both formal and informal roles, are instrumental in doing at least three things: facilitating and sustaining teacher voice; building leadership capacity in schools and communities; and addressing teaching and learning issues and concerns with best practices evidence and research. Research on the intersection of teacher leadership, school culture, and school improvement is extremely limited, particularly as it pertains to school reform efforts that occur in diverse geographical and social contexts. Important factors that affect the work of teacher leaders include, but are not limited to, issues such as race; urban and rural education; socio-economics; ethnicity; politics; and ideological differences. Critical efforts to link teacher leadership with increased power and agency in teachers' work are limited. Teacher leadership that is both transformative and critical serves the purpose of redefining teachers' work to include new roles and responsibilities, such as advocacy leadership and a commitment to the principles of social justice as key components of teachers' work. As such, a better understanding of teacher leadership and the way that it functions in schools and communities has the potential to nurture new conceptualizations of the teaching profession, but also on the work of teachers advocating for both academic and social reform in public spaces for teaching and learning.

Books in the Series

A Cross-Cultural Consideration of Teacher Leaders' Narratives of Power, Agency and School Culture: England, Jamaica and the United States
by Ellie J. Blair, Carmel Roofe, and Susan Timmons (2019)

Bridges Not *Blockades: Transcending University Politics*
by Gayle Maddox and Martha Diede (2020)

Stewardship as Teacher Leadership: Portraits from the Profession
by Carrie Rogers (2020)

Interested authors and collection editors are invited to contact:

Eleanor Blair
ejblair@email.wcu.edu.

Stewardship as Teacher Leadership

Myers Education Press

Published by Myers Education Press, LLC
P.O. Box 424 Gorham, ME 04038

Myers Education Press is an academic publisher specializing in books, e-books, and digital content in the field of education. All of our books are subjected to a rigorous peer review process and produced in compliance with the standards of the Council on Library and Information Resources.

Library of Congress Cataloging-in-Publication Data available from Library of Congress.

13-digit ISBN 978-1-9755-0154-9 (paperback)
13-digit ISBN 978-1-9755-0153-2 (hard cover)
13-digit ISBN 978-1-9755-0155-6 (library networkable e-edition)
13-digit ISBN 978-1-9755-0156-3 (consumer e-edition)

Printed in the United States of America.

All first editions printed on acid-free paper that meets the American National Standards Institute Z39-48 standard.

Cover design by Teresa Lagrange

Stewardship as Teacher Leadership

Portraits From the Profession

By Carrie Rogers

Myers Education Press

GORHAM, MAINE

DEDICATIONS

This work is dedicated to all the teachers
who were willing to speak to me about their work and ideas
on teacher leadership and who allowed me into their classrooms and lives.
Even though the names have been changed and the stories have been
condensed, the voices of those teachers are on every page. You know
who you are. I wrote this for you and the teachers yet to come.

To Misty Sato, my brilliant mentor and friend,
who is a true steward of teaching and learning.

To Mike, for everything.

CONTENTS

FOREWORD

MISTILINA SATO
Christchurch, New Zealand

WHEN CARRIE WROTE TO me in 2018 and asked to talk about her book idea, I was excited to hear about her new project. Carrie and I met when she was pursuing her PhD at the University of Minnesota and I was beginning my career as an assistant professor. We shared many interests, primarily based in our shared experience as teachers. We both had a desire to describe, interpret, and theorize teachers' work in a way that felt authentic to our own experiences as teachers and that offered theoretical concepts that honor the status of teachers' knowledge and wisdom. We found our theoretical roots in the ideas of practical reasoning—the theoretical perspective that the world of the practical has an epistemological character that is as important as abstract social theory.

The epistemological value of practical reasoning was instilled in me through my doctoral supervisor at Stanford University. Emeritus Professor J Myron Atkin, affectionately called Mike by everyone who knows him, always said, and I paraphrase here, his deepest theoretical interest lies in the realm of understanding the practical. He would always pause after saying this, as if waiting for the students or the group of scholars around the table to react to this sentence. I heard him say this dozens of times. I didn't grasp the irony in his statement until a few years into my PhD studies with him. And today, I smile and laugh lightly at the irony in his statement. He was making a tongue-in-cheek reference to how the scholarly study of practical work, everyday decision-making, and the moral drive and impact embedded in teacher-student relationships does not usually hold status in universities as being "theoretical." Educational scholarship often turns to social and literary theory to find abstract constructs for describing social interactions in teaching relationships. The world of the practical—the everydayness of making choices, learning through experience, and engaging in the uncertainties of new situations—is not typically what we imagine in academic circles when theoretical interests are being discussed. Rarely do educational scholars seek to describe and interpret teaching practice and interactions as theoretical in its own right.

In this book, Carrie has picked up on the practical work of teachers through the lens of leadership. Leadership is a pervasive concept—and set of practices—in education. As such, it is a deeply studied and theorized idea for organizations and for individuals in leadership roles. For teachers, leadership is often a taken-for-granted idea. Carrie has taken on the complex task of illustrating how we can understand the daily decisions of teachers through the concept of stewardship and helps us understand these daily actions as leadership. She has a bold agenda, stating, "My hope in writing this book is to center the work of teachers and schools within the philosophy of stewardship and to recognize acts of stewardship as leadership." She has lived up to this hope and given us a new way to imagine, interpret, and illuminate the work of teachers.

The idea of stewardship as it pertains to teachers' work has intermittently haunted me for two decades. When I wrote my dissertation about teacher leadership back in 2002, I put forward the theory of *practical leadership* as a way to understand the everyday leadership enactment that teachers describe in their interviews with me. The undercurrent of the conversations in these interviews suggests something about teachers' choices that serves a greater purpose than simply moving through the day-to-day complexity of teaching. There is a professional and societal collective notion that teachers convey in their stories. I float the idea of stewardship in the conclusion of my dissertation as a way to understand and name what teachers are doing to influence and lead in their schools, districts, and communities.

In a later essay that Carrie and I wrote together, we revisit the idea of stewardship as a way to describe leadership through the lens of practical leadership while trying to also imagine leadership as a re-culturing activity in schools. We briefly explore the concept of stewardship as leadership to try to capture the ways that teachers take care of not only the students who are in their direct care, but also the way that they look out toward a horizon of hope for the community and the profession that guides their choices and gives them purpose.

In this book, Carrie has taken the concept of teacher leadership as stewardship to the next level of theorizing. She does this while continuing to honor teachers' everyday work, maintaining the authenticity of teachers' lives while offering a conceptual framing of stewardship that gives greater clarity to the underlying meaning of the idea. She has clearly articulated and illustrated the four tenets for her theory of stewardship: 1) knowledge, judgement, and deliberation; 2) a vision and support of education as public good; 3) a student-first commitment; and 4) an understanding of the politics of schooling. Through these tenets, she is able to describe features of leadership that are contextual, decisive, moral, collective, client-oriented, and imbued with power dynamics. She brings the tenets to life through the portraits of Owen, Carly, Abigail, and Ben as well as the other snapshots of teachers' work embedded throughout the book.

I am so very glad that Carrie contacted me in 2018 with her idea to write this book. I had just moved to Christchurch, New Zealand to take on a new position at the University of Canterbury and having a familiar colleague with a familiar idea to talk about was very comforting. Now, in 2020, to be able to read the book in its finished form is more than comforting; it is enlightening. Teachers who read this book will see themselves in the portraits and snapshots of the teachers Carrie portrays so elegantly and humanely. They will understand their contributions as teachers not as service and not as saintly work. This book has created a new language for pre-service and in-service teachers to talk about, share, and own their leadership work. By making the case for stewardship, Carrie is giving teachers a way to frame, name, and claim leadership as part of their professional passion and everyday work.

INTRODUCTION

IN THIS BOOK, I have the privilege to share the voices and experiences of teachers that demonstrate how their everyday actions reflect what they believe is morally just and right for their students, colleagues, and schools. These are teachers who care passionately and deeply about the success of children within public schools. They believe intensely in public schools as a public or common good. They also believe that schools are places where teachers can help kids become good, kind, and knowledgeable people. This is the moral purpose of schools. They also care profoundly about the world in which the kids are living. These teachers believe that schools can help mitigate the trauma of life while teaching skills that will help them become the adults they want to be. These teachers believe in helping students see beyond their current horizon. These teachers demonstrate stewardship in and of the profession of teaching. Stewardship is an old but powerful idea. As Sato and Rogers (2017) write,

> The role and status of the steward harkens to a time of kings leaving their lands in the capable hands of a trusted steward—someone with the talents to care for the kingdom's economic well-being and the wisdom to lead the people in the absence of the ruler. From this history, standard definitions of stewardship emphasize the responsible management and care of something entrusted to one in the absence of the owner. (p. 37)

This book argues that teachers function as stewards, and schools are where that stewardship occurs. Parents and the public leave their children in the care of teachers who are entrusted to help prepare children for the world as it is and the future to come. This is a heavy responsibility, yet true stewardship is also a democratizing force in which every adult within an organization is responsible to its core values and mission. The public has entrusted public schools and teachers to have the knowledge and wisdom to care for the future. While teachers are the primary face of schools, there are many adults working within the educational system today. In this book, however, teacher voices are featured. They are not perfect teachers, but they are thoughtful and reflective teachers who put children's futures at the forefront of their decision making. They are new teachers and veteran teachers who have chosen the stance that teaching and schooling is a public good and that their work requires them to be stewards of the children in their care as well as their colleagues and communities in which they work and sometimes live. In these stories, the moral work of stewardship is not only present in the means by which the teachers act "courageously, caring for others, using just practices—but is simultaneously the ends towards which the teacher is seeking to influence others" (Sato, Hyler, & Monte-Sano, 2014, p. 5). Influence is inextricably connected to notions of leadership, but stewardship attempts to influence the culture and profession of teaching through less hierarchal means.

I began teaching elementary school at the turn of the 21st century. I walked into a second-grade classroom in December, was handed math and reading teacher manuals, and was left alone with 22 second graders. I was overwhelmed and unprepared for the attitudes and issues these children brought to me. I was their fourth teacher since September and their first statement was, "You're not coming back, are you?" In the short few weeks before the holiday break, I struggled. I struggled to learn their names, create routines, and set expectations. These children had experienced trauma in a place that was supposed to be safe. Schools and classrooms are often thought to be a safe and welcoming place where routines and order help students learn and grow. The number of teachers that had rotated through the classroom created uncertainty and was certainly unconducive to learning. Throughout the holiday break, I read, planned, and thought about the question, What do these children need when we come back together? They needed to build trust and create community with me and each other. So, that's what we did. At that time, students and teachers were just beginning to be measured by test scores, so the pressure on me and my second graders to perform academically was less than it is today. We had morning meetings, played games, created rules together, and read books about kindness. In six months, we cobbled together a community, and the children began to trust the adults within the school again. It was hard. I will not lie; it was a daily struggle. It wasn't perfect, but it was better. My responsibility to the children was to take care of them, protect them but also help them see the possibilities of their world through reading, talking, and doing.

Since the start of the 21st century, and my life as an educator, I have held true to that idea: adults are responsible for and to the children. Hannah Arendt, a philosopher who fled Nazi Germany, writes about how adults have a special responsibility to children when it comes to preparing them for the world into which they are born. Arendt writes about schools during integration and how the nightly televised pictures of black youths being jeered at or spat upon as they tried to attend school left an impression on her. Arendt is conflicted about the role of public schooling and feels there is a need to protect children from a "world they did not make" (Arendt, 1968, p. 189). Arendt's idea is that children should be protected from politics and political acts or other controversial issues happening in society. Addressing controversial, or larger social and political, issues within the classroom is controversial. Zimmerman and Robertson (2018) review the various policies and public opinion polls on what kinds of issues have been controversial since the 1950s and conclude that, while many teachers are discussing social and political issues, many others are not. Children and youth usually have a very good sense of justice and empathy and can have incredible insights into how people are treated within the classroom, school, and society. Often, this sense of justice and empathy is dulled along the way to adulthood if it is not fully developed in youth through critical discussion and debate. Increasingly, divided public opinions shared instantly through social media challenge teachers' supposed neutrality within the classroom and remind us that teachers have been given a special trust: to help children navigate the world in which they live and to ignite the possibilities of a world in which they can grow into.

This book will not only link stewardship to the concept of teacher leadership, but also argue that stewardship is a more inclusive term for the work of teachers and schools in the 21st century. This book is not an argument against role-based forms of teacher leadership, such as instructional coaches or mentors. In schools, differentiated roles serve purposes within the flat structure of the teaching profession in the United States. This book will argue that a different language for describing teacher leadership can help us actually see what teachers are doing and provide a sense of increased professionalism at a time when teachers are feeling restricted in how much power they really have to make professional decisions. To paraphrase Mistilina Sato's (2005) work that has led to me conceptualize stewardship as teacher leadership, actions, rather than roles, lay at the center of the stewardship as teacher leadership framework.

Stewardship as teacher leadership, or just renaming teachers' work as stewardship, can help teachers both recognize and further refine their work as professionals and lessen some of the resistance from teachers who so adamantly deny their own potential to influence and create change because of the historical and hierarchical images that the word "leader" conjures. Teachers who take a steward leadership stance toward their everyday work may not have a designated position of leadership. They can, however, have a sense that their ideas are important, that they have expertise that can be shared with others, and that they have a responsibility to participate in shaping the work and culture of the school.

Stewardship has been an essential element of some forms of leadership, but it is usually not viewed as leadership in and of itself. Leadership theorists such as Sergiovanni (1992) and Greenleaf (2002) view stewardship as a component of servant leadership (this idea will be explored more in Chapter Two). Peter Block (2013) is the first theorist to provide a model of stewardship as leadership. For Block, stewardship is a more politically oriented way of rearranging how organizations are run. Stewardship requires an examination of power, purpose, wealth, and how those resources are allocated within the organization. Stewardship requires trust that those doing the work will be guided by the organizational moral mission, rather than needing to be coerced and controlled through hierarchal structures to do good work.

For many teachers, enacting stewardship is how they influence and change cultures of schools. Influence and change are hallmarks of leadership, and the stories within this book will advocate, particularly for new teachers, that being and becoming a steward of teaching and learning is leadership. This text is written foremost for teacher candidates and beginning teachers. Teacher leadership is a phrase that is used in teacher preparation, in teaching standards, and in many teacher evaluation processes. For example, North Carolina has teacher leadership as one of the state standards of professional teaching. The state requires classroom teachers to be evaluated on this teacher leadership standard that is comprised of leading in the classroom and school and being an advocate for schools and students (North Carolina Department of Public Instruction, 2018). A coalition of states also created the Model Teacher Leader Standards (2011) "to codify, promote and support teacher leadership as a vehicle to transform schools for the needs of the 21st century" (p. 8). These standards have seven domains ranging from using data to inform instruction to working with parents. It is vital that new teachers understand the various ways teacher leadership is conceptualized (thought about) and enacted (actually done) in research and schools. Chapters Two and Three delve into some important philosophical ideas about leadership that will help the new teacher think about their own ideas of leadership in general and teacher leadership specifically. This book will answer the question of why thinking about teacher leadership is important to new teachers, schools, and students but also why teacher leadership is sometimes problematic for many, especially new teachers. This tension will be explored further in Chapter Three.

This book presents the framework of stewardship as teacher leadership. This framework draws heavily from Sato and Rogers' 2017 work examining practical leadership, as well as a deep reading of Block's theory of stewardship and the research on collective teacher leadership. Practical leadership, collective teacher leadership and stewardship have great similarities, but the language of stewardship explicitly places trust and self-accountability at the center of teachers' work. The argument that stewardship *is* teacher leadership rests on these four tenets:

Tenet One: Stewardship requires knowledge, judgement, and deliberation. Stewards reflect upon and act within a particular context and culture in which one works. The knowledge of how trust, collaboration, and relationship building occur within the school is key. Stewardship requires deliberation and judgement that is practical and situated. Experience and reflective action help teachers develop and refine their abilities to judge and act based on the context. Sato and Rogers (2017) write:

> Deliberation is a process of weighing alternatives and reaching decisions about actions that are both strategic and also reasoned through for what is right for the situation. For a decision to be right does not necessarily mean that it is true or accurate or factual. A decision is right if it is reasonable in light of virtues such as being a just decision, a fair decision, or a fitting decision. (p. 3)

Tenet Two: Stewardship requires a vision and support of education as public good. Stewards are advocates for the enhancement of the profession and support for schools. In acts of stewardship, teachers are trusted to use their professional knowledge in creating rigorous experiences for the children in their care that attend to the notion of public schooling as a cornerstone of democracy and preparing children to take their role within a pluralistic society. Stewards also maintain and advance professional standards through sharing practices and creating or participating in networks that support the work of public schools.

Tenet Three: Stewardship requires a student-first commitment. Stewards make decisions that are best for students. These decisions are made according to the deliberative ideas outlined in Tenet One. Stewards are trusted to make school-wide decisions based upon the best interests of the students and communities within which they work.

Tenet Four: Stewardship requires an understanding of the politics of schooling. Stewards are able to recognize the inherent inequities in education. Stewards work towards helping students and other teachers recognize these political issues that shape experience in public schools. Stewards understand and are unafraid of the power they have within systems and use their power to create more just and equitable spaces for all children in public schools.

Steward leadership is also purposeful. Here, purpose is most linked to the idea of intention. Purpose is not only what drives one toward becoming a steward, but also why one is driven toward action in particular moments or situations. Questions of purpose can be answered with a traditional idea such as a "vision" for teaching and learning, but purposes do not always have to look outward to the future. Purpose can also stem from a deeply held value or moral that requires a response to a current need. Stewardship as leadership may not be located in a single event or connected to a particular role. Stewardship is bound up in the everyday actions and interactions of teachers. Stewardship is a way of being within a particular context. The snapshots and portraits in this book will help illustrate how stewardship can be seen in the everyday work and decision-making of teachers.

Thomas Sergiovanni (1996) notes that schools are unique places as they serve as "transitional places for children" and teachers function *in loco parentis*. He writes, "Teachers and administrators are brought together into a collective practice that resembles a shared stewardship" (p. xii). Schools are unique places and the role of teachers and administrators has always been powerful, but society at large has always questioned the role that this transitional place should fill. The attempt to create homogenous students in the early years of compulsory schooling tried to erase the private, cultural, and language traditions of Indigenous and immigrant students through the process of Americanization. Now, well into the 21st century, schooling is more likely to be viewed as part of creating social cohesion and promoting a pluralistic society through a diversity of ideas and people in classrooms. Schools and teachers, while still trying to provide common experiences, are somewhat more sensitive to preserving private traditions of culture and language. This is why stewardship as teacher leadership is important. Being a steward of teaching and learning requires trustworthiness, talent, and wisdom to lead and take care of children entrusted to public schools. Being and becoming a steward leader within a school also requires the essential disposition of hope. To return to the philosopher Hannah Arendt, we learn that technical knowledge can only get us so far in improving our schools, and something more human is required:

> Arendt's biggest lessons about hope are that we all gain most when we are honest about the challenges we face and open to the unexpectedness of life. What can give us hope, then, are the concrete relationships with our students, our willingness to be there for them and to not be defined by the accountability culture that now saturates schools. (Edgoose, 2010, p. 403)

In interactions with students, parents, and colleagues, teachers encounter many dilemmas that require moral judgement and discernment. When decisions are made within the dilemmas of teaching, the teacher is using their power to influence outcomes. In Chapters Two and Three, power and influence as components of leadership will be explored within the contexts of teachers' work and culture. When it comes to the role that public schools and teachers play within society, we see power and influence often. In this book, we will explore what stewardship as teacher leadership can look like within differing contexts. Through the snapshots and portraits shared in this book, we will see how teachers harness and use their abilities of judgment and power to benefit students and to steward students and schools in the moment and for the future.

My hope in writing this book is to center the work of teachers and schools within the philosophy of stewardship and to recognize acts of stewardship as leadership. This lens may help keep all those involved in education and schooling morally grounded and clearly focused on the task at hand: preparing children for the world as it is and the world as it can be.

A note on the snapshots and portraits of teachers and ways to use this book

Time is required to really know and understand a school culture and a teacher's way of being in the school and classroom. In this book, there are two ways I share the work of teachers in their school: snapshots and portraits. Snapshots are brief glimpses into teachers' thinking about school culture, student success, and the value of teacher leadership to novice teachers. The portraits are longer and required me to spend more time within the schools with the teacher. These snapshots and portraits are interspersed among and between the chapters to give the reader the voice of real teachers working in classrooms and how those voices are voices of stewards. Some of the voices are clearly speaking within a view of schools as hierarchal, patriarchal, and bureaucratic. Other voices seem to transcend the bureaucratic trappings of public schools. Some of the voices seen to find solace in the familiar nature of public schools. Teacher leadership, as naturally hierarchal, is viewed very similarly across these stories, and teacher leadership is defined differently within these teachers' contexts, so teacher leadership is a hard concept to convey or capture because of the contextual nature. Stewardship, on the other hand, can transcend contexts and is a more useful way of talking about the work and ways of being a teacher.

In interpreting these portraits, there are lots of details that can be used for professional conversations within teacher education classrooms or professional learning communities. These portraits, while possibly entertaining, are not meant to simply be examples of types of teachers and their experiences. They should be interrogated. There are four questions following each portrait, but the actual number of questions to be asked of these portraits are numerous. It is my hope that those interacting and intellectually engaging with these teacher portraits will ask more questions of these teachers and hypothesize some answers based on the information given.

The chapters in this book were designed to be flexible in use. The chapters can be read chronologically or independently. Although each portrait has a set of questions associated with it that reflect upon the major themes of the book, the portraits are rich, thick descriptions of teachers work and can be read through many different lenses. The snapshots are situated within chapters for illustrative purposes. The concluding chapter will provide a discussion across these snapshots and portraits. This book was written with pre-service teachers and new teachers in mind. Still, my hope is that the teacher portraits and the ideas of stewardship will resonate across all levels of teaching.

References

Arendt, H. (1968). The crisis in education. In *Between past and future: Six exercises in political thought.* (pp. 173–196). Cleveland and New York: The World Publishing Company.

Block, P. (2013). *Stewardship: Choosing service over self-interest.* (2nd ed.) San Francisco, CA: Berrett-Koehler.

Edgoose, J. (2010). Hope in the unexpected: How can teachers still make a difference in the world? *Teachers College Record, 112*(2), 386–406.

Greenleaf, R. F. (2002). *Servant leadership: A journey into the nature of legitimate power and greatness.* (25th anniversary ed.). Mahwah, NJ: Paulist Press.

North Carolina Department of Public Instruction (2018). North Carolina Teacher Evaluation Process. Retrieved from https://sites.google.com/dpi.nc.gov/ncees-information-and-resource/teachers?authuser=0

Sato, M. (2005). Practical leadership: Conceptualizing the everyday leadership work of teachers. *The New Educator, 1*(1), 55–71.

Sato, M., Hyler, M. E., & Monte-Sano, C. B. (2014). Learning to lead with purpose: National Board Certification and teacher leadership development. *International Journal of Teacher Leadership, 5*(1), 1–23.

Sato, M., & Rogers, C. (2017). Practical leadership: How teachers enact leadership to re-culture their schools. In C. Rogers; K. Lomotey, & A. Hilton (Eds.), *Innovative approaches to educational leadership: Selected cases* (27–31). New York, NY: Peter Lang Publishing.

Sergiovanni, T. J. (1996). *Leadership for the schoolhouse: How is it different? Why is it important?* San Francisco: Jossey-Bass Publishers.

Teacher Leadership Exploratory Consortium (2011). Teacher Leader Model Standards. Retrieved from http://www.nea.org/assets/docs/TeacherLeaderModelStandards2011.pdf

Zimmerman, & Robertson (2018). The controversy over controversial issues. *Phi Delta Kappan, 99*(4), 8–14.

PORTRAIT OF OWEN

Owen's voice booms across the classroom, and if you didn't know him, you would think he was angry. Owen has a deep voice with a rumbling laugh that ripples across the room. When he is laughing, you can't help but laugh. When he is crying, you can't help but cry. Owen teaches English Language Arts and Social Studies to 68 fifth-grade students in three blocks. He has homeroom first thing in the morning and then for a short time again at the end of the day.

A typical day of instruction follows a familiar pattern. The students have a "bell ringer" activity posted on the white board. After settling in, Owen announces where they are going with their common reading book and then asks them to get ready for Quizlet. This pre-reading activity has student teams review book-based vocabulary in an online quiz. They get very excited and work hard on congratulating each other and using positive language when challenged by a team member's behavior. Working together is not always easy, and when Owen hears inappropriate language, he stops the quiz and reminds the class of the expectations.

By December, the class has fallen into a familiar pattern. By now, students listen for the vocabulary as Owen reads aloud from the section of the text. Students raise their hands when they have heard a vocabulary word. Owen often stops to ask questions or explains intricacies of the plot. He is reading The Phantom Tollbooth, *which is part of the Wit and Wisdom Curriculum the county adopted this academic year. Owen likes the literature choices but feels it is hard to stay current with the pacing expectations because he likes to stop to talk with the kids about what they are reading. Every other day, he teaches social studies to the same groups of students. His teaching of social studies follows a similar pattern: a bell ringer, a Quizlet, and then a common reading and discussion.*

The students spend a lot of time on their Chrome Books. They carry them from each subject and often begin and end class on the computer. He often reads the local newspaper with them for the common reading and discussion. Overall, student gender numbers are about equal. His second group of fifth graders, however, sits in less-segregated gender groups because there are fewer boys in this section. Also, the fifth grade is quite diverse for this rural section of the state. Many of these second-generation children come from Russian, Ukrainian, Mexican, and Thai families. Many of the Mexican families arrived only recently to work in the local chicken factory. Owen has learned that many families who speak Spanish can't read Spanish. He reports, "They come from countries where only the rich get an education."

"Ya'll want to do some singing?" Owen likes to sing with his class, whether it seems appropriate or not. The students appear to love this. At one school day's end, he sings "Ice Ice Baby" to the students as they pack up. Earlier in the day, they sing a more relevant song about the 13 colonies. Sometimes they sing as a "brain break" and often it gets loud. Owen's classroom is not quiet, but he calms it by using call and response techniques the kids love. They watch him and are very attuned to his feelings. Owen's view of student success is holistic. He says, "I want them to be good people, be connected to the community, honest and hardworking." He continues, "If you know your kids the data shouldn't surprise you. By the time they get to fifth grade they have internalized school failure. They need love. School isn't a priority for most." He acknowledges the trauma that these kids experience living in an impoverished rural town, so he is actively seeking community connections. Owen says, "They're scared of their community. There are a lot of bad things happening, but it's like, 'Well, you can change it.' And right now, I have several students doing some big things in the community."

As with most schools across the United States, there is a heavy emphasis on reading and math. Owen recognizes the irony in district initiatives of Growth Mindset and the emphasis on single, end-of-year test scores. He says his instruction is driven by love. He has ability-grouped his students based on his knowledge of them as people and found those groups equate to the predicted levels from prior test scores. But yes, test scores do matter to him.

Owen relates a story that demonstrates the school culture: After a field trip Owen was called into the principal's office. He was apprehensive. Owen tells the story, "I started sweating. I knew all the kids got picked up, so what did the principal want? I sat in the office and the principal started talking, 'Owen, your pre-end-of-year tests are bad, only 17% passed.' My stomach just dropped. I know I got nine students who read better than me! Then the principal said, 'April Fool's! 78% passed!' I fell into the chair and starting crying. That's my kids; that ain't my teaching." But his colleagues and administrators would give him more credit than he allows himself. They perceive him as a role model for relationship building within the school and the district. Mentor and administrator observations of his teaching consistently focus on the classroom community and relationships. These evaluators often say to Owen of his students, "They'll do anything for you."

Owen is somewhat dismissive of state regulations and expresses frustration with testing. He has a good support network that he draws upon when faced with instructional conundrums. He often consults his father, a retired school administrator about issues he faces. He also has a district mentor. Another colleague is a former regional teacher of the year. Professionally, he struggles with reading instruction expectations and how the district expects him to use data to create instruction. He sees a bigger picture behind the data. He relates his understanding of data to his time as a baseball player and a fan. "It's numbers, and it can be manipulated any way you want to show it. I played baseball. For example, this guy's batting 375 with runners in scoring position. Yeah, but does that matter when he's facing this pitcher? Every situation is unique. That's an average for it, sure, but just like every student is unique, each situation or interaction is unique. Last year, when they took the test, one student's dog got run over by the bus when it came to pick him up that day. The kid was emotionally broken down that day and it's like, well, sorry your dog died. You still got to take this test." That student scored a three, which is passing, but two levels below previous scores and these scores reflect directly on the teacher. Owen feels that all the things that happen to kids on test days are variables to be considered. What if "the parents had a fight that morning, or they didn't have breakfast, or the kid stayed up too late playing video games. They can't put that in the data."

Owen teaches in one of the farthest western counties of North Carolina. He is from here, really of this place. There is a unique quality to being a teacher in a small rural county. He is known and knows many of his students' families. At about six feet five inches, Owen is a giant teddy bear of a man. He towers above everybody. His father, Coach, is even taller than his son and is something of a county legend as a football coach and school administrator. Owen didn't immediately follow his father's footsteps into public education. Owen first went to college to play baseball, but he flunked out. When his son started Head Start, he noticed only two men worked at his school and "one was the janitor." He saw need and space he felt he could fill. He believed he had knowledge to pass on and that maybe an elementary education degree would help him become a better father. But, he laughs, "It didn't."

Owen is an "older" beginning teacher. He had spent much of his early working years in surveying, a lucrative and in-demand job in the region. He married and had a child. Being a father changed his life. By July 2011, Owen, single and unemployed, faced foreclosure on his house. While painting and staining a log cabin, he reflected, "There's got to be something better" to provide for his three-year-old son. He decided to go back to college but was unsure of what to study.

Owen knew that to take care of his son, he needed a good job. In his part of the state, working within a school system is one of the better jobs available. He went back to the local university, part time, to complete a degree in elementary education. For a single father, getting a teaching degree was no easy process. Initially, he drove 150 miles roundtrip to attend classes. When his son reached school age, Owen moved closer to the university, enrolled his son in school, and took a local job tending bar. The move took him farther away from his support system of family and friends. He says he almost didn't make it, but a few positives, a good faculty mentor during student teaching, experiences with children that "would melt my heart," and support from his peer cohort helped him to stay in the profession.

He returned to his home county. Initially, his mindset was, "They'll give me any job I care to have when I go back home." As the son of a well-respected administrator, he could have used his connections to obtain a favored job or even to fast-track into leadership positions within the county system. But it has not worked out that way.

Instead, he knew, above all, he wanted to be in the classroom. So, he first accepted a job teaching third grade at a very small rural school. For many years, talk in the county was about school consolidation, but nothing ever seemed to happen. Owen remembers, "When I got hired, my dad was the only one to tell me, 'Boy, it ain't going to be around long.'" Owen's experience of the elementary school eventual closing and the county's continued moves towards consolidation certainly impacted him as a teacher, but also as a parent and longtime community member. These lenses give him an almost 360-degree view of the process of school closings and their impact on everyone.

Owen considers the school: "It was small. It was centrally located in the middle of the county. It serviced the most impoverished community in our county but there's just been so many success stories coming out of it. They had a grant to create an outdoor education center there. I used it every day. There was a walking trail along the creek, and a little outdoor amphitheater and everything. I definitely didn't want it to go, because that's where I wanted to be. I wanted those small class sizes, to work with the most challenged students, the low socioeconomic status, and I don't know, it just felt like home. It felt like a big family, it didn't feel like a school. And they worked hard; they did good. My scores were great. I mean, putting all that information together, and it's like you have this theory on that, the classroom size, and then you've got this theory about poverty and education and seeing how it all works."

Rumors about consolidation had been circulating all year and right before testing, the superintendent came in and brought the staff together to announce the school's closing. Owen relates, "It got real quiet. People started crying, I started crying. Only one person said something." Sadness soon gave way to other stages of grief and anger. Owen was upset because it would be his son's fourth school in three years. That night, social media erupted with rallying cries: "We still got a chance, let's go before the school board!" At the next, and last, officially scheduled school board meeting, the county's teacher of the year was announced. That teacher was from Owen's school. Then the school board announced the closing. And then, Owen says, "It became a fiasco."

Apparently, even within small communities without teacher unions, there is a process for the closing of schools which the school board must follow, but the school board did not hold an open public meeting. That was a violation. So, a week later, the board was mandated to hold a public meeting and even the local news came to cover it. Owen says, "I thought it would be standing room only. There were over 100 people, but the church was big, so it made it seem empty." Owen chose not to speak publicly at the meeting. In fact, the entire staff decided not to speak because they wanted parents and the other public members to present their own arguments. Owen says, "I wanted to say something, but I would've been crying. I didn't think I'd really make them any better. I felt like it was already done, there was nothing I could have said that would have made it go any other way."

Owen says, "You still had hope during that last month of school, because we had no idea. We had to wait until the next school board meeting. And just tried to keep doing things as if it wasn't going to happen, or that hadn't happened, and the kids are still asking all kinds of questions and everything. And it's like, 'I don't know. I don't know what to tell you. I don't know what's going to happen. I don't know.' That's the hardest thing to tell a kid."

The consolidation process moved Owen from anger through sadness, and finally, to acceptance. Not once did he lay blame for the school closing at any one person's feet. The consolidation has forced him to ask himself and others to pay attention to who you vote for, recognizing that school funding is political. Again, this year there is talk of consolidation in the county. As a parent, he sees the value in consolidating limited resources for kids at one school, but also, as both parent and teacher, he appreciates the fact that a small school may offer quality instruction and dedicated teachers. Owen acknowledges the county is "doing the best they can" with what they have and that this county is "done taxed out." Most of the dwindling money from the state goes to maintaining structures.

Since beginning at this second school, Owen feels he has been placed where administrators feel he is most needed. He did get to choose whether he would teach fifth or sixth grade. Initially, he did not feel entirely confident, but he always knew he could do it. Consequently, he has learned he has a place in the elementary classroom. The students' liveliness feeds him and gives him energy. He believes his interactions with them contribute to his growth. Like many teachers, he has taken a second job and also works in the summer. He feels that money is always an issue, but he says, "The good outweighs the bad."

Owen feels he is a better person since returning to and graduating from college with his teaching degree. In teacher education courses, he had experience with third, fourth, and fifth grades. He substitute-taught in local schools, gaining experience in kindergarten through 12th grade. He says, "By the time I graduated, I had been involved with thousands of students in the area. I just fed off their energy. I felt that it was helping me grow into this superhuman being. It was just a very powerful feeling. I was learning a lot, too. I was placed with some great teachers in some great schools with some good administrators." He says about teaching, "It's opened my eyes to a lot of things that I never would've cared to pay any attention to. I'd have been one of those people, 'Oh, get a job,' or, 'Learn the language.' It has opened my eyes. I have gained empathy."

An anecdote demonstrates his empathy: On the way to lunch, Owen notices a child storming down the hall. He stops and waits for the kid to approach. He sees the kid is visibly upset, red faced, and holding back tears. A woman hurries behind him. Focused on lunch, Owen's fifth graders are already in the cafeteria. The boy seems to be drawn to him. Owen lightly takes the boy's arms, speaking quietly into his ear, asking him to breathe. He sends the boy to the bathroom and turns to the woman, who is also near tears as she watches Owen speak to her son. He gives her a hug and speaks to her quietly. All this happens in just a few minutes within the main hall of the school as students and teachers move to and from lunch and P.E. There is no scene, no fuss, no loud words exchanged, but Owen is visibly upset, tears welling in his eyes as he joins his class in the lunch line. A few students cheerily tell him of some surprise they were working on. They notice his distress and ask, "Are you crying again?" He says, "Yeah. I'm just a teddy bear." He smiles and listens to his students as they move through the line.

Toward the end of the year, just as many teachers in other states in recent years have done, some teachers in the state in which Owen teaches stage a protest march on the capital. North Carolina is one of the five states that does not have rights to collective bargaining through a teachers' union (Winkler, Scull, & Zeehandelaar, 2012). The state allows an opt-in professional organization that lobbies for teachers in the media and at the legislature. This is a very different kind of organization than other states, such as California or New York, have representing the interests of teachers and public schools. Owen is very aware of the organization and the machination of the state in regard to funding and mandates for public education. His father is very active in the organization and chides his son about participation. Physical and organizational structures prevented the county in which he works to participate in the rally in the capital. The county is isolated. Over-the-air television news comes from the neighboring state. The capital, Raleigh, is more than 300 miles from the school.

Yet, despite the relative geographic isolation and conservative politics, Owen still talks to his students about the teacher activism that is happening and why. It has become a teaching tool for him. "I tell them all the time," he says. "We are lucky because it is the nicest school in the county, but ceiling tiles still fall in heavy rains. We talked about the teachers march and protesting because we are talking about protesting when we learned about Martin Luther King, Jr. I'm like, 'There's some teachers in L.A. right now protesting. That's how things get done.' We've also talked about taking risks, like Harriet Tubman. Everyone gets to decide for themselves if the risk is worth it."

As the holidays approach and the weather turns cooler, the mood changes within a school. Both students and teachers look forward to long breaks. The principal holds an impromptu talent contest during lunch time. The teachers sit together at a table that gives them a good view of all the students and the lunchroom's entrance. It feels festive and casual. Students can visit and walk around and seem aware of their limits of freedom within this space. Owen eats his homemade sandwich. A girl who appears to be Latin approaches the teacher table. She is obviously dressed in a set of green and red pajamas. She asks permission to get another fruit cup from the share table. Owen nods and says, "I like your outfit." The girl replies, "Everyone says it's PJs." She leans her arm on Owen's shoulder. He smiles and responds "Nah, it's a holiday outfit." He watches her skip back to her table and hears her report her peers, "See, Mr. Owen says it's an outfit." He smiles, as if to himself, then resumes finishing his own lunch.

Questions

1. Where is the power in this portrait?
2. What types of deliberation does Owen engage in?
3. How is politics an issue within Owen's work as a teacher?
4. What morals does Owen demonstrate in his life as a teacher?

References

Winkler, A. Scull, J., & Zeehandelaar, D. (2012). How strong are U.S. teacher unions? A state-by-state comparison. Fordham Institute: Washington D.C. Retrieved from https://nccft.org/wp-content/uploads/2018/04/20121029-Union-Strength-Full-Report_7_0.pdf

CHAPTER ONE

Teaching in the 21st Century

THIS CHAPTER WILL EXPLORE some origins of teachers' work and its intensification into the current era. The development of teachers' knowledge through technical training and practical experience will be explored. The chapter will conclude with an exploration of the moral obligation that teachers' work has within a society

A Working Profession

We define ourselves through our work. We are asked, "What do you do?" not, "Who are you?" Although teaching (the what) and teachers (the who) are often inseparable. Yet, the question of whether or not teaching is a profession often hinges on the idea that anyone can teach. People say, "It's not so hard to be a teacher. I went to school, didn't I?" Others will gladly proclaim they could never do it, that it requires certain skills and knowledge. According to Feinberg (1990), the professional model of teaching is that the teacher is able to "define the nature of the child's need" (p. 161) using their judgement and experience and a specialized knowledge. In the bureaucratic/technical model, specialized knowledge is not required (since anyone can teach). The need is defined by "other agencies, and the teacher serves as but a conduit functioning between the planner and the child" (Feinberg, 1990, p. 161). The reality of the teaching profession, still, lies somewhere in between the professional model and the bureaucratic/technical model.

Despite the best efforts of many, teaching is still not a full-fledged profession, such as law or medicine, even though there are many more teachers than people in other professions. Teaching is still unique, and many are called to teach as a part of a higher moral purpose, a desire to give back, to serve. For many, it is a job that they can and want to do, one that offers a sense of job stability in many parts of the United States through collective bargaining. For others, it's the job they can take and still be close to home. In the 300+ years since the first public schools in Massachusetts were opened, teachers' work, at the core, remains essentially unchanged. Teachers help children within the community learn to read, write, think, problem-solve, learn history, math, and science, and become a fully developed, contributing citizen to our still fledging democratic republic. Often, teaching is not only about coming to new knowledge. It also involves understanding the mistakes, or common misperceptions, students have or engage in and working with those kids in ways that don't harm their dignity while also helping them get to the right answers. The content of those areas has certainly changed over the years. The role of who decides the content has changed and the idea of what a democratic citizen is still debated. Yet, the underlying ideas of teaching, learning, acquiring new knowledge, and generating knowledge remain at the heart of public schools within the United States.

As discussed in the introduction, the concept that teachers have been entrusted by the public to care for and prepare children for the world is a somewhat idealized statement. It is well known that teachers and schools are not well funded and often blamed for many of the public's or society's shortcomings. Public schools and their purpose, from their very inception, have been controversial. The most controversial idea is that people are taxed to educate their children *as well as* other people's children. While family, church, and community were the first educators, in time, the idea that a free (supported by taxes) public education could serve to advance the social, economic, and moral well-being of a new nation, such as the Unites States, began to take hold. Up to and through the Civil War, schooling in the United States was a patchwork of small schools and part-time rural schools, all depending on the resources of the community. In the later part of the 19th century, with the rise of industrialization and immigration, schools, particularly in larger cities, began to take on a resemblance to the factories that they were adjacent to while one-room schoolhouses still dominated smaller cities and towns. These one-room schools were non-graded. Children of multiple age groups came together to learn, and the teacher would work with small groups and often used older students to tutor younger ones in particular subjects. By the era of compulsory schooling, almost all schools, even smaller rural schools, became "graded." As Larry Cuban (2019, para. 5), noted education historian, writes:

> As an organization, the age-graded school allocates children and youth by their ages to school "grades"; it sends teachers into separate classrooms and prescribes a curriculum carved up into 36-week chunks for each grade. Teachers cover each chunk assuming that all children will move uniformly through the 36-weeks to be annually promoted (or retained). Obviously, students do not learn at the same pace. If some fail to learn fractions in the allotted time, then algebra becomes a serious problem later in their school career. And just as obviously, all teachers do not cover the assigned content and skills within the time allowed. So, students then become unprepared for the next grade or sequence of academic subjects. These students became "misfits." Educators called them: *pupils of low, I.Q., ne'er-do-wells, laggards, slow learners, occupational learners, slow learners, mental deviates.*

Cuban points out that, as schools morphed into the age-graded bureaucracies we have today, there was little room for students who could not keep pace with this industrial model of schooling. Students who failed to thrive in this environment were blamed. At that time, it certainly wasn't the teacher's or the school's fault. In the United States through the mid-20th century, teachers and schools were simultaneously held responsible for national progress but not for individual or groups of students who were failing. Within about a decade of the 1954 Brown vs. Board of Education desegregation ruling, federal researchers found an "achievement gap" among White students and students of color (Coleman et al., 1966). To this day, the results of the Coleman Report hold true. Economic and family background do play a part in achievement on standardized measures. It is also true that teacher quality and school resources are important in student outcomes. Even just going to school and graduating has a great impact for social and economic outcomes in adulthood for all kids. So, although it has been proven that family social and economic background plays a huge factor in children's success in school, teachers (and schools) have become the focus for trying to alleviate these larger social issues within the United States. Teachers' work has become enlarged in scope and intensified and scrutinized in the last 50 years. Yet, as Hatch (1999) writes, "Teachers' work lives are mainly experienced in the 'gray' areas between 'black and white' alternatives. Paradox and contradiction are inherent components of the teaching workplace" (p. 237). Teachers are asked to teach character education, anti-drug education, fire safety (among others), as well as ensure that all kids meet grade-level expectations or make significant academic growth in one year. Teachers' work balances the needs of society and the individual, while being culturally responsive and inclusive. Teachers' work is hard. So, why do teachers teach?

Phillip Jackson's 1968 book, *Life in Classrooms*, tries to uncover the real experience of teaching through analyzing interviews and observations of classrooms. Jackson conducted this research at the end of the 1960s during turbulent times in schools. He sought to know what it was that motivated teachers to keep teaching. He found that teachers have the "joys of teaching" that are "closely tied to what the teacher sees happening with individual students" (Jackson, 1990, p. 134). The teachers he interviewed also believed that part of the joy of teaching is the mix of individuals in the group that made coming to work every day a new day.

Nearly a decade later, another book established ideas and norms about teachers that persist to this day. *Schoolteacher: A Sociological Study*, by Dan Lortie (1975), analyzed interviews to uncover the meaning that teachers attach to their work. He drew some major conclusions from the data about teachers' wants and rewards. Teachers want more time to teach in their classrooms, and their primary work satisfaction is derived from experiences in the classroom. Lortie calls these feelings "psychic rewards," which are intrinsic rewards that ebb and flow with teachers' self-defined goals and enjoyment of their work. In Lortie's data, this is most often defined by knowing one has "reached" a student in their classroom (Lortie, 2002, p. 103.) Teachers teach because the rewards of helping and seeing children learn are unlike any other rewards available in most professions.

In the late 1980s, Michael Apple's labor intensification theory of teachers' work attempts to explain "the growing separation between conception and execution in teachers' work" (Ballet, Kelchtermans, and Loughran, 2006, p. 210) as an issue of deskilling and deprofessionalization. Teachers' work has been primarily perceived as making decisions about ways to help students learn particular content or concepts. Yet, as the "achievement gap" grew, so did the scrutiny of teachers' work. Increasing external mandates in the late 1980s and the growing reliance on pre-packaged curricula created teachers' work as the "execution of prescription by others that can be monitored and easily assessed" (Ballet et al., 2006, p. 211). At roughly the same time, other researchers were seeing this intensification of teachers work as evidence of increased teacher professionalism since the requirements of the reform movements required more teachers to collaborate for school-wide improvement (Hargreaves, 1994). Either way, as we moved into the late 20th century, teachers' work became enlarged in scope.

In later 20th century analyses of teachers' work, we see some of the same joys of teachers' work but also a fundamental change in the emotional labor of teaching. Andy Hargreaves' 1994 book, *Changing Teachers, Changing Times: Teachers' Work and Culture in the Postmodern Age*, finds that Michael Apple's "intensification thesis" still rings true a decade later. Hargreaves relates the notion of the intensifying but also expanding role of the teacher, which includes "encompassing social and emotional goals as well as academic ones, concerns for the child's welfare at home as well as their performance in school" (1994, p. 126). The teachers in Hargreaves' study speak of this in terms of the notion that one could always do more: Lessons, activities, and student work could always be attended to with more care, thoughtfulness, and detail. This is a concern of teachers to this day.

In the early 21st century, Ballet et al. (2006) offer three refinements to Apple's intensification thesis: (1) there are multiple sources of intensification including the teachers themselves, (2) intensification is mediated, and (3) teachers experience intensification differently. Their first idea notes that parents, school structures, and teachers are sources of intensification. Parents' roles have shifted, in accordance with the business model of schooling, to consumers of educational outcomes for their children. Resourceful parents shop schools and teachers based on achievement outcomes. Parents may still be seen as partners in many schools, but the family and school relationships have become more adversarial than in the past. The continued bureaucratic organization of the school, and even the structure of the school day, binds teachers' autonomy. Finally, teachers can be their own worst enemy. In their efforts to meet external mandates, teachers "keep imposing high norms of pedagogical perfection" on themselves (Ballet et al., 2006, p. 213), which echoes Hargreaves' earlier findings. These self-imposed high standards can often be a source of guilt and self-doubt as test scores become the bottom line for schools.

All the sources of intensification are mediated by what Ballet et al. conceptualize as a "personal interpretive framework" (2006, p. 213). The teachers' responses to and experiences of intensification are filtered through their personal beliefs and immediate school contexts. A second-year teacher responds differently to certain mandates than a 15-year teacher. The administration can also help teachers to manage increasing professional requirements or make the situation worse. Intensification has generally been seen as negative, but the work of Ballet et al. indicates that, with new responsibilities, the development of new skills and knowledge are also gained. For example, whereas teacher research or collaborative planning has intensified teachers' work, it has also led to professional conversations that help improve teaching and learning. Therefore, while the work of teaching has expanded and intensified, individual and school contexts are important in how teachers view or cope with these changes.

Whether the reform movements from the mid-1980s to today are creating increasing professionalism or deprofessionalization is actually still debated. Reform is a strong undercurrent in the empirical research on teachers' work. Research repeatedly asks, How are teachers working in order to support (or thwart) reform initiatives within their schools and districts? The word "reform" is almost always synonymous with student achievement on standardized tests.

Mary Kennedy's (2005) book, *Inside Teaching: How Classroom Life Undermines Reform*, looks directly at the relationship between classroom life and reform movements to improve teaching and test scores. The teachers in Kennedy's study expressed goals and hopes for instruction but also things they wanted to avoid in their lessons, such as avoiding disruptions to the momentum of their lessons and pacing guides. Kennedy (2005) also suggests that teachers may not want students to be engaged too much (i.e., asking deep questions of content) because this will disrupt the momentum of lessons and will impede coverage of tested items. Teachers aspired to be fair or kind. They also felt obligated to the school and students to meet the goals of reform.

The tension of engaging students intellectually (getting to those a-ha moments that Jackson and Lortie wrote about) and keeping up with pacing guides and test pressure is a development of the reform movements that teachers have been facing since the late 1990s. Susan Kidd Villaume (2000) wrote of the "terrible freedom" (p. 21) some teachers felt when they were asked to teach the children and not a program. Some teachers were uncomfortable with this uncertainty. Kidd Villaume indicates that these teachers had a more technical vision of teaching. On the other hand, some teachers embraced this freedom and viewed the change as an "opportunity to venture even more deeply into creating authentic and challenging language and literacy environments" (Kidd Villaume, 2000, p. 21).

Teachers' work, though it sometimes looks easy, requires complex skills and knowledge. It is not dissimilar to that of a plate spinner who moves constantly back and forth while keeping plates spinning in the air. As one wobbles, the spinner rushes to keep that one moving as others begin to wobble. Occasionally, all are spinning nicely, and the joy of teaching pervades the space until the spinner/teacher notices plates beginning to wobble and must use their professional judgement to decide which plate to attend to first.

Teaching Knowledge

We have established the complexity of teachers' work. Now, we will explore the work of educational philosophers or theorists regarding how teachers' knowledge and beliefs in and about their work are developed. What does philosophy or theory have to do with teachers' work? A lot. Teachers have certain ways of doing things in their classroom that reflect their philosophy of living and their theories of learning. These ideas may be very clear to them and others around them (explicit), or they may be evident in the way they do things in their classroom or school (implicit). For example, if social justice and equity are important to them, they may set up their classroom in ways that allow students to interact with each other. Instructional groups may be based on interests and not on ability, thus ensuring each child gets quality, high-level instruction from them. Often, teachers' beliefs about teaching and learning are implicit, meaning that if someone observed their classroom, they could see these equity instruction practices and make a good guess on the values of the teacher. If the teacher clearly tells the students, their parents, and administrators that social justice and equity are important in their classroom and classroom themes, such as equity, are explored by the students, the philosophic approach to teaching would be explicit. Being explicit about the ideas and theories of teaching and learning means no one should need to guess what is valued in a teacher's classroom.

Sometimes, however, teachers' ideas or philosophies are not congruent within the classroom or school. Congruency means one's actions follow their philosophies. If a teacher believes that all students deserve quality instruction, then equity pedagogical strategies would be used in the classroom. If a teacher says they believe in equity but use certain discipline strategies that shame or remove students from learning time, then their actions are not congruent with their philosophies. This teacher may not really believe in equity education, so this incongruence doesn't matter. Another teacher who believes in equity pedagogy may feel pressured to participate in common discipline or academic practices within the school that are contrary to their beliefs. If that teacher continues to comply with school culture at odds with their own belief systems, something called cognitive dissonance can occur. Cognitive dissonance is a very common issue teachers deal with. It is defined as "mental conflict that occurs when beliefs or assumptions are contradicted by new information" (*Encyclopedia Britannica*, 2019). This state causes tension within a person. There are several ways people deal with the dissonance including ignoring new information or evidence that contradicts their beliefs or telling oneself that no conflict really exists. The mental anguish of trying to preserve an illusion of stability can lead to burnout and indifference. In the classroom, perhaps the best way to deal with this pressure is to reconcile the differences between one's beliefs and the evidence of student success and emotional well-being. As a teacher, being explicit (i.e., clear, precise, frank) about the philosophies of teaching and learning that guide classroom decisions is paramount to teacher and student success. Below is an example from a novice teacher who, rather than just following along with her more experienced grade-level team, made a choice to revise the type of rewards and punishments in the classroom to meet her and her students' needs.

Snapshot: Laura

Laura has spent one and half years teaching in third grade, but only a half a year as the primary teacher. Laura believes that student success is about creating life-long learners and providing a non-coercive environment in which students want to learn. Laura believes a lot of learning occurs out of the classroom (playground, home, etc.). She is committed to helping students understand their value to the world. Laura travelled a lot in college, including a semester in Cuba, two weeks in Kenya, and she was the first student to complete their student teaching in an international setting in Peru.

She believes her school supports her idea of school success, sort of. A real stress is test scores, and a lot of practices are driven by test scores. Test scores even determine at what grade level teachers will teach and there are testing bonuses in her county. While pressured to do well on tests, she feels supported by her team and mentors and feels she has enough resources to teach well. Classroom management is something that every new teacher struggles with. But for Laura, there is one moment in which she realized she needs to change her inherited "clip system" into something more beneficial.

Laura knows her students have fairly traumatic home lives. One day, she has to talk to the principal about a student who was swearing at other kids. The principal recommends silent lunch for two days, but Laura knows that would just further traumatize the child. So, after speaking with the student about the inappropriate behavior, she introduces a positive reinforcement system where all students earn craft puff balls for good behavior. Students never lose the earned puffs (as Laura calls them) for inappropriate behavior. These puffs are traded in weekly for extra time in certain activities or for use of special chairs for the day. Within a few weeks, the other 3rd grade teachers change their systems. Prior to changing, Laura speaks with her mentors, but not her administration. After the fact, she informs the principal, but to Laura, the principal seems unconcerned about the change. Yet, Laura has concerns about the student whose behavior needs helped her change her system as he begins fourth grade. She says, "I told him that I loved him every day even though he continued to throw scissors. He needs more than silent lunch. He moved from E to N reading levels during my time with him. I saw lots of growth. I believed in him and he showed me that he began to believe in himself."

Philosophies of Knowing

Often, teaching is called an art and a science. This idea is rooted is basic philosophes of how people come to know something (epistemology). If we go back to Aristotle's philosophy, we learn that he had two ideas about how we come to know. First, there is the knowledge associated with activities of living in relationship with others. This knowledge represents an experiential knowing that is required of practice or *praxis*. The other way of knowing is *techné*, or "technique," which is a knowledge that helps one make something tangible. These Aristotelian ideas, in a contemporary sense, are the "practical" or the "technical" and, in teaching, an "art" and a "science" approach (Sato, Kern, McDonald, & Rogers, 2010). In practice (*praxis*), the means and ends exist together in action. It is what is done. So, the actions one chooses in classroom practices are a representation of not only how one chooses to act, they are also illustrations of how one wants the ends of actions—or outcomes—to be. Put simply, a teacher who wants equity for students in schools chooses actions within the classroom (and the larger society) that are equitable. This definition of the practical *(praxis)*, action that is congruent with personal philosophy, is the one used in this book.

These ancient ideas help us think about teacher knowledge and action. Teachers often crave concrete steps to, for example, implement equity teaching strategies. Knowing the "steps" of equity pedagogy provides teachers a sense of certainty. Having "steps" to implement is a technical approach and to some, like Michael Apple, it can lead to the deskilling of teachers and a less responsive classroom. As a former teacher, I have experienced the technical approach to improving teaching with the newest "research-based" ideas that are designed to improve student achievement. I participated in several staff development sessions and was assured that if I delivered instruction exactly as they told me, my students' test scores would improve. Does that sound familiar? While having steps or guidelines is helpful and appropriate in classrooms, the issue of "teaching with fidelity" (which means to stay on pace and not go "off script") can prevent teachers from spending time with students struggling through thorny problems or a deep-discussion of literature since, as evidenced by the teachers in Kennedy's (2005) research who felt that covering what was going to be tested was of primary importance. If we take an excessively technical approach to teaching, the relational aspect can be stymied. This relational knowing in teaching often comes from a teacher's disposition toward the children they teach, but it also comes from experience.

As we bring the ancient ideas to a more present-day philosophy of teaching knowledge, we are led to John Dewey's pragmatic philosophy. Dewey's pragmatic philosophy focuses on knowing in and through action. Knowledge first lives "in the muscles," and then we translate that knowledge into language or other symbolic forms (Biesta & Burbules, 2003, p. 11). Knowledge is constructed through what Dewey refers to as a *transaction* between a person and their environment. In other words, people learn something in doing as well as by doing something. More recently, Conle and Sakamoto (2002) offer a more responsive way of attaining knowledge through action in the classroom. Rather than offering steps to follow, they encourage teachers to act in a way that "allows inquiry and is connected to personal and cultural histories" (p. 429) in order to help improve teaching and learning. What Conle and Sakamoto are distinguishing here are the differences between teachers' responses to their everyday issues that are stimulated by external or internal mandates. Reflective practice is one way teachers develop ways to respond to students and other issues that arise within their day.

The teachers' portraits shared in this book and the approach to stewardship as teacher leadership is based in the philosophy that teacher knowledge is generated from experience writ large: personal experience, teacher education, professional development, and teaching. Early on in my career, my own teacher knowledge and professionalism was challenged by the school culture in which I found myself. Prior to the beginning of the year, I was placed in a school that was not doing well academically. As the year progressed, it came to the fore that most teachers and administrators had very different philosophies on trying to improve student academic performance. I was initially on the same track with the administration and was working hard to develop relationships with my fifth graders. Once some students began misbehaving, however, directives from the administrators regarding basic classroom management, such as student bathroom and locker use, recess, and curricular and instructional decisions, began appearing in my mailbox. The action of the administration not only impacted my relations with my students, but my relationships with the other teachers and the students' relationships with other students throughout the school.

My focus was on relationships, which was guided by practical knowledge I had developed: if my students trusted me, they would work for me. Even though I was a fifth-year teacher, all my experience was called into question because of the misbehavior of some students. Rather than addressing the issues of those individual students in the fifth grade, perhaps because of the administration's focus on test scores, the whole fifth grade was treated as a problem to be solved. The administration believed that it could *make* the fifth graders do well on the test through the denial of recess and the imposition of curriculum fidelity. I cannot imagine the kind of stress the administration was under to improve test scores, but, as research now supports, ignoring social and emotional learning undermines academic learning. Teachers make decisions based on their previous practical knowledge. This knowledge is not just about "getting the job done" in a colloquial sense of practical. As argued in my earlier research with colleagues (Sato & Rogers, 2017) and supported by other researchers (e.g., Sato, 2005; Korthagen & Kessels, 1999; Sanders

& McCutcheon, 1986), teachers address everyday problems and uncertain situations not solely by understanding situations with theoretical knowledge or by learning a set of steps that will help them get similar outcomes again and again. They must read the situation at hand and act based on what they think would best address that situation with both the desired outcome (ends) and the strategies (means) in mind. The act of teaching requires discernment, judgment, and reflection upon the technical knowledge as well as the practical knowledge of teachers.

Toulmin (1990) speaks of the return to the local and timely in understanding and rendering meaning to existence. Toulmin writes that Aristotle "saw that our chance of acting wisely in a practical field depends upon our readiness, not just to calculate the timeless demands of intellectual formulae, but also to make decisions pros ton kairon—that is, 'as the occasion requires'" (p. 190). What is worrisome is that in many schools within the United States, the focus has become more on the technical approach to issues (school reform such as curriculum fidelity and computer-based testing) that leads to the deskilling of teachers. In schools today, as well as the larger culture, we are seeing "the passive adaptation of citizens in a society whose affairs are increasingly administered according to the standard of technocratic efficiency" (Dunne, 1993, p. 89). This simply means that, as humans and teachers, we have begun to fail to respond to increased technological and micromanaged schools. We fail to act as the occasion requires us to act. Like the proverbial frog in boiling water, we become numb in the underlying messages sent about teacher professionalism and knowledge with each mandate. Even with increased reforms, like professional learning communities and school-based mentoring, many teachers spend much of their time isolated in their classrooms. Teachers are often distanced from their students because of the constraints of mass schooling and high-stakes testing, which often lead to circumstances when passivity is preferred, encouraged, and awarded. Within this 21st century malaise, a return to the idea of teaching as stewardship is crucial. Stewardship frames teaching and schooling as a moral obligation to do what is right. Doris Santoro (2016) writes about the idea of pedagogical responsibility and moral manipulation of teachers when they are asked [coerced] to implement curriculum fidelity. Teachers' pedagogical responsibility, the responsibility to do what is right by the students, is compromised by these types of mandates, argues Santoro. She concludes,

> Continually asking questions about the means, ends and aims of education is the proper use of teachers' intelligence and the only moral stance for those living in a democratic society. The failure to use one's judgment is not simply a failure of intelligence for Dewey, it is a failure to engage morally with the world. (Santoro, 2016, p. 265)

Teaching as Moral Work

In this chapter, teachers' work and its intensification into the current era has been examined. The ways teachers develop knowledge around teaching, such as through training (technical) and experience (practical), has also been explored. In this last segment on the work of teachers, we will explore the moral obligation that teachers' work has within a society. There have been various waves of thought around the role of schools within American society. A traditionalists' view represents the idea that public schooling is a positive force in the development of the American idea and that public schooling is the best venue for solving pressing social problems. About 50 years after mandatory schooling laws were enacted, authors, like Joel Spring, argued that public schools are, and have been, sites of social reproduction. They argued that schools do not help children marginalized by race and class demarcations transcend their social positions, that public schools are an "elite conspiracy" to keep people oppressed (Kelly, 2014, p. 776).

Walter Feinberg's 1990 essay on the moral responsibilities of public schools touches upon the evolution of several arguments on what it means for public schools and teachers to help youth become members of a "public." He speaks to two basic roles for public schools within history: 1) as tools to enhance the position of the United States in competition with other nations and 2) as providers of opportunities that otherwise can only be afforded by wealth and privilege. Both these roles have been proven, at one time or another, to be false. The role of public schools to provide for the country's needs is often diametrically opposed to American notions of individuality and freedom of expression. The role of public schools as an equalizer of opportunity, while primarily the moral force of schooling, has also been problematic. As mentioned earlier, the "discovery" of the achievement gap and the structural racism in schooling that writers like Joel Spring (1972) and Jonathan Kozol (1991) have uncovered points to the failures of schools as places of opportunity. So, where do we look for a renewed moral purpose for teaching and schooling?

Advocates for vouchers, charter schools, and the privatization of public schools use an economic definition of a "public good." Viewing public schools through a purely economic lens misses the larger civic goals of public education that the "founding fathers" imagined. An economic definition of a public good views the goals of public education in purely individualistic outcomes. While individual outcomes are part of the goal of public schooling, civic outcomes are just as important. Public schools, in theory, are good for the public. They are places where diverse future citizens learn how to live in a pluralistic world. As Feinberg (1990) writes, "[B]ecoming a member of the public does not [only] involve learning the 'proper' response to an item. Rather, it involves finding a way to enter the debate about which items are worth considering and how we should think about them" (p. 178). This idea is the moral dimension of teaching. Public schools are good for the public because they prepare children to participate in the "public," and "the development of a public involves entrance into a critical dialog in which respect for the interpretations of others is a part of the rational inquiry" (Feinberg, 1990, p. 178) What Feinberg is saying here is a response to the "Cultural Literacy" movements that suggested if public school students just mastered a list of facts, predominately about Western Civilization, then the students would be prepared to be citizens. Feinberg counters by saying the moral foundation of teaching is not only to help students learn "facts" but to be able to think and wrestle with them in order be able to participate fully within society. Teaching's moral obligation is more about teaching children and youth to think than it is about teaching them what to think.

Public schools are an "imperfect social good" (Kelly, 2014, p. 766). As we have moved in to the 21st century, schools are both providers of opportunities for marginalized children and families as well as sites for violence and oppression. But overall, the public and the teachers who work in these places believe that public schooling as a public good is a promise that can still be made right. To believe that public schools are a public good is a moral stance. It is a value that guides a teacher's decision making. Some authors, such as John Goodlad and his colleagues (1990), would argue that teaching is a moral and ethical activity. In this sense, we are talking of morals, not in a religious sense, though that often comes into play, but in a sense of right, wrong, and justice. Viewing teaching as a moral activity indicates the power behind teachers' actions because the teacher must answer the questions: Whose morals? Right and wrong for who? Justice for who? Maxine Greene (1973) writes about this idea as a paradox that has no solution:

"The tension between the individual and the civilization has been and will be irreducible. Education, because it takes place at the intersection where the demand for social order and the demands for autonomy conflict, must proceed through and by means of the tension" (p. 9).

References

Ballet, K, Kelchtermans, G., & Loughran, J. (2006). Beyond intensification towards a scholarship of practice: Analysing changes in teachers' work lives. *Teachers and Teaching*, 12(2), 209–229.

Biesta, G., & Burbules, N. (2003). *Pragmatism and educational research*. Lanham, MD: Rowman & Littlefield Publishers.

Cole, T. (2012). The white-savior industrial complex. *The Atlantic*. Retrieved from https://www.theatlantic.com/international/archive/2012/03/the-white-savior-industrial-complex/254843/

Coleman, J., Campbell, E, Hobson, C., McPartland, J., Mood, A., Weifeld, F., & York, R. (1966). *Equality of education opportunity*. United States government printing office: Washington: National Center for Educational statistics. https://files.eric.ed.gov/fulltext/ED012275.pdf

Conle, C., & Sakamoto. (2002). "Is-When" stories: Practical repertoires and theories about the practical. *Journal of Curriculum Studies*, 34(4), 427–449.

Cuban, L. (2019, Jan 18.) Whatever happened to the non-graded school? [Weblog Post.] Retrieved from https://larrycuban.wordpress.com/2019/01/18/whatever-happened-to-the-non-graded-school/

Dunne, J. (1993). *Back to the rough ground: Practical judgment and the lure of technique*. Notre Dame, IN: University of Notre Dame Press.

Encyclopedia Britannica. (2019). Cognitive dissonance. In *Encyclopedia Britannica Online*. Retrieved July 11, 2019, from https://www.britannica.com/science/cognitive-dissonance

Feinberg, W. (1990). The moral responsibility of public schools. In J. Goodlad, R. Soder & K. Sirotnik (Eds.), *The moral dimensions of teaching* (pp. 155–187). San Francisco: Jossey-Bass.

Goodlad, J., Soder, R., & Sirotnik, K. (Eds.) (1990). *The moral dimensions of teaching*. San Francisco: Jossey-Bass.

Greene, M. (1973). Identities and contours: An approach to educational history. *Educational Researcher*, 2(4), 5–10.

Hargreaves, A. (1994). *Changing teachers, changing times: Teachers' work and culture in the postmodern age*. New York: Teachers College Press.

Hatch, J.A. (1999). What preservice teachers can learn from the studies of teachers' work. *Teaching and Teacher Education*, 15(3), 229–242.

Jackson, P.W. (1990). *Life in classrooms: Reissued with a new introduction*. New York: Teachers College Press.

Kelly, M. G. (2014). The mythology of schooling: The historiography of American and European education in comparative perspective. *Paedagogica Historica: International Journal of the History of Education*, 50(6): 756–773.

Kennedy, M. (2005). *Inside teaching: How classroom life undermines reform.* Cambridge, MA: Harvard University Press.
Korthagan, F., & Kessels, J. (1999). Linking theory and practice: Changing the pedagogy of teacher education. *Educational Researcher, 28*(4), 4–17.
Kidd Villaume, S. (2000). The necessity of uncertainty: A case study of language arts reform. *Journal of Teacher Education, 5*(1), 18–25.
Kozol, J. (1991). *Savage inequalities: Children in America's schools.* New York: Random House.
Lortie, D. (2002). *Schoolteacher: A sociological study* (2nd Edition). Chicago: University of Chicago Press.
Sanders, D. P., & McCutcheon, G. (1986). The development of practical theories of teaching. *Journal of Curriculum Studies and Supervision,* 2(1), 50–67.
Santoro, D. (2016). "We're are not going to do that because it's not right": Using pedagogical responsibility to reframe the doublespeak of fidelity. *Educational Theory, 66*(1-2), 263–277.
Sato, M. (2005). Practical leadership: Conceptualizing the everyday leadership work of teachers. *The New Educator, 1*(1), 55–71.
Sato, M., Kern, A., McDonald, E., & Rogers, C. (2010). On the rough ground: Instantiations of the practical across the teacher professional continuum. *Teacher Education & Practice,* 23(1), 66–87.
Sato, M., & Rogers, C. (2017). Practical leadership: How teachers enact leadership to re-culture their schools. In C. Rogers; K. Lomotey, & A. Hilton (Eds.), *Innovative approaches to educational leadership: selected cases* (27–31). New York, NY: Peter Lang Publishing.
Spring, J. (1972). *Education and the rise of the corporate state.* Boston: Beacon Press.
Toulmin, S. (1990) *Cosmopolis: The hidden agenda of modernity.* New York, NY: The Free Press.

CHAPTER TWO

Leadership and School Culture

LEADERSHIP IS AN IDEA that most people understand in some way. But like other diffuse concepts like love or democracy, leadership can be defined quite differently by people in different contexts. Who is, and can, be a leader and what constitutes leadership is often in the eye of the beholder. While leadership is a complex concept with many different theoretical approaches, Northouse (2016) describes four components as central to any theory of leadership: process, influence, groups, and common goals. According to Northouse, the study of leaders and leadership theory has had different focuses over the years. In the first half of the 20th century, obedience, influence, interactions, and group think theories were examined in light of hierarchal models of leadership. In the latter half of the 20th century, the focus was how effective leaders were at helping organizations create goals and change. Towards the end of the 20th century, there became a clear distinction between leadership and management. Management focuses on the efficient use of money and human resources, whereas leadership theory and research became focused on this guiding definition of leadership: "Leadership is a process whereby an individual influences a group of individuals to achieve a common goal" (Northouse, 2016, p. 6).

A person's assumptions about leadership influence their ability to see something as leadership. In most peoples' minds, leadership is usually about one person: the great leader phenomenon, such as Abraham Lincoln or Martin Luther King, Jr., someone who inspires and influences others to act. There is also the business model of leadership with chief officers, general managers, and company presidents (upper management) who have a whole slew of middle managers and workers below them that they supervise. This is the hierarchical notion of management, and it's the blueprint of the school bureaucracies in which most teachers work.

Leadership in Education

Traditional school leadership consists of ideas about traits, skills, and behaviors. The trait approach in leadership across the board indicates that people are "born leaders" or have what it takes. Research on traditional leadership examines people who are already good or great leaders and asks: What traits (or dispositions) do they have? What strategies or skills do they use to get stuff done? What do they do (behaviors)?

People who believe in the need to find the "right" leader often use instruments to measure traits or skills. Northouse (2016) indicates that the major leadership "traits" are: intelligence, self-confidence, determination, integrity, and sociability (p. 15). Traits are seen as integral to one's personality. Skills and behavior are what leaders do as opposed to who they are (traits). Skills can encompass technical, human, and conceptual. In other words, leaders have the knowledge about the work that they lead. They know how to work with people, and they understand the larger conceptual ideas of the work that they do and lead. So, an educational leader would know how teaching and learning works and how schools are run. They would know about teachers' lives and be able to communicate with the children and families within the school community. These leaders' skills would also include understanding the big ideas—or vision—of the school and district in which they work and have the ability to communicate that vision to those they "lead." Other skills, such as problem-solving, are key as well. Examining a leader's behavior is an extension of their skills. These are the actions that motivate a group to accomplish tasks and behaviors. They also help "followers" feel comfortable within the place of work. The underlying idea is about the focus of the leader, whether that includes accomplishing tasks, creating a comfortable work environment, or finding, of course, a balance.

Some principals or administration teams may have some of these traditional characteristics of leaders: they may be exceptionally smart and friendly, have a good handle on the work of teachers (maybe they used to be one!), and know the students and families. They may be the relational leader who greets students and teachers each day, making themselves known in the lunchroom and on the playground. Or, they may be exceptionally smart and friendly and have a good handle on the work of teachers, but they spend time organizing teams and committees to accomplish tasks and working the phone and email to get the school new supplies. An administration team may encompass both of these types or somewhere in between. Some principals prioritize relationship building and focusing on the larger, long-term vision of the school, whereas others might prioritize short-term goals that are to be accomplished within the school year.

The next three ideas about leadership will speak to what may be the principal's leadership "style" or philosophy: transformational, authentic, and servant.

Transformational leadership is one that focuses on intrinsic motivation. A principal who is a transformational leader focuses on what makes their staff work well, a leader who is concerned about satisfying the physical and emotional needs on the staff. This type of leadership motivates staff to go beyond what is usually expected because they are inspired to do so by their leadership team or principal. Transformational leadership is different from transactional leadership. Within organizations that have a transformational model, both leaders and staff are moving together towards better outcomes. Transactional is a traditional and common model where leaders make promises or exchanges for better outcomes. Principals or administrative teams use the transactional model quite a bit, particularly around evaluation measures. Teachers often engage in transactional models in the classroom when they incentivize behavior or academic work for their students. In simple terms, transformational leadership occurs when others are intrinsically motivated to do better and transactional is an external motivation strategy. A key component of transformational leadership is charisma. Charismatic leaders are able to motivate others to do things they may not otherwise do. This can be either positive or negative. For example, there have been many cult leaders that have influenced people to commit violence or to leave their family. Perhaps the ultimate example is Adolph Hitler, whose charismatic speeches and style motivated the unquestioned genocide of Jews in Europe. Researchers call this negative transformational leadership psuedotransformational, or "fake" transformation, because true charismatic transformational leaders have high moral standards. Examples of transformational leaders are people such as Mohandas Gandhi, Martin Luther King, Jr., and Jimmy Carter. Transformational leaders have many of the hallmarks of a steward, but their main goal is to motivate people to accomplish shared goals.

In "a world bereft of trust and awash with accountability," (Hargreaves & Fink, 2006, p. 510) there is a need to rebuild trust and confidence. The "confidence-sapping conditions of standardized reform" (p. 511) create a call for transformational and authentic leadership. Authentic leadership is a relatively new phenomenon in leadership studies as it focuses on the genuine and trustworthiness of leaders within organizations. This idea of authenticity stems from transformational leadership but is coming into play at a time where many people that have been seen as great leaders have let their companies and their organizations down. A recent phenomenon that reminds us of the need for trustworthy leaders is that of Elizabeth Holmes, the founder of Theranos, who is currently on trial for misleading investors and using investors' money for her own lavish lifestyle. In 2015, 11 educators were convicted of tampering with standardized tests, often referred to as the "Atlanta Cheating Scandal." Over several years, there was an elaborate scheme among teachers and administrators to change students answers on standardized tests. This scheme was uncovered when a local newspaper began noticing dramatic rises in test scores within some Atlanta public schools.

Servant leadership theory is popular in educational settings. This theory is premised on the idea that leaders put others first and values and ideals above all else. A servant leader is the type who stands behind their employees, whether they be teachers or engineers, to help them develop their own capacities for problem solving and leadership. Rather than serving their own self-interests, a servant leader listens to and put the issues of their followers first. Servant leaders serve in ways that are ethical and serve the greater good of their organization and society at large.

The servant leader is not only a leader of people, but more precisely a leader whose actions serve the ideas that connect the leader and the follower. In theory, the servant leader has earned the trust of the followers or staff because they have put the values and ideas of the organization before their own, and others' interests. In Chapter Four, a deeper discussion of the relationship between servant and stewardship theory is presented.

Distributed Leadership

The three preceding ideas were about styles or philosophies. Distributed leadership is the most-often cited type of leadership within 21st century schools. It can also be referred to as a "style" or "philosophy," but it has more to do with the organizational structure within schools than the previous three ideas. It is also often called "shared leadership" or "shared governance." It is more of a stance towards leadership by leaders that acknowledges "that there are multiple leaders" within organizations and that the model focuses on "interactions, rather than the actions, of those in formal and informal leadership roles" (Harris & Spillane, 2008, p. 31). This form of leadership within schools is seen as one way to manage the school reforms demanded of 21st century learning. Distributed leadership claims a less hierarchical model of leadership than any of the other ideas presented in this chapter. Stewardship, which will be explored more in depth in a later chapter, is also less hierarchical but inverts the leadership paradigm to one where leaders are those who earn the privilege of leading through their actions as opposed to the traditional administrative teams placed at schools, with or without the consent of the staff and community. Under the idea of distributed leadership, other ideas, such as shared leadership or collaborative leadership, have been grouped. The originator of the term, James Spillane, argues that distributed leadership is more of an analytic tool than a leadership style. Harris and Spillane (2008) encourage teachers and administrators to ask key questions about leadership at the organizational level like: How is leadership distributed among stakeholders such as staff, students, and families?

Often, in the name of "distributed leadership," what happens is the creation of another structure that is less hierarchical or delegated to ad hoc committees. Harris and Spillane (2008) warn that, "Flattening the hierarchy or delegation of leadership does not necessarily equate with distributed leadership, nor does it automatically improve performance. It is the nature and quality of leadership practice that matters" (p. 33). Organizations that claim to value distributed leadership have a perspective on school leadership that "involves a decentralized, devolved and shared approach to leadership in the school" (Harris & Mujis, 2005, p. 7). Marya Levenson's (2014) book, *Pathways to Teacher Leadership: Emerging Models, Changing Roles*, demonstrates what distributed leadership around instruction looks like in her case of Northern High's Critical Friends Group. After some initial volunteer meetings, the administrative team decided that departments in this large high school would create collaborative groups. To help these groups meet and succeed, the administration created time within the weekly schedule for these teams to meet and appointed a teacher as the lead facilitator. This lead teacher was relieved of some duty (like study hall) to prepare for and run the meetings. The meetings were confidential. Teachers could share instructional challenges and get help. Departmental chairs, who oversaw teacher accountability, were not in attendance at the meetings. Therefore, a peer group came together to discuss and take responsibility to improve their instruction. One of the teachers called this a "top-down collaborative mandate" but also found the group's authority to decide the topic and focus of the weekly meetings refreshing. The teachers also felt they benefited by being able to see "how successful we were in achieving those [instructional] goals and measures by looking at examples of student work" (Levenson, 2014, p. 25).

Distributed leadership requires social cohesion with a shared vision. It also requires trust and the belief in human potential because, as Harris and Mujis (2005) contend, distributed leadership is a "way" of thinking about leadership and deals with finding leadership and expertise where it exists rather than just relying on formal positions and roles (pg. 28). In Levenson's case above, we can see how the administrators were able to create a space within the school day and structure where teachers could discuss and reflect on instructional decision-making. They could trust that this time was well spent. There are barriers to this kind of leadership because it challenges the status quo, which is the formal hierarchy of leadership, and forces school structures and divisions to rethink their decision-making processes. Other teachers may also push back against the idea of other teachers' having leadership capacities to enforce or encourage different practices within the classrooms. Another example in Levenson's book, the science department welcomed the weekly meetings and discussions of data and instruction. But when they were presented with the opportunity to observe other's classroom practices, they became recalcitrant, believing observations were done only by those who evaluated their teaching.

Gender and Leadership

Examining the ways gender identity influences leadership practices is a new branch of leadership studies. In most educational settings, as in corporate settings, there is a gender imbalance within leadership structures. Today, as at the turn of the 20th century, the core staff of schools are often women. While recently, more and more men are being recruited into teaching, men were the only teachers in the earliest days of schooling in the United States. Community-based schools were often overseen by village elders who hired young men on leave from college to work a season or two within the school. Women did not enter the profession of teaching in the United States until the late 19th century. With the movement from an agrarian economy to the industrial age, women moved from the home to factories as workers and secretaries, to shops as the face of retail clerks, and to schools as the face of elementary school teachers. As women moved into the classrooms, men moved into the levels of bureaucracy created around the graded schools. Men were principals, supervisors, and educators at normal schools for women. There have been notable women educators over the last century, and women have also become principals, school superintendents, and state heads of education. But they entered these positions in small numbers compared to men.

Understanding the gender history of teaching helps make sense of why "teacher leadership" is at once an important issue and also highly problematic. As we move through the 21st century, our ideas of gender are being opened and expanded. Yet schools, as institutions, have a lot of historical baggage around what is appropriate for genders. For most of the past century of schooling, teachers have been women, and their social lives, bodies, and minds have been orchestrated by rules that men have made. Leadership positions in schools, historically in the United States, have been dominated by men.

In the first half of the 20th century, young women were seen as good role models for young children. Young women teachers would instill ideas of honesty, purity, and hard work in elementary classrooms. Many of the young children first educated in graded common schools were immigrants who also often worked. Child labor laws and compulsory schooling increased the number of children attending schools and increased the need for more teachers. Women, for the most part, expressed their leadership within the classroom. Some of these children would go on to high schools dominated by faculties of men, elite preparatory places for college-bound students. While we are well past the days when women could not even earn advanced degrees, the issue of gender and gender roles within leadership remains an important one as we examine the types of leadership theories and styles that school administrators take up and the kinds of cultures that are created and sustained within school settings.

School Culture

School culture and administrative leadership approaches go hand in hand. School culture, sometimes referred to as climate, is that feeling a person gets after spending a few days within a school. Usually within a teacher education program, assignments are given to the pre-service teacher to observe and document the school culture. Assignments like these often ask for the pre-service teacher to notice what is hanging on the walls in the hallways and to notice the language used among staff and among students and staff. These observations of school culture are often superficial since truly knowing a school culture requires one to be immersed within it for months. Yet, these assignments and observations can hint at some of the cultural norms of the school. When referring to school "norms," we are speaking of the ways of being, acting, and speaking that are acceptable within that place. It can be referred to as a cultural or social norm, which is a standard of behavior shared by members of a group, more specific than values or ideals. For example, honesty is a general value, but the rules defining what is honest conduct in a particular situation is a social norm. Schools, classrooms, and churches have norms. Observing these social and cultural norms within schools demonstrates parts of the school culture. For example, if students call teachers by their first name within a school, that is a norm that points to a more democratic, and perhaps informal, school culture. School culture can be demonstrated implicitly and explicitly. Stolp and Smith (1999) define school culture as a system of meanings that shape what people think and how they act. This system of meanings includes norms, school traditions, and routines. Something that seems unremarkable and mundane, like bus duty, may be a very valuable routine within the school culture. It has also been known for a long time (Cheng, 1993) that stronger school cultures have better motivated teachers. Cheng's study found that teachers experienced higher job satisfaction in a school with strong shared belief systems, shared participation, good leadership, and caring among staff and students.

Administrators *and* teachers shape school culture. During my first four years of teaching, I had three principals. While each principal had their own method of leadership, the school culture had been strongly created by the teachers who had been there for years. We had teachers across the grade levels that had taught at the school for many years prior to my arrival. They were the leaders in the school when it came to school norms, particularly around behavior and instructional approaches. These teachers influenced me in the way I worked within my classroom. At staff meetings, I also observed how they influenced discussion about new curriculum and ideas from each new principal. The school culture was strongly rooted within the concept of teacher professionalism and expertise. Those teachers who knew the "history" of the school (i.e., families, ways of doing events, working with kids) had voices that were valued by each principal during my four years there. It was an ideal place to spend my early years learning to become a teacher.

School culture has also been called the "hidden curriculum" of the school organization. The hidden curriculum is the unseen, unplanned learning that occurs implicitly within schools and classrooms. This can either be positive or negative. What value is implied (implicit) when children are expected to walk down the hall silently? What value is implied (implicit) when children are given silent lunch for not bringing in their homework? Questions like these help uncover the hidden messages, the implied cultural norms, of schools.

While principals and administration are often tasked with "shaping" school culture, teachers are key actors within this shaping. Teachers can resist, ignore, and participate deeply or superficially. The level of resistance or participation is often due to two things: the principal's approach to leadership and the teachers' beliefs in leadership.

In my story from Chapter One about the disconnect between my beliefs and my administration's regarding best instructional practices can also be viewed as an issue of school culture. I was hired three days before the school year began into a fifth grade (tested grade) position. I reached out to the fourth-grade teachers for information on the school, families, and students. They were kind but not very helpful, deferring to the curriculum coordinator. In the first few staff meetings, I learned about which teachers had been at the school the longest, and I learned that the administration was new. The stakes were high for all of us in this low-performing school. I had come from a strong, professional teacher culture in which co-planning and professional learning communities happened. None of that was happening at this school. Teachers closed their doors. The administrative team set your schedules for reading, math, and remediation time for reading and math (and nothing else). Every morning, staff and students walking into the building saw a large countdown clock to the test date. It's no wonder my student said to me in late May, after testing, "Why are we still coming to school?"

The school principal and administration team are powerful forces in shaping school culture and opportunities for teacher leadership. Depending on their beliefs about leadership and the role of teachers in decision making processes, there is a wide variety of ways that schools may be organized and run. A principal who has very traditional views of leadership can create a culture in which community voices—teachers, students, parents—are less valued than those of a superintendent or other principal. This principal may believe that the responsibility for the success of the school resides on their shoulders. These types of leaders tend to entice or coerce faculty and staff into participating in reform agendas imported from outside the school. Teacher leadership in this type of culture will be recognized as those teachers who participate and engage in the vision of the principal or administrative team. Teachers can either find this type of leadership comforting or oppressive. While principals may give lip service to the teacher as professional in traditional authoritarian-based models of leadership, there are clear demarcations of professional responsibility: the classroom is the teacher's realm and the school is the principal's realm.

In schools were the principal or administrative team believe in less traditional models of leadership, there will be many more seats at the table of decision making. There will be more meetings and more committees. Principals within these models may view teacher leadership in managerial ways, such as chairing a committee. Teacher leadership may also be viewed as a willingness to step into conversations about whole school issues. In these more decentralized cultures, teachers may thrive if they feel they are being asked to contribute with all their professional knowledge, while others may feel uncomfortable because they are being asked to speak up as professionals for the first time in their work lives.

As Blair (2016) writes, "Teacher leadership requires conditions and opportunities that facilitate the work of teacher leaders, but, simultaneously, teachers must be prepared to make commitments and take risks that will lead to new definitions of what it means to be a teacher today" (p. 180). In my early years of teaching, I looked to the experienced teachers to question what was happening, to make a stand. But in my final years of teaching, they closed their doors to the hard problems. When experienced and novice teachers open their doors and begin to take seriously the collective responsibility for the children in our care, school culture will change. And all the work done to help a child feel safe and loved in school will not be completely undone in the next grade. In the next chapter, teacher leadership will be reviewed and the idea that teachers can step into their power and lead in multiple ways will be explored.

References

Blair, E. (2016). *Teacher leadership: The "new" foundations of teacher education.* New York, NY: Peter Lang.

Cheng, Y.C. (1993). Profiles of organizational culture and effective schools. *School Effectiveness and School Improvement,* 4(2), 85–110.

Hargreaves, A., & Fink, D. (2006). Resourcefulness. In M. Grogan (Ed.), *The Jossey-Bass reader on educational leadership (3rd ed,* pp. 492–519). Jossey-Bass San Francisco.

Harris, A., & Mujis, D. (2005). *Improving schools through teacher leadership.* Berkshire England: Open University Press.

Harris, A., & Spillane, J. (2008). Distributed leadership through the looking glass. *Management in Education,* 22(1), 31–34. https://doi.org/10.1177/0892020607085623

Levenson, M. (2014). *Pathways to teacher leadership: Emerging models, changing roles.* Harvard Education Press: Cambridge MA.

Northouse, P. (2016). *Leadership: theory and practice* (7th ed.) Thousand Oaks, CA: Sage.

Stolp, S., & Smith, S. (1999). *School culture and climate: The role of the leader.* OSSC Bulletin. Eugene: Oregon School Study Council.

PORTRAIT OF CARLY

Carly holds her long, blond hair in her hands and leans across the table to listen to one of her third graders read. Her blond hair is a contrast to all the dark-haired heads around her. Carly is in her second year of teaching at an elementary school in the Southeastern United States that predominately serves Native American students. Carly is White and from the middle part of the state, which is demographically White, yet poor. She comes from a long line of teachers. The instruction that is happening is somewhat of a review. Students pair up and sit in different parts of the room to work on sequencing. She asks them to tell her about the expectations for partner work. Students respond with comments like "quietly," and "make sure you're talking about sequence." A kid pipes up and says, "You should try and talk to your partner even if you get partnered with someone you may not want." Carly agrees and says, "We all work together very well in this class."

Carly student-taught across the hallway three years ago. She says, "It was the most amazing" experience. Her cooperating teacher, a very experienced Native American educator, embraced Carly's ideas for content as long as they fit into the instructional and standard expectations. Carly is a history lover and almost became a high school history teacher like her dad. She knew she was "called" to teach when she taught Sunday school. During her junior and senior years in high school, she was able to assist in a kindergarten classroom, where her love of teaching was solidified. Her high academic standards were set by her experience attending an International Baccalaureate high school, which requires six rigorous content exams for the diploma.

She realized the lack of social studies and historical content in elementary schools and wanted to be an advocate for social studies. She firmly believes civic education needs to begin in the early grades: "The issues [we face] in the world today are due to the lack of what history kids know. We don't understand our history." She believes that the developing young minds in elementary schools are more open to learning how to have civil conversations. She says there are parts of the United States' history that are "hard to talk about, but we need to talk about otherwise history repeats itself." While the third-grade curriculum doesn't call for conversations about topics such as slavery, a key standard asks third graders to look at how historical events shaped current communities. Carly works with mostly Native American students, so conversations about the Unites States' policies of genocide and forced assimilation of Native Americans do happen. To achieve this within the curriculum she says, "I say we do reading and we read history." Her third-grade team supports her in this passion. Each teacher steps up in different content areas to plan curriculum for the grade level and Carly takes on social studies integration with enthusiasm. However, she is not actually sure if her plans and assessments are implemented in the other classrooms because most of the grade level focus is on reading and math instruction. For Carly, however, making connections among the content areas is a key goal for her social studies planning and instruction.

Carly's classroom is brightly decorated. The chairs at the guided reading table have seat covers that look like basketballs, soccer balls, and baseballs. They spin and have wheels. The kids enjoy sitting in them during small group instruction. She is working with three kids at this table. One boy is not responsive to her prompts. He is slowly sliding off and almost falls out of his chair. She keeps the prompts on sequence and does not reprimand the boy for not responding or sliding out of his chair. Carly gets up from the table, circulates around to the partners working in various places, and leaves the boy staring at the book. She comes back to the boy and does a picture walk. She turns a few pages as he looks at the pictures. He begins to thumb the pages, wrinkling the corners. She takes the book from him and says, "We know how to turn pages correctly." She moves the book closer to him and says, "Try again." And he does. He begins turning pages correctly, looking at each page.

Separated by a few seats, two little girls work at the back table as well. They are doing something slightly different. The boy starts drawing on his sheet and Carly encourages him to continue. Again, she gets up to circulate around the classroom. The three students continue working. The boy sneezes and the girl next to him hands him a tissue and tells him to blow his nose. He does. The girl then moves the trash can near him as well. Carly returns to her chair. The little boy touches her hand and says "pumpkin" and she nods. Ten minutes after the group begins, he starts talking to Carly, retelling the story and working on sequence. He knows that the seeds were left and that they became pumpkins. This boy has high-functioning autism, spending an equal amount of time in and out of the classroom.

Carly agrees with the common perception that the first year of teaching is about surviving. "I felt that I couldn't really get into the curriculum until the third quarter of last year." This year, she feels she can go deeper into the curriculum expectations, but she also feels limited by her lack of knowledge on how to help her student with autism and the large number of children dealing with trauma. These third graders are called the "Peacekeepers" within the school, but their lives seem to be anything but peaceful. Carly shares that many of her students have a lot of trauma, which she feels influences classroom behavior. The causes of student distress are many, including deceased or absent parents. Regardless of the reason, the kids miss their parents. On top of absent parents, many students have ailing caregivers, such as their grandparents. Carly has noticed that her kids are starting to process these traumas and recognize their actions are often related to their emotions. Carly has sought help from the school counselor to help kids process some of these sadly common issues. She has asked for someone to come in to do a lesson on coping strategies to deal with emotions. As much as Carly works on her relationships with her students, she knows the limits of her own skills and that she cannot help them when they say to her, "I've been sad a long time. I'm depressed."

Carly tries within her own skills and limits to provide a safe place for her students. Her classroom is full of "I can" statements, anchor charts, and quotes such as "Dreams don't work if you don't." Currently, the class pursues a Dr. Seuss theme, as well as seasonal books and Native stories like The Rough Face Girl, Loon Spirit, *and* Lady Slipper. *Books are everywhere. Achieve3000 is a recently mandated program for students. It is a "just-right, just-on-time" computer-based comprehension program designed to move "Lexile measures up steadily, level by level" (Acheive3000, para. 1). Carly has displayed the Achieve 3000 goals, but not prominently. The school stresses that achieving these "official" measures are important. The goal is 75 and her class average is 55. Carly wants all her kids to be on grade level, but last year, while 60% of her students met their growth goals, many were not on grade level at the end-of-year assessments.*

Carly teaches at the school just outside of the town for which it is named. The new campus was built in 2009. It houses all levels and school administration. In 2018, just over 91% of students were Native American. While the school is funded by a mixture of federal and tribal resources, federal, state, and local education policies and initiatives shape the curriculum. Grade level teams used the relatively new state standards to write their curriculum as they taught last year. This year, they meet weekly to review, revise, and update their last year's work. The administration team consists of an instructional coach, an assistant principal for curriculum, another assistant principal who focuses mainly on behavior, and the head principal. Carly has two mentors, one provided by the school (a highly regarded kindergarten teacher) and a regional mentor from the state-wide beginning teacher mentoring program. Carly asked to be mentored into her second year by the regional mentor. Carly leverages these people to help her solve problems.

The majority of Carly's teaching experience has been at this school. In her junior year, her instructors placed all elementary education teacher candidates at the school to learn from the schools' diverse population and culture. After Carly's ten-week practicum, she petitioned the college to place her there for her two-semester student teaching experience. She now teaches the same students she had in her practicum course. During that ten-week course, the school staff led several sessions, and during one on the school's classroom management philosophy, Carly found she had fallen in love with their message: "This was a community and kids are more than just a test score." As a beginning teacher, it resonated with her belief system.

As Carly's pre-service year ended, the entire third grade team knew an opening was coming to their level. There was lots of chatter about whether or not Carly would stay to be a classroom teacher. The instructional assistant (IA) said, "I sure hope she's my teacher next year." The assistant was enthusiastic for many reasons, perhaps because of Carly's enthusiasm for teaching, her reliability, her kindness, the known qualities she had demonstrated in her internship, or the credit she shared schoolwide for the third-graders' achievements.

That IA got her wish for two years. However, in Carly's second year, issues and tensions arise. While all parties are discreet, their observable relationship in the classroom moves to a much more formal and professional manner than the previous year. While professionalism is maintained in the classroom, the tension between them is not a secret within the school. The IA is a longtime school employee and community member, someone with a lot of community power. But, and Carly knows this clearly, as the classroom teacher, she is ultimately responsibility for what happens in the classroom in academics and well as behavior.

At the end of her second year, Carly says that having an IA is both an asset and a challenge. Carly plans for the IA to do guided reading groups and math groups during station rotation. Since Carly believes in a spiral cur-

riculum, a method in which students continually revisit previous ideas and concepts, she has the IA lead these review sessions. The IA works alongside lower students during whole group instruction. This year, the IA has often been absent for health reasons, but Carly tries to provide the stations. While Carly does all the planning, she believes her IA has "good instincts" on what students need and has created a communication folder so Carly can access information on students. There is not much time to chat because the IA is off to other assigned duties before and after school as well as during planning time.

The school and community are integrally tied, but Carly feels that perhaps not knowing so much about the families could be a strength. She believes her outsider status may allow her to focus on academics along with, and in spite of, some of the issues occurring at home. She has noticed that her students struggle with retelling a story even though they understand the print (meaning decoding, definitions, and literal comprehension). She asks her state mentor for help and the two begin a book study on reading instruction. She realizes that when the kids struggle with retelling, they do not picture the story in their heads. She tries something new: working on mental and pictorial representations of their readings. Summarizing and retelling are essential and tested skills, so she aims to help them know they have the power to picture the passages in their heads. Now, they focus on chapter books they can read more than once in a week. Students can "go to the movies" in their head. Reflecting on her practice later in the year, she recognizes what she learned in the book study is actually making a difference.

Carly begins lessons with questions, always seeking to tie new learning to previous learning. One day during math, when her IA is absent, she begins: "What did we do last week?" Children respond, a few pointing to anchor charts, "Graphing!" In a quick review of the graphs they have learned, she asks questions such as: "Could we have a sideways graph?" When students suggest different ways to label bar graphs, she responds, "I see what she's saying. That's a good idea." Then, when they decide upon the graphing interval, she prompts an extension from a student, "Why would we go by 2s?" Others get excited and suggest different intervals. As usual, she follows up, "Do you think going by 3s is a good number?" Students decide on their own intervals after much debate. Carly chooses a number and models one graph. On their own, they work the rest of the problems. When they finish, they work on their computer-based math program. She differentiates in math by setting students to one task while pulling others into small groups who may still need additional teaching. Here, Carly focuses on a small group that does not work on graphs, but on addition and subtraction. As Carly observes the students working, she says, "I like how we are using mental math. That is a good strategy, but I want us to show how we get that." To monitor all students, she sits at the back of the room. She plays soft music. Carly rarely uses negative language like "don't" or "wrong." She redirects students by saying "slow down" and "review." She uses every minute for instruction.

At the end of one day, the class engages in a discussion on ancient Egypt and pyramids. They are animated and excited about this topic, but the school intercom constantly interrupts the flow of discussion. The loudspeaker frustrates students because they cannot hear each other. They sigh. They look at the speaker and yell, "C'mon stop it." Once the loudspeaker settles down (between car pick-ups and buses), they do a turn and talk about what they learned that day.

As with most beginning teachers, Carly struggles to balance behavior management with instruction. This year, she says, "has been tricky." Throughout the school, there is a web of connections. Many students are related to peers, a teacher, an instructional assistant, or another staff member. Carly has had to negotiate teaching her IA's family member, a student with autism, and navigate students' emotional issues. At times, Carly has not always felt her behavioral expectations have been supported by her IA or the administration. Carly says her "behavior management approach is different than what is commonly done in school. I do not do rewards for negative behavior. I have this different way that I want to handle it." She is concerned that her classroom authority is undermined, that "students will repeat rewarded behavior no matter what it is." In this school, what she has experienced is that undesirable behavior is often resolved with a quick fix that allows students to avoid doing the hard work. She says students are taken for a walk and given snacks to help them calm down. She feels this approach isn't helpful.

This year, Carly deals with a coalition of girls pressuring each other to disrespect her. They accused her of yelling in the classroom and denying them ice cream. Some of these students seek consolation and a different response from the IA or principal. One day at lunch, a girl wants ice cream, but Carly has a rule that they need to eat "real" food first. Parents know about this healthy food expectation. Carly already spoke with one mother about her daughter's pattern of choosing unhealthy food for lunch. This child asks the

IA to take her to the principal, where the girl complains that Carly would not let her have ice cream. The assistant principal interrupts Carly's teaching to pursue the issue. Carly's defense of her policy costs half an hour of instruction. To the young teacher, the administrative questioning is nerve-wracking, and the disruption of her instruction feels even more demoralizing.

Also, Carly is, for a short time, the subject of an unfounded rumor. A female student reports to the IA that Carly yelled at her and the charge soon circulates among students, families and, most likely, school board members. The principal hears about it at a basketball game and brings Carly into her office the next day. Carly is at a loss, especially when she learns that her IA did not come to her about the accusation first. In reflection with her mentor, Carly feels that perhaps others could interpret Carly's enthusiasm and the daily excitement of her classroom as yelling. Carly acknowledges that this incident is part of learning to navigate the culture of the school and community. She understands the need to build bridges to be able to convey the beliefs that guide her practice and expectations. Eventually, Carly and a few of the girls' parents have a two-hour long conversation. She believes this meeting marks a turning point because she is able to communicate her class-wide high expectations and the parents seem to understand. Reflecting on this incident, she concludes, "I am a young teacher. I am not from here. I am an outsider, and I have clashed with parents because of my strict discipline policy, but I follow through."

Carly climbs a steep learning curve in shaping her teaching practice with her student with autism. She invests many hours exploring what would help him. She recognizes his academic potential and wants to make sure he grasps the content and knows he is expected to complete the work. Often, he resists leaving the classroom to attend art, music, or gym. Carly goes with him, reinforcing that he is held to the same expectations as other students. This boy has hit her, yelled at her, and often refuses to move from his seat. One week, after sacrificing her planning time all week to support this boy in moving through the school day, another third-grade IA removes him from her classroom and said, "Ms. Carly has had enough." Carly appreciates the IA's support and validation of how much she has given, but she does not feel she can surrender. But, Carly says, "Eventually I walked down there and dealt with it because it is my responsibility."

Carly has a checklist in her head about what may be causing a child's behavior. She believes children want to be perceived as good and their behaviors are manifestations of the need of control when external things seem out of control for them. The boy with high-functioning autism has an on-and-off-again relationship with his mother. At year's end, Carly realizes, "I just can't take those things personally anymore ... the physical stuff ... it's not out of anger toward me but anger toward their inability to expresses emotions appropriately."

This high-resource school struggles with support for trauma. Carly says, "There are just not enough people [counselors]. Each teacher needs to step up in his or her own way to help. Like today, I gave up planning." Carly pauses for a minute then continues, "What's the answer? What is a teacher supposed to do? I don't mind leaving grading or paperwork [at the end of the day] but planning for the kid's emotional needs that cropped up in the day—that's when I need to do research and create a plan to deal with it."

At the end of the year, Carly knows she is leaving the school, but she says her move is not because of what has or not happened at the school. "I'm not petty. I don't leave because it gets tough. I know that these issues will be at other schools." She continues, "My heart is in three different places." She means here at the school, where all her teaching experience has been, with her fiancé and his family three hours away, and, of course, hours away in her hometown with her family.

The last few weeks after her decision to leave have been hard. She hasn't shared that she is leaving with many of her colleagues or students because testing is coming. She informs the administration as well as her informal mentor, her "school mom," who was her cooperating teacher and someone she feels is a great friend. There are a lot of tears. She emphatically states that her team has been so supportive. She saw herself grow and believes other classroom teachers did not judge her. She also feels that the school has held true to their vision in her three years there. She hopes to secure a position in another school that also loves its students. Her own small-town background prompts her to teach in a small school.

She volunteers that she will miss the Native American culture and miss the experience of being the minority. "I love being somewhere I can learn and that the kids and school are open to learn about other cultures. Learning about others' culture helps you know about your culture."

Questions

1. Does Carly demonstrate a student-first disposition?
2. Where is the power in Carly's portrait?
3. How is Carly trying to shape school culture?
4. How does the school culture shape Carly's work?

References

Achieve3000. (2019). *Why Achieve 3000?* Retrieved May 5, 2019 from https://www.achieve3000.com/why-achieve3000/

CHAPTER THREE

The What and How of Teacher Leadership

THIS CHAPTER EXPLORES HOW the concept of teacher leadership evolved as a key component of school reform. As the work of teachers went under the microscope, the notion of teacher leadership evolved to bring teachers into the discussion about their profession and student achievement. Teacher leadership has also presented a conundrum for many within the field of education. While more calls for teacher leadership have gone out, the research on and the practice of teacher leadership has struggled to agree on a common definition of what teacher leadership looks like in schools. While the argument of this book is that the language of teacher leadership is potentially problematic, calls for teachers to step into their power as professionals, whether in formal leadership roles or by enacting stewardship through student-first decision making, teachers' voices are an integral piece of the educational puzzle.

Importance of the Idea of Teacher Leadership

Teacher leadership, as with instruction, is not a one-size-fits-all concept. Teachers engaging in becoming teacher leaders do so within the specific contexts of their locations in time and space. Teachers who began teaching in the 1990s would have a very different response to teacher leadership than teachers who are now entering the profession. Harris and Lambert (2003) argue that teacher leadership skills encompass three areas: personal, professional, and collaborative. Personal dispositions are listening to feedback, self-reflection, self-evaluation, showing concern, and respect. Teacher leaders have professional skills and knowledge such as responsiveness, communication, influence, and collaborative skills like decision making, team building, problem solving, and resolution of conflicts. Teacher leadership skills also require being an excellent teacher of children and youth. Many concepts of teacher leadership often gloss over this idea or take it for granted that someone who could be a good leader is also a good teacher.

Being an excellent teacher is important because calls for teacher leadership are rooted in school reform. Since the mid-1980s, the belief has been that the work of teachers, rather than larger societal issues or inequities in school funding, is the primary avenue to increasing student achievement. The calls are to "ignite," "leverage," or "awaken" the powers of teacher leadership in order to improve outcomes in public education. It seems that calls to and for teacher leadership (in the varying ways it has been conceived over the decades) is the tonic that will cure what is ailing schools. Yet, teacher leadership hasn't been the panacea that reformers thought it would be. Any growth of professional autonomy is limited to the organizational structure. When decisions about curriculum materials, assessment procedures, and adoption of standards of practice occur through legislative action, and not teacher, educator, or school-based leadership, then professional growth is limited. We know teachers are important, highly engaged in their work, and passionate about what they do. But when teachers do not even sit at the table where decisions are made, then true teacher leadership is hard to achieve. Despite structural difficulties, engaging in professional decision making with adequate power is essential to sustain and grow practices that are critical to student achievement and wellbeing.

This chapter shares the history of teacher leadership through broad policy and research ideas of the previous decades. This is by no means an exhaustive history of teachers and their roles within the organizations of schooling but rather an overview of big policy ideas and reform movements that have brought us to the idea of teacher leadership within 21st century schooling. Why is knowing this history important to both new and experienced teachers? Knowing the previous policy and reform movements helps teachers understand current reform initiatives. Teaching and schooling, as organizations, have remained relatively stable since the invention and adoption of graded schools in the early 20th century. Understanding the ebb and flow of reform, particularly around the teaching profession, will give teachers a sense of how the profession has evolved into what it is today.

From one-room schoolhouses to "egg-crate" schools and site-based management and professional learning communities, the true ability of teachers to shape and influence schools and educational discourse has varied with the times. In the latter half of the 20th century, there came more and more calls for "teacher leadership" within schools and research communities. But very few schools have discarded hierarchical models for more democratic ones.

Origins of Teacher Leadership

The term teacher leadership has been around for a long time. At varying points in the past, larger society as well as those involved in education have looked to teachers to be leaders, leaders as role models but also leaders in educational decision making. Yet, it wasn't until the late 1980s that teacher leadership became the *thing* that was seen as a way to change teaching and schooling for the better. Why does this shift that happened in the 1980s—most likely way before you were teaching or even alive—matter? What happened in the 1980s is still impacting your everyday life as a teacher. Professional learning communities, lead teachers, mentor teachers, and school improvement committees all come from the reform movement sparked by a government report in the 1980s.

In 1983, the federal government, in trying to rid itself of the Department of Education, issued a report that did the opposite. *A Nation at Risk: The Imperative for Educational Reform* sounded an alarm that indicated without significant improvement in K-12 school outcomes, the economy and the strength of the nation would collapse. This document, much criticized and applauded over the years, created the accountability and reform movements, from a federal level, that we contend with today. Prior to this, the role of the federal Department of Education (prior to 1979, it was the Office of Education) was to ensure that students were obtaining access to equal education and coordinating any federal funds that schools received. After a *Nation at Risk*, the federal government took on a bigger policy mandate and oversight role, while most of the money to actually run schools still came from state and local taxes. The role and purpose of the Department of Education is still being debated into the 21st century. However, the narrative that schools are responsible for and essential to national success persists.

Interestingly, the report's recommendations suggest some fundamental changes in the way schools operate in the United States: increasing the school year, moving teachers to an 11-month contract, creating career ladders for teachers, increasing salaries for teachers and the development of a peer-evaluation system, among many others. The recommendations conclude with the statement:

> This Commission calls upon educators, parents, and public officials at all levels to assist in bringing about the educational reform proposed in this report. We also call upon citizens to provide the financial support necessary to accomplish these purposes. Excellence costs. But in the long run mediocrity costs far more. (National Commission on Excellence in Education, 1983, p. 33)

The cost of mediocrity was the hallmark of this report. But it turns out that schools and students in the United States were doing all right. The narrative of mediocrity and failure has remained consistent despite data. Since 1983, a lot of things have happened, not without controversy, that the report would support: a movement toward better standards with the adoption, albeit not uncontroversial, of Common Core standards across multiple states, and peer evaluations of the profession, such as the Teacher Performance Assessment (edTPA) for teacher candidates and the National Board for Professional Teaching Standards (NBPTS). Yet, what has had most of the focus since 1983 is the role of how teachers are improving student outcomes, which is often measured through "value-added" measures like test scores. Sadly, the report's call to increase the financial support to combat mediocrity has not been heeded either.

Prior to a *Nation at Risk*, the role of teachers within schools was not as scrutinized as it is today. Between the World Wars, the intelligence quotient (IQ) dominated schools. Any student, if they did not learn, was just thought to be deficient. The public did not fault the teachers. Also, many students were denied access to public school until the 1975 Individuals with Disabilities Education Act (IDEA), and preparation for teachers varied widely with each state, similar to today, having comparable yet differing requirements to teach in public schools (Ravitch, 2003). In 1974, a report published by the Association of Teacher Educators proposed that teachers be prepared differently in order to create change in education. The report defined a teacher leader as "a competent educator with special skills in analyzing teaching, working with students, implementing change, and developing curriculum" (Andrew, p. 8). Not surprisingly, this call was in response to Charles Silberman's *Crisis in the Classroom: The Remaking of American Education* (1970), which was one of the numerous books in the late 1960s and 1970s that called into question what was happening to children in U.S. schools. The main criticism of schooling in this era was that it was oppressive, teacher directed, and not responsive to the students' culture and background. This new attention to human relationships in teaching and learning was also a move away from traditional rote learning and behaviorist techniques that had gained popularity in the post-World War II era.

Within schools in the 1970s, teacher leadership was studied as a set of behaviors documented through observation and surveys that were created for examining research in business settings. Research articles at the time also praised the idea that teachers can learn from business management principles (Ames, 1979). Other researchers believed that there were some teachers who had great influence over students and school culture that led to changes. They also thought that these teacher leaders had distinct characteristics including the ability to bring about change, pedagogical content knowledge, positive relationships, age, experience, communication skills, and years within the context (Brownlee, 1979). These characteristics have persisted as a way to define teacher leadership into much of the 21st century's research and thought on teacher leadership.

In the previous chapter, we learned that leadership is often defined in the eye of the beholder and that ideas, such as influence and common goals, are key to leadership definitions. Similarly, the definition of teacher leadership that is most commonly used in research is one offered by York-Barr and Duke (2004): "Teacher leadership is the process by which teachers, individually or collectively, influence their colleagues, principals, and other members of school community to improve teaching and learning practices with the aim of increased student learning and achievement" (pp. 287–288). This definition sets increased student learning as the goal to be achieved in teacher leadership. How that learning is determined is not defined. Other conceptions of teacher leadership exist, such as Lieberman and Miller's *Teacher Leadership* (2004), which breaks down York-Barr and Duke's definition into three separate roles teachers can take: advocates who concern themselves with student learning, innovators who are the change agents, and stewards who are the models of continued improvement of the profession. The concept of teacher leadership is a robust field of study focusing on the roles and areas of influence that teachers have in their schools and the larger educational community. Much research in teacher leadership has described distinct formal roles and differentiated paths (Margolis & Huggins, 2012) as well as subtler acts of leadership in interpersonal relationships (Sato, 2005). Regardless of the nuances in definitions, the idea that teachers should engage in processes that guide policies that impact the school and students is an old concept (Dewey, 1946). Currently, there are many ways teachers can influence the public discourses about schooling. One way is the management concept of teacher leadership: helming committees, producing professional development, managing a wide array of school-based events, having data-based decision-making capabilities, and influencing others to get on board with curriculum changes. Wider definitions of teacher leadership see advocating for policies that benefit students, communication with elected representatives, doing independent research and writing, and leading communities of practice (that benefit students and school communities) as authentic teacher leadership. The advent of social media has allowed teachers' voices to enter the news cycle. Stories of why teachers are leaving the profession and pictures of poor school conditions that have gone viral or trending end up on the nightly news. One of the earliest examples is from 2015, when Wendy Bradshaw posted her resignation from the Polk County Florida school system on Facebook. The post indicated the reasons for her resignation as the mandates of developmentally inappropriate evaluation measures for young children (Einenkel, 2015). In subsequent years, many similar posts followed. In 2018, teachers in states such as Oklahoma, West Virginia, and North Carolina began staging one-day protests and strikes for better school systems. In 2018, Jill Bradley-Levine, noted scholar on teacher leadership, wrote about the relationship between advocacy and teacher leadership. She calls advocacy a "practice of teacher leadership" (p. 47). Advocacy for schools and students requires that teachers understand that schools are places of empowerment *and* oppression for students: the essential dilemma of public schools. While schools are seen and spoken of as a public good, funding and support from the public doesn't often follow.

Leadership and the Professional Status of Teaching

There are two basic thoughts about teaching out there in the wider world. They may sound familiar. One idea is that anyone can teach. Teaching is about implementing curriculum, reading the script, and following along with the daily and/or weekly plans provided by the textbook company. Teaching is only about knowing content, telling students that content, and testing the students. Repeat. Another idea is that teachers are professionals. The teachers as professional idea indicates that there is a specialized knowledge of how to teach certain groups of kids (pedagogy), and of certain kids (developmental psychology). Teachers are creators of learning experiences that foster curiosity and create critical thinkers. They reflect on what their students know and need to know and create curriculum to get their students to achieve those goals. Now, as with most things in our lives, the reality occurs somewhere in between two opposites. After reflecting on one's own experience with classrooms and fellow teachers, what is the reality of teaching? Teachers, many teachers, are accountable to something more than test scores. Some moral imperative pulled them into teaching, the public mission of schooling, the calling to care for the knowledge development of other people's children, the call to serve. This call to serve, to teach, is at odds with "the disorder in the system" (Einenkel, 2015, para. 4) that is found in most U.S. schools.

Smulyan (2016) situates current public schools and the clamor for "teacher leaders" within the neoliberal framework, where schooling has gone from a "public good" to a focus on individual prosperity. Smulyan argues that real teacher leaders keep the public good as their focus. Smulyan and her colleagues have created the idea that teacher leader is a stance rather than a role or types of behaviors. Teacher leadership, according to Smulyan's group, has three key perspectives: it (1) is firmly rooted in teaching as a professional, intellectual act; (2) occurs on a political landscape for democracy and social justice; and (3) requires collaborative networks to work for the common good (p. 9). Teacher leadership emerges in three areas as well: instructional, curricular, and policy. The teacher leadership that emerges is "deeply local and broadly political" (p. 22). It is about teachers stepping into their power and "harnessing this power that exists in every teacher" (p. 8). Webb (2002) writes that, "Teacher power refers to teacher's professional discretion and is considered to be the foundation upon which to professionalize teaching" (p. 47). This power, this professional discretion, is the one thing that many accountability reforms stifle as Bradshaw's resignation letter states: "The disorder is in the system which bars teachers from differentiating instruction meaningfully, which threatens disciplinary action if they decide their students need a five minute break from a difficult concept, or to extend a lesson which is exceptionally engaging" (Einenkel, 2015, para. 4).

Teachers have power, a lot of power. If one thinks back to teachers they've had or known, what teachers choose to say in the classroom has power. What teachers choose to teach, to ignore, and to simplify is based within their power. If one believes teachers ought to just comply with curriculum mandates, follow the script, and repeat, then teacher power is particularly frustrating. Santoro (2016) notes many teachers enter the profession for moral reasons and are sustained in their work through joys of teaching. She argues that asking teachers to implement curriculum fidelity (stick to the script) often presents a moral dilemma to teachers. She writes,

> Teachers who challenge or do not follow the plan may be characterized not only as insubordinate, but as traitors to the aims of equitable education. The threat of moral reprobation may be especially damaging to educators for whom teaching is a significant source of their moral identity. (2016, p. 9)

Thinking that teachers have a moral imperative to do what is right for kids can make the idea of teacher power liberating. Most often, teacher power, or professional discretion, occurs within accountability and evaluative structures. Teachers become conduits and negotiators. They negotiate standards and curriculum mandates to allow their students to grow and show what they know. They reflect on their teaching and change—or mediate—expectations to fit student needs. Teachers develop their judgement through their teacher education courses and within their years of teaching in order to implement their professional discretion. Two profession-created performance assessments, the edTPA and the NBPTS, were developed to help improve and refine a teacher's professional judgment. While these assessment systems are not without their critiques and controversy, they are one step to professionalization, which allows more teachers to exert influence and steward the profession to the benefit of students and communities.

In the snapshot below, we meet Katherine, a third-year middle grades English Language Arts teacher, who is confident and thrives within professional norms at her school.

Snapshot: Katherine

Katherine is the youngest teacher in the school at the age of 24. She has reoccurring dreams of her class being out of control, yet, when one enters her room, there is a low hum of conversation. Everyone seated and working on something. When one enters her rectangular-shaped classroom, she is hard to find since she looks very similar to her seventh graders. She is sitting at a desk, talking with a student, while the students are working, at various stages on a writing assignment. Katherine works in one of three middle schools in a dis-

trict that serves just over 7,000 students. It is a mixed rural setting that spends about $9,400 per pupil per year. Half the district population qualifies for free and reduced lunch. There are about 550 students at Katherine's school and 60% of the students at her school are deemed proficient in English language Arts per state expectations.

Katherine is teaching in the county where she grew up, although she lives nearly 45 miles away with her partner. Katherine wants school to be a safe place and believes that student success is about growth but also very much about meeting the state standards. Katherine pays attention to data. She, and her students, did well in her first year with state assessments. In her second year, she set a goal for her Gifted kids to exceed growth. This year, her focus is on those "middle" kids to make growth. She "loves" the short assessment practices provided by the state as she feels she gets good data on her students.

Katherine and her colleagues are treated as professionals by their administrators. Once, each nine weeks, content area teams get a planning day. Content area department heads bring information or help teachers examine some specific skill. Katherine has a big binder with planning documents because teachers design their own curriculum. As long as they are successful and making growth on assessments, the administration hasn't seen a need to create any curricular mandates.

Katherine is a team leader for seventh grade this year, but she is also considered a beginning teacher because she is just in her third year. She feels that she has received this leadership role because she has been willing to invite her principals into her classroom and shared her students' growth. Katherine thinks that it is important both to be confident in one's decisions around instruction and to also "show leaders that you are willing to grow."

Teacher Leadership as a Role

Many teachers see teacher leadership as a role that they are given with certain tasks to accomplish. Many "Lead Teachers" in schools function as assistant principals with managerial types of responsibilities. Leadership and management are different things. Teachers who are given "leadership" roles that focus on reducing the chaos of the school day or the increasing efficiency of the organization are managers, not teacher leaders (Northouse, 2016, p. 13). Sommerness, York-Barr and Hur (2008) reinforce the qualitative difference between leaders and managers by indicating that teacher leaders share leadership with the administration (i.e., principal) to "enact the school's vision of advancing teaching, rather than just being communicators or coordinators" (p. 1). Teacher leadership requires an "expanded set of capacities and skills, beyond those required for excellence in classroom instruction" (Sommerness, York-Barr, & Hur, 2008, p. 8). But even if we have teachers who have this set of skills, there are contextual constraints in demonstrating teacher leadership.

Teachers are not attracted to leadership roles that are incongruent with existing norms of professionalism among teachers. This is evidenced by Margolis and Deuel's study (2009) that shares deep portraits of teacher leaders in a grant-sponsored initiative. Margolis and Deuel also found that a moral imperative (doing what is right for students and schools) is a large motivator to engage in leadership beyond the classroom. Other intrinsic motivators are sharing and helping others growth, which is a similar to a finding of a study on nationally board-certified teachers shared below. The teachers in Margolis and Deuel's study were designated, formally, as teacher leaders within a two-year grant initiative focused on content area literacy practices. The researchers found that "doing" teacher leadership is more important than being called a teacher leader. Doing teacher leadership includes having professional, peer-to-peer conversations on how and what teachers do in the classroom impacts student outcomes. One important aspect to this study is that these teachers were compensated with a stipend for their leadership roles. Initially, these teacher leaders found the stipend to be ranked as a secondary motivator for leading their initiatives within their school. However, by the end of the grant, many teacher leaders found the stipend to be as important in recognizing their extra work and professional knowledge as the formal designation. The researchers concluded that intrinsic and extrinsic motivators are synergistic, but teacher leadership will still be underutilized because of the professional norms and allocation of time within teaching (Margolis & Deuel, 2009, p. 283).

Teacher Leadership as Influence

A two-year project in a small, rural high school in British Columbia found that teacher leadership emerges to address a need based on a school or teacher goal, skill, and/or desire. Cherkowski and Schnellert (2017) worked with the school to develop a placed-based professional development. A key part of the work is that the teachers, in teams, created their own common goal for improving teaching and learning. This process took several months, but the common goal allowed teacher leaders to emerge at different stages of the professional learning process. One teacher became so energized by the ownership around the goal that she found articles to share and organized meetings to discuss research. Others felt supported to try new teaching strategies modeled by other teachers. This study found that teacher leadership emerges naturally when teachers are in control over their own professional learning and are given the time to truly collaborate.

A study by Sato, Hyler, and Monte-Sano (2014) of a small group of National Board-Certified Teachers (NBCT) found that the teachers became more grounded personally and professional through their NBCT process and were more able to articulate a moral purpose in which to engage in leadership. Becoming an NBCT requires a teacher to submit a portfolio that is aligned with the National Board of Professional Teaching Standards (NBPTS) within the teacher's desired area of certification. The portfolio consists of teacher planning documents, student work samples, and videos of practice. For the participants in the study, the NBCT process created a language in which they were able to clearly articulate what is good for student learning. These teachers then were able to help others within their schools locate evidence of student learning in their work. The NBCT portfolio continually asks teachers to reflect and write about: Why do I do what I do, and how can I do it better? These teachers continued to use this question to frame their conversations with colleagues and administrations within the school. One teacher explained that, when she was asked to reflect within the portfolio on how her professional work beyond the classroom impacted student learning, she realized that many of the committees she was on had no good "case as to why that [committee] was really benefitting kids" (Sato, Hyler, & Monte-Sano, 2014, p. 17).

Teacher leadership can be constructed as practical actions that a teacher takes within their context based on a value system or purposes that drive one to act. These actions are where a teacher is exercising professional discretion, or exerting their power, in choosing which items to act on and to lead based on the teachers' professional knowledge of the needs. This is in contrast to a technical manager that is placed into a teacher leadership role at the discretion of others, mainly administration. Sato and her colleagues (2014) found that there was no real pattern to these teachers' acts of leadership. Being an NBCT was not necessarily favorable to their opportunities to become formal teacher leaders since some administrators saw little value in the certification process. The results show that these teachers "saw a need" within the specific context in which they worked and decided to act to address the need rather than be appointed to fix a need determined by someone else. For example, one teacher began a lesson sharing time because she felt teachers at her school needed more time to talk together about what was working, or not, within their instruction.

This study also supports the ideas that teacher leaders *choose* to lead. These teachers choose their pursuits based on their own professional and personal identities. The researchers also noted that after becoming an NBCT, the teachers felt an obligation to help improve teaching and learning within their school contexts, either by mentoring others who wanted to become NBCT or just by sharing their experiences and personal growth in informal ways. Sato, Hyler and Monte-Sano (2014) use the idea of "professional stewardship" as way to name this commitment to other teachers: "...a driver of teacher leadership could be finding purpose in preserving and supporting professional ideals. To be members of the profession of teaching means to uphold a set of responsibilities and behaviors" (p. 17).

Role of Teacher Preparation

The idea that teacher education has a significant role to play in creating teacher leaders is fairly new. York-Barr and Duke (2004) reference two studies on pre-service education for teacher leadership. Since their review, teacher leadership at the pre-service level has become an emerging field of research. Wenner and Campbell's (2017) review of the literature on teacher leadership concludes there is a "dearth" of detailed research on how teachers become leaders (p. 20). Many studies on pre-service teacher leadership suggest ideas and strategies for allowing teacher candidates to demonstrate leadership within their undergraduate work (Turnbull, 2005; Mangin & Stoelinga, 2009). For example, Bond and Sterrett (2014) promote the idea that pre-service teachers who serve as officers of student professional organizations, such as Kappa Delta Pi, are better prepared to be teacher leaders. Holland, Eckert and Allen (2014) premise their research on the idea that teacher education must help pre-service teachers understand school culture and have mentors that are teacher leaders in order to be fully prepared to implement the "fourth wave" of teacher leadership: impacting policy rather than following mandates (p. 436). However, much research finds current novice teachers viewing teacher leadership as involvement in school-based decision making, a path to tenure, and administrative responsibilities rather than as opportunities to influence policy towards better outcomes for children (Rogers & Scales, 2013; Scales & Rogers, 2017).

Bank Street College of Education met limitations in meeting its goal for their graduates to "be leaders in the creation of a better world for all of our children" (Snyder, 2015, p. 7). In a serious self-evaluation process, Bank Street found that, while their candidates took on leadership roles in classrooms and schools and "walked the talk" about advocacy, their principals reported that Bank Street graduates had trouble "fitting in" to the school culture, though they were excellent classroom teachers (Snyder, 2015). Reading between the lines, the trouble fitting into the school culture may have been because the culture did not support a vision of teacher leaders that was similar to Bank Street's. The developing research on pre-service teacher leadership is that helping students understand the culture of schools, offering mentors, intentionally using the language of leadership across courses, and encouraging students to be leaders in organizations may impact their ability to be teacher leaders.

Teacher Leadership and New Teachers

For new teachers, the opportunity to be seen as a teacher leader, whether in a formal or informal role, has the potential to increase retention (Donaldson, 2007), the sense of self-efficacy (Chew & Andrews, 2010), and student learning (Leithwood, Louis, Anderson & Wahlstrom, 2004). The examination of leadership development and capacity in the early years of teaching is crucial for retention, as many teachers leave the profession within those first five years and 55% leave because of dissatisfaction with their profession (Carver-Thomas & Darling-Hammond, 2017). Margolis and Deuel (2009) note that, as early as the fourth year, new teachers are yearning for more challenges beyond the classroom.

The ideas of who can and cannot be a "teacher leader" are changing, but examinations of early-career or novice teacher leadership are rare. As mentioned above with the Bank Street graduates, many new teachers are finding it hard to "walk the talk" of leadership and change in their early years. One of the reasons this may be is because many definitions of teacher leadership, either of the managerial kind or the more informal ideas, lean on a concept of expertise acquired through classroom experience and/ or advanced education. Opportunities for formal teacher leadership are limited for new teachers, yet as Levenson (2014) points out the eagerness of new teachers often leads them into being asked to do "teacher leadership," even when they are not ready. One teacher interviewed for this book was invited to sit on the school leadership team during her first year. After the first few meetings, Monica realized that she wasn't ready for this type of responsibility. She told her principal that she felt the leadership team was taking her away from her focus on student achievement and asked to be released from the committee. The principal understood and let Monica return to lead in her classroom.

As teachers enter their first teaching assignments and work in their first schools full time, their ideas of teacher leadership change. In North Carolina, student teachers were required to complete a Teacher Leadership assignment as part of their licensure requirements. In a study of one North Carolina university teacher education graduates Scales and Rogers (2017) found that many of the pre-service teachers couldn't remember the assignment, and those that did viewed the assignment as merely a task to complete for licensure that did not apply to the actual classroom. In survey responses, other new teachers felt that, after a year of teaching, teacher leadership made more sense to them as a key part of being a teacher. One teacher says, "I am more aware now that I need to have a voice in the school and the community. I feel as though I fight for the rights of my kids to be as ready to learn as possible" (p. 6).

Early-career teachers also move along a continuum from classroom to community when it comes to teacher leadership. Another teacher writes,

> I see the importance of being a leader in the community and school much more now. In college, I viewed it as more of a leading in the school. But as teachers, we are affecting the generations coming after us who will be in charge of our communities, cities, and maybe even country one day. We are leading on a much bigger scale. (Scales & Rogers, 2017, p. 6)

Others note that teacher leadership in schools is different than previously held conceptions as one participant writes, "I have also realized that there are subtle ways that teachers lead among their peers that I did not recognize during my time as [a student teacher]. Also, it's [leadership] not as simple as I probably thought prior to graduation" (Scales and Rogers, 2017, p.6).

In their study Scales and Rogers (2017) find four themes in the new teachers' definitions of teacher leadership: risks (being open or vulnerable), perceptions from others, advocate, and planner. These ideas are similar across the literature on novice teacher leadership. New teachers believe that becoming a teacher leader early in one's career requires some risk. Novice teachers engaging in teacher leadership, as it is defined within their context, run the risk of alienating their administrators or other teachers. Yet, having an open or vulnerable disposition can lead to increased learning for novice teachers.

The perceptions of others in the school, mainly other teachers, is important for a new teacher to be seen as a leader. One participant in the study comments that she does not feel like a teacher leader despite her colleagues' inquiries. She says that she is open to being a teacher leader by putting herself "out there" and concludes that she is a teacher leader "[a] s much as I can be as a first-year teacher. I'm not ready to train the whole school or anything" (Scales & Rogers, 2017, p.8). Her response indicates that teacher leadership, in her school, is seen as role or task that one is given to fulfill. She puts herself out there to be noticed but is not ready to "train" the school, which reveals her perception that teacher leadership requires advanced expertise and being recognized for that expertise.

Other new teachers interviewed for this book express a range of ideas about what teacher leadership is and their role to play in it. Eleanor, a third-year teacher at a charter school in a large metropolitan area, says that she feels she can influence her colleagues through relationships and collaboration activities such as cross-grade planning. She acknowledges that she works in a small school and that her context is different. She sees teacher leadership as occurring within one's own classroom, team, school, and then outside. She says, "Teacher leadership looks different for teachers depending on what they want to do. Running meetings, facilitating conversations." She also believes it is "Hard to be a leader and stay in the classroom. It's taking on too much. It looks different." Katherine, a middle-grades Language Arts teacher, agrees with Eleanor's ideas and says, "It [teacher leadership] is different for each teacher because it depends on what they want to do." Connor, a second-year upper elementary teacher, defines teacher leadership as "going out of their way to do things for kids." He says, "You don't have to do it all to be a leader. You are watched by everyone else and you see what teachers are good at certain things and then they are viewed as a leader." Morgan, a fourth-year elementary school teacher, says that if you are doing the best for kids and are recognized for it, then you are a leader. For her, recognition comes from parents, administration, and other teachers—in that order. She is very careful and knows that she is young and new but says, "When I preface my concerns about what's best for children, I am heard."

Critiques of Teacher Leadership

Since the school reform movement began in earnest in the late 1990s, public schools have been moving more and more towards a business model of leadership and management. Ideas imported from business, such as increased competition, lean management, incentive pay, mission statements, and outcomes, have permeated public schools. The "bottom line" has become student test scores as opposed to profit margins in the corporate world. While there have been critiques of restructuring schools into a business model, there have been few direct critiques of the notion of teacher leadership. It is a term that teachers seem to simultaneously welcome and distrust. Though many teachers want to be a leader, they question what it means to be a "teacher leader" and what kinds of sacrifices are required to be one.

In an interesting piece, two authors from Australia take a critical stance regarding teacher leadership, one that is not often heard but is worth talking about. Fitzgerald and Gunter (2008) write that leadership is a "ubiquitous term" since it is used in a lot of places in a lot of different ways. It is hard to know what someone means by leadership. As another scholar on leadership writes, leadership cannot really be defined unilaterally, meaning that, while there is a general sense of what leadership is, the definition is often based on one's previous experience with leadership (Northouse, 2016).

Fitzgerald and Gunter (2008) write that the use of teacher leadership is essentially about school reform, and that it is a management strategy rather than something radical that will improve teaching and learning in the school. This is an important critique. Often, schools will entice teachers into doing more work without compensation, all in the name of being a "teacher leader." The authors also argue that neoliberal visions of schools, which impose private business models on to public schools through performance management and evaluation of teachers against standards, just reinforce that teacher leadership is about using teachers to do management work rather than the work of teaching students. In other studies, the proliferation of school committees and events that teachers are asked to "lead" are really management roles with little to do with student learning. This is the bigger idea that Fitzgerald and Gunter (2008) are writing about and other scholars caution against: as a teacher, be vigilant about what you devote your time to. Teachers need to ask themselves how is this task about helping students? If the answer is satisfying to the teacher, then it is worth giving precious time to.

Teacher leadership is important and problematic. It's important because teachers are well educated, thoughtful, and loving people and ought to have an influence on the policies and practices that guide their daily work. Teacher leadership is problematic because the structures that teachers work in are not responsive to the calls of teacher leadership. A teacher interviewed for this book, who taught from the early to mid-2000s, remembers all the calls to leadership within her school to sit on committees or attend workshops. But she still felt little "leadership, or the ability to make decisions about what actually happened at the school."

It seems to be common sense that engaging teachers in the work of leading schools (making decisions about curriculum, instruction, scheduling, and even allocation of resources) would increase student achievement. Any person who is highly engaged in their work, who is stimulated and challenged but also supported, may be better at what they do. Teachers teach kids. So, engaging teachers in decision making, research, and conversations around curriculum and instruction would help teachers become better engaged and perform better at their work. Theoretically, teacher leadership is a positive concept. Practically? In the United States, we have not altered the basic structure of public schools to allow real teacher leadership to happen, even though research points to increased student achievement with more teacher involvement in decision-making processes (Ingersoll, Sirinides, & Dougherty, 2017). More often than not, new teachers will work in schools that are traditionally structured. This means that there are 180 school days, and time for professional development occurs before and after the school year begins with a few days sprinkled throughout. Often lumped into "teaching duty" is bus and lunchroom supervision combined with a 50-minute prep per day. In addition, required meetings after school often impede professional conversations about instruction.

There are school leaders (by this I mean principals and superintendents) who engage in an enlightened type of leadership that may try to structure school days differently and hire substitutes to allow teachers to do peer-coaching/observation. These principals know that their teachers are the best resource in improving teaching and learning. Yet, the essential structure of teacher duty and school days remains unchanged. For many teachers in U.S. classrooms the school day and structure limit opportunities to traditional leadership roles such as mentor or coach and even these roles are constrained by the school day and structure. For new teachers, who are required by traditional structures to prove they can teach and manage their classroom first, opportunities for leadership are often limited to the classroom where a teacher can influence students and families.

Margolis and Deuel (2009) write about "fracturing the head from the heart" when teachers are asked to engage in professional development or placed into leadership roles that don't align with personal or professional values. This fracturing can lead to dissatisfaction with the profession and can drive teachers to leave. The next chapter will examine how the concept of stewardship can prevent this fracture between head and heart and change the way schools are structured, allowing teachers to lead through stewardship at any point in their career.

References

Ames, M. (1979). What teachers can learn from managers. *Educational Horizons*, *57*(3),107–111. https://www.jstor.org/stable/42924323

Andrew, M. (1974). *Teacher leadership: A model for change.* Association of Teacher Educators, Washington D.C.

Bond, N., & Sterrett, W. (2014). Developing teacher leaders through honorary professional organizations in education: Focus on the college student officers. *Education*, *135*(1), 25–38.

Bradley-Levine, J. (2018). Advocacy as a practice of critical teacher leadership. *International Journal of Teacher Leadership*, *9*(1), 47–61.

Brownlee, G. (1979). Characteristics of teacher leaders. *Educational Horizons*, *57(3)*,119-122.

Carver-Thomas, D., & Darling-Hammond, L. (2017). *Teacher turnover: Why it matters and what we can do about it.* Palo Alto, CA: Learning Policy Institute.

Cherkowski, S., & Schnellert, L. (2017). Exploring teacher leadership in a rural, secondary school: Reciprocal learning teams as a catalyst for emergent leadership. *International Journal of Teacher Leadership*, *8*(1), 6–25.

Chew, J. O. A., & Andrews, D. (2010). Enabling teachers to become pedagogical leaders: Case studies of two IDEAS schools in Singapore and Australia. *Educational Research for Policy and Practice*, *9*, 59–74. https://doi.org/10.1007/s10671-010-9079-0

Dewey, J. (1946). *Problems of men.* New York: Philosophical Library.

Donaldson, M. L. (2007). To lead or not to lead? A quandary for newly tenured teachers. In R. H. Ackerman & S. V. Mackenzie (Eds.), *Uncovering teacher leadership: Essays and voices from the field* (pp. 259–272). Thousand Oaks, CA: Corwin Press.

Einenkel, W. (2015). Teacher's Facebook resignation post goes viral because she is 100% right. Retrieved from https://www.dailykos.com/stories/2015/11/5/1445148/-Teacher-s-Facebook-resignation-post-goes-viral-because-she-is-100-right

Fitzgerald, T., & Gunter, H.M. (2008). Contesting the orthodoxy of teacher leadership. *International Journal of Leadership in Education*, *11*(4), 331–340.

Harris, A. & Lambert, L. (2003) *Building leadership capacity for school improvement*. Buckingham, UK: Open University Press.

Holland, J., Eckert, J., & Allen, M. (2014). From preservice to teacher leadership: Meeting the future in educator preparation. *Action in Teacher Education*, *36*(5-6), 433–445.

Ingersoll, R. Sirinides, P., & Dougherty, P. (2017). School leadership, teachers' roles in school decision making, and student achievement. *CPRE Working Papers*. Retrieved from http://repository.upenn.edu/cpre_workingpapers/15

Leithwood, K., Louis, K. S., Anderson, S., & Wahlstrom, K. (2004). *Review of research: How leadership influences student learning*. New York, NY: Wallace Foundation.

Levenson, M. (2014). *Pathways to teacher leadership: Emerging models, Changing roles*. Harvard Education Press: Cambridge MA.

Lieberman, A., & Miller, L. (2004). *Teacher leadership*. San Francisco: Jossey-Bass.

Mangin, M., & Stoelinga, S. R. (2009). The future of instructional teacher leader roles. *The Educational Forum*, *74*(1), 49–62.

Margolis, J., & Deuel, A. (2009). Teacher leaders in action: Motivation, morality, and money. *Leadership and Policy in Schools*, *8*(3), 264–286. https://doi.org/10.1080/15700760802416115

Margolis, J., & Huggins, K. S. (2012). Distributed but undefined: New teacher leader roles to change schools. *Journal of School Leadership*, *22*(5), 953–981.

Northouse, P. (2016). *Leadership: Theory and practice* (7th ed.). Thousand Oaks, CA: Sage.

National Commission on Excellence in Education. (1983). *A nation at risk: the imperative for educational reform. A report to the Nation and the Secretary of Education*. United States Department of Education. Washington, D.C.

Ravitch, D. (2003). *A brief history of teacher professionalism*. White House Conference on Preparing Tomorrow's Teachers. Retrieved from https://www2.ed.gov/admins/tchrqual/learn/preparingteachersconference/ravitch.html

Rogers, C., & Sales, R.Q. (2013). Pre-service teachers' perceptions of teacher leadership: Is it about compliance or understanding? *Issues in Teacher Education*, *22*(2), 17–37.

Santoro, D. (2016). "We're are not going to do that because it's not right": Using pedagogical responsibility to reframe the doublespeak of fidelity. *Educational Theory*, *66*(1/2), 263–277.

Sato, M. (2005). Practical leadership: Conceptualizing the everyday leadership work of teachers. *The New Educator*, *1*(1), 55–71.

Sato, M., Hyler, M. E., Monte-Sano, C. B. (2014). Learning to lead with purpose: National Board Certification and teacher leadership development. *International Journal of Teacher Leadership*, *5*(1), 1–23.

Scales, R.Q., & Rogers, C. (2017). Novice teacher leadership: Determining the impact of a leadership licensure requirement after one year of teaching. *Professional Educator*, *41*(1). http://wp.auburn.edu/educate/wp-content/uploads/2017/05/Scales-spring_16-accessible.pdf

Silberman, C.E. (1970). *Crisis in the classroom: The remaking of American education.* New York: Vintage.
Smulyan, L. (2016). Symposium introduction: Stepping into their power: The development of a teacher leadership stance. *Schools: Studies in Education, 13*(1), 8–28.
Snyder, J. (2015). Teacher leadership and teacher preparation: a personal narrative. *The Educational Forum*, *79*(1), 5–11.
Sommerness, J., York-Barr, J., & Hur, J. (2008). Teacher leadership. In T. Good (Ed.), *21st century education: a reference handbook* (pp.12-20). Thousand Oaks, CA: Sage Publications.
Turnbull, B. (2005). Facilitating early career leadership through pre-service training. *Teachers and Teaching: Theory and Practice*, *11*(5), 457–464.
Webb, P.T. (2002). Teacher power: the exercise of professional autonomy in an era of strict accountability. *Teacher Development, 6*(1), pp. 47–61.
Wenner, J.A., & Campbell, T. (2017). The theoretical and empirical basis of teacher leadership: A review of the literature. *Review of Educational Research*, *87*(1), 134–171.
York-Barr, J., & Duke, K. (2004). What do we know about teacher leadership? Findings from two decades of scholarship. *Review of Educational Research*, 74(3), 255–316.

PORTRAIT OF ABIGAIL

Abigail looks like she is ready to do some serious work. Attired in work boots and jeans, she moves around the classroom to check with students before she settles at her desk. Abigail teaches agricultural education at the middle school in a rural county in the Appalachian Mountains. The school resides in a wide valley that runs along a river. The area was originally inhabited by the great Cherokee Nation prior to removal in the 1840s. The land contains rich, river-nourished soil and wide valleys for crops, which is why it was valued by the Cherokee Nation. In the 21st century, the ground remains fertile, but agriculture is not a primary economic force here, nor is subsistence farming that White settlers engaged in after removal of the Cherokees. In fact, a large part of the teaching that Abigail engages in helps students and their families reconnect with the land. She has students bring in items from home and do research on how those foods got into their refrigerator or cabinets. Abigail works in one of the poorest counties in the state, hundreds of miles from the capital in which laws are passed for schools. Yet, Abigail is well connected to the capital, where the state Future Farmers of America (FFA) is headquartered and where she attends school online for her teaching credential. She is what is called a "lateral-entry" teacher. She has a degree in agricultural science and experience, but she lacks the specific state teacher licensing requirements.

Where she teaches, median household income is around $40,000. While 80% of the county has graduated from high school, only about 20% continue on and finish a college degree. College wasn't in Abigail's plans initially. While she thought about teaching, her initial career path led her down a different route. In Abigail's classroom, learning and challenging oneself to be better are clearly communicated. But she doesn't fuss over students' futures as much as she fusses about their current work.

Abigail is young, but she is a non-traditional teacher. She's a "farm girl" from a nearby state who worked for agricultural corporations, the United States Department of Agriculture, and the State Agriculture Extension offices before being called to teach Agriculture Education (Ag Ed). Ag Ed includes vast content within earth sciences such as soil and water issues and conservation as well as biological sciences, which include plant life, crop development, and animal life cycles. Her curriculum is driven by FFA standards and then aligned with grade level science and English language arts standards. She realizes that other teachers see her as having much more freedom to do "fun" teaching. While being able to structure her classes in more non-traditional ways, the curriculum and expectation contain much rigor. She is considered a "Career and Technical Education" (CTE) teacher. Her class is an elective chosen by students among options such as Bible, band, and art, among others. Her class sizes are small, but she sees sixth, seventh, and eighth graders throughout the day. As part of the class, she starts a garden. Although she doesn't require students to work in the garden, she definitely incentivizes working and growing crops in the garden. The garden is an amazing source of pride for the students and the middle school. Growing and selling food has revolutionized the way some kids think about their futures now. They have become curious about what kinds of food they can raise to feed their own families and ways that growing food can supplement their family income.

Abigail is good at promoting her students work in the garden and within the FFA. This skill, and the praise she and her students receive by the school and county administration, has put her in awkward positions with her colleagues. Some teachers, despite her attempts to coordinate curriculum standards, don't see her as a real teacher. Also, some teachers have seen her as the "pet" of the principal because the work of the FFA group and the garden has brought positive press to the school. The school, as most in poor rural areas, struggles with meeting the state achievement expectations. Yet, this past year, science test scores increased dramatically for the first time. While she doesn't teach every student, she does work with students in every grade level who have brought their Ag Ed knowledge back to their science classrooms. One day, the principal came into her room and said to her, "I'll watch your class. You need to go to the seventh grade science classroom." When Abigail arrived, she saw that Ag Ed students were being "fought" over to be on quiz teams because they knew and remembered more than the other students about the science content being quizzed that day.

What is interesting about this story is that many of these Ag Ed students are not normally sought out as teammates for academic activities. Many of the students have Individualized Education Plans (IEPs) or 504 plans. Many are low performing academically and are drawn to the project-based learning of the Ag Ed class. In her first year, Abigail only had sixth grade classes. The following year, her class was open to all grades. For two years, she has cultivated leaders for the class, for the FFA, and for the garden. The FFA was instrumental to her own development in high school, and she is passionate that its values will help other students see themselves in a different light than they might within math, English, or science class. She says, "These kids [with severe or profound development issues] may not be able to pass the math test, but they can weed the garden with everyone else." She believes her students are learning hard work and showing the community that they are capable.

Student success for Abigail is measured relationally. She says, "It is definitely not by a grade." Abigail relates the story of a kid that was in day treatment and came to middle school afraid and non-talkative. This "type" of student is often placed into Abigail's class because of its project-based nature and Abigail's reputation. He lashed out at her violently but was able to be successful by the following year. He matured and let Abigail know she was a key part of him feeling at home and safe in school. She has a vision board for what Ag Ed can look like and be like at the middle school. The variety of kids throughout the grade levels and their growth give her what she calls "the fire in my belly" to keep teaching.

While leadership is something she helps her students understand through the character-building standards of the FFA, she would not necessarily consider herself a teacher leader in terms that most research would support. She does influence the school culture and the other teachers. Some see her course as beneficial to a certain segment of their students. She sees leadership in herself in the ways she connects with the wider community. This could be because of her prior relationships with many organizations, such as the FFA and the County Agriculture Extension, or her relative isolation as a teacher within her school.

While Ag Ed may be an elective, there is a lot of hard work that occurs within the classroom. Students take quizzes on content, such as aquatic systems. They write papers, design hybrid vegetables based on their content knowledge, and write and give speeches on environmental topics. Abigail often monitors their work via Google Classroom, where she can see if they are writing or not and give immediate feedback. She knows where they are in their FFA quiz progress. She also knows where they are with the other parts of their lives. She knows their track schedules. She knows their parents and speaks to them regularly. Her mentor calls her a "natural" teacher. She understands the big picture of her content but also her relational work with the students. She calls the boys "son" even though she has no children of her own. She jokes and teases in a way a big sister would without ever making it too personal. She is also often a "mom" figure to many of the students who lack mothers, and she assists the single dads in helping their daughters navigate puberty. She has made this work with her middle grades' students her life. This is also something her mentor worries about. How is this kind of commitment sustainable? She says the kids sustain her, even though "they may drive me crazy."

Questions

1. Where is the power in Abigail's portrait?
2. How does Abigail's teaching shape school culture?
3. What morals does Abigail demonstrate in her life as a teacher?
4. What kinds of deliberation does Abigail engage in?

CHAPTER FOUR

Stewardship in Schooling and Teaching

TEACHING IS POWERFUL. TEACHING is political. Many new (and experienced) teachers heartily agree with the first statement. They will share stories of the teachers they had that transformed their lives, or they will share stories of how a child was transformed by the care from the school and classroom community. The second statement, teaching is political, might cause some hesitancy in agreement among new and experienced teachers. Why this hesitation? Bree Picower (2013) writes that many teachers are unaware of the political dimensions of schooling. Yet, as Chapter One points out, the goals or outcomes of public schools are highly contested among people in the Unites States, and many decisions are made by elected or appointed officials within government structures. The distance between the classroom and the Congress or Department of Education is vast and creates a veil that many teachers choose not to move aside.

Why do many teachers ignore the obvious political component of public schooling? It's not often explored explicitly in teacher education programs. There is this sense that early career teachers need to learn their "craft" prior to learning about the organization in which they practice. Others believe that they are called to teach children, and larger issues are of little concern to their daily practice and relationships with children. This chapter argues that stewardship and its encompassing ideas about trust and power should frame the work of schools and teacher leaders. Grounding daily practices and long-term school goals in stewardship helps teachers and schools align their action with more just social goals.

Throughout this book, the concept of stewardship has been defined, connected to the role of adults in schools, educational leadership, and the profession of teaching. In this chapter, we take a deep dive into stewardship as Peter Block defines it in his book and connect his ideas back to the possibilities of 21st century teaching and schooling. It will be argued that adopting stewardship as a way of being a teacher *is* leadership since it leads to increased moral and, possibly, real responsibility for all aspects of schooling. Prior to exploring stewardship as it applies to teachers' roles in school, it is important to define what stewardship is not.

Servant, Savior and Steward

Servant

In educational leadership, stewardship is predominantly associated with the servant-leader theory of leadership by Robert K. Greenleaf. Other leadership theorists have also articulated that stewardship is a key component to moral and ethical leadership. In his discussion of stewardship, Sergiovanni (1992) focuses on the idea of servant leadership as the type of leadership needed within the unique places that are schools. In his 1977 essay, Greenleaf describes that servant leadership emanates from

> the natural feeling that one wants to serve first. This conscious choice brings one to aspire to lead. The difference manifests itself in the care taken by the servant—first to make sure that other people's highest priority needs are being served. (p. 15).

The ultimate goal of servant leaders is that those who are being led grow as people and in turn become servants themselves. Greenleaf's theory came to him while reading a novel in which a mythical group of travelers go on a journey with a servant. This servant, the person who cleaned, cooked, and tended the group of travelers, disappears, leaving the travelers adrift and the journey ends. After many years, one of the travelers arrives at a monastery only to be reunited with the servant, who is actually a great leader within the monastery. This concept of servant leadership can be applied to the teaching profession since many teachers and schools put the needs of those being served (the students) first. Yet, schools also have simultaneous commitments to teacher needs and the moral responsibility to the public to attend to as well. This is why stewardship as leadership is a more appropriate lens in which to view the work of teachers and schools.

Stewardship (and its moral and ethical underpinnings) is applied to secular and religious life, but its basic premise appears across almost all cultures. The dictionary definition of stewardship is "the careful and responsible management of something entrusted to one's care" (Merriam-Webster, n.d.). Environmental protection organizations and advocates have often used the term stewardship to remind us of our responsibility to preserve resources, and also the obligation to nurture, sustain, and improve the earth's environment (which belongs to none of us) so that we, as well as future generations, benefit from our forethought today.

Stewardship, within Judeo-Christian theology and practice "is defined as one's responsibility for systematically sharing time, talent, and possessions in the service of God and for the benefit of mankind" (Sato & Rogers, 2017, p. 37). Pieterse (2002), a theologian, argues that it makes sense that the notion of stewardship has cropped up in non-theological matters:

> The concept resonates with a set of moral and ethical assumptions about what is required for all life on our planet to flourish (indeed, to survive)—assumptions that are increasingly shared among religious and nonreligious folks alike. Two of these assumptions suggest themselves with particular urgency today: (1) All life, human as well as nonhuman, is interconnected in a fragile and increasingly threatened ecology of relationships. (2) Precisely because of this, all of us bear direct responsibility for nurturing and caring for this delicate web. And this responsibility must penetrate and find expression in all aspects of our life together—from personal relationships to financial institutions and the market to our interaction with the nonhuman creation. (p. 331)

As stewardship is explored further in this chapter, concepts like faith, values, justice, and trust will be used in the more secular notions of the ideas. But is it clear, as Pieterse writes, that one can embrace stewardship from a religious as well as a non-religious lens. Block (2013) refers to stewardship as a "spiritual, values-based anchor in an era that constantly drives us in the direction of speed, control and efficiency" (p. 10). Approaching stewardship within one's place of work and using it as an organizing framework to improve working conditions will focus on the idea of spiritual renewal or of reconnecting the head and the heart. Many teachers approach teaching as a calling to serve and be of service. While this calling is morally sound, to steward the profession of teaching, we must see the work of schools as valuable and worthy of investing money and resources from society at large. Stewardship in teaching is not about volunteering teachers' time or asking teachers to do more with less. It is about recognition of the work that teachers do to prepare children for the world. Stewardship is not being a "servant" to the school, nor is it about being a "savior" to marginalized children and families. Also, focusing on the collective responsibility of all members of an organization to attend to how decisions and actions shape the culture removes the individualistic notion of teachers as servants or saviors.

Servant-leadership was described in an earlier chapter as an educational leadership philosophy in which leaders put those whom they serve first: children, families, and teachers. Perhaps the most expressive example of a servant leader is Sergiovanni's (1992) portrait of Madeline Cartwright, a principal in Philadelphia. Cartwright bought a washer and dryer to clean kids' clothes who came to school unwashed, visited and cleaned families' homes, brought in families to clean up the school, all while holding high academic expectations for her students. Cartwright believed that service to those who were in need encompassed many things. Cartwright stepped up to help her school community in ways that other services failed. It is, some would contend, heroic and brave to serve one's community in those ways. The idea of the "hero" teacher or the savior of a class of kids is one that is rare in real life but common among media representations of teachers. In particular, the White savior mentality is one that families and youth of marginalized communities suffer from the most. Nearly all teachers enter the profession to do good. As mentioned before, many see public schools as a public good, as a democratizing place in which all kids can learn. Unfortunately, many teachers, young teachers in particular, enter into schools in which they unconsciously enforce White, middle-class values and expectations on to their students in order to "save" them from their current lives. Many teachers enter into classrooms with assumptions about who their students are and what their students need.

Savior

In 2012, Teju Cole coined the term White Savior Industrial Complex (WSIC) in a series of tweets in response to a viral YouTube documentary showing a White man's charity, Invisible Children, making a difference in war torn Uganda under the rule of the despot Joseph Kony. The controversy is well documented (just Google Kony 2012). Cole's eloquent and prescient criticism of White saviors in African nations is about how often White people "see no need to reason out the need for the need" (Cole, 2012), meaning that, while well-intentioned organizations attend to the readily apparent horrors, such as starvation or lack of clean water, these organizations do not interrogate why there is famine and lack of clean water. Natural disaster does account for many of these needs, while other needs are the surface problems of much deeper structural inequities. Many of the reasons are related to policies implemented by the United States and other countries and monetary policies created by organizations like the International Monetary Fund (IMF) (Masters & Chatzky, 2019). Natural resources and who controls those resources also come into play. Cole writes,

> There are more complex and more widespread problems. There are serious problems of governance, of infrastructure, of democracy, and of law and order. These problems are neither simple in themselves nor are they reducible to slogans. Such problems are both intricate and intensely local. (2012, para. 15)

What role do outside, particularly White and American, charities involved with Uganda's problems play in teaching? Cole's notion that inequities run deep in organizations in Uganda parallels the status of many U.S. institutions, particularly schools. Since many teachers do not see themselves as working within a political system, they are not questioning the need for the *need* in schools today. Why do we have an opportunity gap? Why do we need culturally relevant education? Why do we need trauma-informed practices? Many teachers simply believe in the power of their own good work to transform the lives of their students. Recognizing that one is called to teach or to serve is important, but it is just as important to recognize the structures in which one serves.

Jill Flynn (2019) explores the media portrayals of teachers through a critical literacy lens with her students. Using questions about how students and teachers are portrayed and what work of teaching is not portrayed in the representations, Flynn begins a fruitful dialogue with her students, mostly nice, White people, who feel that they are called to teach to make a difference. Critiquing teachers like Mr. Schue in *Glee*, Mr. Keating in *Dead Poets Society*, Ms. Gruwell in *Freedom Writers*, and Ms. Johnson in *Dangerous Minds* provokes

Flynn's students into asking, How can nice, White teachers make a difference? The difference lies in attending to race, identity, power, and representation. Flynn uses this quote to start the discussion with her students:

> Teachers must study how the world that is unjust by design shapes the classroom and the relations between teachers and students. By doing this, teachers can begin to discern concrete manifestations of the abstract concept of a world unjust by design. Here critical teachers make use of this knowledge not to "save" marginalized students but to provide a safe space for them and to learn with them about personal empowerments, the cultivation of the intellect and the larger pursuit of social justice. (Kinchloe, 2008, p. 25, cited in Flynn, 2019, p. 59)

After the completion of the assignment, one of the students in Flynn's class, who was inspired by the movie *Freedom Writers* to become a teacher, writes,

> This [movie] creates an unrealistic image of what teachers are supposed to be doing in the class. Sure, it is great to inspire each one of your students, but will teachers get discouraged if they can't be a superhero? Will they think they are failing? (Flynn, 2019, p. 63)

Flynn concludes that a "nice white lady can be an effective teacher of any group of students, but she has to commit to growing and learning alongside her students and continuing to employ critical literacy tools for questioning the world around her" (2019, p. 65). Nice teachers who want to make a difference need to see the world as it is (unjust) and also see the world as it can be.

Limits of servant and savior models

As Cole points out (2012), the savior model attends to many surface issues within schools. The notion that a single teacher can change the educational outcomes of their students is a powerful, but mainly mythological, narrative of the work of teaching. Teaching and learning occur within schools with many teachers, administrators, and other educational workers. Teaching is really a team effort. While individual relationships among a teacher and her students are powerfully mitigating factors in achievement, the sustained inadequacy of schools and school resources, particularly among poor and immigrant communities, are often stronger than individual relationships. Servant roles are also problematic because of how they are equated with low pay and low skill in the popular imagination. The original servant leader, Jesus of Nazareth, while full of love and light, is poor and depends upon his disciples and followers for food and shelter. If, as a country, we take the idea of public schooling seriously, we should provide appropriate funding for teachers to at least feed and house themselves and their families. In the spirit of service, many teachers feed and clothe their students while also spending their own money on school supplies. Churches and community organizations try and make up the difference with backpack drives and toy drives during certain times of the year.

While welcomed by many, these intermittent acts of service by outside organizations or even acts like paying off the debt of college graduates (Seale, 2019) spins a narrative that what matters are "great acts" of service and somehow those great acts can offset years of educational neglect or institutional racism. These great acts are connected to the great leader hypothesis, which says that there is one great leader out there that can come and "make a difference" in a school. What school reform says is that great leadership is needed, but others argue that schools and teachers need to reform themselves and that teachers should be trusted as professional educational stewards, not servants or saviors. Servant and savior models do nothing to move the dialogue about what matters in schools beyond simple acts of courage. Stewardship enlarges the conversation about achievement and student success across the whole organization: students, parents, and everyone who works within a school.

Stewardship

In late 1993, Peter Block, whose work has mostly been in organizational theory and design, published a book. This book was heralded as "radical" and "revolutionary." Twenty years later, he published a second edition. In 2013, the book is still heralded as revolutionary. His rallying cry is that, despite all the reform movements in business in the 1980s and in education in the 1990s and 2000s, nothing has fundamentally changed. Businesses are still profit driven. The gap in wages between CEOs and hourly workers has skyrocketed. Consolidation of services has reduced customer choice. There is an increasing malaise among workers as finding value and meaning becomes a struggle in their daily work. Through increased technology, human workers become obsolete. Businesses have become lean machines with their eyes on the profit line and not the hearts and minds of their workers. For example, while Amazon seemingly provides everything, it does not always provide a safe and secure working environment for its employees (Evans, 2019). What does Amazon have to do in a book about public schooling and teaching? Part of the school reform movements of the 1990s was to import business models into public schools. The language in schools began to change around this time. Schools became data driven, using "scientifically-based practices" with "fidelity" to ensure outcomes on standardized tests while also keeping wages and costs down, as any other for-profit business would. Alas, public schools are not for profit. (The for-profit charter movement also shows a lot of bad business practices *and* poor student outcomes [Strauss, 2019].) Schools are non-profit government entities supported by mainly local and state taxes, with a small amount of funding coming in at the federal level. Schools also are not factories, at least they are not intended to be factories. In theory, we left behind the factory model of schooling when increased accountability arrived for all students under federal laws like Individuals with Disabilities Education Act (IDEA, 1990) and No Child Left Behind (NCLB, 2002). Schools are places of teaching and learning. While research can approximate what a child should know and be able to do by a certain age, we all know that learning something new is hard and not everyone learns at the same rate. These factors make teaching pretty exciting at times. They also make teaching a profession, similar to other professions that are human relation based. Often teachers have similar experiences from year to year but some years they may also have all sorts of new experiences and, in turn, learn and grow as teachers.

Peter Block has offered his organizational theory of stewardship to the world for over 20 years. The United States has a relentless churn toward progress and the individual acquisitions of those signs of progress: more money, new technology, more things to have and own as devices become immediately obsolete. Block asks us to stop and ask, Don't we have enough? Don't we have enough talent within our organizations to be able to meet our needs? If the ultimate cost of continual progress means emotional and environmental break down, shouldn't we just stop? One reviewer (Tucker, 1994) called Block's theory revolutionary because stewardship is not just about service, it's political. Block's ideas call for a redistribution of power and wealth in organizations. It's a redistribution that follows redefining the purposes of an organization. Now, this is not an anti-capitalist argument, but an argument to find a more humane and just form of capitalism. So, how does Block's revolutionary theory of stewardship work in organizations?

> Stewardship begins with the willingness to be accountable for some larger body than ourselves—an organization, a community. Stewardship springs from a set of beliefs about reforming organizations that affirms our choice for service over the pursuit of self-interest. When we choose service over self-interest, we say we are willing to be deeply accountable without choosing to control the world around us. It requires a level of trust that we are not used to holding ... Stewardship questions the belief that accountability and control go hand in hand. We can be accountable and give control to those who are closer to the work, operating from the belief that in this way the work is better served. (2013, pp. 6–18)

Stewardship is predicated on trust. Block refers to this as partnership rather than patriarchy. People within an organization trust each other to do the right thing by the whole organization. Each person understands what they are accountable to and for and will meet those expectations without the external and rigid control of a boss.

In his revised 2013 edition of the book, Block reiterates the urgency for organizations to take up stewardship. He argues that in the new digital age in which we work and live, the work weeks are longer, we are always available, and we have more options to learn and work from home. However, the flip side is that people are becoming increasingly isolated, and social media produces as much fear and anxiety as any other media. The premise that what is good for business is good for the world dominates, and it has led to increasing gaps in wealth and opportunities.

While stewardship is tantalizing as an organizational framework, it would take a seismic shift to change the bureaucratic nature of public schools. However, on a school level or team level, stewardship is achievable. There are movements to take back the profession of teaching, but I would argue that taking back the profession in the language of for-profit business models can be detrimental to this movement. Instead, a return to the moral argument that public schools are a public good refocuses the argument on whether or not schools are doing good by society at large rather than are they doing well on tests with the amount of funding they get. Through stewardship, all teachers and those who work in public schools would be attuned to all the factors: finances, social and emotional outcomes, and academic achievement. Accountability systems would look different based on context, but the overall (i.e., state) goals could still be met. Trusting those closest to the work with children to do their best work is what true stewardship is all about. If the work is not done well, then the peer group (grade or department-level) either help them get better or help them find a new career.

Stewardship as teacher leadership

The argument for moving away from the hierarchical and corporate language of teacher leadership is that stewardship as leadership is inherently communal, as is schooling. Organizationally, the concept of nested stewardship applies to schools. As Thomas Sergiovanni (1992) writes,

> Stewardship represents primarily an act of trust, whereby people and institutions entrust a leader with certain obligations and duties to fulfill and perform on their behalf. For example, the public entrusts the schools to the school board. The school board entrusts the school to its principal. Parents entrust their children to teachers (p. 373).

This concept of nested stewardship highlights the role of trust within stewardship. Organizationally, schools who commit to a stewardship (trust-based) approach to decision making also become living examples of many "character education" programs (Leader in Me, Character Counts, etc.) as schools and teachers examine themselves through a moral lens of stewardship. Every member of the community asks themselves the questions: "What are we about? Why? Are the students being served? Is the school as a learning community being served? What are our obligations to this community? With these questions in mind, how can we best get the job done?" (Sergiovanni, 1992, p. 277).

A key problem of the "teacher leadership" concept is that it is often seen as either a role or a member of a team that has a hierarchal relationship to others within the school. Teaching is an egalitarian profession. Leadership and leaders have very specific meanings within each school context. Even though teachers may want to and learn more from each other (Margolis & Duel, 2009) teachers who are designated "leaders" within schools may be seen as operatives of the administration or curriculum mandates (Sato, 2005). Research finds that "teacher leadership" emerges when teachers have control over their own profession and are given time and space to collaborate (Cherkowski & Schnellert, 2017; Levenson, 2014). Research also indicates that "teacher leadership" occurs in relation to immediate and local needs (Bricker & Tracy, 2017; Smulyan, 2016). These descriptors of teacher leadership are also clear descriptors of stewardship. For new teachers, stewardship, as opposed to leadership, lowers the risk felt by many new teachers as they try and share practices and ideas to help improve teaching and learning. Reframing leadership as stewardship may also help prevent the burnout of teachers as they are allowed to "lead" and contribute in ways that match their personal and moral obligations. The language of stewardship is more inclusive and the concept itself (as opposed to leadership) is rooted in the language of professionalism. Being a steward means one has the best interests of the profession at the forefront of their actions. The profession of teaching is about working with students to help them grow in numerous ways: into being able to participate fully in society through accruing the skills and knowledge to navigate, sustain, and recreate this world.

While stewardship is a communal notion, individual teachers can begin to reframe their work within the language of stewardship. Teacher education can also begin to rename the landscape of teaching and move away from corporatized language into a more morally-based language of teaching. Being a steward means that the youth of the nation are entrusted to the teacher until they come of age. As a teacher, one is only partially accountable, but it is still often one of the most important roles in a child's life.

The early decades of the 21st century have been fraught with traumatic national and regional events. Terrorist attacks, mass shootings, hate crimes, and family violence are all part of our daily news feed. It is hard to be a public-school teacher now, but, now, more than ever, it is a sacred and important task. Teachers these days are better educated than ever before, with just as big of hearts as always, and they want the institutions to trust them to do their job-to teach children and work together to benefit the students and community—therefore benefiting society as a whole. The problem is that society (along with teachers and principals) has allowed schools to be run in a "for-profit" management style. In schools these days, "test scores" or "data" are the bottom line. Though early graded schools were run in a factory-like way, the end result wasn't "profit" or test scores. Students were sorted, and graded teachers did their best to impart skills, such as reading, math, and American history, to help students be functionally literate within society. Over the decades, society has asked schools to educate a more diverse student body with a wide ranging of expectations beyond traditional subjects (from fire safety to personal finance) without adding adequate resources.

In undergraduate teacher education programs, there are essentially two years of coursework/preparation for teaching. Many states require graduate degrees to teach, which requires two more years of preparation. Two or four years is not enough time to adequately prepare teachers for the myriad of issues they may face in teaching content. Two or four years also is not enough time to help candidates acquire all the other skills required of teachers today such as understandings of equity, culturally sustaining pedagogy and social emotional learning. Increasing pressure to do well on tests leads to the deprofessionalization of teaching but also the demoralization of teachers. The pay and benefits are not good enough for teachers with advanced degrees to continually pour their hearts and energy into other people's children. The best evidence of this is straight from the teachers. Social media campaigns such as #imhumantoo or the Facebook page *Just Let Me Teach* share thousands of stories about teachers seeking work-life balance while doing the good work of teaching.

This business/management model of teaching is not working, and it is not working because teaching is about more than the "bottom line" of test scores. The language society uses around teaching, particularly the language of teacher leadership, needs to shift to the language of stewardship, which encompasses the moral language of trust and virtue in the profession. I encourage all teachers and administrators to start looking at the work of schools through the lens of stewardship as outlined in this book and to bring trust and the moral imperative of public-school teaching back to the forefront of everyone's mind.

Teaching can be taught. There are skills and strategies that great teachers use that have been well documented and codified into high-leverage practices. With experience and support, teachers can become better at their work. There is one thing that cannot be taught explicitly but must be present and developed as well and that is love: love of the world, of the children, and of learning. Teacher leadership relies too much on the individual notion of the teacher, and many of the configurations around what teacher leadership is move teachers away from their main work: teaching and learning. This includes teaching children and helping children learn, but it also includes learning themselves and refining their craft of teaching through professional conversations on issues of teaching and learning. The question we should be asking is, What kinds and at what levels of stewardship are our teachers engaging in? This concept honors the egalitarian nature of teaching but does not let it stagnate. It also honors the various levels at which teachers feel they are contributing to the children, community, and profession. Stewardship asks teachers to reflect upon their actions and ask, What am I doing to make the world better for the children, community, and profession? Stewardship is not a lack of leadership. It is a moral and heart-based leadership that calls for a decentralizing method that engenders trust and a more inclusive language that allows teachers who engage in anything that is a service to their students or the profession of teaching to be seen as a way of leading.

References

Block, P. (2013). *Stewardship: Choosing service over self-interest* (2nd ed.) San Francisco, CA: Berrett-Koehler.

Bricker, P., & Tracy, K. (2017). Elementary teachers leading from the classroom: Cases of practical leadership. In C. Rogers, K. Lomotey, & A. Hilton (Eds.), *Innovative approaches to educational leadership: Selected cases* (pp. 95–104). New York, NY: Peter Lang Publishing.

Cherkowski, S., & Schnellert, L. (2017). Exploring teacher leadership in a rural, secondary school: Reciprocal learning teams as a catalyst for emergent leadership. *International Journal of Teacher Leadership*, 8(1), 6–25.

Cole, T. (2012). *The White-savior industrial complex*. Retrieved from https://www.theatlantic.com/international/archive/2012/03/the-white-savior-industrial-complex/254843/

Evans, W. (2019). Ruthless quotas at Amazon are maiming employees. The Atlantic. Retrieved from https://www.theatlantic.com/technology/archive/2019/11/amazonwarehouse-reports-show-worker-injuries/602530/

Flynn, J.E. (2019). What's a nice White lady to do? In M. Dalton & L. Linder (Eds.), *Teachers, teaching, and media: Original essays about educators in popular culture*, (pp. 57–65). Leiden & Boston: Brill Sense.

Greenleaf, R. F. (2002). *Servant leadership: A journey into the nature of legitimate power and greatness*. (25th anniversary ed.). Mahwah, NJ: Paulist Press.

Levenson, M. (2014). *Pathways to teacher leadership: Emerging models, changing roles*. Cambridge, MA: Harvard Education Press.

Margolis, J., & Deuel, A. (2009). Teacher leaders in action: Motivation, morality, and money. *Leadership and Policy in Schools*, 8(3), 264–286. https://doi.org/10.1080/15700760802416115

Masters, J., & Chatzky, A. (2019). The IMF: The world's controversial financial firefighter. Council on Foreign Relations. Retrieved from https://www.cfr.org/backgrounder/imf-worlds-controversial-financial-firefighter

Merriam-Webster. (n.d.). Stewardship. *Merriam-Webster.* Retrieved February 13, 2020, from https://www.merriam-webster.com/dictionary/stewardship.

Picower, B. (2013). You can't change what you don't see: Developing new teachers' political understanding of education. *Journal of Transformative Education, 11*(3), 170–189. https://doi.org/10.1177/1541344613502395

Pieterse, H. (2002). Like good stewards of the manifold grace of God. *Quarterly Review,* 22(4), 331–332.

Sato, M., & Rogers, C. (2017). Practical leadership: How teachers enact leadership to re-culture their Schools. In C. Rogers, K. Lomotey, & A. Hilton (eds.), *Innovative approaches to educational leadership: Selected cases* (pp. 27–31). New York, NY: Peter Lang Publishing.

Sato, M. (2005). Practical leadership: Conceptualizing the everyday leadership work of teachers. *The New Educator, 1*(1), 55–71.

Seale, C. (2019). $40 million for 400 students: Morehouse donation highlights an inequitable new normal. *Forbes.* Retrieved from https://www.forbes.com/sites/colinseale/2019/05/28/40-million-for-400-students-morehouse-donation-highlights-an-inequitable-new-normal/#482d3fea1bc3

Sergiovanni, T. J. (1992). Leadership as stewardship. In M. Grogan (Ed.), *The Jossey-Bass reader on educational leadership* (3rd ed., pp. 372-392). San Francisco: Jossey-Bass Publishers.

Smulyan, L. (2016). Stepping into their power: The development of a teacher leadership stance. *Schools: Studies in Education, 13*(1), 8–28.

Strauss, V. (2019). A report that detailed up to $1 billion in wasted federal funds on bad charter schools may have underestimated the problem. *The Washington Post.* Retrieved from https://www.washingtonpost.com/education/2019/06/24/report-that-detailed-up-billion-wasted-federal-funds-bad-charter-schools-may-have-underestimated-problem/

Tucker, M. (1994). Stewardship: Choosing service over self-interest by Peter Block Review. *The Academy of Management Review,* 19(3), 592–595.

PORTRAIT OF BEN

Ben is a small man with ruddy cheeks and a slight beard. He is the only classroom teacher that is a man at Frog Creek Elementary, which is located in a first-ring suburb of a large, upper-Midwest city. Ben's philosophy of teaching is professionalism-based and he says, "I, in order to do the best job possible, need the freedom to do my job—to practice my art." Ben is a fifth-grade teacher in his 19th year of teaching in the middle 2000s when the full impact of No Child Left Behind *(*NCLB, 2002*) is being felt.*

Ben became a teacher later in life. He simply says, "And then came a kind of a life-changing experience for me and that's when I got sober" and stopped drinking. He had been a lead nursing assistant, training new people and felt he was talented in that area. Previous college professors had mentioned those talents to him. Many things aligned for him when he chose to look into teaching as a career, including an information session on the program and finding a program that met his needs. He says, "It's just like everything fell into place." The timeline was "perfect" for him to become a teacher. Ben believes that teaching is an art and a science. He believes it is the responsibility of a teacher to bring the curriculum to the students in a dynamic and engaging way and that mandates from districts and administrations need to be examined critically. Teaching to the test seems to go against the very fiber of Ben's teaching soul. He says, "We are creating these beings that are going to go out there and be, you know, useful members of society, so, they need to know science. They need to know everything. They need to know as much as we can tell them."

Ben wants to always say "yes" to his students when it comes to their learning and well-being. As a child, Ben's family was troubled. He received poor grades, became the class clown, and no one knew what was going on at home. He says, "I've kind of become sensitive to what the kid might be going through and if they're going through rough things outside of school, I understand that." For the first time in his 19 years of teaching, Ben decides to visit all his students' families in their homes. He is the only teacher at the school who does this and hopes it will help him and the students make great progress.

One day at school, Ben has hiccups after lunch during the math review time before a test the students are going to take. He decides to teach his students how to cure hiccups. He says, "I am teaching you something you often don't get to learn in school." He goes to the back of the room and fills a coffee cup with water. He leans over forward and then drinks from the other side of the cup. The class is quiet. It seems successful and he returns to his chair to explain what hiccups do to you and why the trick works. He then asks for more questions and a flurry of hands goes up. The students want to know more about hiccups or share their own stories. He lets this proceed for a few questions then reiterates, "When I say, 'any questions?' I mean about math." Most hands go down and the math review continues.

Later in the year, Ben arrives at school in jeans and a sweatshirt, which is unusual for him. He looks tired, worried, and constantly runs his hands over his face and into his very thin hair. He had to take his dog into the emergency vet early that morning. Ben breeds Japanese Akita dogs, one of the more expensive breeds in the United States. He does not tell his students about this at any point, but he does tell other teachers. Later in the staff lunchroom, he confirms with his colleagues that his dog is better. Curiously enough, the students don't seem to notice Ben's distracted behavior that morning, perhaps because the routines of the classroom help Ben put aside his emotions for a little bit.

While Ben's 19th year of teaching is going well, he often remembers the most unpleasant year of his teaching career that occurred just a few years earlier. Ben chalks it up to a leadership issue. Ben, being tenured, is also the school's teachers union representative. He speaks of several things the administrator did: removing a student teacher without warning, suspending students from his class, appropriating his students' materials, and not allowing union representation during disciplinary meetings. Ben elaborates on a particular moment that sums up the issue in a very public manner.

He says that everyone knew what was coming as the staff huddled into the library after work. The school had not made adequate yearly progress (AYP) on state assessments recently and the principal presented an opportunity for a large grant that would possibly lead to more resources and better scores. If the school didn't make their goals the next year, the consequences would be severe. Ben says, "Everybody [was] just totally freaking out and feeding into this frenzy of all the awful things that would happen to us. The other teachers would say, 'Oh they're going to move us, we're going to lose our jobs.' Then if you throw in the mix teachers that are not tenured who can't speak up without fear of losing their jobs—that's another reason why I spoke up, we had a lot of non-tenured teachers in the building." The text of the grant was left in the teachers' lounge for teachers to review prior to the meeting. The principal, a proponent of the grant, assumed all the teachers had a chance to review it but began the meeting with a call for questions.

Ben felt he needed more information and the staff needed more time to make an informed decision. Taking his role as union representative seriously, he asked about what kinds of work and meetings would be expected. The principal indicated that more work would be required, but she did not give details. She then, according to Ben, proceeded with a voice vote, or roll-call vote. Ben expresses disbelief and wondered if that was a valid way to measure commitment to the grant and the work it would require. He knew that he would have to answer out loud, in front of the principal and everyone, and he was afraid. Reflecting upon the answer he gave, Ben feels there were many reasons for his answer, including the values his grandfather passed onto him as he heard stories about protecting the railway workers. His grandfather represented the union in railroad strikes. Ben also thought about the other teachers who were afraid. Ben understood his responsibility to them and the values passed onto him. He told the principal that he didn't believe they had enough information to make an informed decision. Ben voted "no."

What ensued, according to Ben, was, a public disagreement in which Ben maintained he did not have enough information to vote yes and the principal said, "Then maybe this isn't the right place for you." Ben was transferred to another school within the district the following year. He admits he was devastated, but after he had the space and time for reflection, he came to the conclusion that his career was not based in a room or school. He says his work is "based in those kids that come through the door. And it doesn't matter where the door is; it's the kids that matter. That's really where the focus lies and you got to do what's best for them. Not necessarily what you think is best for you."

Questions

1. Where is the power in this portrait?
2. What types of deliberation does Ben engage in?
3. How is politics an issue within Ben's work as a teacher?
4. Why is there a lack of trust between Ben and his principal?
5. What "big ideas" guide Ben's life as a teacher?

CHAPTER FIVE

Stewardship in Action

THIS CHAPTER WILL DISCUSS the benefits of professional conversations around teacher narratives of experiences and will offer some potential ways to answer the questions posed at the end of the portraits of Owen, Carla, Abigail, and Ben. Differences and commonalties across the portraits, as well as the snapshots, will be discussed and evaluated through the lens of the stewardship framework.

In this book, I have attempted to provide some foundational ideas on educational leadership and teacher leadership. I have also presented an argument as to the limiting nature of the term "teacher leadership," particularly to new teachers. In turn, I have offered a stewardship framework as an alternative and more inclusive way of describing the cognitive, social, and emotional work of teaching. The language of stewardship also returns the moral purpose of schooling to the center of the work that is done in schools. Block (2013) suggests that the concept of stewardship be used in lieu of leadership. I hope I have and will illustrate that, for many teachers, enacting stewardship is how they use their power to build relationships and influence and change school culture in order for them to become organizations that prepare all children for success. Influence and change are hallmarks of leadership, and the portraits within this book demonstrate, particularly for new teachers, that being and becoming a steward of teaching and learning is leadership. This book has reviewed important philosophical ideas about leadership that have helped the reader think about their own ideas of leadership in general and teacher leadership specifically. The four tenets of the stewardship framework also help new and experienced teachers situate and name the work they are doing to improve the profession.

These four tenets of the stewardship framework were outlined in Chapter One. To review briefly, stewardship requires knowledge, judgement, and deliberation to guide acts within the context and culture in which one works. Judgement is born out of experience and reflective action on the part of the teacher. Stewardship requires great cognitive and intelligent reflection upon the part of the teacher (tenet one). Stewardship requires a core moral value of public education as a public good. Stewardship requires professional knowledge in creating rigorous experiences that attend to the notion of public schooling as a cornerstone of democracy and preparing children to take their role within a pluralistic society (tenet two). Stewardship requires a student-first commitment in which decisions are made for what is best for students, teachers, and communities within which they live and work (tenet three). Finally, stewardship requires an understanding of the politics of schooling, paying particular care to the inherent inequities in education and using power to create more just and equitable spaces for all children in public schools (tenet four).

Professional conversations

The snapshots and the four portraits and their accompanying questions within this book are useful for professional conversations. The importance of professional conversations cuts across all four tenets of the stewardship framework. Professional conversations are essential because without talking about what is happening in schools, it can be impossible to find a place to begin actions aimed towards the common good. Whenever sharing teacher stories or stories of teachers, it is important to attend to the power of the narrative, but also what is unvoiced or unwritten in the narrative. Mary Louis Gomez (1996) and Frances O'Connell Rust (1999) explore the impact of listening to and telling stories among and between experienced and novice teachers. Gomez's work focuses on the self-reflective, empowering nature of telling one's story. In her work, she has student teachers share stories of classroom experiences and finds that the teller and listener are transformed through the telling and sharing of stories. She does indicate, however, that to have this practice influence how the teachers respond to and improve their own practice, it must occur in a trusting community. O'Connell Rust (1999) grounds her work in focusing "on the ways in which conversation, story, and narrative enable us to understand the complex work of learning to teach" (p. 370). The stories and findings she shares come from the New York City participants in the Sustainable Teachers Learning and Research Network Project, which is a community of learners (novice, pre-service, and experienced educators) exploring how conversation supports the development of knowledge. Her research finds that these conversations and the space provided for the listening and telling of stories acknowledge the complexities of teachers' work. They also allow teachers to move out of their daily concerns and engage in larger conversation across classrooms and schools.

There are several researchers who advocate story, or narrative, as a way to reveal multiple ideas about teaching as well as the teacher and their context, or across different landscapes such as the personal and professional (Clandinin & Connelly, 2000). Cheryl Craig's (2007) work focuses on the meaning made through teachers' experience of reform. Craig conceptualizes this knowledge as "story constellations," which demonstrate how teachers' stories are related across the professional, personal, and practical knowledge landscapes.

Olson and Craig's (2001) work with narrative in what they call "teacher knowledge communities" focuses on the idea that "profound meaning can be found in teachers' everyday experience" (p. 671). Whelan, Huber, Rose, Davies, and Clandinin (2001) examine the story told and retold by Annie Davies, a teacher. This story is about an incident with a student, parent, and principal, which gets told and retold across different settings. The researchers conclude that, in the simple recounting of stories, there is little to be gained. What happens, they argue, is that stories are simply affirmed, reified, and become closed to the possible knowledge in the stories. The researchers advocate for the re-imagining of the story in which different readings and questions are asked in order to make the story and experience knowledge generating since "examining experience is the key to education" (Clandinin & Connelly, 2000, p. xiii).

Kienholz (2002) writes that stories help make the familiar strange and make "explicit" the connection between theory and practice, between belief and experience. He writes that stories "provide a venue where our own perhaps unchallenged assumptions about how things ought to be collide with scenarios of how things actually are" (p. 38). He cautions, though, that the power of these stories to transform beliefs can only occur if readers attend to these stories "as something other than entertainment" (p. 38). The snapshots and portraits in this book are provided as a way to see inside the life of regular teachers. They are stories of particular experience, but they are also more than stories. In the next part of the chapter, we examine how Katherine, Laura, Owen, Carly, Abigail, and Ben tell us about the power and limitations of stewardship and teacher leadership in schools.

Stewardship within the snapshots and portraits

While questions aren't included with the snapshots, they do help illustrate some ideas of stewardship and the potential for teacher leadership within professional settings. Katherine, who we meet in Chapter Three, illustrates what most would consider typical within the United States: a focus on data and test scores. But Katherine's school provides time and space for teachers to meet together and create curriculum. Providing this professional time and space helps us understand another dimension of the school culture beyond data and test scores. Katherine is a student-first teacher within a school culture that simultaneously upholds norms of professional practice and traditional ideas of academic achievement.

Laura, who we meet in Chapter One, helps us understand the extent of teacher power to make choices to benefit student outcomes. Laura reworks an inherited discipline system to create a positive, rather than punitive, classroom environment. This environment not only aligns with Laura's belief system but also with research on best practices for equity. While the school culture remains focused on consequences, such as silent lunch, Laura's grade level has completely changed. There is a hope that continued good outcomes in third grade will eventually influence the rest of the school culture.

The portraits provide deeper understandings of teachers work and leadership as stewardship. The questions at the end of Owen's portrait align with all four tenets of the stewardship framework. Questions of power and politics reside in tenet four, which requires an understanding of the politics of schooling that includes the personal power or micropolitical dynamics within a school and the larger political atmosphere in which schools operate. Questions about deliberation and morals are at the heart of tenet one, two, and three in which knowledge of local contexts, reflective action, and a student-centered approach to teaching all intertwine in Owen's daily actions. There are a few ways to answer the question of power in Owen's experience. Owen has a lot of power or influence among the students and the culture of the school. Being a large, older man and a teacher who is not afraid of his emotions sets a tone for the students he works with. His power lies in his own self-aware emotional state. Power is also located within the traditional hierarchy of administration as well as seen through Owen's reaction to being called into the principal's office after a field trip. The power to close a school in a community is also experienced by Owen. The closure leads him to a process of deliberation and action that seemingly conflicts with his vision of himself as a teacher. Deliberation on instruction, politics, role, and influence are all evident in this portrait. Owen engages in daily deliberations and makes choices based on context and knowledge of those that will be impacted by his choices. Often in his relationships with students and families, these actions are reflexive, automatic, as seen in his encounters with the angry child and mother in the school hallway or in his response to the Latina girl and her holiday outfit. Owen preserves the dignity of his students as best as he can. Politics, the understanding of inequities in students' lives, the large impact of poverty on his students, and their access to a good education resonate throughout Owen's daily decision making. The politics of curriculum mandates also impact him and his students as evidenced by his struggle with the Wit & Wisdom pacing guides and his desire to engage students in discussion. Owen's values are clearly influenced by his practical knowledge from his prior experience that led him in making a career choice later in his life. His experience as a father, parent, and member of the community in which he works as well as the influence of his informal mentors, such as his father and other teachers, help shape Owen's actions within the classroom. While much of his decision making is guided by what he believes is right for his own son, he also realizes that access to a good education is deserved by all students in the school system.

The questions at the end of Carly's portrait align with the tenets of stewardship. As with Owen's portrait, Carly's issues of power and politics reside in tenet four, which requires an understanding of the politics of schooling that includes the personal power or micropolitical dynamics within a school and the larger political atmosphere in which schools operate. Carly's portrait is also much about culture shaping, which is centered in tenet one, two, and three. Carly's vision of schooling and her student-first commitment require much reflection and deliberation as she makes judgments about how she supports students. Carly clearly demonstrates a student-first disposition, almost to her own detriment. Her goal of being "the one" that holds students accountable is a burden that one person, one teacher, should not bear alone. Carly often enacts the "savior" mentality, particularly with her student with autism. While she does seek help from others, such as her mentor and the special education staff, she envisions herself as "the one" responsible for his behavior and growth. Carly, as a new teacher, is in the space of trying to prove herself to others (and herself) that she can be that teacher who makes a difference. While Carly claims that the school culture is one of family, her belief in the idea of the classroom teacher as sole responsible adult resonates throughout her portrait. Carly believes that the power of her good work in the classroom can change lives, but that idea is often challenged by others within the school. Carly is a good teacher, yet the power dynamics of the school culture influence Carly's work in trying to shape the culture. Carly is focused on academics and wants her students to do well, but she acknowledges that the students she works with are very much below grade level. Carly's practice of giving critical, yet positive, feedback and encouraging persistence in tasks is a very different approach than others use in the school. In this way, she is thinking about the power of education to help transform these children's lives. Carly is stewarding the profession of teaching through her focus on increasing her own professional knowledge and holding students to high standards.

Abigail's unique position as an Agricultural Education teacher gives us insight into how the culture of schools are shaped by someone who is not seen as a classroom teacher. Her deliberation, reflection, and action are all centered and aligned with tenet three of the stewardship framework: a student-first vision of schooling. Abigail has a lot of power in her elective class since her students are not tested on end-of-grade tests. She uses this power to help students know that they are capable. Students' work in the garden does not rely on their ability to pass math or reading tests but does require them to apply the reading and math skills they have. The garden and the students who work within it plan, plant, weed, harvest, and sell their goods to local restaurants and individuals. Tenets two and four undergird that the work Abigail does is shaping school culture by allowing other teachers and the public to see the middle-grade students that may struggle with academics and behavior as capable students who can contribute to society now and in the future. Abigail engages in intellectual deliberation by working with other teachers to support the mastery of state standards (tenet one). This is something Abigail doesn't necessarily need to do as she has her own state and Future Farmers of America standards to guide her instruction. Yet, she will reach out to other teachers about particular content standards or students to find ways she can help. It is clear that Abigail values public education and her work as a way to help students see their potential rather than their failings.

Ben's portrait is also unique in that he has been teaching for the longest time and in a place that has a very difference political dynamic (union-supported school) than the other three teachers. Trust is an essential component of stewardship, and Ben's portrait suggests the kind of relationship that can occur when trust is absent. In other ways, Ben's portrait exemplifies the notion of tenet one and four of the stewardship framework as he clearly deliberates within a political climate but aligns his actions with his vision of schooling and student first commitment. Ben's most important deliberations come the year the school votes on the grant. Ben draws upon his experience and knowledge as a teacher and makes a judgment to say "no" in public. To some, it may seem to be a risky decision, but as Sato and Rogers (2017) write, "A decision is right if it is reasonable in light of virtues such as being a just decision, a fair decision, or a fitting decision" (p. 32). For Ben, this clearly is the right decision. This deliberative decision comes not only from his experience, but also his vision for schooling, the experience of students, and the work of teachers within schools. This issue is clearly tied to the politics within Ben's portrait. In Ben's portrait, there are micropolitics and macropolitics at play. The pressure to perform on standardized tests creates a tense situation for Ben and the rest of the teachers at the school. Ben's knowledge of what teachers can be asked to do as result of outside pressures makes him reflect on the power (tenet four) he has to push back against something that he feels may not be well thought out in how it impacts students and teachers. He clearly represents the principal as wanting to get the money without thought to how that money supports the larger goals of the work of teaching and learning. There is obviously an adversarial relationship between Ben and his administration. The reasons as to why is not fully answered within the portrait. We could hypothesize that Ben is a fairly confident and independent teacher who feels that teachers' professional knowledge should drive decision making, particularly around curriculum. We could also hypothesize that, as the union representative, he may be particularly disliked or distrusted by administration. It is unclear, but what is clear is that a lack of trust of his administration leads him to become stronger about what his professional obligations are and where his "loyalty" lies. Trust is the key component of stewardship, so a lack of trust between administration and even one teacher can create discord in a school. Ben trusts himself and trusts that his actions are what is best for the students and school. Tenet two and three align with the values that guide Ben's work as a teacher: education is a public good and a student-first commitment. His vision is for his students to be able to become "useful members of society" that know more than just how to take a test. He wants the measures of success to be attuned to students' lives outside of class. He wants students to feel safe and successful in school. Therefore, it doesn't matter to him what classroom he is in. As long as he is working with kids, he knows what he is doing is right.

Stewardship across the portraits and snapshots

The six teachers in the snapshots and portraits have a variety of professional and lived experiences. Owen, Carly, and Abigail are all within their first few years of teaching and Ben has been teaching for nearly 20 years. Carly is the youngest, barely 24 at the time of her portrait. Abigail is almost 30 and Owen and Ben are in their 40s and 50s, respectively. While their cumulative teaching average is low on number of years teaching, they have rich and varied lived experiences that have brought them into teaching. These teachers all demonstrate stewardship as an essential component of ways of being a teacher. If we were to look at these portraits for "teacher leadership," many of the teachers' actions, particularly the early-career teachers like Owen and Carly, may be labeled as potential or emergent leadership because they lack the experience and work beyond the classroom that is considered "teacher leadership" within the research literature. Worse yet, their actions may be labeled as "just teaching." Yet, their deliberations within the walls of the classroom reverberate through the school and community. It's more than just teaching that they do every day. Abigail is a good case of this as well. She teaches students the required FFA curriculum but also, through the work in the school garden, she is changing their lives and their families' lives in immeasurable ways. There is not a formal role for Abigail beyond Agriculture Education teacher in this portrait. Using the theoretical framework of stewardship as teacher leadership allows teachers' work that is enacted in and out of the classrooms, that defies roles and titles given to more experienced teachers, to be seen and valued. The language of stewardship recognizes that early-career teachers, in fact, all teachers, act with intent and fit their actions to the local context.

Ben's story perhaps most clearly illustrates the notion of professional stewardship in a "community of practitioners that hold something in common—practices, ideals, purposes" and that part of his reason for action is "linked to helping others live and work within those same professional expectations" (Sato, et al., 2014, p. 17). Ben's stewardship enactment is about his students, but also about the profession. Ben has a clearly articulated role as building union representative. Although that leadership role puts him at odds with administration, that relationships does not have to be antagonistic. If stewardship is holding something in trust for another person and building the "capacity of the new generation to govern themselves" (Block, 2013, p. xxiv), then Ben's actions can be read as modeling for newer teachers that there are types of action that can be taken.

Another key component in stewardship is relationships. These relationships are genuine and non-coercive. In this aspect of stewardship, new teachers can be validated that their daily work with students, families, and communities is important. In these portraits, all the teachers receive professional satisfaction by working with students and families, similar to the findings of Jackson and Lortie over 40 years ago. Owen's self-awareness of the role he plays as a man in an elementary school guides many of the decisions he makes in building relationships with his students. Owen also knows the power he holds as the son of a well-known educator in the county. Owen can choose to step into that power when he needs to, but as with the closing of the school, he realizes that using his power may not be the right action. Perhaps he is biding his time, but in his everyday interactions with his students and colleagues, he demonstrates the four stewardship tenets. Unsurprisingly he does not consider these aspects of his daily work to be leadership. He equates leadership with experience, roles, and hierarchy.

Block (2013) sets up stewardship in opposition to leadership in his book. Stewardship, as Block writes, "is meant to be a choice to (1) act in service of the long run, and (2) act in service to those with little power" (p. 1). It is clear that all the teacher's portraits reflect choices they have made in the service of their students and colleagues with less power. However, making some of these choices has resulted in power struggles, which are really struggles over how to answer the question, What is best for the students? Bradley-Levine (2018) sees teacher leadership as ethical leadership within an ethic of care: placing student needs at the center of the work and choosing the just, right action. While Bradley-Levine calls action in the best interests of students teacher leadership, many teachers balk at the idea that they are teacher leaders. When the teachers in the portraits are asked if they are teacher leaders there is, as one would expect, some initial hesitation from the novice teachers. The newer teachers feel that they are helpful within their schools by creating useful tools such as a curriculum maps or through a distinct action such as offering afterschool activities. None of the four teachers call themselves teacher leaders. Ben sees himself as serving a role that required certain behaviors, rather than as a teacher leader. This is not a surprising result since teaching is a profession that has a historic resistance to competition and hierarchy amongst teachers (Tyack & Cuban, 1995; Goldstein, 2014). The realm of influence, or leadership, for these teachers is in the relationships they have with students, parents, and colleagues.

The language of stewardship is also apparent in their views of student success, which include long-term and short-term goals such as social and emotional growth and academic achievement, respectively. They also serve their students, who have little power, by focusing on classroom instruction and management that is good for their students rather than what is easy for them. This is reflected in Carly's portrait and the snapshot of Laura, who starts teaching by inheriting a classroom halfway through the year and decides to change her classroom management system from an inherited "clip down" system to a positive-reinforcement model and to stop using silent lunch as a consequence. Other teachers in the grade level decide to change as well because they feel the current system isn't working and is just part of the school's culture of behavior management they inherited.

Closing & opening thoughts about stewardship

As many teachers leave the profession within the first five years and 55% leave because of dissatisfaction with their profession (Carver-Thomas & Darling-Hammond, 2017), the opportunity to be seen as a capable teacher, whether in a formal or informal role, has the potential to increase retention in the profession. Stewardship allows for teachers to demonstrate their capabilities and capacity in ways that traditional teacher leadership roles do not. This can lead to a greater sense of self-efficacy for teachers and increase student success.

Teacher leadership is a well-researched concept and has been seen as a critical component of overall school leadership (Spillane & Diamond, 2007) where most teacher leaders are experienced, veteran teachers who often take on roles and responsibilities beyond the classroom. Yet, teacher leadership, regardless of how we try and reshape its meaning in educational contexts, connotes hierarchical relationships. Formal teacher leadership roles often require expertise acquired through years of experience. Therefore, the language of teacher leadership is limiting to early career teachers because they do not possess experience or expertise in the eye of many other teachers and administrators. The language of teacher leadership is also problematic for experienced teachers since many choose to focus their time and energy within the classroom and school.

There are many good teachers doing the hard work of stewarding the profession. Stewardship language broadens pre-service, novice, and experienced teachers' beliefs about their own agency and leadership actions in the re-culturing and improvement of schools. Being seen and recognized as stewards of the profession through their everyday actions in creating and sustaining relationships that serve the interests of their students and families gives new teachers, and even experienced teachers who wish to remain in the classroom, opportunities to be leaders within the important work of teaching, which could lead to increased job satisfaction and the retention of good classroom teachers.

The concept of stewardship also describes a professional stance toward leadership enactment that is rooted in the belief that teachers' contributions and actions can make a difference for the larger community—the students, the school, and the profession. In the portraits provided, we see that teachers do not only look out for themselves and the students in their classrooms, they see themselves as part of a larger educational endeavor. They contribute to the betterment of the school and uphold the covenants of being a teacher. Not only are the teachers acting as stewards of the students they serve, they are also stewards of the school and stewards of the profession of teaching.

Stewardship as teacher leadership, or just renaming teachers' work stewardship, can help teachers both recognize and further refine their work as professionals and lessen some of the resistance from teachers who so adamantly deny their own potential to influence and create change because of the historical and hierarchical images that the word "leader" conjures. The language of stewardship reminds us that teaching is an important moral responsibility within our culture, and all teachers have a right and a responsibility to shape the work and culture of their schools and their profession for the sake of the children they teach. Teachers who take a stewardship stance toward their everyday work may not have a designated position of leadership, but they will know that they have expertise that can be shared with others and that they are deserving of good pay and support for the hard work of helping students learn to navigate the world in which they live and also see the possibilities of a world they can create.

References

Block, P. (2013). *Stewardship: Choosing service over self-interest.* (2nd ed.). San Francisco, CA: Berrett-Koehler.

Bradley-Levine, J. (2018). Advocacy as a practice of critical teacher leadership. *International Journal of Teacher Leadership, 9*(1), 47–61.

Carver-Thomas, D., & Darling-Hammond, L. (2017). *Teacher turnover: Why it matters and what we can do about it.* Palo Alto, CA: Learning Policy Institute.

Clandinin, D.J., & Connelly, F.M. (2000). *Narrative inquiry: Experience and story in qualitative research.* San Francisco: Jossey-Bass.

Craig, C. (2007). Story constellations: A narrative approach to contextualizing teachers' knowledge of school reform. *Teaching and Teacher Education, 23*(2), 173–188.

Goldstein, D. (2014). *The teacher wars: A history of America's most embattled profession.* New York: Anchor Books.

Gomez, M. (1996). Telling stories of our teaching, reflecting on our practices. *Action in Teacher Education, 18*(3), 1–12.

Kienholz, K. (2002). "Let me tell you a story": Teacher lore and pre-service teachers. *Action in Teacher Education, 24*(3), 37–42.

O'Connell Rust, F. (1999). Professional conversations: new teachers explore teaching through conversation, story, and narrative. *Teaching and Teacher Education, 15*(4), 367–380.

Olson, M., & Craig, C. (2001). Opportunities and challenges in the development of teachers' knowledge: The development of narrative authority through knowledge communities. *Teaching and Teacher Education, 17*(6), 667–684.

Sato, M., & Rogers, C. (2017). Practical leadership: How teachers enact leadership to re-culture their schools. In C. Rogers, K. Lomotey, & A. Hilton, (Eds.), *Innovative approaches to educational leadership: Selected cases* (pp. 27–31). New York, NY: Peter Lang Publishing.

Sato, M., Hyler, M. E., & Monte-Sano, C. B. (2014). Learning to lead with purpose: National Board Certification and teacher leadership development. *International Journal of Teacher Leadership, 5*(1), 1–23.

Spillane, J.P., & Diamond, J.B. (2007). *Distributed leadership in practice.* New York, NY: Teachers College Press.

Turnbull, B. (2005). Facilitating early career leadership through pre-service training. *Teachers and Teaching: Theory and Practice, 11*(5), 457–464.

Tyack, D., & Cuban, L. (1995). *Tinkering toward Utopia: A century of public school reform.* Harvard University Press: Cambridge, MA.

Whelan, Huber, Rose, Davies, & Clandinin. (2001). Telling and retelling our stories on the professional knowledge landscape. *Teacher and Teaching: Theory and Practice, 7*(2), 143–156.

AUTHOR BIO

Carrie Rogers is an associate professor at Western Carolina University in the School of Teaching and Learning. She earned her doctorate from the University of Minnesota-Twin Cities after being a classroom teacher in Minneapolis for several years. In her research, Carrie strives to demonstrate the thoughtful, intellectual, and critical actions of teachers in helping students understand and transform the world. Her areas of expertise are action research and teacher leadership. She has published extensively on the constraints and affordances of the concept of early teacher leadership.

INDEX

The dialogue of the Church with the Jews and with the Jewish tradition that has begun on many levels since the council and that needs to continue, despite immense "problems over language," is, as a constitutive element of the Church's life, an act of return to the roots—*and* a search for companionship with contemporary Judaism along the way. Whoever speaks here—superficially, without understanding, or cynically—of philosemitism or sees at work here merely the Church's bad conscience has not comprehended the depth dimension of the bond that indissolubly binds the Church and Judaism (with *vinculum* the council used a concept of marital law!) and that "obligates the Church to dialogue with the Jewish community," as John Paul II expressed it on October 28, 1985, to the participants at the annual gathering of the International Commission for the Relationships between the Catholic Church and Judaism.[5]

By means of the council declaration in 1965 the Church has begun to cart off the wretched rubbish littering the history of its relationship with Judaism and to pave new ways for requisite solidarity with the Jewish people. The expression *ecclesia semper reformanda* is appropriate precisely at this point, as the Pope shows in the talk I have just quoted:

> It was repeatedly said that the content of this section . . . was epoch-making, changing the existing relationship between the Church and the Jewish people and opening a new era in this relationship. It gives me joy here twenty years later to be able to give assurance that the fruits that we have harvested since then . . . confirm the truth that lies behind these assertions. The Catholic Church is always ready, with the help of God's grace, to revise and renew everything in its attitudes and modes of expression which turns out not to correspond sufficiently to its identity. . . . It does that not out of any expediency or to gain any practical advantage, but out of a deep consciousness of its own "mystery" and out of a renewed readiness to put this mystery into action.[6]

The principal declarations of the council are a renunciation of what could be found for centuries on the lips of Christian theologians, in the decrees of Church and state, but also in the thought and speech of the so-called common people. The "new" declarations on the Jews and on the relationship of the Church to the Jews can be summarized in two fundamental theses:

1) The Church and the Jewish people are connected to one another in manifold ways—to this very day! In particular, the Church has Jewish roots: it dare never forget that it "is nourished (present tense!) from the root of the good olive tree, into which the Gentiles are grafted as wild shoots."

[5] Ibid., 106.
[6] Ibid., 104.

2) In explicit repudiation of false teachings in the history of Christianity, especially in catechesis and preaching, it is expressly emphasized that it is a contradiction of biblical truth to say that the Jews are "rejected or cursed by God." On the contrary, with a quotation of Rom 11:28-29 the council emphasizes that the Jews "continue to be loved by God," who has chosen them with an "irrevocable call."

Among the Lutheran churches the revision of theological and ecclesial thinking came to expression even earlier. The Berlin-Weißensee Synod of the EKD [Evangelical Church in Germany] pointed the way in 1950 with this formulation: "We believe that God's promise to Israel, the people whom God chose, has continued in effect even after the crucifixion of Jesus Christ." Since then numerous member churches of the EKD have followed along this path. And the EKD itself has published two of the studies written by its study commission on "Church and Judaism"—*Christen und Juden* [Christians and Jews] *I"* (1975) and *Christen und Juden II* (1991), which mark out the kinds of questions that go beyond the consensus reached so far and that have to be worked on more in the future.[7]

If the "new" thinking, which definitely wants once and for all to overcome all the variations (including the subtle and "pious" ones) of the Church's teaching about the rejection of Israel, is labeled—somewhat pathetically, to be sure—as a "change," "rethinking," "reversal" that, indeed, brings to expression the reality that on this issue a rupture needs to take place in the history of Christianity—a paradigm shift. Whoever at this point, *a priori* and for whatever reason, opposes the thought of a "rupture" should understand this: Christianity's vitality has shown itself not least in its interruptions, ruptures, demolitions. Theologically, persisting in positions known to be false would be precisely what the New Testament calls the "sin against the Holy Spirit." The opposition to the "new" thinking precisely in wide circles of theological scholarship is, on the one hand, understandable if one is aware of the long tradition of theologically motivated hatred of Jews. On the other hand, however, it is inexcusable if one considers the fatal consequences of the alienation and hostility. That theological discrimination against the Jews was *one* of the roots of modern anti-Semitism can scarcely still be seriously disputed by anyone today.

With respect to the relationship of the Church to Judaism we thus stand before a new theological beginning: the "rediscovery" of the ongo-

[7] An excellent overview is offered by Rolf Rendtorff, *Hat denn Gott sein Volk verstoßen? Die evangelische Kirche und das Judentum seit 1945. Ein Kommentar* (Munich: Kaiser, 1989), as well as the study of the EKD, *Christen und Juden II. Zur theologischen Neuorientierung im Verhältnis zum Judentum. Eine Studie der Evangelischen Kirche in Deutschland* (Gütersloh: Mohn, 1991) 9–19.

ing theological significance of Israel requires, as it confronts the traditional teaching about the Church (ecclesiology), a powerful change of perspective that Rolf Rendtorff has aptly characterized as follows:

> What matters . . . is maintaining Israel's identity undiminished. The theological problem is thereby reversed: it is no longer a matter of defining Israel from the perspective of Christian theology, thereby finding a place for Israel in Christian thought-structures, but much more, given the continuing existence of biblical Israel, defining the Church without coming into conflict with the biblically based statements about Israel that maintain their unaltered validity.[8]

It dare no longer be a matter of what sometimes appears as a "Christian theology of Judaism" that wishes to "evaluate" Judaism with categories that are "allegedly" Christian and alien to what is Jewish.[9] In the final analysis these categories cannot be used because they correspond neither to historical nor theological reality. Rather, what is required is a reflection and, if possible, also a conceptual world that goes back to the common root in which, on the one hand, Jews find themselves again *as* Jews, *and* in which, on the other hand, the Church holds on to what distinguishes it from Judaism (its so-called *proprium Christianum*) as well as what binds it to Judaism.[10]

That appears to be putting a square peg in a round hole, and yet it is not, when we open ourselves to the necessary *and* possible change of perspectives that has already begun—both in official and theological attitudes—at the place where definitions of the relationship are sought with the help of concepts and metaphors that come from the biblical tradition *common* to Christians and Jews, namely, the Tanakh.

On the one hand no one will deny that in the search for a new understanding of the relationship Israel—Church recourse to the language and thought patterns of the Jewish *as well as* the Christian Bible is necessary.

[8] Rendtorff, *Hat denn Gott,* 114.

[9] Cf. on this the critical "report on trends" by Julie Kirchberg, *Theo-logie in der Anrede als Weg zur Verständigung zwischen Juden und Christen,* Innsbrucker Theologische Studien 31 (Innsbruck/Vienna: Herder, 1991) 64–72.

[10] On this cf. also Edna Brocke, "Von den 'Schriften' zum 'Alten Testament'—und zurück? Jüdische Fragen zur christlichen Suche einer 'Mitte der Schrift,'" *Die hebräische Bibel und ihre zweifache Nachgeschichte: Festschrift für Rolf Rendtorff zum 65. Geburtstag,* ed. Erhard Blum et al. (Neukirchen-Vluyn: Neukirchener Verlag, 1990) 594: "Where possible . . . a way can be travelled that . . . notes the differences, does not perceive them as necessarily (or at least not exclusively) divisive, and seeks constructive ways of filling the boundaries and demarcations with a positive meaning, with a 'Yes' to one another despite the differences—bearing in mind the fact that nearly two thousand years ago there was a common point of departure." Precisely for Christianity what counts today is to recognize *and* honor the *proprium Judaicum* in its *particular* dignity. Only when *what is different* is first viewed with respect can what unites become visible.

Especially helpful would be categories that occur in the Tanakh, as well as in the deuterocanonical books and in the New Testament, as the (self) designation of Israel and the Church. On the other hand the problem cannot be solved in a biblicistic manner, since in the terminological precision *Israel—Church* (and Jews—Christians) it cannot be present as yet in the Tanakh, and since even in the New Testament it appears at best only in the latest books, in which it is dealt with in part in the context of historically conditioned polemics—precisely what we today wish to overcome. So at first we have to be satisfied with seeking biblical "models" that can be developed in such a way that they produce a paraphrastic description of their relationship usable by Jews and Christians, a description that lets Israel and the Church maintain their respective identities and yet relates them to one another in a way that is in accord with their respective biblical testimonies. We see such "accord with Scripture" primarily in two biblical textual and thematic domains: in the biblical theology of the covenant and in those texts that reflect on Israel's relationship to the nations/Gentiles or the relationship of the God of Israel to the nations/Gentiles. The individual studies collected here have as their intention treating both themes in such a way that as a result of the exegetical investigations systematic-theological perspectives for a determination of the relationship Church–Israel emerge that can be characterized as scriptural.

Covenant theology thrusts itself forward for our question first of all from the *Christian* Bible. The category of covenant appears to us indispensable for the discussion because it represents a constitutive element of the definition of the Church as it legitimates itself biblically, especially in taking up the biblical talk about the "new covenant." Three recently published offerings on the theme are meant to illustrate that on this issue there is currently much to talk about for a Christian theology that is also concerned about the renewal of the relationship between Christians and Jews.

First, in volume III of his *Systematic Theology,* which appeared in 1993, Wolfhart Pannenberg devoted a separate section to the question of "The Church and Israel." Therein he expressly criticized the thesis about the participation of Christians in God's covenant with Israel:

> . . . it [is not] enough to say with the synod's declaration 4 (4) that by Jesus Christ the church has been taken up into God's covenant with his people . . . , for this might leave the impression that the church is taken up into the old covenant and that proper note is thus not taken of the constitutive difference between the new covenant and the old.[11]

[11] Pannenberg, *Systematic Theology,* vol. 3, trans. Geoffrey W. Bromiley (Grand Rapids: Eerdmans, 1993) 472, n. 100. For the text of the resolution passed by the Rhineland Synod of the Evangelical [Lutheran] Church cf. Rendtorff and Hendrix, *Die Kirchen,* 593–96.

Rather, on the basis of Romans 9–11 Pannenberg finds it necessary to conclude:

> The new covenant, in which, according to Rom 11:27, Israel is to have a share at Christ's return is no other than the new covenant established, according to 1 Cor 11:25, in the blood of Christ, to which the cup offered at the Lord's Supper grants a share. This means that the church, which in table fellowship with Jesus is made one as his body, shares already in the new covenant that will be granted to Israel as a whole (Rom 11:26) when Christ returns as the eschatological Redeemer whose coming Israel awaits. Only in terms of this eschatological destiny, and on the basis of the new eschatological covenant, may we see Jews and Christians as parts of one and the same people of God. The unity of the people of God, then, does not rest on the fact that in the form of Christianity the peoples are brought into the covenant history of Israel that dates back to Moses. Instead, it rests on the fact that in the new covenant which Jewish prophecy promised, and which will renew the covenant relationship of the Jewish people with its God, the old people of God will be united with the church of Jesus Christ, which by its fellowship with Jesus Christ shares already in this new covenant. As Paul sees it, for the Jewish people no less than for Christians, the basis of the new covenant is Jesus Christ, who at his coming again will show himself to his people as their expected Messiah.[12]

Second, the *Catechism of the Catholic Church* published in 1993 also expressly takes up covenant theology categories in order to describe *the relationship of the Church with the Jewish people*:

> When she delves into her own mystery, the Church, the People of God in the New Covenant, discovers her link with the Jewish People, "the first to hear the Word of God."[13] The Jewish faith, unlike other non-Christian religions, is already a response to God's revelation in the Old Covenant. . . . And when one considers the future, God's People of the Old Covenant and the new People of God tend towards similar goals: expectation of the coming

[12] Pannenberg, *Systematic Theology,* vol. 3, 473–74 [the first sentence of this quotation is my translation of Pannenberg as quoted by Lohfink, since the English is very different here. Trans.]. Cf. also the "classical" position of Ernst Käsemann in his commentary on Rom 11:27: "Whereas Christianity is already living in the new covenant, Israel will begin to do so only at the parousia, and it will do it through the same Giver, Christ, and with the . . . gift . . . of the forgiveness of sins"—*Commentary on Romans,* trans. and ed. Geoffrey W. Bromiley (Grand Rapids: Eerdmans, 1980) 314.

[13] *Catechism of the Catholic Church* (Washington, D.C.: United States Catholic Conference, 1994) sections 839 and 840. Cf. also section 674: "The glorious Messiah's coming is suspended at every moment of history until his recognition by 'all Israel,' for 'a hardening has come upon part of Israel' in their 'unbelief' toward Jesus (Rom 11:20-26). . . . The 'full inclusion' of the Jews in the Messiah's salvation, in the wake of the 'full number of the Gentiles' (Rom 11:12, 25; cf. Lk 21:24), will enable the People of God to achieve 'the measure of the stature of the fullness of Christ,' in which 'God may be all in all' (Eph 4:13; 1 Cor 15:28)."

(or the return) of the Messiah. But one awaits the return of the Messiah who died and rose from the dead and is recognized as Lord and Son of God; the other awaits the coming of a Messiah, whose features remain hidden till the end of time; and the latter waiting is accompanied by the drama of not knowing or of misunderstanding Christ Jesus.

Third, how extensively the category of the new covenant is sometimes used in Christian theology to dissociate the Church and Israel is shown in the posthumously published *Biblische Theologie des Alten Testaments* of A.H.J. Gunneweg. He diminishes the covenant theology in Exodus 19–34 and overemphasizes the alleged semantic differences in the New Testament Lord's Supper tradition over against Jer 31:31-34 and Exod 24:8. Both are supposed to prove that at this point, on the basis of the New Testament, Israel's self-understanding is destroyed:

> With the help of some concepts taken from the Old Testament—from sacred scripture—the opposite of what was originally meant by these concepts is said! Whoever takes issue with this way of dealing with texts as historically and methodologically invalid today needs to expand and further sharpen their historical knowledge and also in addition understand the methods of interpretation in use at that time: common concepts that are important in the context of the Old Testament as Sacred Scripture are filled with an entirely new content that bursts—and is fully intended to burst—the "old wine-skins." The exclusivity of God's covenant with Israel (and Judah) is broken through, and in place of the genealogically and nationally defined people of God appears the inclusivity of the many, for whom the blood of Jesus is poured out.[14]

Gunneweg reads even Rom 9:4 against Israel: ". . . It is noteworthy that the enumeration of Israel's privileges passes over in silence two parts of the ancient promise, land and posterity (the people's origin and national existence) and says nothing about an exclusive covenant of God with Israel."[15] Since Gunneweg reads the covenant texts in the Bible in this way (against the grain) it is no longer surprising that he, one of the initiators of the critique of the Rhineland Synod that came from Bonn, concludes:

> In the light of this finding, the view, occasionally also advocated by Church authorities, that the new covenant entails the incorporation of the Gentiles into the covenant with Israel shows itself to be blatant heresy. The opposite of the "German Christian" heresy, with its declaration that Jesus was an Arian and the requisite abrogation of the Old Testament, it is itself an equally obvious false teaching—even from the standpoint of authentic Ju-

[14] Antonius H. J. Gunneweg, *Biblische Theologie des Alten Testaments. Eine Religionsgeschichte Israels in biblisch-theologischer Sicht* (Stuttgart: Kohlhammer, 1993) 73.

[15] Ibid., 74.

daism, for which proselytes are not integrated into Israel through the covenant blood of Jesus.[16]

The extent to which "covenant" as a "canonical" category can provide the fundamental perspective from which the dynamic-dramatic alliance of Israel and the Church as two instruments of God for the coming of God's reign can be described is shown by the first of the studies collected here, "The Concept of 'Covenant' in Biblical Theology" (Norbert Lohfink). That this "alliance" is established as a "pilgrimage of the nations to Zion" will be developed in the next two studies, "Covenant and Torah in the Pilgrimage of the Nations to Zion" (Lohfink) and "The Covenant Formula in Psalm 33" (Lohfink). How intensively the biblical tradition understands Zion as the source of life for the nations and as the place of revelation for the universal reign of YHWH will then be elaborated in the studies "Zion as Mother of the Nations" (Erich Zenger) and "The God of Israel's Reign over the World" (Zenger).

With regard to methodology our individual studies take up the concerns of canonical criticism and the more recent reader response theory. They do not reject the historical-critical questions about the origin of the texts, even taking these up at times, but they strive for a productive conversation with the "document" that now lies before us as the "final text" and with its theological thought world, in order to arrive in this conversation at perspectives relevant *for today,* which are to be indicated at the end of the book in chapter 7.

[16] Ibid., 73.

CHAPTER 2

The Concept of "Covenant" in Biblical Theology[1]

As Pope John Paul II in 1980 at his address in Mainz contrasted the "people of God of the old covenant that has never been revoked by God" with the people of God of "the new covenant,"[2] he spoke of two "covenants" and of two "peoples of God." Is this way of speaking biblical? At least the twofold "old" and "new" covenants is; the talk of two "peoples of God," on the other hand, hardly so.[3] Since, then, "biblical" theology is under discussion in what follows, only the keyword "covenant" is taken up. What will be asked is how one can work with the concept "covenant" theologically, particularly also with an eye to Jewish-Christian dialogue, given the current state of biblical scholarship.

[1] This chapter was presented at a conference in August 1990 at Nemi, near Rome. That paper has been published as Lohfink, "Der Begriff 'Bund' in der biblischen Theologie," *ThPh* 66 (1991) 161–76. For this book the text has been reworked.

[2] Address to the Central Council of the Jews in Germany and the Rabbinical Conference on November 17, 1990 in Mainz: "The first dimension of this dialogue, namely, the meeting between the people of God of the old covenant that has never been revoked by God [note: cf. Rom 11:29] and the people of God of the new covenant is at the same time a dialogue within our Church, between the first and second parts of her Bible." The text is given from Rolf Rendtorff and H. H. Henrix, eds., *Die Kirchen und das Judentum: Dokumente von 1945 bis 1985* (Paderborn: Bonifatius-Druckerei; Munich: Kaiser, 1989) 75.

[3] There are a few texts that come close to such a way of speaking, for instance Isa 19:25; Zech 2:11 [MT 2:15], 9:7; Ps 87:4-7 (on this, see ch. 5 below). That they were perceived as difficult is shown by the way old translations manipulated them: cf. Walter Groß, "YHWH und die Religionen der Nicht-Israeliten," *ThQ* 169 (1989) 38–39. Yet even the Masoretic text cannot be understood in the sense of several "peoples of God" existing alongside one another—for reasons that vary from text to text.

Since they knew the Bible, Christian theologians have always spoken not only of the "old" and "new" covenant but also of many other "covenants"—of God's covenant with Noah, Abraham, or David, for example. The "old" covenant often meant for them the covenant at Sinai. The other "covenants" of which Israel's Bible speaks are not, however, simply identical with this one.

There was soon also an attempt to systematize the various "covenants." Already in the Hebrew Bible, indeed in its preliminary stages, the priestly source's two categories of a covenant with Noah and one with Abraham or Jeremiah's juxtaposition of the broken Exodus covenant with the promise of a "new" covenant are something like systematizations. Then Jesus Sirach went still further in his "Praise of the Fathers" (Sirach 44–47).[4] He sets Israel's history into periods by means of seven "covenants," the Greek text using the word διαθήκη twelve times in this passage. These are the "covenants" with Noah, Abraham, Isaac,[5] Jacob, Aaron, Phinehas and David. The emphasis is on the covenants with Aaron and Phinehas. Jesus Sirach mentions neither the "new covenant" of Jeremiah 31 nor the Mosaic covenant at Sinai that this presupposes (the Sinai event, at least in the Hebrew text of Sirach, is simply law-giving).[6] The historical perspective is decidedly "priestly," and the system of "covenants" that is presented does not uniformly structure the entire history, but rather a kind of foundational epoch. Nevertheless, just by characterizing history through "covenants" the "Praise of the Fathers" could have served as the biblical stimulus for later salvation-historical theologies of the covenant. Comparable outlines, even if laid out differently in details, are found in Jubilees and in the *Biblical Antiquities* of Pseudo-Philo (first century C.E.).

Most Christians engaged in Jewish-Christian dialogue probably have salvation-historical sketches of this kind in their minds. Therefore we point out some things in such thought patterns that are not supported by the biblical statements.

[4] On this, most recently, see Johannes Marböck, "Die 'Geschichte Israel's' als 'Bundesgeschichte' nach dem Sirachbuch," *Der Neue Bund im Alten: Studien zur Bundestheologie der beiden Testamente,* ed. Erich Zenger, QD 146 (Freiburg: Herder, 1993), which has references to the earlier literature.

[5] Here the word "covenant" is missing. However, in Sir 44:22 the word הקים / ἔστησεν ("he gave assurance"), the same term used in v. 21 with reference to the oath to Abraham, likely is a reference to the concept. Only if this interpretation is correct are seven covenants discussed.

[6] In 45:5 in the Greek Sirach, however, חקיו, "his laws," which Moses teaches (as the preserved Hebrew text has it) has become διαθήκη, "covenant."

Often a covenant of God with "Adam" is presupposed. The Bible knows nothing of this. The biblical covenant at Moab (cf. Deut 29:1 [MT 28:69]), on the other hand, often goes unmentioned, as is true of the covenants with Aaron and Levi. Moreover, evolutionary categories are often introduced, for example, the idea of a continued concentration by God on ever smaller and more specifically chosen groups. That even contradicts the Bible, because in the Bible, for example, the covenant with David (2 Samuel 7) that is restricted to a dynasty comes after the Sinai covenant extended to the entire people of Israel, but non-Israelite populations also live in David's kingdom, and Isa 55:3-4 applies the covenant with David precisely to these circumstances. So this covenant, when compared with the one at Sinai, expands rather than narrows.

These, however, are critical observations about certain superficial aspects of the theory. The problems that biblical scholarship presents today, if one wishes to speak about the "covenant," lie deeper than that. They are connected with contemporary biblical scholarship's methodological starting points.

For this reason we intend to start with a history of the research into the problems biblical scholarship has with the concept of "covenant." Then, in a second part, we shall indicate how one can perhaps speak of "covenant" from a biblical-theology perspective in a way that is tenable for biblical scholarship and useful for Jewish-Christian dialogue. The point is that one has to inquire about the "canonical theology of the covenant."

I. The "Covenant" in Modern Biblical Scholarship[7]

1. Assumptions in Thinking about "Salvation History"

Salvation-historical sketches structured by means of God's covenants preceded modern biblical scholarship. It is precisely from such conceptions that this scholarship has distanced itself. In the Protestant circles in which they were developed in the last century one was aware of major theologians who had structured salvation history through "covenants," Cocceius or Johann Christian Konrad von Hoffmann, for example.

In such sketches the Bible is taken to be a single, cohesive book of history. Contradictions are harmonized by attempts to discover what really

[7] For further details refer to Erich Zenger, "Die Bundestheologie—ein derzeit vernachlässigtes Thema der Bibelwissenschaft und ein wichtiges Thema für das Verhältnis Israel—Kirche," in Zenger, ed., *Der Neue Bund.*

happened. Then this alleged "history" is divided into periods by various "covenants" instituted by God and following one another.

Biblical scholarship, by contrast, uses only historical and literary criticism.[8] Therefore it cannot designate "Adam" or "Noah," for example, as historical figures. Neither can be precisely located in a chronology. They belong to the genre "primal history." The statements made with the help of these figures rest on something other than certain historical details. If Abraham turns out to be a historical figure that does not make the covenant with Abraham a fact of history.[9] The Sinai tradition probably spoke originally only of a theophany. The themes of "covenant" and "law" came into it during the monarchy at the earliest. It is difficult to determine what events stood at the beginning of the Sinai tradition. "Covenant at Sinai" is an unlikely historical reality. The covenant of God with the Aaronic priests is a late construction as well. It is no different with the covenant at Moab in Deuteronomy.

Such findings sweep the feet out from under every string of "covenants" understood as historical.

2. *"Covenant" as a Late Interpretive Symbol*

The classical counter-thesis to such salvation-historical sketches of covenants following one upon another is found in the work of Julius Wellhausen. In his view "covenant" was not spoken about until the waning days of the monarchy and in the Exile. At that time Israel had begun to orient itself to the "law" but had at its disposal no theory about the "law," so its obligatory nature was explained by means of an agreement that God and Israel freely made with one another. That was projected back into Israel's primal era in the form of a narrative. Thus the "covenant" or the "covenants" were not historical realities but a theological interpretation turned into history.[10] But this theory of Wellhausen's could not be maintained even among historians.

[8] On the history of statements about covenant in Israel see Norbert Lohfink, "Bund," *Neues Bibellexikon: Band I: A–G,* ed. Manfred Görg and Bernhard Lang (Zürich: Benziger, 1991) 343–48. Further literature there.

[9] I once advocated the idea that the tradition of the covenant with Abraham was very old (Lohfink, *Die Landverheißung als Eid: Eine Studie zu Genesis 15,* SBS 28 [Stuttgart: Katholisches Biblewerk, 1967]). I have been frequently criticized for this, partly with counterarguments worthy of consideration. I do not agree at all with the current tendencies to a late dating of Genesis 15. Nevertheless, I would now be more cautious with theses about the antiquity of the text.

[10] The most recent and a good history of the research, also for what follows, is Ernest W. Nicholson, *God and His People: Covenant and Theology in the Old Testament* (Oxford: Clarendon, 1986) 3–117. He provides references to the sources.

3. The Theory of a Historical Covenant Institution

For example, Codex Hammurabi was discovered. Thus a prominent culture of law already existed long before Israel, accompanied by theories about law that did not contain any kind of idea about an "agreement" with the divinity. And so even in Israel the concept of "covenant" was unnecessary to explain the obligatory character of law. In addition a new understanding of cultic institutions took over. Ethnology and sociology provided new models for understanding Israel's primal era.

And so in the first half of this century, and until about 1970, the older "salvation-historical covenant theology" returned, fully altered. It had now become presentable historically as a kind of religious and cultural history of Israel for which the category of "covenant" exercised regulative functions. That was, to be sure, no "salvation history" structured by means of "covenants," and yet, according to this view, there had always been a "covenant institution" in the history of the people of God on the societal and cultic level. One built on the assumption that Israel had begun as a "tribal covenant" that at the same time was understood to be a "covenant with God," and that the heart of its worship had been a celebration of this double "covenant."[11]

The covenant with Noah would then be a theological projection into the past, of course, and perhaps the covenant with Abraham as well—as would covenants in general in the sense of divine revelatory interventions. But at least from the moment in which there was a tribal covenant for Israel, and through its entire history until the time of Jesus, there would also have been a "covenant institution," with individual aspects such as "covenant worship," "covenant festivals," "covenant documents," "covenant-renewal," and "covenant theology." Israel's self-understanding would have borne the decisive stamp of all of this. Israel would then also have interpreted the decisive junctures of its history as "covenants." Walter Eichrodt could sketch out his *Theology of the Old Testament*[12] as a "theology of the covenant."

This theory was meant to be a historically verifiable assumption. In the end it did not stand up to the historical test. For a short time it appeared as though it would receive brilliant confirmation through the linguistic and

[11] The prime impetus for the new view appears to have been Max Weber. On him cf. Christa Schäfer-Lichtenberger, "Von Nebensatz zum Idealtypus: Zur Vorgeschichte des 'Antiken Judentums' von Max Weber," *Die hebräische Bibel und ihre zweifache Nachgeschichte: Festschrift für Rolf Rendtorff zum 65. Geburtstag,* ed. Erhard Blum (Neukirchen-Vluyn: Neukirchener Verlag, 1990) 419–33.

[12] 2 vols., trans. J. A. Baker (Philadelphia: Fortress, 1961–1967 [first German edition 1933]).

formal proximity of biblical texts about the covenant to ancient oriental treaties between states from the second millennium B.C.E. But on closer examination an opposite conclusion emerged. The deuteronomic covenant theology was instead connected with the substance of neo-Assyrian loans, oaths, and treaties; it was thus a literary and theological phenomenon of the waning days of the monarchy.[13]

4. An Interpretive Theological Symbol Once Again?

Today it probably cannot be proven that there existed from Israel's beginnings an all-encompassing "covenant institution." Much evidence points rather in the opposite direction—even if particular conceptions of a relationship with God bestowing on Israel legal privileges may be old, several covenant rituals may have existed early and the inner core of Israel's whole self-understanding, the "legally privileged" conception of its relation to God, may also go back to the primal era.[14] A "covenant institution" encompassing the whole of Israel's worship and embodied in the liturgy probably did not even exist in late periods. The periodic public proclamation of the deuteronomic law ordered in Deut 31:10-13, for which we have no contemporary witnesses to implementation, hardly suffices for such an assumption.[15] The only possible exception was the Qumran community: the beginning of the Rule of the Community (1QS 1-2) contains a ritual for "entrance into the covenant." But even at Qumran (in the Hodayot) the word "covenant" can also simply mean the "faith" in the heart of the indi-

[13] Cf. especially Dennis J. McCarthy, *Treaty and Covenant: A Study in Form in the Ancient Oriental Documents and in the Old Testament,* 2d ed., AnBib 21A (Rome: Biblical Institute Press, 1978).

[14] On what can now be said cf. Lohfink, "Bund," 345–46. The end of the theory about the covenant institution was brought about primarily through Lothar Perlitt, *Bundestheologie im Alten Testament,* WMANT 36 (Neukirchen-Vluyn: Neukirchener Verlag, 1969). The book should be read critically, it is true: cf. Norbert Lohfink, "Bundestheologie im Alten Testament: Zum gleichnamigen Buch von Lothar Perlitt," *Studien zum Deuteronomium und zur deuteronomistischen Literatur I,* SBAB 8 (Stuttgart: Verlag Katholisches Bibelwerk, 1990).

[15] William L. Holladay believes that he can explain a series of "deuteronomistic" prose texts in Jeremiah as stylistically consistent with prophetic reactions to these proclamations of Deuteronomy. He reckons with readings of this kind in the years 615, 608, 601, 594, and 587. Cf. Holladay, "A Proposal for Reflections in the Book of Jeremiah of the Seven-Year Recitation of the Law in Deuteronomy (Deut 30:10-13)," in *Deuteronomium: Entstehung, Gestalt und Botschaft,* ed. Norbert Lohfink, BEThL 6 (Louvain: University Press; Peeters, 1985) 326–28; cf. idem, *Jeremiah, 2: A Commentary on the Book of the Prophet Jeremiah Chapters 26–52,* Hermeneia (Minneapolis: Fortress, 1989) 27. Yet that remains extremely hypothetical, because for Deuteronomy itself there is once again a difference between this reading of the law and Israel's actual worship.

vidual person. And then there were also, of course (seen with Jewish eyes from that period), the followers of Jesus of Nazareth, who understood their central rite, the breaking of bread, as the actualization of the "new covenant" instituted in the death of its inaugurator.

In Israel's Scriptures the word ברית = διαθήκη = "covenant" shows itself again, as it did for Wellhausen, to be a secondary, theological symbol denoting past and present. It came into the foreground only at the end of the monarchy and in the exile, probably in the intellectual conflict with the new Assyrian cultural pressures.[16] Even later in Israel the concept of "covenant" never ruled the field of theological thinking on its own.

Nevertheless, we are not once more simply back to Wellhausen. We have moved beyond his assumption that the idea of a covenant with God was a first attempt to legitimize the new (according to the view in Wellhausen's time) phenomenon of national law.[17] Rather, decisive salvation-historical experiences of Israel have been interpreted by means of the concept of "covenant."

For some time there has been considerable semantic investigation of the terms ברית and διαθήκη [18] and of the theological conceptions in which these words play a role. With reference to semantics, ברית as well as διαθήκη do not *mean* "agreement, covenant" but "obligation" or "commitment," often also "oath." These are also words of normal speech and not simply technical theological terms. And yet in many occurrences they are used in *reference* to a presupposed preferential or contractual relationship between God and Israel or specific people in Israel. Even the reference to contractual relationships and signing contracts was presupposed in normal speech. Such references, if present, must be individually explained at each occurrence.

[16] Cf. Norbert Lohfink, "Theology as the Answer to Plausibility Crises in Emergent Pluralistic Situations, Taking the Deuteronomic Law as the Basis for Discussion," in idem, *Great Themes from the Old Testament,* trans. Ronald Walls (Edinburgh: T&T Clark, 1982) 17–37.

[17] Even if Wellhausen's assumption stands quite near that of Lothar Perlitt, for example. Wellhausen continues to be correct to the extent that the covenant concept took over the function of establishing the law at the time in which the earlier systems no longer held their ground against societal relationships being transformed into higher complexity. Thus Eckart Otto in more recent works.

[18] Primarily in two monographs by Ernst Kutsch—*Verheißung und Gesetz: Untersuchungen zum sogenannten "Bund" im Alten Testament,* BZAW 131 (Berlin: de Gruyter, 1973) and *Neues Testament—Neuer Bund? Eine Fehlübersetzung wird korrigiert* (Neukirchen-Vluyn: Neukirchener Verlag, 1978)—and in many prior articles by the same author. The problem with all these analyses, of course, is that apparently no distinction was made between "meaning" and "reference."

In other places ברית appears to be a designation for the ten commandments or the first commandment, the command to worship YHWH alone.[19] The word ברית is not synonymous with תורה, "teaching, instruction, law."[20]

In many late passages the word has lost color. It means something like what we mean when we speak of "religion" or "faith," especially in Daniel.

In the various theological sketches in the Hebrew Bible ברית is employed in very different ways. The sketches in part even consciously oppose one another. Thus in the priestly writing "the theology of the covenant" is a theology of divine "promises" that cannot be abrogated. As it uses for this the word ברית and introduces it into history not at Sinai but with Abraham, it wants to offer a corrective to the deuteronomistic ברית theology of an "agreement" between God and the people of Israel.[21] This contrast between two literary works and their fundamental theological positions paves the way for the uncertainties in the (Pauline) teaching about justification.

In late texts in Israel's Bible, and in the New Testament as well, statements using the word ברית are often given definition through allusion. In this case reference is made to an existing fundamental canonical passage. Thus in the New Testament when reference is made to the "new covenant," it is often an allusion to Jeremiah 30–31. At least implicitly it is then also asserted that the promise in the passage has been fulfilled. Other New Testament texts using διαθήκη allude to other passages, for example to the promises to Abraham. In that case the word naturally has a shade of meaning and a reference different from those in passages that allude to Jeremiah 31.[22]

So when responsible historical and literary scholarship cannot start its interpretation of the Bible with the presupposition that wherever the words ברית or διαθήκη occur the same thing is spoken of, what can still be done in terms of biblical theology?

[19] Cf. Georg Braulik, "Die Ausdrücke für 'Gesetz' im Buch Deuteronomium," *Bib* 51 (1970) 39–66; reprinted in idem, *Studien zur Komposition des Pentateuch,* SBAB 2 (Stuttgart: Verlag Katholisches Bibelwerk, 1988) 11–38; further details in Lohfink, "Bundestheologie," 338–40.

[20] Only the parallelisms in Isa 24:5; Hos 8:1; and Ps 78:10 could be alleged in support, and these must be read in light of other passages in which the terms are distinguished. Cf. especially Lev 26:45-46; Deut 29:20; 31:9, 26: Josh 24:25-26; 2 Kgs 17:34-35, 37-38; Mal 2:5-10; Ezra 10:3.

[21] Cf. Walther Zimmerli, "Sinaibund und Abrahambund: Ein Beitrag zum Verständnis der Priesterschrift," *ThZ* 16 (1960) 268–80.

[22] An attempt to demonstrate this in detail: Norbert Lohfink, *The Covenant Never Revoked: Biblical Reflections on Christian-Jewish Dialogue,* trans. John J. Scullion (New York: Paulist, 1991), ch. III: "An Auxiliary Notion—And No More," 20–34.

5. The Question about the Next Steps

Systematic theology is, of course, always free to designate a particular subject matter, in this case the special relationship between God and the chosen people, with a biblical word that is somehow applicable, in this case the word "covenant," and even free, perhaps, to work with a concept given precise definition when it is introduced. Perhaps one cannot then draw upon all biblical texts in which ברית or διαθήκη occur. On the other hand, one may need to draw upon many passages in which these words are lacking.[23] But the undertaking is legitimate.

Something of this kind no doubt happened already with the so-called "federal theology" initiated by Zwingli and carried to a high point by Cocceius,[24] which greatly influenced pietistic movements. Covenant theology also plays a large role in the Baptist churches.[25]

A covenant theology of this kind is compatible with modern exegesis. In a certain sense even a "biblical" theology never escapes translating into a new "language"; it has to become systematics. No one can stop it from using biblical words in the process, even if these (at least *sub rosa*) are then redefined. Thus systematic theological sketches of this kind could even be characterized as "biblical" theology. Yet they would not be "biblical theology" in the sense of a thought form already discoverable in the

[23] This will be clearly seen, for example, if one analyzes Camille Focant and André Wénin, "L'alliance ancienne et nouvelle," *NRTh* 110 (1988) 850–66. In this essay the examples that tend toward the priestly writing's concept of covenant are virtually eliminated, and from the New Testament many texts are drawn upon in which the word "covenant" does not appear at all. As far as this way of operating is concerned, the essay is to be regarded as "systematic," even if it appears to be almost entirely a string of biblical statements. This is true, similarly, of Paul Beauchamp, "Propositions sur l'alliance de l'Ancien Testament comme structure centrale," *RSR* 58 (1970) 161–93, except that in this case the standard is supplied not by a word but by a form-critical structure, that of the Hittite vassal treaties, which, as is known, help to clarify several deuteronomistic covenant texts. Here as well one should speak of a (thoroughly legitimate) systematic form of presentation.

[24] Cf. Willem Jan van Asselt's recent work *The Covenant Theology of Johannes Coccejus (1603–1669): An Examination of Its Structure,* SHCT 58 (Leiden: Brill, 1994). The work is unfortunately not available to me.

[25] In these communities the word "covenant" appears to play an important role in the translation of συνειδήσεως ἀγαθῆς ἐπερώτημα εἰς θεόν, 1 Pet 3:21. Luther, for example, translated this passage, "The covenant of a good conscience with God." This translation is not all that far off: ἐπερώτημα could be—as a response of the parties involved with reference to the individual obligations—a *pars-pro-toto* designation for the making of an agreement. In that case the baptismal vow with which the candidate responded in the early Church would be primarily in view. Luther himself had written in a marginal note in the edition of 1545: "a stipulation to which God by grace obligates us and which we accept." Perhaps he thought here of Genesis 9.

Bible itself. Often, however, only a historical-descriptive investigation preceding along these lines is designated as "biblical theology." In Jewish-Christian dialogue, perhaps, precisely something of this sort would be sought.[26]

Despite all the problems we have sketched, doors still appear to be open for this approach even within modern historically and literarily oriented biblical scholarship. Although it has to this point barely been considered, there appears to be in the Bible a kind of "canonical covenant theology" that overarches all the individual biblical theologies, differing from one another, that operate with the concept of "covenant." The pages that follow can, of course, offer only some preliminary observations on this issue, suggesting a plan rather than following through on it.

II. Observations on the "Canonical" Theology of Covenant

1. The Concept of a "Canonical" Theology of Covenant

In essence exegesis actually becomes theology only when it undertakes *the interpretation* of the canonical text. Only the meaning that the biblical texts acquire within the unity of Scripture is their inspired and inerrant meaning. Theology must proceed from this meaning alone; everything else, however important and indispensable it may be, is only preliminary study.[27]

This Christian view corresponds in other respects to the way traditional Judaism deals with the Hebrew Bible. There as well, even though with different canonical boundaries, the Bible is always read as a unity, that is, synchronically. To that extent modern exegesis on our question becomes more interesting also for Jewish-Christian dialogue.

[26] In my book *The Covenant Never Revoked* I expressed the view that the concept of "covenant" is not especially helpful for conversation with Judaism that bears a rabbinic stamp, since it does not play much of a role there. Since then Jewish dialogue partners have corrected me. In rabbinic literature the concept is not actually very important, but the situation is different in liturgy and in prayer-life. Cf. Alan F. Segal, "Covenant in Rabbinic Writings," *The Other Judaisms of Late Antiquity,* Brown Judaic Studies 127 (Atlanta: Scholars Press, 1987).

[27] This is the perspective of the Vatican II Constitution *Dei Verbum*. Cf. Norbert Lohfink, "Über die Irrtumlosigkeit und die Einheit der Schrift," *StZt* 174 (1964) 161–81, reprinted in idem, *Studien zur biblischen Theologie,* SBAB 16 (Stuttgart: Verlag Katholisches Bibelwerk, 1993) 13–39, and "Der weiße Fleck in *Dei Verbum,* Artikel 12," *TThZ* 101 (1992) 20–35. It is true that Erhard S. Gerstenberger writes, "The final redaction can claim . . . no special status of any kind over against the redactions that preceded it," "Der

To be sure, one can still approach even the canon with a variety of methods, even with those that modern exegesis would not accept. Yet modern exegesis' own methods are totally appropriate for investigating configurations of canonical expressions. It is only that this type of investigation is uncommon among exegetes, as is shown by the reaction that Brevard Childs' program of "canonical criticism" has evoked.[28] But that is a problem about interests and not about methods.

2. "Canonical Covenant Theology": Reviewing the Data

What Scripture expresses in its canonical totality does not need to be "covenant theology" out of any kind of *a priori* necessity. Whether the canon, read synchronically, offers a "covenant theology" is a factual issue that must be established *a posteriori.*

One could naively say that the case is really clear, that the Bible appears before us as "Old" and "New Testament." Yet that clarifies nothing whatsoever. For we are not dealing here with the Bible's self-designation but with a characterization created by theologians—even if quite early—that is then used by the Christian tradition. It is true that in this process biblical words were used. But in the Bible itself these words do not yet designate the two parts of the canon of sacred books. Thus a review of the data is still called for.

3. In the "New Testament" "Covenant" Is Not the Primary Category

For a Christian reading of the Bible the New Testament provides the ultimate basis for establishing meaning. Thus if the New Testament would

---

Psalter als Buch und als Sammlung," *Neue Wege der Psalmenforschung: Für Walter Beyerlin,* ed. Klaus Seybold and Erich Zenger, HBS 1 (Freiburg: Herder, 1994) 8; a footnote at that place shows that he is specifically thinking of me. By contrast he would like "to distinguish the various stages of the tradition" and then "to value, . . . also theologically," all of them together, including the final redaction (ibid., 9). Indeed that is what I do and would like as well, and the insinuation hovering between the lines that what I and other colleagues have found in analyzing the final text is the product of "reading a theological concern back into the text" (ibid., 8), I would like to regard as a derailment arising in the heat of the moment and thus pardonably small. It is only that I do not yet confer such "theological valuing"—for the speech act of real "theology" in the sense of the Christian tradition—on a historical narration, called a "narrative-assertive" utterance in speech act theory, coming from texts that at best previously functioned in a social context and that, moreover, were reconstructed only hypothetically by a historian or literary critic. Theology in the sense of the Christian tradition presupposes a community of faith and the sacred Scriptures this community acknowledges. Only in this sense do I speak of theology at this place in my text.

[28] For the most recent major discussion of the problem cf. Günter Stemberger and Ingo Baldermann, eds., *Zum Problem des biblischen Kanons,* JBTh 3 (Neukirchen-Vluyn: Neukirchener Verlag, 1988).

present the entire message of the Bible as covenant a Christian reading would be obliged to treat even the older part of the Bible in this way, regardless of how often and in what manner the concept was used there. Thus the first question is whether the New Testament actually has covenant as its primary category.

The answer appears to be "no." The passages that use διαθήκη are not numerous. They are varied and not necessarily connected with one another. Standing beside them are other texts using different categories with at least the same importance, such as "the reign of God" and "righteousness." If the message of the New Testament as a whole is reduced to a single term it would be to a name, Jesus, the Christ.

Besides, where the καινή διαθήκη, the "new covenant/testament" is mentioned, this is in the first instance always an allusion to Jeremiah 31, not to the totality of Israel's Scriptures. In the two passages that, starting with the concept of the καινή διαθήκη, also develop the concept of an old or first διαθήκη—in 2 Corinthians 3 and in Hebrews[29]—this is not identified as the totality of our Old Testament books but only one of the parts. Second Corinthians 3 speaks only about the books read in Jewish or Jewish-Christian synagogues—and that was only the Pentateuch, perhaps the

[29] The concept πρωτη διαθηκη, "first testament," in Hebrews perhaps has a connection to the LXX text of Lev 26:45: καὶ μνησθήσομαι αὐτῶν τῆς διαθήκης τῆς προτέρας ὅτε ἐξήγαγον αὐτοὺς ἐκ γῆς Αἰγύπτου ἐξ οἴκου δουλείας ἔναντι τῶν ἐθνῶν τοῦ εἶναι αὐτῶν θεός, "I will remember the former covenant with them when I brought them out of Egypt, from the house of slavery, in the sight of the nations, to be their God." In any case the text here reads not πρωτη, "first," but προτερα, "former, earlier." The Greek text has reconceptualized the statement in comparison with the Hebrew text known to us. There we read, "I will remember in their favor the covenant with their ancestors (ברית ראשנים), whom I brought out of the land of Egypt in the sight of the nations, to be their God." In the Hebrew text it is fully possible to think of the covenant at Sinai as a comprehensive event connected with the Exodus (in the sense of the already more or less definitive Pentateuch), which is added as a supplement to the patriarchal covenants mentioned in Lev 26:42 (against Ernst Kutsch, *Verheißung und Gesetz: Untersuchungen zum sogenannten "Bund" im Alten Testament,* BZAW 131 [Berlin: de Gruyter, 1973]). In the Greek text what is in view is a covenant made at some time in the past with the Israelites who now find themselves in exile. The added temporal clause can refer to the establishment of this covenant. Nevertheless, it is possible the reference is to the patriarchal covenants mentioned in the priestly texts (cf. "to be their God") and the temporal clause points to a covenental remembrance on God's part that already took place earlier, in the context of leading the people out of Egypt (cf. Exod 6:5). Besides, the formulation ברית (ה)ראשנים occurs here alone in the Hebrew Bible. Jeremiah 11:10 can hardly be compared with this, since there the "ancestors" were precisely not the "ancestors" with whom the covenant was made. In any case, inasmuch as the "former covenant with them" in Lev 26:45 is not contrasted verbally with any new or present covenant, as is done with the "first covenant" in Hebrews, there exists here at best a loose stimulus for the formulation, but not a connection in terms of the subject matter.

"prophets" as well (as *haftara*), but the "writings" were not included. Hebrews is referring only to the cultic regulations in the Pentateuch, not to all the Scriptures of Israel.

So the New Testament does not compel us to see Israel's Scriptures as a whole as testimony to an old or a first covenant. Covenant is one category of meaning among many. It does occupy, to be sure, an important place in the Lord's Supper tradition. As a category that is already significant in the New Testament διαθήκη (covenant/testament) is picked up later by Christian theology and tradition and made the central category of many interpretive systems. Yet on the basis of the New Testament one can also describe the subject matter of which it speaks by using totally different concepts.

Now it could be the case, of course, that the New Testament offers the category of covenant as only one possibility among many for understanding the canon as a whole, and yet that covenant, at least for the canon of the sacred Scriptures of Israel (the Palestinian or the Alexandrian canon), is the decisive category of meaning in one or the other delineation. Then there would perhaps still be a reason to grant a preferential status to the term "covenant" in the theological interpretation of the New Testament. Is that the case?

4. Against "Covenant" as a Dominant Category in the Scriptures of Israel

First of all, this question is, of course, related to that other much-discussed question about the "center of the Old Testament,"[30] although they are not identical. The question about the center of the Old Testament, at least for those who have discussed it up to now, has not been about the canon read synchronically. Moreover, it has not necessarily sought a keyword that appears in the biblical writings themselves. But we are concerned with both of those issues here.

The term that occurs in the Tanakh itself to signify the unity of the canon is, of course, not "covenant" but "torah." It is true that the word תורה, "torah," is less common than the word ברית, "covenant."[31] But within the Bible the Pentateuch is already viewed as תורה or νόμος, "law." When

[30] Cf. Henning Graf Reventlow, *Hauptprobleme der alttestamentlichen Theologie im 20. Jahrhundert,* EdF 173 (Darmstadt: Wissenschaftliche Buchgesellschaft, 1982) 138–47. D. H. Odendall, "Covenant—the Centre of the Old Testament," *NGTT* 30 (1989) 143–51, which according to *OTA* 12 (1990) 79 defends the view that covenant is the center of the Old Testament, was unfortunately not accessible to me.

[31] The statistical details about the words are easily accessible in Francis I. Anderson and A. Dean Forbes, *The Vocabulary of the Old Testament* (Rome: Editrice Pontificio Istituto Biblico, 1989). For ברית cf. p. 295, for תורה p. 444.

Chronicles speaks of the "torah of Moses" it already has the entire Pentateuch in mind.[32] If in the New Testament ὁ νόμος, "the law," designates the Pentateuch, in Rom 3:21 for example, then in 3:19, by contrast, it actually designates all of the Scriptures of Israel, as the quotations that precede it show. The "prophets" of the Hebrew canon are, in fact, literarily framed by corresponding torah motifs at the beginning and end (Joshua 1 and Malachi 3) and thus present themselves as a kind of prophetic commentary on the torah, in a sense as the realization of the promise of the deuteronomic prophetic law (Deut 18:15-18). The Psalter opens with a torah-Psalm that is linked by keywords with Malachi 3, indeed even with the end of the torah itself.[33] That is characteristic of the Psalter as a whole. Through Deut 4:6-8 "wisdom" is connected with the realm of torah[34] and is probably already identified in Proverbs 1–9 with torah's way of living.[35] These are literary signals. Behind them stands the intention to make a canonical assertion. In the LXX canon, at the climax of a book newly added to this canon, the identification of divine wisdom with the torah of Moses is expressly asserted (Sir 24:23).[36]

Literary methods thus bring out that the theological keyword for Israel's Scriptures, read canonically, is "torah" rather than "covenant." That is true even if thereby a specific theme of the biblical writings that in literary terms is only one among many is shoved into the foreground at the

[32] Cf. Georg Steins, *Die Chronik als kanonisches Abschlußphänomen: Studien zur Entstehung und Theologie von 1/2 Chronik,* BBB 93 (Frankfurt am Main: Hain, 1994).

[33] On this last point Midrash Tehillim already indicates the connection of the last word of Moses (Deut 33:29) with the first word in the Psalter (Ps 1:1) through the beatitude form. Cf. Erich Zenger, "Der Psalter als Wegweiser und Wegbereiter: Ps 1–2 als Proömium des Psalmenbuchs," *Sie wandern von Kraft zu Kraft. Aufbrüche, Wege, Begegnungen. Festgabe für Bischof Reinhard Lettmann,* ed. Arnold Angenendt and Herbert Vorgrimler (Kevelaer: Butzon & Bercker, 1993) 29–47.

[34] Cf. Georg Braulik, "'Weisheit' im Buch Deuteronomium," in Bernd Janowski, ed., *Weisheit außerhalb der kanonischen Weisheitsschriften.* Veröffentlichungen der Wissenschaftlichen Gesellschaft für Theologie 10 (Gütersloh: Kaiser/Gütersloher Verlagshaus, 1996) 39–69.

[35] Cf. Georg Braulik, "Das Deuteronomium und die Bücher Ijob, Sprichwörter, Rut. Zur Frage früher Kanonizität des Deuteronomiums," in Erich Zenger, ed., *Die Tora als Kanon für Juden und Christen.* HBS 10 (Freiburg: Herder, 1996) 61–138.

[36] It is true that βίβλος διαθήκης appears there as well. Exodus 24:7 and Deut 33:4 are combined. Yet the focus on "torah" is probably in the foreground. And beyond that, since διαθήκη in Sirach reproduces two Hebrew words, ברית, "covenant," and חק, "law," and since the Hebrew text of 24:23 has not been preserved, we do not even know whether the word ברית originally appeared in this place. The evidence in 45:5 more likely supports חק. Cf. Johannes Marböck, "Die 'Geschichte Israels' als 'Bundesgeschichte' nach dem Sirachbuch," in *Der Neue Bund im Alten: Studien zur Bundestheologie der beiden Testamente,* ed. Erich Zenger, QD 146 (Freiburg: Herder, 1993) 186. For further literature see ibid., n. 40. On Sir 24:23 as a whole cf., in addition, Bar 4:1.

expense of others, such as "history" or "promise." Precisely that would indeed be a canonical decision, to raise a specific theme above all the rest.[37]

In the Hebrew canon the word ברית does not have a role comparable to תורה in framing and in accenting and interpreting the individual parts of Scripture.

To be sure, "covenant" and "torah" belong closely together. One could say: the Hebrew canon intends to be a "torah" issued in the context of "covenant."[38] In this sense one could, then, perhaps designate the Old Testament as a whole *also* as "a testimony about the covenant." This "covenant" would be thought of from the perspective of Mount Sinai. "Covenant" as promise, "covenant" as God's saving activity, God's covenant with Noah (and all of humanity) would remain subordinate ways of speaking about covenant.

This, of course, does not correspond to the way the New Testament takes up the word "covenant." By no means does the New Testament think only about the covenant at Sinai and the law. In Galatians, for example, it uses the word διαθήκη to refer to the covenant with Abraham, which it actually contrasts with "the law."[39] So has the New Testament reconsidered an Old Testament canonical decision, as becomes visible precisely by the opposition of the words תורה and ברית?

The possibility must not be excluded *a priori.* But *a posteriori* it is another matter entirely. The stress on Israel's canon as תורה remains. Yet the connection with the word ברית has the function of giving the word torah a more comprehensive frame of reference on the canonical level. I now offer some observations in support of this thesis.

5. *For "Covenant" as a Dominant Category in the Scriptures of Israel*

It is probably not necessary to offer here evidence for what forms the basis of everything that follows, namely, that at least in the Deuteronomistic History ברית and תורה belong together. Israel receives the תורה precisely in the context of the ברית. The same תורה as in the covenant established at the time of the Exodus will also be in effect in the promised new ברית. We would like to show right away that this in the first instance deuterono-

[37] The objection could be raised here that the concept of torah includes historical narrative in any case. That is true, and yet precisely in the passages that here come into question the giving of the law is pushed to the conceptual center.

[38] As a key text here, in addition to Exod 19:3-8, cf. above all Deut 29:1 [MT 28:69]. There what happens in the narrative "description" to this point and subsequently through the performative speech-acts of Moses, the elders, and the priests is brought to this concept by the narrator of the book in the process of "reporting." On this see Norbert Lohfink, "Die Fabel des Deuteronomiums und der Bundesschluß" (to appear shortly in the *ZAW*).

[39] Cf. Lohfink, *The Covenant Never Revoked,* 28–34.

mistic connection has been fused together in the canonical process with everything else otherwise connected with the word ברית in Israel's Scriptures. Here as in other instances the deuteronomistic perspective has put its special mark on the canon.

All the key texts are present in the Pentateuch. That is especially important, since from the Jewish perspective the Pentateuch does to a certain extent serve as the "canon within the canon." That permits us in what follows to touch on the relevant passages in the rest of the Hebrew canon only in passing and also to omit further treatment of the changes in the order of the books in the LXX.

What are all the things that depend thematically on the word ברית, "covenant"? The word ties together—to say it quite briefly—several other decisive themes in the biblical writings. Through the covenant with Noah and with Abraham, and through the making of other covenants in the course of history, it becomes connected with the *portrayal of the entire history of salvation.* Through the passage about Sinai and through Deuteronomy it becomes connected with the entire *torah.* Through Jeremiah 30–31 and its textual parallels it becomes a catchword for the "messianic" *promises.* As a designation for the decalogue or its first commandment it evokes the core of the *relationship with God.*

The one word ברית thereby belongs, as already said above, to systems of expression that are disparate, indeed that in part are consciously in conflict with one another. Yet with respect to this some things have already been changed in the process that led from individual writings to canonical unity.

In Deuteronomy the core text 26:17-19 shows that the deuteronomic law is understood as an actual "agreement" between God and Israel.[40] In Deut 29:1 [MT 28:69], as a "covenant in the land of Moab," it is declared to be an addition to a first ברית, the decalogue given at Horeb. Chapter 29 then offers texts of the agreement ritual,[41] and chapter 28 contains the broadly developed conditional blessing and curse texts of the agreement.[42]

And yet, in chapters 7 and 8 of the present book another ברית concept is inserted: the unconditional promise of the land, sworn by an oath to the

[40] Cf. Lohfink, "Deut 26:17-19 und die 'Bundesformel,'" *ZkTh* 91 (1969) 517–53; reprinted in Lohfink, *Studien zum Deuteronomium und zur deuteronomistischen Literatur I,* SBAB 8 (Stuttgart: Verlag Katholisches Bibelwerk, 1990) 211–61.

[41] Cf. Lohfink, "Der Bundesschluß im Land Moab: Redaktionsgeschichtliches zu Deut 28:69–32:47," *BZ* 6 (1962) 32–56; reprinted in Lohfink, *Studien zum Deuteronomium I,* 53–82.

[42] Cf. now Hans Ulrich Steymans, "Deuteronomium 28 und die *Adê* zur Thronnachfolgeregelung Asarhaddons: Segen und Fluch im Alten Orient und in Israel" (Dissertation, Vienna, 1994).

ancestors, now obtains this designation (cf. Deut 7:9, 12; 8:18).[43] Chapter 4 expressly focuses on the imposition of the curse in the Exile, looks at the covenant with the ancestors, and promises for the time that is coming that God will once more turn to the people (Deut 4:31).[44] As Deuteronomy is composed chapter 30 relates to chapter 4 as its mirror image.[45] It is true that in Deut 30:1-14, the passage at issue here, the word ברית is lacking, yet the text speaks of God's renewed compassion after the Exile, in that it takes up the prophetic statements about the "new covenant."[46] Thus already in Deuteronomy itself deuteronomic covenant theology has been encased in the priestly and prophetic perspectives.

Something similar happened with the covenant theology of the priestly writings—keyed to unconditional promise—in the blessing and curse text of the holiness code. That is, in Lev 26:3-13 the promises of the covenant with Abraham, given in Genesis 17 without any conditions whatsoever, become the contents of the blessing whose coming or continuance depends on Israel's obedience to the law.[47]

In the same chapter, to be sure, the curse is set in the future. In a guarded parallel to the prophetic promise of the new covenant God announces at Sinai that after Israel's breaking of the covenant (Lev 26:15) and the coming of all the covenant curses (26:25) God will remember the old covenant with the ancestors and the covenant with the Exodus generation

[43] Cf. Norbert Lohfink, *Das Hauptgebot: Eine Untersuchung literarischer Einleitungsfragen zu Deuteronomium 5–11,* AnBib 20 (Rome: Pontifical Biblical Institute, 1963) 88–89, 167–218.

[44] Cf. Norbert Lohfink, *Höre, Israel! Auslegung von Texten aus dem Buch Deuteronomium,* WB 18 (Düsseldorf: Patmos, 1965) 87–120 = Lohfink, *Studien zum Deuteronomium I,* 167–91 (Verkündigung des Hauptgebots in der jüngsten Schicht des Deuteronomiums [Deut 4:1-40]); Georg Braulik, *Die Mittel deuteronomischer Rhetorik erhoben aus Deuteronomium 4:1-40,* AnBib 68 (Rome: Biblical Institute Press, 1978).

[45] Cf. Dietrich Knapp, *Deuteronomium 4: Literarische Analyse und theologische Interpretation,* Göttinger Theologische Arbeiten 35 (Göttingen: Vandenhoeck & Ruprecht, 1987) 154–57, though with attention to the extensive critique in Georg Braulik, "Literarkritik und die Einrahmung von Gemälden: Zur literarkritischen und redaktionsgeschichtlichen Analyse von Deut 4:1–6:3 und 29:1–30:10 durch D. Knapp," *RB* 96 (1989) 266–86.

[46] Cf. Gottfried Vanoni, "Der Geist und die Buchstabe: Überlegungen zum Verhältnis der Testamente und Beobachtungen zu Deut 30:1-10," *BN* 14 (1981) 65–98; Georg Braulik, *Deuteronomium II: 16:18–34:12,* NEB (Würzburg: Echter, 1992) 216–20.

[47] Cf. Norbert Lohfink, "Die Abänderung der Theologie des priesterlichen Geschichtswerks im Segen des Heiligkeitsgesetzes: Zu Lev 26:9, 11-13," *Wort und Geschichte: Festschrift für Karl Elliger zum 70. Geburtstag*, ed. Hartmut Gese and H. P. Rüger, AOAT 18 (Kevelaer: Butzon & Bercker; Neukirchen-Vluyn: Neukirchener Verlag, 1973) 129–36; reprinted in Lohfink, *Studien zum Pentateuch,* SBAB 4 (Stuttgart: Verlag Katholisches Bibelwerk, 1988) 157–68.

(26:42-45).[48] Thus the priestly covenant, despite its "deuteronomization," continues to be a ברית עולם, an "everlasting covenant."

Even a final theme with which the word ברית is associated in Isaiah and the Psalms in a manner that is at times quite sublime and indirect[49] comes to expression in the Pentateuch itself: the hope for the eschatological pilgrimage of the nations to Zion. For Exod 19:3-6, God's first word in the entire Sinai passage, interprets the "covenant,"[50] which singles Israel out from the nations, as a priesthood on behalf of all nations.[51] Thus already here in the Pentateuch even the covenant with Israel established at

48 Cf. note 28 above.

49 For more detail on this issue cf. the next chapter of the book.

50 Let it remain open whether this is only a proleptic reference to the soon-to-be-concluded covenant at Sinai or—already on the level of the redaction of the Pentateuch—a reference to the existing covenant with Abraham (by this time viewed as conditional), which now is to be taken to its high point at Sinai.

51 The more important older literature is given in Brevard Childs, *The Book of Exodus: A Critical Theological Commenary,* OTL (London: SCM, 1974) 340. In addition, cf. Henri Cazelles, "Royaume de prêtres et nation consacrée (Exod 19:6)," in *Humanisme et foi chrétienne: Mélanges scientifiques du centenaire de l'Institut Catholique de Paris,* ed. Charles Kannengiesser and Yves Marchasson (Paris: Beauchesne, 1976) 541–45 = Cazelles, *Autour de l'Exode: Etudes,* SBi (Paris: Gabalda, 1987) 289–94; idem, "Alliance de Sinaï, alliance de l'Horeb et renouvellement de l'alliance," in *Beiträge zur alttestamentlichen Theologie: Festschrift für Walter Zimmerli zum 70. Geburtstag,* ed. Herbert Donner et al. (Göttingen: Vandenhoeck & Ruprecht, 1977) 69–79 = Cazelles, *Autour de l'Exode,* 299–309; Rudolf Mosis, "Exod 19:5b, 6a: Syntaktischer Aufbau und lexikalische Semantik," *BZ* 22 (1978) 1–25; Domingo Muñoz León, "Un reino de sacerdotes y una nación santa (Exod 19:6)," *EstB* 37 (1978) 149–212; André LaCocque, *But as for Me: The Question of Election in the Life of God's People Today* (Atlanta: John Knox, 1979); P. Sandevoir, "Un royaume de prêtres," in *Études sur la première lettre de Pierre: Congrès de l'ACFÉB,* ed. Charles Perrot, LeDiv 102 (Paris: Cerf, 1979) 219–29; J. H. Le Roux, "A Holy Nation Was Elected (The Election Theology of Exodus 19:5-6)," in *The Exilic Period: Aspects of Apocalypticism,* ed. Wouter C. van Wyk, OTWSA 25 (1982) and 26 (1983) (Pretoria: University of Pretoria, 1984) 59–78; R. R. Ellis, "An Examination of the Covenant Promises of Exodus 19:5-6 and Their Theological Significance for Israel" (Dissertation, Fort Worth SW Baptist Theological Seminary, no date); Hans F. Fuhs, "Heiliges Volk Gottes," in *Unterwegs zur Kirche: Alttestamentliche Konzeptionen,* ed. Josef Schreiner, QD 110 (Freiburg: Herder, 1987) 154–60; T. B. Dozeman, *God of the Mountain: A Study of Redaction, Theology and Canon in Exodus 19–24,* SBLMS 37 (Atlanta: Scholars Press, 1989) 106–13; Gianni Barbiero, "*mamleket kohanîm* (Exod 19:6a): I sacerdoti al potere?" *RivB* 37 (1989) 427–46; Erhard Blum, *Studien zur Komposition des Pentateuch,* BZAW 189 (Berlin: de Gruyter, 1990) 51–52; Bernard Renaud, *La théophanie du Sinaï. Exode 19–24: Exégèse et théologie,* CRB 30 (Paris: Gabalda, 1991) 142–55; Christoph Dohmen, "Der Sinaibund als Neuer Bund nach Exod 19–34," in *Der Neue Bund im Alten: Studien zur Bundestheologie der beiden Testamente,* ed. Erich Zenger, QD 146 (Freiburg: Herder, 1993) 70–72; Jean L. Ska, "Exod 19:3-8 et les parénèses deutéronomiques," in *Biblische Theologie und gesellschaftlicher Wandel: Für Norbert Lohfink,* ed. Georg Braulik et al. (Freiburg: Herder, 1993) 307–14.

Sinai acquires a connection with the universal reign of God, that in its fullness is for the endtime. How this is to come about is portrayed by the prophetic books and the Psalms primarily with the image of the pilgrimage of the nations. In one of the most important texts about this pilgrimage it is also interpreted with the category "sacred—profane" (Isa 61:4-9),[52] and here also in proximity to the word ברית.[53]

That leads to the place from which there emerges the specific character of the canonical synthesis of all the varied ברית statements from the older writings, a synthesis carried out in the Pentateuch itself. It is not a matter of a subsequent assertion that the particular self-contained systems of expression in the varied biblical writings in which the covenant is discussed are, after all, really a single system of expression and as such logically no longer contradictory at all, as long as one does not look at them too closely. Nor is it the case that in a manner of speaking there has now come into being a full "canonical" text that is in every respect in harmony within itself.[54] Rather the canon, with its different systems of expression that are to be distinguished from one another all along the line, has been put together to address a specific unified situation. It is meant to address post-exilic Judaism awaiting the coming reign of God.

The people are still living in the diaspora or once more in Jerusalem, which by no means exudes eschatological splendor. They have experienced in their own persons the breach of covenant and the imposition of the curse. They believe in God's faithfulness and in God's promise, but they are still waiting for it to be fulfilled. In this situation they can be addressed by diverse covenant theologies at the same time; the deuteronomic, because it convicts of guilt and offers that torah that will be in force also at the end; the prophetic, stepping out into the universal, because it contains hope; the priestly, because it offers the ultimate ground for hope: God's eternal faithfulness that no human unfaithfulness can destroy.

For Israel everything depends on turning anew to the torah it has been given. To that extent תורה remains the decisive word for the entire canon. Yet this word shines forth only because it has been illumined by the word ברית in all its varied colors.

[52] On the connection with Exod 19:3-6, cf. Hans Fuhs, "Heiliges Volk Gottes," 159–60; Erhard Blum, "Israël à la montagne de Dieu," in *Le Pentateuque en question: Les origines et la composition des cinq premiers livres de la Bible à la lumière des recherches récentes,* ed. Albert de Pury, Le monde de la Bible (Geneva: Labor et fides, 1989) 288–90.

[53] Cf. Isa 61:8. For an understanding of Isa 61:4-7, cf. Norbert Lohfink, art. "יקש," *Theological Dictionary of the Old Testament,* ed. J. Johannes Botterweck and Helmer Ringgren (Grand Rapids: Eerdmans, 1977–) 6:396.

[54] This seems to be the implication in Rolf Rendtorff, "'Covenant' as a Structuring Concept in Genesis and Exodus," *JBL* 108 (1989) 385–93, and in Dohmen, "Sinaibund," 76–81.

It is clear that this constitutes the situation to which the Pentateuch is addressed. For at the end of the five scrolls Israel does not find itself in the promised land but stands instead on its threshold. When this point is reached in the synagogue reading of the Pentateuch it is time to start over at the beginning. Many inner structural elements of the work are also clarified by this assumption about the situation: for example, that already right at the beginning of the wandering in the wilderness there is a passage about obedience to the law and Israel's testing (Exod 15:23-26),[55] or that the Sinai pericope is marked by the sequence "covenant—breach of the covenant—promise and covenant renewal," which is already mirrored in advance with respect to all humanity in the primal history, as Rolf Rendtorff has shown.[56]

In the Hebrew canon this foundational situation, which the entire canon addresses, is also made clear once again at the end. The last sentence of the last book is the word of Cyrus: "All those among you who belong to God's people, may YHWH their God be with them! Let them go up (to Jerusalem)" (2 Chr 36:23). Immediately before that (36:21), through an allusion to Lev 26:34-35, reference was made to the conclusion of the holiness code, where, indeed, all covenant theologies are themselves tied together at the center of the torah with a crucial knot.

6. *The "New Testament" in the Light of the Canonical Covenant Theology of the "Old Testament"*

Now the New Testament is also addressed to a comparable situation. It is, of course, read and heard from a new point of view. No longer is it said, "God's hoped-for full compassion will come, and with it God's new and eternal covenant." Rather it is said, "They have come." And yet the reality remains the same; there is only a new perspective for viewing it.

Thus it is not now necessary for the New Testament to present itself in its entirety as a theology of the "new covenant" and in some fashion to make διαθήκη its univocal central concept. Much rather, in full freedom, according to the interests of its individual writings, it can take up first this and then that form of the Old Testament covenant statements and enter into discussion with them. The only condition is that now the discussion must proceed from the standpoint of its eschatological fulfillment.

55 Cf. Norbert Lohfink, "'I am Yahweh, your Physician' (Exodus 15:26). God, Society and Human Health in a Postexilic Revision of the Pentateuch (Exod. 15:2b-26)," in idem, *Theology of the Pentateuch. Themes of the Priestly Narrative and Deuteronomy,* trans. Linda M. Maloney (Minneapolis: Fortress, 1994) 35–95.

56 Cf. Rendtorff, "'Covenant' as a Structuring Concept."

In Jewish-Christian dialogue the Christian participants dare never forget, of course, that the essential canonical keyword in the Bible of their conversation partners is not ברית, "covenant," but rather תורה, "torah." Since according to Jer 31:31 the ברית remains the same in the new covenant as in the old, we Christians also must not hesitate to make precisely this a theme for ourselves once again.

The fact that the Old Testament can be summed up under the double symbol "covenant—torah," in any case justifies, on the level of the whole Christian canon, granting to the symbol "new covenant" a greater, even decisive importance, also in the section that is ultimately determinative for the canon, namely the New Testament. At least that appears to be the case. In this way a scriptural basis would also become visible for the fact that the designation "Old—New Testament" has prevailed in Christian terminology and in Christian theology.[57]

With all the descriptions presented in this chapter it has naturally only been clarified *that* it is possible to support a biblical theology of the "covenant." Where it could begin and how it could look has been shown at best in very preliminary outlines. The following chapters have to go more fully into the details. And even that will happen only with respect to a single aspect, the right to use the category of "covenant" not only with reference to Israel but also with reference to the "nations." This is the most difficult aspect. At the same time, however, this above all must be dealt with in Jewish-Christian dialogue.

[57] This consideration would be just as valid if the devalued, indeed defamed connotations that easily attach to the word "old" on the basis of today's evolutionary sensibilities should lead to the replacement of the traditional terms "Old Testament—New Testament" by the terms "First Testament—New Testament." There is also evidence for "Old Testament—New Testament" in the New Testament: in Hebrews, where through the context the concept is, to be sure, much more negatively laden than in the pairing "Old Testament—New Testament" in its place of origin in 2 Corinthians.

CHAPTER 3

Covenant and Torah in the Pilgrimage of the Nations (The Book of Isaiah and Psalm 25)[1]

In the Hebrew Bible there is a pattern of statements in which two "covenants" of God are related to one another, a first with all humans and animals, a second with Israel alone. It is found in the "priestly history." The two "covenants" are the "covenant with Noah" (Gen 9:1-17) and the "covenant with Abraham" (Gen 17:1-22). And yet, apart from this double image, "covenant" appears to be a prerogative of Israel's in the Hebrew Bible as well as the LXX. This is true also of the "torah" in the sense of the law given at Sinai. It is not even different with respect to the "new covenant" that is promised in Jer 31:31 for the "days that are coming soon":

> The days are surely coming, says the LORD, when I will make a new covenant with the house of Israel and the house of Judah (Jer 31:31).

Thus even for that onrushing future Jeremiah speaks only of Israel.[2] There is no reference to the nations. This is also the case in the parallel texts

[1] This a chapter is based on a lecture given at the Christian-Jewish theological conference of the Sisters of Zion in January 1991 in Ammerdown, England. The lecture was published as Norbert Lohfink, "Covenant, Torah and Pilgrimage of the Nations to Mount Zion," *SIDIC* 24/2–3, English ed. (1991) 3–15. The sections on the texts about the pilgrimage of the nations have already appeared in German in an abbreviated version as Lohfink, "Der neue Bund und die Völker," *Kirche und Israel* 6 (1991) 115–33. The present version has been substantially enlarged and thoroughly reworked.

[2] To be precise, the passage actually speaks about the two states of the divided kingdom ("house" must have the meaning of "state" here), Israel and Judah. Contrary to the meaningless "addition" in the textual apparatus of the BHS for ואת־בית יהודה, "and the house of Judah," the transmitted text is clear. Its prehistory is not a topic for textual criticism. The

Jer 32:37-41; 50:4-5; Ezek 16:59-63; 37:21-28; 43:23-31, which are also about a future covenant.

Even the principal text about the pilgrimage of the nations, transmitted in two places, Isa 2:2-5 and Mic 4:1-4, makes it sound as though all that will be expected of the nations that in the future (in "days to come")[3] will come to Zion is that they worship there the God of Israel and that they learn on Zion to make peace with one another. The final item could by all means be attributed to the Noah material in the priestly writings. There is no mention of a "covenant."[4]

When Jewish-Christian dialogue has addressed theological issues it frequently revolves around the word "covenant," as explained in the first chapter of this book. At this point we Christians often do not have the foggiest notion how strange the conviction that is so self-evident to us, that we are in the "new covenant," must sound to Jewish ears.

There is already a question of whether the Jeremiah text actually speaks of a "messianic" event or, rather, more likely of something that was soon fulfilled in the history of the people of Israel and that can be fulfilled again and again.[5] But even aside from that, in no biblical text that promises a pilgrimage of the nations to Zion is it clearly stated that the nations on Zion would be taken into Israel's covenant.

If we Christians, despite that, apply to the nations the promise in Jeremiah, then apparently only the writings of the New Testament give us a warrant for that. They apply the new covenant that they believe has come with Jesus to all who follow Jesus, even to those who come from the nations. They interpret the Lord's Supper, which is celebrated by all Chris-

---

double entity Israel-Judah is probably introduced here because an oracle about Israel and an oracle about Judah were at hand for the primary redaction of the text. They were taken by this redaction into the text and from Jer 31:31 on had to be carried further and interpreted. Then in 31:31 the double entity Israel-Judah is transformed into the future entity of a single בית ישׂראל, "house of Israel," that embraces both entities. Cf. Winfried Thiel, *Die deuteronomistische Redaktion von Jeremia 26–45: Mit einer Gesamtbeurteilung der deuteronomistischen Redaktion des Buches Jeremia,* WMANT 52 (Neukirchen-Vluyn: Neukirchener Verlag, 1981) 21–22.

[3] While in Jeremiah 30–31 there is reference to ימים באים, "days" that will "come" (soon), the time reference in Isaiah 2 and Micah 4 reads באחרית הימים "In days to come." That is less imminent but not necessarily eschatological in the usual sense. Cf., finally, Ludger Schwienhorst-Schönberger, "Zion—Ort der Tora: Überlegungen zu Mic 4:1-3," in *Zion—Ort der Begegnung: Festschrift für Laurentius Klein zur Vollendung des 65. Lebensjahres,* ed. Ferdinand Hahn et al., BBB 90 (Bodenheim: Athenäum Hain Hanstein Verlagsgesellschaft, 1993) 115–16.

[4] The word ברית, "covenant," does not occur in the entire book of Micah.

[5] On this cf. Norbert Lohfink, *The Covenant Never Revoked: Biblical Reflections on Christian-Jewish Dialogue,* trans. John J. Scullion (New York: Paulist, 1991) 52–57.

tians and not only Jewish Christians, with the formulation from Jeremiah 31. If one traces the word "new" in the words of institution back to Jesus and views the Lord's Supper from a perspective that from the beginning goes beyond Israel to include the nations, then Jesus himself also understood the word from Jeremiah in this way. If that is not the case, his followers, at least, did that very soon.

Speaking theologically we Gentile Christians could also live with the idea that extension to the nations of the promise of a "new covenant" only became clear with its fulfillment. A theological discussion with the Jews would also be possible in that case. For Israel's Bible speaks both of the pilgrimage of the nations to Zion and of the "new covenant," and promises both with a view to the future. So even starting from Israel's Bible there is no way to avoid the discussion about how the two declarations relate to one another and whether they are somehow related.

But it will actually appear, contrary to everything said to this point, that this discussion has already begun in Israel's Bible itself. The Hebrew Bible is already occupied with the question whether, in the endtime pilgrimage of the nations, all who come to God on Mt. Zion will also observe the torah and become part of God's covenant with Israel. Contrary to first impressions the answer actually appears to be "yes."

To be sure, this is by no means a loud and clear yes. Rather, Israel's Scriptures barely whisper it. But they do say it. Indeed, they already prepare for it secretly in the core of the Jewish canon, the torah, at the beginning of the Sinai pericope in Exod 19:3-8. We have already spoken of that above in chapter 2. They then say it in the Psalms, in an extension of the statements about the pilgrimage of the nations, about which both the prophetic books and the Psalms speak. We must now speak about this. Apparently contemporary biblical scholarship has still not really taken this matter into consideration.[6]

This discussion will be carried out as follows: On the basis of Jeremiah 31 it will be presupposed that torah and covenant belong together, even with respect to the "new covenant." Therefore the texts about the pilgrimage of the nations will be investigated not only with respect to the covenant but also with respect to their statements about the torah. Moreover, in keeping with this book's starting point, the Hebrew Bible must be read synchronically, in the canonical intertextuality of all the books. Nevertheless, the investigation remains consciously on the level of the

[6] For a precise summary of what scholarly exegesis is saying at the moment about the participation of the nations in Israel's salvation according to Israel's Bible, cf. Walter Groß, "YHWH und die Religionen der Nicht-Israeliten," *ThQ* 169 (1989) 34–44. Exodus 19:3-8, for example, is not discussed there.

Scriptures of Israel and so does not draw the New Testament into the intertextuality. The clarification of the issue of a historical stage that precedes the New Testament is precisely what is at stake.

In crucial matters the starting point corresponds with that in Jewish Scripture interpretation, although in its traditional mainstream this operates, in detail, with a different hermeneutic and methodology. This also offers the hope that the observations and reflections that now follow can be helpful for Jewish-Christian dialogue.

After an analysis of the principal passages on the pilgrimage of the nations it first needs to be shown, also in the interest of complete honesty, that—contrary to what is sometimes supposed[7]—in the entire book of Isaiah the "covenant" is related to Israel alone and never, not even for the future, promised to the nations.[8] Next we intend to follow a particular line in the Psalter, leading finally to Ps 25:14. We would not want to exclude that in the Hebrew Bible there are perhaps still other lines that one could follow with the help of the word ברית, "covenant."[9] The so-called covenant formula can offer an additional trail, which we intend to pursue in chapter 4 in an examination of Psalm 33.

I. The Torah in Isaiah 2 and Micah 4

1. God's Torah for the Nations

Just as the decalogue appears twice in the Pentateuch, the text about the pilgrimage of the nations to Zion appears twice in the prophetic canon.

[7] From more recent work, with full attention to the way the problem is being stated here, cf., for example, Aarre Lauha, "'Der Bund des Volkes': Ein Aspekt der deuterojesajanischen Missionstheologie," in *Beiträge zur alttestamentlichen Theologie: Festschrift für Walter Zimmerli zum 70. Geburtstag,* ed. Herbert Donner et al. (Göttingen: Vandenhoeck & Ruprecht, 1977) 257–61. For the preliminary stage of the text in which the word is introduced into the tradition cf. Odil H. Steck, "Der Gottesknecht als 'Bund' und 'Licht': Beobachtungen im Zweiten Jesaja," *ZThK* 90 (1993) 117–34.

[8] The book of Isaiah is important for these questions also especially because both in Qumran and in the New Testament Isaiah is "the author of choice, especially with regard to the sections that are called Second Isaiah. [. . .] Especially in the Gospel of Luke and in Acts the tendency to refer to Isaiah increases, but already long before that the call of the Gentiles was an important area for the influence of Isaiah on the New Testament"—so says Klaus Berger, *Theologiegeschichte des Urchristentums: Theologie des Neuen Testaments* (Tübingen/Basel: Francke, 1994) 24–25.

[9] In this context Isa 56:1-7 is often mentioned, even in the Jewish tradition. However, this passage does not seem to be speaking about the nations but about individuals from the nations. Moreover, the word ברית, "covenant," appears to be used in reference only to the Sabbath command (in the version given in Exod 31:13-17). See below.

That shows its importance. As previously stated, it does not contain the word ברית, "covenant." And yet the word תורה does appear, best translated here as "instruction"—though it is to be noted that in Hebrew the word is the designation for the foundational books of the entire sacred collection. Before this word and leading to it stands the verb ירה, "teach," which has the same root:

> that he may[10] teach us [from the storehouse of] his ways (ירנו מדרכיו),[11]
> and that we may walk in his paths (בארחתיו).
> For out of Zion shall go forth instruction (תורה),
> and the word of the LORD (דבר־יהוה) from Jerusalem (Isa 2:3 = Mic 4:3).

In the Masoretic text this word sketches a consistent picture. God is the one who acts. God's teaching (and therewith God's "torah") consists in or continues by rendering judgment (ושפט) and in God's speaking (והוכיח) that calls forth new ways of acting. An oracle is sought and issued, and the nations act as it directs: they end their wars and make future wars impossible through disarmament and by renouncing instruction in the ways of war.

[10] 1QIsa[a] reads ויורנו, "They (or one) will teach us," Mic 4:2 LXX, δείξουσιν ἡμῖν, corresponds to this. The original consonantal text must have been that of the MT. Yet there apparantly was for both prophetic books a tradition that read the form as a plural. This, by comparison with the singular, is the *lectio difficilior,* since it makes the text more complicated. While this reading would accommodate the interpretation that is developed in what follows, for safety's sake let the Masoretic understanding, more difficult in the context of the present question, be presupposed.

[11] The introduction of the object of ירה Hifil with מן is unique in the entire Hebrew Bible (2 Sam 11:20, 24 has מעל, and the verb is used in a totally different sense). The partitive interpretation is the first to suggest itself, which then in German requires a somewhat awkward formulation. With respect to the construction Franz Delitzsch, *Commentar über das Buch Jesaia,* BC 3.1 (Leipzig: Dörffling & Franke, [4]1889) 71, points to Isa 47:13 (with ידע Hifil) and Ps 94:12 (with למד, Piel). The most recent interpretation in this sense is given in Joseph Jensen, *The Use of the Word tôrā by Isaiah: His Debate with the Wisdom Tradition,* CBQ.MS 3 (Washington, D.C.: Catholic Biblical Association, 1973) 92–93. Hans Walter Wolff, *Dodekapropheton 4: Micha,* BK 14.4 (Neukirchen-Vluyn: Neukirchener Verlag, 1982) translates, "that he teach us on the basis of his ways." For this sense of מן he points to Carl Brockelmann, *Hebrew Syntax* (Neukirchen: Erziehungsverein, 1956) 111. Yet it is hardly evident how one can use this as the basis. If that were possible, one would naturally need to ask what was to be understood concretely by the "ways" of the God of Jacob, "on the basis of which" he teaches the nations. Wilhelm Rudolph, *Micha—Nahum—Habakuk—Zephanja,* KAT 13.3 (Gütersloh: Mohn, 1975) 80, who advocates the partitive interpretation, thinks that what is meant is a piece of the "divine plan of salvation." But the text is about instructions. Thus, in the final analysis, someone adopting Wolff's translation will surely have to say that in the post-exilic period the "ways" could only mean Israel's torah, which God himself interprets. The further explanations we are about to offer would in that case be superfluous. However, because of the difficulties of this translation the issue should be pursued more closely.

2. *Torah for the Nations and the Torah of Moses—Text Analysis*

The "torah" of the pilgrimage of the nations, as the parallelism shows, is the "word of YHWH" that now goes forth. At first glance, up to this point the word "torah" does not need to designate Israel's torah contained in the Pentateuch, particularly as this appears in the prevalent references in the Bible as the torah *of Moses* rather than as the torah *of God*.[12] This can be a reference to an entirely new eschatological "teaching" by the God of Zion that orders the social structure of humanity.[13] But does it have no relation whatever to that torah that Israel was given in its covenant?

At second glance—to which the impetus is perhaps given by the underscoring of the word תורה, "torah," through the verb that precedes it, ירה, *yārāh*, "teach"—there really are connections.

The word about the pilgrimage of the nations begins with the symbolic picturing of mountains and hills. The world landscape changes. Zion becomes the highest of the mountains. Next to Zion there are only hills that do not attain its height. What is the significance of this picture?

It is not meant to describe the enduring nature of the Temple, as do comparable statements in Mesopotamian temple dedication texts.[14] Even if there should be a tradition-historical dependence, the statement does not yet apply in the present, when the Temple is already standing. Only in the future will something change. Thus its abiding nature cannot be in view here.

It is customary to interpret the text from the start on the basis of the oracle that later controls the passage. The reason that Zion will surpass everything else is that it will become the most important, or the only, locus of oracles in the world. In that case one need not take into consideration any kind of reference to the social reality of Israel that lives there. Instead one needs to regard the lower hills—which are self-evidently succeeded in the same verse by the nations—as analogous to the temples and oracle loci of other gods throughout the world. And here as well this can be done without needing to take into account the nations living there at any given

[12] Cf. Norbert Lohfink, "Das Deuteronomium: Jahwegesetz oder Mosegesetz? Die Subjektzuordnung bei Wörtern für 'Gesetz' im Dtn und in der dtr Literatur," *ThPh* 65 (1990) 387–91. Special attention should also be given to the fact that in Josh 1:7-8 and in Mal 4:4 [MT 3:22] the association of the entire prophetic canon with the torah happens through a framing that uses the term "torah of Moses."

[13] Hartmut Gese, starting precisely with this text, speaks in this sense of an endtime "torah of Zion" that is a thoroughly "new torah." See his *Zur biblischen Theologie: Alttestamentliche Vorträge,* BEvTh 78 (Munich: Kaiser, 1977) 75.

[14] Cf. Fritz Stolz, *Strukturen und Figuren im Kult von Jerusalem,* BZAW 118 (Berlin: de Gruyter, 1970) 79 and 110–21.

time. What would be in view, ultimately, is God and the gods. The gods of these oracle loci would have become powerless at the envisaged point of history, for no oracles offering help would go forth there any longer.

The starting point for the word about the pilgrimage of the nations would thus be the impending disappearance of the gods outside Israel. As is known, that is a theme from Isaiah 40 onward. But is that really the point of view that controls the text in Isaiah 2 and Micah 4?

As this text continues it clearly presses forward to questions of human conflict. At least as one reads further, when the picture that perhaps at first is open to a variety of interpretations yields to closer inspection, the surpassing height of Zion must have something to do with the peace that the nations are unable to find among themselves, but which they seek and then obtain from Zion. The issue of the disappearance of the presence of the gods in the temples of the world is implied, but it does not become thematic.

Thus the hills in the picture at the beginning very likely must also have been a reference to the nations: as realities among whom there exists strife or peace, that is to say, as social entities. But if the hills stand for the nations, why would Mt. Zion that towers over all not also stand, correspondingly, for the inhabitants of Jerusalem?

Now if in this context the word torah is so clearly emphasized, that suggests that the torah that is directed to the nations from Jerusalem is connected with that peace-establishing torah possessed by Israel that lives on Zion. By the time they get to Isaiah or Micah, readers of the Bible have also long since known which torah is meant. Moreover, all of this is even more clear if וְיֹרֻנוּ, "they will instruct us" (with a plural subject) is to be read, which probably really was the original reading. In that case the instruction is no longer directly connected to YHWH. The people in Jerusalem, whether individuals who impart the word of YHWH or everyone, are directly in view.

That in future days Zion will stand higher than all other mountains for the reason that in Jerusalem torah reigns becomes even more clear if one looks at the verse with which the prophetic word closes. Isaiah 2:5 calls upon the "house of Jacob" to walk in the light of YHWH. In use here is the metaphor of the Sun-god—who is also the God of righteousness.[15] The house of Jacob must begin to become a just society. This demand is

[15] Bernd Janowski, *Rettungsgewißheit und Epipanie des Heils: Das Motiv der Hilfe Gottes "am Morgen" im Alten Orient und im Alten Testament. Band I: Alter Orient,* WMANT 59 (Neukirchen-Vluyn: Neukirchener Verlag, 1989). Birgit Langer, *Gott als "Licht" in Israel und Mesopotamien,* ÖBS 7 (Klosterneuberg: Österreichisches Katholisches Bibelwerk, 1989). Mark S. Smith, *The Early History of God: Yahweh and Other*

made now, and it is made in view of what is promised for the "days to come" (2:2). The logic is: we must now become a just society so that what God will bring about in days to come can thereby begin. That the mountain with the house of YHWH towers above the other hills is dependent on the fate of the torah in Israel. Only when it begins to give light there can the Zion-torah go forth from Israel into the world of the nations.[16] Thereby, at least in Isaiah, the conclusion of the word makes it clear that the torah of 2:3 also has an inner connection with the torah given Israel by its God.

Micah 4:4 gives the oracle a different conclusion. It puts the picture of peace among the nations explicitly into the context of home and family. Moreover, v. 5, which follows the concluding formula, sounds less ethically and more cultically oriented than Isa 2:5. Its climax appears to be the exhortation to a life of faithfulness and endurance during the time in which what had just been prophesied for the days to come is not yet visible, since the other nations are continuing to worship their old gods.[17] In this respect the verse is not an interpretive key for vv. 1-4 that precede it. But even if it were, the entity "we," meaning Jacob-Israel, would come into view for the interpretation of the picture of high-towering Zion, if only formally with regard to the faithfulness to the God of Jacob. Israel's enduring faithfulness to YHWH would be important in view of the truth of 4:1-4. Even for Micah's

Deities in Ancient Israel (San Francisco: Harper & Row, 1990) 115–24. Othmar Keel and Christoph Uehlinger, *Götter und Gottessymbole: Neue Erkenntnisse zur Religionsgeschichte Kanaans und Israels aufgrund bislang unerschlossener ikonographischer Quellen,* QD 134 (Freiburg: Herder, 1992) 318–20 and 464–65. Glen J. Taylor, *Yahweh and the Sun: Biblical and Archaeological Evidence for Sun Worship in Ancient Israel,* JSOR.SS 111 (Sheffield: JSOT Press, 1993).

[16] The Targum of Jonathan uses the repetition in 2:5 of what is in the Hebrew text of 2:3, לכו, "Up! Go!" as the impetus to interpret the image of the light of YHWH in 2:5 through אלפן אוריתא דיוי, "instruction of the law of YHWH." In doing that it not only refers to the formulations in 2:3 but with אלפן, "instructions," it also produces a contrasting connection to the "learning" of war in 2:4. This appears to be a completely appropriate interpretation. On light as an image of the torah cf. Geza Vermes, "'The Torah Is Light,'" *VT* 8 (1958) 436–38.

[17] כי is to be understood as concessive ("Even if" [so that instead of the NRSV's "For all the peoples walk, each in the name of its god," the text would read "Even if all the peoples/nations. . . . trans.]. Cf. Hans W. Wolff, "Schwerter zu Pflugscharen—Mißbrauch eines Prophetenwortes? Praktische Fragen und exegetische Klärungen zu Joël 4:9-12, Jes 2:2-5 und Mi 4:1-5," *EvTh* 44 (1984) 288, who appeals to Theodorus C. Vriezen, "Einige Notizen zur Übersetzung des Bindewortes *kî,*" in *Von Ugarit nach Qumran* (Festschrist for Otto Eissfeldt), ed. Johannes Hempel and Leonhard Rost, BZAW 77 (Berlin: de Gruyter, 1958) 266–75. Vriezen does not actually treat Mic 4:5.

version of the saying it could not be said that not even "by a word is there an indication of" any kind of "participation by Israel in this event."[18]

3. The Torah for the Nations and the Torah of Moses—Context Analysis

Everything becomes even clearer from the material leading up to the prophetic word, and that is the case in both books.

The book of Isaiah deals with the lost righteousness of the "city" from 1:21 on. From 1:24 on, YHWH intervenes to restore righteousness once more. The downfall of the unfaithful is portrayed once again in 1:28-31, after which the theme of Zion is picked up once again in 2:2. That is the text we are discussing, and it begins with the picture of Zion and its towering height. After a lead-in such as this can one interpret this picture from any point of view other than "righteousness"? But then the torah proceeding from Zion must from the start be connected with that torah from which the inhabitants of the city know how they can live righteously. As was said at the beginning, we are dealing here with a synchronic analysis of the final text of the books that are joined together in the Tanakh.

In Micah (un)social behavior is a theme again and again beginning at 2:1.[19] Prior to our text, in 2:12-13, there was an insertion contrasting what was to come with the present reality, but in that case the future appears to be much closer at hand than in 4:1-4. After 2:12 the climax comes in 3:9-11a, an accusation against Zion because of injustice.[20] In 3:12 the sentence is given: Zion shall be plowed like a field; moreover, Jerusalem shall become a pile of rubble, the "mountain" of the "house" a wooded height. Thus there is no longer a proudly towering temple mount, crowned by a "house." This is the release mechanism for the oracle—associated with it by stark contrast—of the mountain, towering over all other mountains, of the "house of YHWH" that is going to appear "in days to come."[21] The intervening thought in 3:11b, that even when injustice reigns there, YHWH is

[18] This is the view of Walter Groß, "Wer soll YHWH verehren? Der Streit um die Aufgabe und die Identität Israels in der Spannung zwischen Abgrenzung und Öffnung," in *Kirche in der Zeit: Walter Kasper zur Bischofsweihe: Gabe der Katholisch-Theologischen Fakultät Tübingen,* ed. Hermann J. Vogt (Munich: Wewel, 1990) 39.

[19] For what follows see especially the synchronic analysis by Alviero Niccacci, *Un profeta tra oppressori e oppressi: Analisi exegtica del capitulo 2 di Michea nel piano generale del libro,* SFBA 27 (Jerusalem: Franciscan Printing Press, 1989).

[20] In that passage, in 3:11a the verb ירה, "teach," (used negatively) occurs for the first time in Micah.

[21] Cf. Julius Wellhausen, *Die kleinen Propheten, übersetzt und erklärt* (Berlin: Reimer, ^{3}1898) 142: "It is clear that 4:1 follows 3:12 with a sharp contrast: first Jerusalem will be destroyed; in days to come it will be the magnet for all the nations." On the next page he states that 4:1-4 is meant to be "a healing salve applied to the wound opened by 3:12."

still in the midst of Jerusalem is, by the way, the utterance of prophets paid to lie.

Thus by the time the reader reaches Mic 4:1-4 the social conditions in Jerusalem have long since become the theme. The impossibility of YHWH's presence in the midst of Jerusalem while injustice reigns on Zion has been long declared. So when, according to 4:1-4, YHWH is without any doubt in the midst of Zion in days to come, because of which the mountain towers so high over the other mountains = nations, this is unthinkable apart from the reestablishment there of the reign of righteousness. The torah that the nations are seeking must be connected with this righteousness, and thereby also with Israel's torah that is directed to it.

Thus, in conclusion, we can in all probability say that the foundational text about the pilgrimage of the nations to Zion promises the nations a torah as fruit of their pilgrimage, and that this torah is related in some way to Israel's torah.[22] No more than that. Not, for instance, that it is the torah of Moses that would be given to the nations. And, let it be noted, there is not a single word about covenant. But what it does say is already a great deal.

II. Torah, Covenant, and the Nations in the Book of Isaiah

The theme of "Israel's relationship to the nations" plays a greater role in the book of Isaiah than in other biblical books.[23] The problem this theme poses must have been a burning issue again and again during the book's long redactional history, but especially in its last phases.[24] The classic text

[22] A more radical argument in the same direction is offered by Schwienhorst-Schönberger, "Zion," 117–21. In addition to context analyses he also offers primarily reflections on the meaning of the word תורה, "torah," during the period in which the text is said to have been composed. A further argument in favor of the thesis offered here can be developed on the basis of the redactional structure of Mic 4:1–5:14 as this is worked out by Eckart Otto, "Techniken der Rechtssatzredaktion israelitischer Rechtsbücher in der Redaktion des Prophetenbuches Micha," SJOT (1991/2) 140–43. For in that case 4:1-5 and 5:9-14 are related to one another structurally and in that respect are complementary. Nevertheless, 5:9-13 portrays the establishment of the torah in Jerusalem by YHWH.

[23] Cf. Graham I. Davies, "The Destiny of the Nations in the Book of Isaiah," in *The Book of Isaiah: Les oracles et leur relectures, unité et complexité de l'ouvrage,* ed. Jacques Vermeylen, BEThL 81 (Louvain: University Press/Peeters, 1989) 93–120.

[24] On this cf. Groß, "Wer soll YHWH verehren?" The essay only deals with late phases of the book of Isaiah. It focuses on redaction history while in what follows we intend to undertake a synchronic consideration of the final text. On pp. 150–51 Groß offers information on and an evaluation of the status of redaction-historical work on the book of Isaiah. Groß follows the wide-ranging construction of hypotheses by Odil Hannes Steck (and Steck's

about the pilgrimage of the nations to Zion has already brought us to the book of Isaiah. Thus it might well make sense, at least briefly, to see what this book has to say with reference to the relationship the nations have to Israel's torah and Israel's covenant in the promised future.[25] The two words תורה, "torah," and ברית, "covenant," each occur twelve times in the book of Isaiah.[26] Perhaps these numbers are already a sign of the significance of the two words.[27]

1. Torah at the Opening of the Book

A reader who trusts the guidance the book itself provides is confronted right at the start with a twofold torah. Torah is given to Israel (1:10) as well as to the nations (2:3), and in each case it is described in a parallel phrase as "the word of YHWH."[28] Naturally the torah directed to Israel in 1:10 is first of all the word that then follows in 1:11-17. Yet this word does not demand any particular action but evaluates Israel's whole manner of life by asking what Israel's central concern is, the cult or righteousness? The text

---

pupil R. G. Kratz). On this the best source of information now with respect to the point at issue here is probably Steck's "Gottesvolk und Gottesknecht in Jes 40–66," *JBTh* 7 (1992) 51–75. There one will also find many references to the individual investigations on which the work is based. In a somewhat different formulation of the question Walter Groß has integrated the theses of the article cited above into his essay "Israel und die Völker: Die Krise des YHWH-Volk-Konzepts im Jesajabuch," in *Der Neue Bund im Alten: Studien zur Bundestheologie der beiden Testamente,* ed. Erich Zenger, QD 146 (Freiburg: Herder, 1993). In that essay he makes reference to an earlier version of this chapter. I am grateful to him for the thoughtful exchange of ideas we have had on this theme. For material on this theme in the second half of Isaiah see also Lothar Ruppert's recent article, "Das Heil der Völker (Heilsuniversalismus) in Deutero- und 'Trito'-Jesaja," *MThZ* 45 (1994) 137–59.

[25] For all that follows, insofar as it concerns the word תורה, I refer to Irmtraud Fischer, "Die Bedeutung der Tora Israels für die Völker nach dem Jesajabuch," in *Die Tora als Kanon für Juden und Christen,* ed. Erich Zenger, HBS 10 (Freiburg: Herder, 1996) 139–67. Our investigations arose independently of one another, making the broad covergence all the more gratifying. It was not until the AGAT conference in Bonn in 1994 that we became aware of each other's work and exchanged manuscripts just about ready for publication.

[26] תורה: 1:10; 2:3; 5:24; 8:16, 20; 24:5; 30:9; 42:4, 21, 24; 51:4, 7. ברית: 24:5; 28:15, 18; 33:8; 42:6; 49:8; 54:10; 55:3; 56:4, 6; 59:21; 61:8.

[27] To be sure, with reference to our issue, the following ברית references need to be set aside right away: 28:15, 18 (about the covenant people have made with death) and 33:8 (presumably about a political treaty). The divergent use of the word does not prevent counting these passages when indicating the symbolic significance of the number of occurrences of the word in the text.

[28] On the question about the torah statements of the historical prophet Isaiah and the texts ascribed to him as authentic, cf. P. L. Smith, "The Use of the Word תורה in Isaiah, Chapters 1–39," *AJLS* 46 (1929) 1–21, and Jensen, *The Use of tôrā*, 65–121.

that follows characterizes the issue by singling out the words משׁפט, "justice," and צדק, "righteousness,"[29] which are already known from the instructions given in the Pentateuch for the system of administering justice (Leviticus 19 and Deuteronomy 1 and 16). Also here in First Isaiah the administration of justice is the center of attention. There is an intertextual connection. On the other hand, what is at issue is not just the administration of justice but Jerusalem's whole manner of life. To that extent Israel's entire torah, long familiar to the reader of the prophetic canon, is put in a new light and characterized by the word pair צדק ומשׁפט.

In recent interpretation of Isaiah it has been sufficiently elaborated that here at the beginning of the book there is much that calls Deuteronomy to mind, from the appeal to heaven and earth as witnesses in 1:2 (cf. Deut 32:1) to the address in 1:10 itself.[30] This address to the "rulers of Sodom" and the "people of Gomorrah" does, on the one hand, refer to the book of Genesis (18:20; 19:24-25), but also, on the other hand, to the solemn ending of the torah. For in Deut 29:23 [MT 29:22], when the laying waste of the land and the burning of the cities of Israel is threatened—over which Isaiah 1:7-9 laments—the names of the two cities appear as well.[31]

A new torah goes forth from the prophet's mouth, and yet it is only the actualization of *the* torah of Israel. Beside this torah there appears at once the torah that according to Isa 2:3 will go forth from Zion to the nations in days to come.

Thus we find at the beginning of the book a dramatically charged prelude in which all that is to follow is already laid out, even if at first only under the rubric "torah." The word "covenant" has yet to put in an appearance.

2. *Torah Up to Isaiah 39*

Up to the section of the book that begins with chapter 40, with respect to statements pertinent to the topic under discussion, we continue to see only

[29] Isaiah 1:21, 26-27. With respect to the context: the word משׁפט already appears in 1:17, and in 1:17 and 1:23 the theme of care for the rights of orphans and widows (this is the deuteronomic order of the two words, in contrast to that in Isa 10:2!) ties the two passages together. On the word order with respect to orphans and widows cf. Lohfink, "Gibt es eine deuteronomistische Bearbeitung im Bundesbuch?" in *Pentateuchal and Deuteronomistic Studies: Papers Read at the XIIIth IOSOT Congress Leuven 1989,* ed. Christian Brekelmans and Johan Lust, BEThL 94 (Louvain: University Press/Peeters, 1990) 96–100.

[30] The material is developed in greatest detail by Otto Kaiser, *Das Buch des Propheten Jesaia Kapitel 1–12,* ATD 17 (Göttingen: Vandenhoeck & Ruprecht, 5th, completely rev. ed., 1981). My interest here is only in the fact that there are analogies, not in the literary- and redaction-critical explanations that are now usually given for them.

[31] Cf. also Deut 32:32.

the word "torah," not the word "covenant."[32] With one exception "torah" is used only with reference to Israel.[33] In all the passages Israel has a negative relationship with the torah. With disdain they reject it (5:24; 30:9), and the prophet has to rescue the torah in the future through a circle of disciples (of YHWH? 8:16, 20). In Isaiah 8 and 30 the teaching of the prophet himself is in view in the first instance, and yet at least at the level of the final text this teaching might point in a transparent way to Israel's torah.

3. Torah and Covenant in Isaiah 40–55

From chapter 40 on the book devotes itself fully to this future.[34] Among the five occurrences of the word torah in this section, the whole fate of the torah[35] in Israel shines forth in three. These passages address the humbling of Israel in the exile; Israel is the servant who is blind. YHWH had planned to magnify the torah and make it glorious (42:21). And yet YHWH had to hand Israel over to plunderers and robbers, because the Israelites did not walk in God's ways or obey God's law (42:24). Then, in exile, the situation changes. When God tells the people[36] that the nations will receive torah (51:4), God's own people need to be reminded of it at the same time, so that *they* know what righteousness is, because they can call the torah to mind (ידעי צדק עם תורתי בלבם,

[32] In this part of the book תורה occurs a total of seven times. For the references see n. 26 above.

[33] The exception is 24:5, where, in addition to תורה, ברית appears as well. According to this verse the inhabitants of the earth have sinned against ברית, חק, and ברית עולם, "torah, law, and everlasting covenant," so that the curse must go into effect. Here it might refer—at least with respect to the intertextuality of the canon—to the Noachic laws and the covenant with Noah, and thus not to the ברית with Israel. Therefore we can exclude this reference to תורה and ברית from our consideration.

[34] On the texts that now follow cf. Paul E. Dion, "L'universalisme religieux dans les différentes couches rédactionelles d'Isaïe 40–55," *Bib* 51 (1970) 161–82; D. W. Van Winkle, "The Relationship of the Nations to Yahweh and to Israel in Isaiah XL–LV," *VT* 35 (1985) 446–85; and Ruppert, "Das Heil der Völker." The last-mentioned text is interesting insofar as one can see there what is revealed about our question by Steck and Kratz's construction of hypotheses and by pure redaction-historical methodology, and what is not revealed.

[35] On the plurals in 1QIsa[a] 42.4, 24, cf. Dominique Barthélemy, *Critique textuelle de l'Ancien Testament: 2. Isaïe, Jérémie, Lamentations,* OBO 50/2 (Fribourg: Editions Universitaires; Göttingen: Vandenhoeck & Ruprecht, 1986) 302–303.

[36] In 51:4, for text critical reasons, Israel is to remain as the one addressed: Barthélemy, *Critique textuelle: 2,* 374. In all of ch. 51 the nations are never addressed. Cf. Franz Delitzsch, *Commentar über das Buch Jesaia,* BC 3.1 (Leipzig: Dörffling & Franke, [4]1889) 499: "Address of the Gentiles (Syriac text) is counter to the consistent character of this entire discourse."

"you who know righteousness, you people who have my teaching in your hearts")[37] and God can announce to them the end of their misery (51:7-8).

In none of these three passages is attention specifically directed at the prophetic proclamation. It is simply a matter of YHWH's torah, which had been given to the entire people. In the last of the three statements, for the first time in the book of Isaiah, Israel relates positively to the law that had been given to them—if one leaves aside the implication of the material that lies behind Isa 2:3. Moreover the talk of Israel's torah is connected here with talk of a torah that "will go out" (51:4, תצא, as in 2:3) to the nations.

Already prior to this the first so-called servant song spoke of a torah for which the nations wait. According to this song, God's servant Israel[38] has received the task of "bringing forth justice" (42:1, 3, יוציא משפט) to the nations, of "establishing" (42:4, ישים) it for them. Thus the verb יצא from Isa 2:3 reap-

[37] I interpret "heart" here, in parallel with "know," as the seat of memory. The reader of the prophets, when coming later upon Jer 31:33 and then looking back on this passage, will perhaps notice talk about the "new covenant" already here. For what this passage is about is the moment in which God forgives and turns once again toward God's people in exile. That is precisely the time, according to Jeremiah 31, when God writes the torah on their hearts.

[38] Regardless of whether one accepts (in whichever of its forms) or rejects Bernhard Duhm's hypothesis about the servant songs, the great majority of interpreters are in agreement that in Isaiah 40–55 the *definitive* textual reading of עבד יהוה, "servant of YHWH," is to be understood as a reference to Israel. This is also correct and can here be presupposed. Beyond that, I myself doubt that servant song hypotheses have been conclusively proven for earlier stages of the present text. Cf. Norbert Lohfink, "'Israel' in Jes 49:3," in *Wort, Lied und Gottespruch, II: Beiträge zu Psalmen und Propheten. Festschrift für Joseph Ziegler,* ed. Josef Schreiner, fzb 2 (Würzburg: Echter, 1972) 217–29. More recently Tryggve N. D. Mettinger argues along similar lines, though he supplies a clearer counter-thesis to the servant song hypotheses: "Die Ebed-Jahwe-Lieder, ein fragwürdiges Axiom," *ASThI* 11 (1977/78) 68–76; idem., *A Farewell to the Servant Songs: A Critical Examination of an Exegetical Axiom,* Scripta Minora Regiae Societatis Humaniorum Litterarum Lundensis 1982/83, 3 (Lund: Gleerup, 1983). The counter-argument by Hans-Jürgen Hermisson, "Voreiliger Abschied von den Gottesknechtsliedern," *ThR* 49 (1984) 209–22, who wants to establish the servant songs once again, does not convince me on the decisive point. Ruppert, "Heil der Völker," 146, n. 29, appeals to the "criticism of *Norbert Lohfink's* counter-position . . . by *Kratz*"—Reinhard G. Kratz, *Kyros im Deuterojesaja-Buch: Redaktionsgeschichtliche Untersuchungen zu Entstehung und Theologie von Jes 40–55,* FAT 1 (Tübingen: Mohr, 1991) 136, n. 519. This "criticism," in fact, consists merely in the observation that in order not to have to regard "Israel" in 49:3 as a gloss Lohfink declares "v. 5 to be secondary in an offhand manner." That is a painfully false summary of a many-sided argument, in which, with respect to various hypothetical levels of viewing the problem, the arguments for and against various positions are weighed in detail. Among other things contained in the argument it is also stated that, if one assumes a tension between 49:3 and 49:5, other observations speak more for 49:5 as extraneous than for "Israel" in 49:3. On this issue cf. also Manfried Weippert, "Die 'Konfessionen' Deuterojesajas," *Schöpfung und Befreiung: Für Claus Westermann zum 80. Geburtstag,* ed. Rainer Albertz (Stuttgart: Calwer, 1989) 104–15.

pears here as well. In a certain sense the word תורה comes onto the stage at the end of a towrope hauled along by משפט, the word that dominates everything. One is reminded of Isaiah 1. What is clear up to this point is that we are dealing with the heart of the matter and not necessarily all the concrete details of Israel's torah. The combination of keywords will recur in 51:4.[39] In 2:3 the torah goes forth from Zion when the nations make their pilgrimage there. Here, on the other hand, the nations wait for the torah of the servant of God (42:4) and for the arm of YHWH, which creates justice on their behalf (51:7). They are not (yet) going to Zion, for it lies desolate and mourning. Nevertheless, the reader perceives the reference to Isa 2:1-5. Thus the theme of the torah going forth to the nations, touched on only briefly at the beginning of the book of Isaiah, in Isaiah 42 and 51 is taken up with the same keywords and with the parallel word משפט, "justice."

In both passages another expression is attached, "light to the nations." The word "light," if in the context it already relates to Israel and the nations, also naturally reminds one of Isaiah 2, of 2:5, that is, where we have established a reference to torah. Is "light" a substitute for torah here as well? Isa 51:4 hints at a somewhat more complicated connection:

> for a teaching will go out from me,
> and my justice for a light to the peoples.[40]

Besides in 42:6 and 51:4, the expression "light to the nations" also occurs in 49:6.[41] It is not connected directly with talk about the torah for the nations until 51:4. In 42:6 and 49:6 (cf. 49:8) it is associated by way of contrast and elaboration with the expression ברית עם, "covenant to the people"—through which the word "covenant" makes its appearance in the context.

[39] In this case, however, the word order has תורה first, and the root יצא, which is coupled with משפט in 42:1, 3, links up with תורה. A direct juxtaposition of משפט and תורה in parallel statements happens in the entire Hebrew Bible only in Isa 42:4 and 51:4, according to Felix García López, "תורה," *ThWAT* VIII (1995) [in press], the galleys of which I have seen thanks to Heinz-Josef Fabry. This justifies interpreting with precision even fine points of word usage in these passages.

[40] For the meaning of the difficult רגע, cf. the שׂים in 42:4.

[41] In 42:6 and 49:6 אור גוים occurs, while 51:4 has אור עמים instead. This change in the clearly important expression is striking, and yet we probably do not need to assume any difference in meaning. That גוים are spoken of in 42:6 is connected, first of all, with the strict coordination to the expression ברית עם. Beside עם the word גוי must naturally occur as the parallel. This association of the terms may also be at work in 49:6, although in this case ברית עם doesn't occur until 49:8. Maybe it is only the absence of this parallel expression in 51:4 that is now the reason for the use of עמים, in itself possibly the more obvious word. Perhaps in addition there needed to be a contrasting analogy to Israel, addressed just prior to this as עמי.

Naturally in what follows no exhaustive analysis can be made of all these interdependent statements. There just needs to be an indication of the way the individual concepts relate to one another within the scope of the problem we are examining.

In 42:1-9 the talk about justice going forth to the nations and about the torah for which they wait is brought to an end after v. 4. In vv. 6-7 the statement about the "covenant to the people" and about the "light to the nations" is expanded by means of a string of infinitives that enlarge on the light metaphor:

> to open the eyes that are blind,
> to bring out the prisoners from the dungeon,
> from the prison those who sit in darkness.

The broader context shows that God's action on behalf of exiled Israel is described here.[42] For all its brevity the statement about the light thus makes quite subtle distinctions. When Israel, sitting in the darkness of the nations, is brought out into the light, the nations will be enlightened precisely by this event. At the same time a "covenant to the people" comes into existence. Since Exodus typology is in the air (cf. 42:7, לְהוֹצִיא, "to bring out, to lead out"), one must probably think about something like a new covenant for Israel, which is connected with the exodus out of Babylon in the sense of a synthetic parallelism. Of course, the parallel "light to the nations" and "covenant to the people" could also be interpreted in the sense of a synonymous parallelism in the direction of a "covenant with humanity," that is, with all nations (cf. 42:5, לָעָם עָלֶיהָ, "the people upon it" = "on the earth"). The conflict over these two interpretations has gone this way and that for a long time.[43] The conflict cannot in my opinion be resolved on the basis of this terse passage, but from the next occurrence of the two terms in 49:6 and

[42] On the subject of infinitive statements of this kind in these chapters cf. Lohfink, "Jes 49:3," 222–24.

[43] In addition to the commentaries cf. Johann J. Stamm, "Berît ʿam bei Deuterojesaja," *Probleme biblischer Theologie: Gerhard von Rad zum 70. Geburtstag,* ed. H. W. Wolff (Munich: Kaiser, 1971) (earlier literature on 517–20); Lauha, "Bund des Volkes"; Delbert R. Hillers, "Berît ʿām: 'Emancipation of the People,'" *JBL* 97 (1978); Mark S. Smith, *Bᵉrit ʿam/bᵉrit ôlām: A New Proposal for the Crux of Isa 42:6, JBL* 100 (1981); Steck, "Bund und Licht." Stamm has noticed a more recent tendency to decide more and more for the nations and not for Israel. That probably relates to the fact that the discussion is carried on more and more not in terms of the meaning of the present text but of inferred earlier stages. Even Stamm thinks that in 49:8bα we have an insertion inspired by 42:6, and that for that reason this second text "can be appealed to only with reservations" when interpreting 42:6 (511). Then he still goes ahead and appeals to it. Even the most recent treatment—Ruppert, "Heil der Völker," 143—discusses an earlier stage of the text (in which, in dependence on Kratz and Steck, Cyrus is understood to mean Darius) and decides for the nations.

8 it probably can. Here in 42:6 the reader at first experiences the two statements "covenant to the people" and "light to the nations" as erratic blocks of material and keeps them in mind as images awaiting interpretation.

In 49:1-9, the second so-called servant song,[44] God's servant Israel[45] introduces himself to the nations. The structure of this longer passage is important for understanding it. God's servant speaks of having been called and formed by God in his mother's womb (1-2) . Then he reports on a kind of dialogue that he had with his God. It begins with the call. God spoke (3). Then the servant complained about the futility of his efforts (4). This is answered by a confirmation, indeed an expansion, of his assignment by God (5-9).

This last word from God within the address to the servant has within itself once again a clear structure. After a solemn prelude to the address (v. 5 and the first word of v. 6, ויאמר) it begins in v. 6 (all but ויאמר) with an introduction that sketches out everything in advance. To the assignment already given to God's servant, to lead Israel home from Babylon (6a, cf. 5), it attaches an additional element: the servant is appointed as the "light to the nations" (6b). After this introduction the two elements that have been announced are developed in two words from God, each formally introduced with a messenger formula. The messenger formulas stand at the beginning of vv. 7 and 8. The two words from God are arranged chiastically with the preview appearing in v. 6.[46] So in the first passage, in v. 7, the theme "light to the nations" is developed. God's servant functions as "light to the nations" when the kings and princes see how God deals with Israel. Then they prostrate themselves in adoration, thus becoming worshipers of YHWH. In the second passage, in 8-9, there is an elaboration of the theme announced first, the Exodus of Israel from Babylon (9, צאו, "Come out!") and the new land distribution (8). In the middle of this development the expression "covenant to the people" returns, namely as a defining of the same verbs as in 42:6. Thus what we have is clearly a continuation of the statement there. God will "keep and give" the servant "as a covenant to the people" (8, ואצרך ואתנך לברית עם).[47]

[44] Usually, following Bernhard Duhm, *Das Buch Jesaja,* HK 3.1 (Göttingen: Vandenhoeck & Ruprecht, [1892] ^{5}1968) 367, the song is limited to 4:1-6, which is then generally assumed to have been inserted secondarily between chapter 48 and 49:7-9. But in view of the construction of Deutero-Isaiah as a whole out of building blocks that are joined together in conscious contrast to one another, this argument is very weak. In our context, in any case, the present text is under discussion, and there 49:6 is, *mirabile dictu,* now a chiastic preview of 49:7-9.

[45] The servant is expressly introduced as "Israel" in 49:3. Cf. above, n. 38.

[46] Ruppert, "Heil der Völker," 146, fails to recognize the overall structure when he thinks that 42:6b is "cited incompletely in 49:8b" and suspects in this a reinterpretive "intention."

[47] In the context of "covenant" it is more natural to derive ואצרך from נצר than from יצר. On the vocalization of the *yiqtol* forms, cf. Barthélemy, *Critique textuelle 2*, 303–305.

The structure we have analyzed makes it clear: this is about Israel. The repetition of the Exodus and of the conquest of the land points to the covenant with Israel traditionally associated with these themes. Israel is preserved by God and at the same time (newly) established. That is a statement that can be fully compared with Jer 31:31-34 but is also distinguishable from it. In any case Israel's covenant is associated here with the turning of the nations to the God of Israel. And yet in the process it continues to be the covenant *with Israel.*

This becomes even clearer in Isaiah 54 and the beginning of Isaiah 55, where the statement about the covenant for Israel occurs for the third time in the book of Isaiah[48] and is developed most broadly. Presumably the themes about marriage, widows, rejection, and subsequent reconciliation with which ch. 54 begins belong to it as well. Or, more precisely: it brings up the talk about the covenant. The keyword "compassion" (רחמים) in v. 7 effects the transition to the explicit covenant theme. Taken up verbally in the following sentence, it is developed by the characterization "with everlasting love" (בחסד עולם). The word חסד, "steadfast love," especially in connection with עולם, "eternity," opens up the verbal field of covenant.

That is shown at once in v. 9 by the comparison made there to the covenant with Noah, which was actually designated in Genesis as ברית עולם, an "eternal covenant" (Gen 9:16, cf. 9:12). By analogy to the oath which God then swore to all living creatures (אשר נשבעתי, "Just as I swore"), God now swears (כן נשבעתי, "so I have sworn")[49] never again to be provoked to anger against Israel, God's spouse who has been brought back home. The oath also belongs to the semantic field of covenant. Thus it is not surprising that in the following verse, still in the context of the conceptual material connected with the covenant with Noah (the shaking and quaking of the cosmos), in parallelism with the previously used word חסד, the decisive keyword "covenant" (ברית) itself now also finally appears:

[48] An interesting observation that is derived more from the prehistory of the book of Isaiah: if one divides Deutero-Isaiah—excluding the prologue (40:1-11) and epilogue (55:8-13)—into nine principal sections on the basis of the hymns with which each ends (42:10-13; 44:23; 45:8; 48:20-21; 49:13; 51:3; 52:9-10; 54:1-3), then the word ברית appears in the first and last section as well as in the central section. On the structure assumed here, cf. Mettinger, *Farewell,* 18–28. If Isaiah 40–55 is meant to occupy the central position in the composition of the book of Isaiah as a whole—as, for example, Rolf Rendtorff assumes, *Das Alte Testament: Eine Einführung* (Neukirchen-Vluyn: Neukirchener Verlag, 1983) 210–12—this circumstance is still important also for the level of the text we are examining.

[49] While the first נשבעתי makes a statement about the past, the second statement is to be understood in a performative sense. At work here is the old faithfulness springing the bounds of time, but it happens in a completely new setting.

my steadfast love (חסדי) shall not depart from you,
and my covenant of peace (ברית שלומי) shall not be removed.

The passage, which employs Noah terminology, is framed and defined through the root רחם, "to have compassion" (54:7, 8, 10). When readers of the Bible later come to Jeremiah they will meet the word again in Jer 31:20, in an emphatic form and in a very similar context, and it will impart its tone to the word "forgive" (סלח) in Jer 31:34, which ends the prophecy about the new covenant.

It is curious that in Isaiah 54 the prophetic word about the pilgrimage of the nations from Isaiah 2 is brought constantly to mind through the use of keywords, although here Israel is under discussion and the theme "covenant" does not occur in the oracle from Isaiah 2. The "nations" are mentioned already in 54:3. In 54:5 it is emphasized that the "Holy One of Israel" is called "the God of the whole earth." Jeremiah 54:10 speaks of the shaking and quaking of the "mountains" and "hills," terms used in the image that opens the oracle in Isaiah 2. Jeremiah 54:11-12 describes the precious treasures that will adorn Zion when it is built anew. In 54:13 the keyword "peace" is taken from 54:10, and this theme, together with the theme of "weapons" (54:17), defines the rest of the chapter, which corresponds to the theme of Isa 2:2-5.

"Covenant" is no longer under discussion here (or in the opening verses of ch. 55), and the perspectives of the text are different from those in Isaiah 2. Nevertheless it is striking how close this text appears to stand to the statements of Isaiah 2. One has the impression that the "covenant of peace" can be thought through only if it is connected with the statements from Isaiah 2.

The theme "covenant" is explicitly present once again in 55:3. Since חסד, עולם and ברית, the three decisive keywords from 54:8, 10 recur, there is no doubt that the issue is taken up again and developed further. However, in place of the name Noah we have the name David. Moreover, after the previous statement of comparison, a prediction about the future is made here. The words are also combined in a new way. No longer do we hear about ברית שלומי, "covenant of peace," and about חסד עולם, "everlasting love," but about ברית עולם, "everlasting covenant," and חסדי דוד, "steadfast . . . love for David."[50]

Apparently there is now going to be a development of the implications for Israel of YHWH's oath that YHWH's faithfulness to Israel will no

[50] On the question of whether דוד is a subjective or objective genitive, cf. the discussion in Norbert Lohfink, *Das Jüdische am Christentum: Die verlorene Dimension* (Freiburg: Herder, 1987) 251, n. 82.

longer be in question when it is viewed with relation to the nations of the world. Verse 5 transfers to Israel the covenant with David in such a way that Israel steps into David's place. Into the place of the non-Israelite nations incorporated into David's kingdom step all the nations of the earth.[51]

On the basis of this covenant Israel exercises three functions with respect to the nations of the world. First, Israel is עד, "witness"—to be heard in the background here are the calls to Israel in Isa 43:10, 12 and 44:8 to witness, in confrontations with the nations, to YHWH's dealings with Israel. Second, Israel is נגיד, *nāgîd*—probably here the royal title found in the David stories is taken up. Perhaps the intention is to avoid the word מלך, "king." Thus God puts Israel into the position of ruler with respect to the nations. Third, Israel is called מצוה לאמים, "commander for the peoples"—the participle מצוה is found almost exclusively in Deuteronomy, where it occurs in profusion.[52] There it constantly brings to mind anew the proclamation of the torah through Moses by means of the "promulgation statement." The baton would be passed from David to Moses, David having served only to emphasize the covenant's relationship to the nations. Now, however, what would be at issue is the function of Israel over against the nations that results from this covenant. Is this the way Israel is to be "witness," by interpreting the "davidic" position of ruler over the nations that it has attained to mean that it, Israel, Moses-like, proclaims the torah to them?

In that case v. 5 that follows would only show the beginning of the activity that is in view. Israel would call to the nations from afar, and they would come on the run. Thus Israel would be setting in motion the pilgrimage of the nations in Isa 2:2-4. The nations would come because YHWH has adorned Zion "with jewels." And then would begin—this is not developed further but can be imagined—Israel's role as Moses for the nations. At long last the torah would go forth from Zion, even though the word torah does not occur here.[53]

In their final form the chapters of Deutero-Isaiah cannot be read in any other possible way than this: behind the many voices that sound through we have here a story according to which, toward the end, by virtue

[51] It should be noticed that already in Isa 11:10 the future shoot from the root of Jesse undertakes a comparable function for all the nations of the world. He also stands in the position of David.

[52] It is unnecessary to ask about occurrences of צוה, "to command," with the plural "nations" as its object, since the only other occurrence in Lam 1:10 cannot be considered a parallel in light of its subject matter. On the Deuteronomic "promulgation phrase" cf. Lohfink, *Das Hauptgebot: Eine Untersuchung literarischer Einleitungsfragen zu Dtn 5–11,* AnBib 20 (Rome: Pontificium Institutum Biblicum, 1963) 59–63.

[53] The words in 54:13, וכל־בניך למדי יהוה, "All your children shall be taught by the LORD," might already be an allusion to the torah; cf. 8:16, and, as a keyword bridge, 50:4.

of the renewal of the covenant with Israel, the pilgrimage of the nations is set in motion, in which Israel's torah displays its effect beyond Israel. What then follows in the context of so-called Third Isaiah is a continuation, but also perhaps in part merely a more in-depth look at the details of the story.

4. Light and Covenant from Isaiah 56 on

The word torah does not occur again in the entire book, which is a notable finding about the book of Isaiah because the theme of the pilgrimage of the nations to Zion is going to sound throughout right up to the final chapter, and as it stood at the beginning of the book, so it also stands at the very end. But the talk about the torah is not carried there along with it. Is the insight growing that the Israel that has returned home is making a mess of the law and that righteousness has to come into the world in a way different from a "model Israel"?

The talk about the torah had, to be sure, become connected with the talk about the light to the nations. The latter puts its heavy stamp once again on ch. 60, which also speaks about the pilgrimage of the nations.[54] Here as well the word ברית, "covenant," also occurs once more to provide a frame. But then the themes "light" and "covenant" also disappear.[55] Toward the end of the book, after the last judgment over Israel as well as over the nations, there finally appears to be an eschatological unity between Israel and the nations through which these terms become superfluous. In 66:23 it simply speaks about "all flesh" (כל־בשׂר) that keeps coming to Zion to worship. Perhaps this is—even if surely only hinted at—really more than merely an "announcement of a" still-unsolved "problem."[56] For כל־בשׂר is a leading term in the primal biblical history (Genesis 6–9).

But now for more on individual details! Through several keywords Isa 56:1-8 is connected with the beginning of ch. 55.[57] For an instant one has the impression that in this text the concept of the covenant, to this point only applied to Israel, now indeed does move beyond the borders of Israel. It deals with groups of people that as far as the law is concerned cannot belong to Israel. They are "foreigners" (בני־הנכר) and "eunuchs"

[54] The connection with the statement given in 55:5 about the pilgrimage of the nations that results from the covenant with David that is transferred to Israel is shown by the appropriation, as a leitmotiv of Isaiah 60, of the root used in the solemn conclusion in Isa 55:5—פאר, "adorn, glorify": cf. 60:7 (twice), 9, 13, 19, 21.

[55] משפט also fades away with 61:8.

[56] Thus Groß, "Israel und die Völker," 165.

[57] For details cf. Davies, "Destiny," 118.

(סריסים)[58] who want to be attached to Israel and observe the law, especially the sabbath.[59] They are given assurance that they belong to the people of YHWH. The behavior of these people, where it is described (56:4, 6), after various statements with reference to the different groups, is uniformly characterized at the end of each section with the participial statement ומחזיקים בבריתי, "holding fast my covenant."[60]

Of course in both cases the subject is a more extensive devotion to the will of YHWH, but everything centers on the sabbath, even in the introductory text in 56:2. The reader oriented to the canon will scarcely be able to proceed without hearing an allusion to Exod 31:13-17.[61] That speaks against the assumption of many commentators that with ברית a reference to circumcision in Genesis 17 is intended.

In any case what is discussed here is an integration of individuals into the people of Israel, not the transfer of the covenant to the nations. The covenant remains with Israel. That is true even though with "my house" (56:5), "my holy mountain," "my house of prayer," "my house," "a house of prayer," and "for all peoples" (56:7) several keywords remind one of Isa 2:2-4, and right at the beginning in 56:1 Israel is called to attend to משפט and צדקה.

Two light passages in 58:8, 10 and 59:9 form a bridge to the great light chapter, Isaiah 60. According to the first passage Israel's light will break forth when they begin to act justly; according to the second Israel

58 For "eunuchs" cf. Deut 23:2; the word for "foreigner" is not the usual word גר.

59 Cf. Herbert Donner, "Jesaja lvi 1–7: Ein Abrogationsfall innerhalb des Kanons—Implikationen und Konsequenzen," *Congress Volume Salamanca 1983,* ed. John A. Emerton, VT.S 36 (Leiden: Brill, 1985).

60 In view of 56:2, where חזק in the Hifil follows עשׂה, "do, act," the interpretive nuance "hold fast" is probably to be preferred over the other possible meaning, "take hold of." חזק in the Hifil + ב + ברית occurs only in this passage, however. We do not know whether it was a common way of speaking. If not, then the reader of the book of Isaiah could perhaps be reminded of 4:1, where seven women "take hold of one man" (והחזיקו באישׁ אחד). These women, thrown out of the community because of a skin disease (cf. 3:17), demand of the man nothing other than regaining a "name" through marriage with him. But the motif of "name" is also central to 56:1-8: cf. 5, יד ושׁם, "a monument as name = a memorial" and שׁם עולם, "an everlasting name" (circumcised); 6, לאהבה את־שׁם יהוה, "love the name of YHWH" (foreigners). If this consideration of the matter is valid, then the translation "take hold of" is preferable.

61 The other occurrences of שׁמר + שׁבת are: Exod 31:13-16; Lev 19:3, 30; 26:2; Deut 5:12. Yet only in Exod 31:13-17 do the following terms shared with Isa 56:2, 4, 6 occur: עשׂה, חלל, and ברית. Perhaps one could still consider the deuteronomic sabbath command as a whole, in which in corresponding framing statements there appear, in Deut 5:12, שׁמר + יום השׁבת and, in Deut 5:14, עשׂה + יום השׁבת. In deuteronomic terminology the decalogue can be designated as הברית. But חלל is absent, and Exod 31:13-17 sounds on the whole more closely related.

confesses that they are devoid of light because they are acting unjustly.[62] For this reason it is YHWH who acts, and according to the final statements in chapter 59 he comes to Zion as redeemer. With the people of Jacob YHWH makes a new covenant, which consists in the gift of the Spirit and the gift of words put in the mouth, gifts that shall never depart, even in the coming generations (59:20-21):

> And he will come to Zion as Redeemer,
> to those in Jacob who turn from transgression, says the LORD.
> And as for me, this is my covenant with them, says the LORD: my spirit that is upon you, and my words that I have put in your mouth, shall not depart out of your mouth, or out of the mouths of your children, or out of the mouths of your children's children, says the LORD, from now on and forever.

One is tempted to think of the torah here (cf. Deut 30:14). But the word does not occur. And even if it did occur, it would not be one lived out by Israel but, counter to Israel's own behavior, a torah given in the Spirit and only as such able to be handed on.

In Rom 11:26-27 Paul will cite the text of Isa 59:20-21 at the climax of an argument that is decisive for him.[63] The detailed formulations in v. 21 can, of course, only be understood as explications of what had earlier been designated as an "everlasting covenant." Several elements in the verse will come to the reader's mind again when she or he reads about the future new or everlasting covenant in the corresponding passages in Jeremiah or Ezekiel. Here as well it is emphatically a covenant with Israel. Its (repeated) evocation now unleashes the light chapter, Isaiah 60, and thereby the most grandiose description of the pilgrimage of the nations to Zion in the entire book of Isaiah.

This chapter is framed by two passages that are defined by the light metaphor, and the root אור, "shine," occurs seven times in all.[64] Zion's light is the divine light. Nevertheless it can in a real sense be called Zion's light. It makes it possible for the nations and their riches to stream in. On the basis of the bridge texts we have just discussed this light concerns Israel's righteousness. But that actually was not present, and the light was given to Israel despite that. The gift of light itself has the effect that all in Israel are righteous (60:21).

[62] The word משפט also appears again in both passages: 58:2 (// צדקה); 59:8, 9, 11, 14, 15 (here as well frequently in parallels to צדקה: 59:9, 14, 16).

[63] On this cf. Lohfink, *The Covenant Never Revoked*, 58–74.

[64] If one considers the ten strophes, 1-3; 4-5; 6-7; 8-11; (12); 13-14; 15-16; 17-18; 19-20; 21-22, then the two light passages, 1-3 and 19-20, actually form the first and ninth strophes, and in this respect the designation of "frame" is not fully accurate.

This is developed further in chapter 61, and then the keyword "everlasting covenant" (ברית עולם) also appears here, for the last time, corresponding to Isa 59:21 as a kind of frame. Here as well ברית, "covenant," is still clearly connected with Israel. The context actually underscores the difference between Israel and the nations, who have joined with Israel by virtue of the pilgrimage. On the one hand it amounts to a kind of overlapping. For just as the nations have streamed to Israel, so Israel will be able to acquire for themselves a "second possession" in their territories (61:6b-7).[65] On the other hand, however, a clear distinction emerges. Israel will become priests, and the other nations the secular working community (61:5, 6a). This will of course immediately call to the Bible-reader's mind the introductory passage of the Sinai pericope, where precisely this had been announced as the effect of the covenant discussed there (Exod 19:5-6).

In this way a question now arises once more for the reader of the book of Isaiah at its very conclusion. For Isa 66:21, one of the last verses of the entire book, can at least be read to say that God will also join people from the nations to the priests and Levites of Israel.[66] Should it thus be the case that that distinction which the consistent reservation of the word "covenant" for Israel had sought to maintain no longer was available at the end of the story? The reader will perhaps call to mind that, already in the oracle about the nations in Isa 19:25, Egypt had been designated for the future as YHWH's people and Assyria as the work of YHWH's hands. Does the word ברית, "covenant," disappear because it was a word that made a distinction and now, at the end of the story, a distinction dare not be made any longer between the redeemed of Israel and the redeemed from the nations? In that case this disappearance of the word "covenant" would say a great deal. We would have a significant, literarily attested place available into which another version of the same interpretation could be inscribed: namely, that the "covenant" at the end of the story was no longer reserved for Israel

[65] On the difficult task of deciphering the statement in Isa 61:6-7 cf. Norbert Lohfink, "ירשׁ *yāraš*," *TDOT* 6:368–96.

[66] The text from Isa 66:18 onward, which doubtless had a troubled prehistory, is very difficult. I connect מהם, "of them," in 66:21 with the "nations" at the end of 66:19—who also could already be the subject of the statement in 66:20, rather than connecting it with כל־אחיכם, "all your brethren," in 66:20, which, according to the usual interpretation, is a reference to diaspora Jews who are now returning home. Yet this is by no means certain. It could also now be that from among the distant nations people of these nations will be brought to Jerusalem as an offering by the "survivors" of the judgment of the nations. They would come as "brethren," a designation they could have without for that reason being Jews. Then also from them people could be joined to the priests and Levites. Still worth reading as a careful and balanced analysis of the text we are now considering is Delitzsch, *Jesaja,* 633–37. In his analysis, in any case, it becomes clear that connecting מהם with the diaspora Jews who have been brought back still creates the most difficulties.

alone. This is precisely what the redactional intention of Psalm 25 appears to be. To this psalm we turn in what follows.

III. Nations, Torah, and Covenant in Psalm 25

If one sets aside the possible elimination of any statement about the covenant at the end of the book of Isaiah, then the covenant, whenever it comes up in connection with the pilgrimage of the nations to Zion, is reserved for Israel, while torah also goes to the nations. In Psalm 25 almost the opposite appears to be the case. While it avoids the word "torah" for the nations despite all emphasis on the subject, it promises the nations a share in the "covenant."

Yet before that can be developed exegetically we must demonstrate why Psalm 25 can be read at all in the context of the theme "pilgrimage of the nations." The psalm does not in any way express that openly. We are dealing rather with a nuance of meaning the psalm acquires only through the sequence of the psalms in which it finds itself in the Psalter. For some years the redactional level has once again been in view more strongly in research on the psalms.[67] On this level there is an interesting connection between Psalm 25 and Psalm 24, which precedes it.

[67] Among the initial studies in German we mention Christian Barth, "Concatenatio im ersten Buch des Psalters 4, 9," in *Wort und Wirklichkeit: Studien zur Afrikanistik und Orientalistik I: Eugen Ludwig Rapp zum 70. Geburtstag,* ed. Brigitta Benzing et al. (Meisenheim am Glan: Verlag Anton Hain, 1976); in English, Gerald Wilson, "Shaping the Psalter: A Consideration of Editorial Linkage in the Book of Psalms," in *The Shape and Shaping of the Psalter,* ed. J. Clinton McCann, JSOT.SS 159 (Sheffield: JSOT Press, 1993). Information about more recent research can be found in David M. Howard, "Editorial Activity in the Psalter: A State-of-the-Field Survey," in *The Shape and Shaping*, ed. McCann; Jean-Marie Auwers, "Le psautier hébraïque et ses éditeurs: Recherches sur une forme canonique du livre des Psaumes" (Dissertation Louvain, 1994) 40–46. The first commentary to follow these issues systematically is Franz-Lothar Hossfeld and Erich Zenger, *Die Psalmen I: Psalm 1–50,* NEB 29 (Würzburg: Echter, 1993); cf. ibid., 23–24 on the principle at issue. A series of essays in Klaus Seybold and Erich Zenger, eds., *Neue Wege der Psalmenforschung: Für Walter Beyerlin,* HBS 1 (Freiburg: Herder, 1994) takes up the question; among them, negatively, Erhard S. Gerstenberger, "Der Psalter als Buch und als Sammlung," 3–13. From the publications of Norbert Lohfink, cf. *Lobgësange der Armen: Studien zum Magnifikat, den Hodajot von Qumran und einigen Späten Psalmen,* SBS 143 (Stuttgart: Katholisches Bibelwerk, 1990) 101–25; "Einige Beobachtungen zu Psalm 26," in *Ein Gott, eine Offenbarung: Beiträge zur biblischen Exegese, Theologie und Spiritualität: Festschrift für Notker Füglister OSB zum 60. Geburtstag,* ed. Friedrich V. Reiterer (Würzburg: Echter, 1991) 189–204; "Der neue Bund und die Völker"; "Psalmengebet und Pssalterredaktion," *ALW* 34 (1992); "Die Lieder in der Kindheitsgeschichte bei Lukas," in *Nach den Anfängen fragen. Gerhard Dautzenberg zum 60. Geburtstag,* ed. Cornelius Mayer, Karlheinz Müller, and Gerhard Schmalenberg, Gießener Schriften zur Theologie

1. The Linking of Psalms 24–26

Psalm 24:3 takes up anew the well-known question, already familiar from Ps 15:1 to one who prays the psalms, about the conditions for entry into the holy place on Zion:[68]

> Who shall ascend the hill of the LORD?
> And who shall stand in his holy place?

As in Psalm 15 the conditions are enumerated by way of reply. Of course the list is shorter here than there. In 15:2-5a there are ten conditions.[69] In 24:4

---

und Religionspädagogik 8 (Gießen: Selbstverlag des Fachbereichs Evangelische Theologie und Katholische Theologie, 1994); "Psalmen im Neuen Testament: Die Lieder in der Kindheitsgeschichte bei Lukas," in *Neue Wege der Psalmenforschung,* 105–25.

[68] Therefore it is customary to assume for these two psalms a category of "Entrance Liturgy." The essential literature about this is found in Erhard S. Gerstenberger, *Psalms: Part I with an Introduction to Cultic Poetry,* FOTL 14 (Grand Rapids: Eerdmans, 1988) 89 and 119. Missing from there are Reinhard Grieshammer, "Zum 'Sitz im Leben' des negativen Schuldbekenntnisses," in *XVIII. Deutscher Orientalistentag vom 1. Bis 5. Oktober 1972 in Lübeck: Vorträge,* ed. Wolfgang Voigt, ZDMG.Suppl 2 (Wiesbaden: Steiner, 1974), an essay that would force the consensus about the category "Entrance Liturgy" to be rethought a bit, and Nicholas Tromp, "Jacob in Psalm 24: Apposition, Aphaereses or Apostrophe?" in *Von Kanaan bis Kerala: Festschrift für Prof. Mag. Dr. Dr. J.P.M. van der Ploeg O.P. zur Vollendung des siebzigsten Lebensjahres am 4. Juli 1979: Überreicht von Kollegen, Freunden und Schülern,* ed. W. C. Delsman et al., AOAT 211 (Kevelaer: Butzon & Bercker; Neukirchen-Vluyn: Neukirchener Verlag, 1982) 271–82, an essay on the basis of which one can seriously question whether the psalm was a formulation for actual liturgical use, since it allows non-Israelites to enter the Temple. The two psalms may go back to available knowledge about entrance rites or ordination rites, but they are hardly texts from a liturgical agenda. It seems to me quite presumptuous to derive a history of the development of the ethos in Jerusalem from an alleged chronological order of the two psalms (according to which Psalm 24 would be earlier because of its brevity, Psalm 15 more recent). This is what is done by Eckart Otto, "Kultus und Ethos in Jerusalemer Theologie: Ein Beitrag zur theologischen Begründung der Ethik im Alten Testament," *ZAW* 98 (1986). While he parallels the development of the law in the book of the covenant and the difference between the two psalms, he forces "the Psalms into a Procrustean bed," according to Franz-Lothar Hossfeld, "Nachlese zu neueren Studien der Einzugsliturgie von Ps 15," *Die alttestamentliche Botschaft als Wegweisung: Festschriftt für Heinz Reinelt,* ed. Josef Zmijewski (Stuttgart: Katholisches Bibelwerk, 1990) 143. For the shorter form of the entrance conditions in Psalm 24 explanations other than greater age are also conceivable. Given that in this book we confine ourselves to looking at the material synchronically, however, all these questions can remain open.

[69] The number is not completely certain, especially because of v. 4. And yet the most likely arrangement consists of three positive, three negative, then again two positive and two negative statements. Cf. Peter Craigie, *Psalms 1–50,* WBC 19 (Waco, Tex.: Word Books, 1983) 150. As an example of another arrangement, with a total of twelve elements, cf. Otto, "Kultus und Ethos," 167–68.

there are only four statements, all of them in a single verse. If one takes the two statements put together in the first colon as a single condition developed in a twofold way, there are actually only three conditions named.

The second of these reads:

> אשר[70] לא־נשא לשוא נפשו
> who do not lift up their throat[71] to what is false.

This condition corresponds to the opening of Psalm 25:[72]

> אליך יהוה נפשי אשא
> To you, O LORD, I lift up my throat.[73]

In the first place this makes it clear that we are not to understand "what is false" in 24:4 as a reference to false statements or the like[74] but to false and vain gods.[75] Above all, however, by opening this way Psalm 25 declares itself

[70] This is probably the reading to be chosen, in agreement with the *Kethib* of the majority of manuscripts from the Middle Ages.

[71] In this phrase, for נפש, originally "neck, throat," I consider the translation "voice" appropriate rather than the usual translation "soul." On נשא in the phrase, cf. קול נשא, "to lift up the voice." In view of the full translation of Psalm 25 that follows below and in which the more important Hebrew words are to be given translations that agree with those here, I also write "throat" here as well.

[72] The difference in prepositions (ל and אל) can be disregarded. Perhaps one can assume the haplography of an aleph in Ps 24:4, along with Michael L. Barré, "Mesopotamian Light on the idiom *nāśā' nepeš*," *CBQ* 52 (1990) 46, n. 2.

[73] Drawing on Akkadian parallels, Barré, *"nāśā' nepeš,"* 53, argues for the translation "To you . . . I flee for protection" in Ps 25:1. Apparently Barré has discovered the (only) context in which the expression was used when it was connected with a deity. That is very important exegetically. Yet the *meaning* does not necessarily follow from this restricted *usage*. The expression still probably means, "To you . . . I lift up my voice." For Ps 24:4 Barré assumes a different translation, since שוא here does not designate a person. But that is precisely the question we are about to take up.

[74] Cf., for example, the German *Einheitsübersetzung:* "der nicht betrügt" ("who does not deceive"). Nor should the following colon be translated "(der) keinen Meineid schwört" *(Einheitsübersetzung)*—"(who) does not swear falsely." It would be better to translate: "who makes a vow to no figment of the imagination (= no non-existent god)." On נשבע ל in the sense of "to swear falsely (to a god)," cf. Ps 132:2. The phrase can even simply mean "to worship a particular god"—cf. Isa 19:18; 45:23; Zeph 1:5; 2 Chr 15:14. It is true that the LXX already had swearing falsely in mind in 24:4 [LXX 23:4]. But it has harmonized with Ps 15:4 [LXX 14:4], for which it had presupposed a different vocalization, as is shown by the expansion τῷ πλησίον αὐτοῦ.

[75] On this interpretation cf. also Sigurdur Ö. Steingrimsson, *Tor der Gerechtigkeit: Eine literaturwissenschaftliche Untersuchung der sogenannten Einzugsliturgien im AT: Ps 15; 24,3-5 und Jes 33,14-16,* ATSAT 22 (St. Ottilien: EOS, 1984) 86 and 93. In the last century this interpretation was advocated, for example, by Heinrich Graetz, *Kritischer Commentar zu den Psalmen nebst Text und Uebersetzung,* 2 vols. (Breslau: Schottlaender, 1882–1883) 41, n. 1. The scholarly commentaries of that period also constantly polemicized against this understanding: thus they were aware of it, although they named no one who advocated it.

to be a prayer for those people who according to Psalm 24 gain entrance to the holy place on Zion. The psalms were edited to enable the reader to see from Psalm 25 how these people prayed or could have prayed.

For the sake of giving a full picture let it be said that this is true also of the psalm that follows. As is so often the case, announcement and description are arranged chiastically. Psalm 25 was announced through the second entrance condition from Ps 24:4. The first condition named there,

> נקי כפים ובר־לבב
> those who have clean hands and pure hearts,

on the other hand, is taken up in the second of the psalms that follow, Psalm 26. Already in its opening section the request appears:

> צרופה כליותי ולבי
> test my heart and mind (26:2).

What the picture envisions is that God put to the test the suppliant's deepest feelings. The turning point of the psalm then begins with the statement:

> ארחץ בנקיון כפי
> I wash my hands in innocence (26:6).

Thus the suppliant in Psalm 26 is sure of having fulfilled the conditions of Ps 24:4.

A series of other observations shows that Psalms 25 and 26 are closely connected.[76] Thus it might follow that as the psalms were edited these two psalms were intended to make clear to the person reciting them in meditative prayer[77] what the people admitted to the holy place on Zion, in accord with Ps 24:3-6, were saying there in their prayers. The one meditating can inwardly associate with them in their praying.

[76] For details see Lohfink, "Psalm 26," 201–202.

[77] On this purpose of the Psalter as a literary genre (not on the purpose of individual Psalms in their prehistory), cf. Georg Fischer and Norbert Lohfink, "'Diese Worte sollst du summen': Dtn 6, 7 *w^{e}dibbartā bām*—ein verlorener Schlüssel zur meditativen Kultur in Israel," *ThPh* 62 (1987) 59–72; Notker Füglister, "Die Verwendung und das Verständnis der Psalmen und des Psalters um die Zeitenwende," in *Beiträge zur Psalmenforschung: Psalm 2 und 22,* fzb 60 (Würzburg: Echter, 1988); Lohfink, "Psalmengebet und Psalmenredaktion"; Hossfeld and Zenger, *Psalmen I,* 25. That in meditative recitation the individual psalms were not normally picked out like fruit from a basket but that one recited the whole text in a connected way can be inferred not only from later Jewish practice and early Christian monastic practice (later unfortunately abandoned), but also from the textual connection the psalms display. To pay attention to this connection and to the development it supplies to the meaning is anything but making out of the psalms "applesauce" or "mixed fruit preserves"—that is the rhetorically polemical image and counter-thesis of Gerstenberger, "Buch und Sammlung," 12.

But now we must ask with greater precision who these people are. So back to Psalm 24!

2. *Psalm 24 Is about the Pilgrimage of the Nations to Zion*

The people discussed in Psalm 24, after an enumeration of the conditions for entrance (v. 4) and a promise of blessing and vindication (v. 5), are in 24:6 directly addressed once more:

> זה דור [78]דרשיו מבקשי פניך יעקב
> Such is the company of those who seek him (= YHWH),
> who seek your face, O Jacob.

The verbs are known to the reader for their use in parallel contexts.[79] They parallel one another here as well. And yet their objects are not parallel. The second shatters the reader's expectation—evoked by the first—of a designation for God. Unless one shuns the reading in favor of that in the LXX,[80] which (or the text on which it was based) offers the *lectio facilior* and apparently has not preserved what this verse says, then those whose entrance into the holy place is discussed here can only be non-Israelites, people from the "nations." Since they wish to see "Jacob's face" they cannot themselves belong to Jacob (= Israel).[81] There are also in Psalm 24 clear verbal reminiscences of the pilgrimage-of-the-nations texts in Isaiah

[78] This is the *Qere*.

[79] Cf. Deut 4:29; Judg 6:29; Isa 65:1; Jer 29:13; Ezek 34:6; Zeph 1:6; Pss 38:12 [MT 13]; 105:4; Job 10:6; Prov 11:27; 1 Chr 16:11.

[80] The LXX [23:6] has τὸ πρόσωπον τοῦ θεοῦ Ιακωβ, "the face of the God of Jacob." Frank M. Cross, "The Divine Warrior in Israel's Early Cult," in *Biblical Motifs,* Studies and Texts 3 (Cambridge, Mass.: Harvard University Press, 1966) 20, makes conjectures that really are quite dubious about an original text of 24:6, but his conjecture that the Hebrew text read by the LXX had פני אביר יעקב, "the presence of the bull of Jacob" (cf. Ps 132:2—ibid., n. 23), is noteworthy. But that has still not clarified which text is older. Most commentaries and translations make their text-critical decisions more or less on the basis of the LXX. An improbable ad hoc syntactical solution is turning the passage into three phrases, which (by rearrangement) may be assumed to lie behind the NJPSV ("such is the circle of those who turn to him, / Jacob, who seek your presence"—after each of the two commas here an ellipsis of זה דור, "such is the circle of [those]," would be postulated). A radical solution adopted in a highly-regarded work on the concepts for "seek" can be omitted from the discusion: Claus Westermann, "Die Begriffe für Fragen und Suchen im Alten Testament," *KuD* 6 (1960) 2–30; reprinted in idem, *Gesammelte Studien II,* 25, translates, "That is the generation that holds to him, that seeks your face, Yahweh."

[81] For the analysis of the MT, cf. Tromp, "Jacob in Psalm 24." He, however, considers the LXX reading to be the original.

2 and Micah 4.[82] It is certain, then, that the Masoretic wording of Psalm 24 is about the eschatological pilgrimage of the nations to Zion.[83]

That is probably why it also begins with an acknowledgment of YHWH, the Lord of the entire world and all its inhabitants (1-2). That is perhaps the reason the only things indicated as entrance requirements are purity of heart and hand and then worship of the one true God, without, as in Psalm 15, going over to things that relate specifically to Israel, the prohibition against lending money at interest, for example.[84]

3. The Pilgrimage of the Nations Between Psalm 22 and Psalm 24

That Psalm 24 deals with the pilgrimage of the nations to Zion becomes even more plausible if one considers that the theme no doubt begins earlier. To treat this briefly:[85] After the theme of the nations was struck right at the beginning of the Psalter (Psalm 2), it remains in the background at first. Only in Pss 7:7-9; 9:5-13; and 18:43-45 [MT 44-46][86] are there reminders of it, without its becoming the principal theme. That changes in

[82] Reference can be made to a dissertation on Psalm 24 and the pilgrimage of the nations texts that is being written by Jerzy Seremak (Hochschule Sankt Georgen, Frankfurt am Main). Thus we can omit providing the evidence here. Yet in addition we still wish to call attention to Isa 11:10. There the verb דרשׁ, "seek, turn to," is used for the procession of the nations to the future messianic king and his glorious מנחה, "rest, peace"—a unique word constellation (an observation by Erich Zenger). One can hardly avoid seeing a triangular connection between Isaiah 2, Isaiah 11, and Psalm 24.

[83] Only in passing we indicate the consequences of this for the interpretation of Ps 24:7-10. Psalm 24:6 serves as the transition to the passage, or it is actually already its beginning—cf. זה in 24:6, 8, 10. The ones who would be coming were the nations. They were coming in order to turn to YHWH on Zion. Yet it turned out that YHWH is coming to Zion with them. This complete reversal of the matter is not so unimaginable as it at first appears. Also with respect to Isa 62:11, a resumption of Isa 40:10, one can ask who is coming to Zion here along with YHWH: the Jews returning home from exile, as in Isa 40:10, or the nations, whose coming is the theme of Isaiah 60–62. In that case the identification of the God seeking entrance with the nations in two stages would perhaps actually be the reflection of a learning process on the part of the nations: they are led by YHWH, the war hero, to the genuine king of glory. On the interpretation of Psalm 24 as a reference to the pilgrimage of the nations, with special attention to the book of Isaiah, cf. James D. Smart, "The Eschatological Interpretation of Psalm 24," *JBL* 52 (1933).

[84] This would be an alternative reason for the terse wording of the conditions in Psalm 24 that does not touch on certain aspects—which Otto had made the basis of his argument in "Kultus und Ethos" (cf. n. 68 above).

[85] For a more detailed treatment see Lohfink, "Psalmengebet und Psalterredaktion," 15–20.

[86] Notice here the synchronic, intertextually significant accord with Isa 55:3-5.

Psalm 22 in a way that is highly surprising, given the psalm-genre to which it belongs.

The vow to praise God that begins with v. 22 [MT 23] of this individual lament,[87] a vow at first totally oriented to the congregation, from v. 27 [MT 28] on extends to the universal sphere and becomes a vision of the end-time conversion of the nations to YHWH.[88] To it belongs the prostration of all nations in worship before YHWH (v. 27 [MT 28]); it remains uncertain whether that will happen in their own places (cf. Zeph 2:11, one of the related texts) or on Zion (in accord with the majority of comparable texts).

One of the ways psalms are linked together is that at the end of a psalm the following psalm or even a number of them are announced, by a promise to offer praise, for example.[89] So now at the end of Psalm 22 it is also announced that future generations will be "told" (ספר) and have it "proclaimed" (נגד Hifil) to them. Thus the person praying the Psalter must at least reckon with the fact that Psalm 23, which begins with the acknowledgment (by a convert?)[90] of YHWH as shepherd, thus as king, makes

[87] At least at the level of the final text, to be sure, it might be understood as a prayer of the king; cf. Patrick D. Miller, "Kingship, Torah Obedience, and Prayer: The Theology of Psalms 15–24," in *Neue Wege der Psalmenforschung,* 136–39. That also expedites the transition to the perspective about the nations at the end of the psalm.

[88] This is probably the response to the summons in Ps 9:11-12 [MT 9:12-13].

[89] Someone who has prayed the psalms up to this point has already been able to observe this at least once—by the example of Psalm 7, along with its following psalms, 8 and 9/10. Cf. Lohfink, "Psalmengebet und Psalterredaktion," 9-10.

[90] The usual translation, "The Lord is my shepherd," leads to an understanding in which the statement about the shepherd is what is new and important about the sentence. And yet both placing the name for God first in the noun clause as well as the continuation of the thought (which presupposes that there are shepherds whose sheep go hungry and others who find good pastures for theirs—YHWH as shepherd obviously guaranteeing the second option) compel us to see here an acknowledgment of YHWH in contrast to other gods who could offer themselves as shepherds. As an acknowledgment by an individual person in Israel—in contrast to Mesopotamia and Egypt—that is unique in the Hebrew Bible; cf. Hermann Spieckermann, *Heilsgegenwart: Eine Theologie der Psalmen,* FRLANT 148 (Göttingen: Vandenhoeck & Ruprecht, 1989) 266–67. The problem of the location of the predicate in this nominal clause has been reflexively formulated, apparently for the first time, by Ludwig Köhler, "Psalm 23," *ZAW* 68 (1956) 228–29. On the basis of consideration about the context he decided for shepherd as predicate and, on account of the consequent inversion of the words, made the entire clause into a temporal or causal dependent clause. The counterview that takes YHWH as predicate is stated by the following: Albertus H. van Zyl, "Psalm 23," in *Studies on the Psalms: Papers Read at the 6th Meeting of Die Ou Testamenties Wergemeeskap in Suid-Afrika Held at the Potchefstroom University for C. H. E., 29–31 January, 1963* (Potchefstroom: O.T.W.S.A., 1963) 64–83; Hans-Joachim Kraus, *Psalmen,* 2 vols., BK 15/1 and 15/2 (5th ed. Neukirchen-Vluyn: Neukirchener Verlag, 1978) 1:337 (who, along with E. Pfeiffer, "Eine Inversion in Psalm xxiii 1ba?," *VT* 8 (1958) 219–20 has defended this counterview against Köhler, Kraus indeed making the

good on this announcement. Accordingly are those who speak here the nations who are being coverted? The reader's expectant question at first goes unanswered.

In any case Psalm 23 is about the pilgrimage to Jerusalem, to the "house of the LORD" (v. 6).[91] If an individual person is not the one praying, but the nations, then their worship of YHWH, the king of the world, announced in Ps 22:27-29 [MT 28-30], is actualized as a conclusion of a pilgrimage to Zion. That this is the understanding imposed on the text redactionally will become more clear as soon as the suppliant has reached Psalm 24. For it is also no longer puzzling that in 24:7-10 YHWH himself demands entry to Zion, although YHWH has for a long time already been there: in Psalm 23, as the shepherd of those newly won, YHWH has come with them to Zion.

The texts are interwoven. One can assume that in the two psalms that follow, 25 and 26, at the level of the definitive text of the Psalter we are dealing with prayers of people from the nations. This is how they will speak when they come to the holy place on Zion in the "days to come." Yet if that is true, many statements in the psalm that interests us here, Psalm 25, that otherwise almost sound like platitudes out of a collection of later psalm motifs, take on new colors. One must try to learn to read the psalm in a somewhat new way.[92]

---

assertion that his own view is the "up to now standard" one); Gianfranco Ravasi, *Il libro dei Salmi: Commento e attualizzazione,* 3 vols. (Bologna: Edizioni Dehoniane, 1986) 1:439 ("una proclamazione kerygmatica e polemica al tempo stesso: il Signore, e nessun altro, è il mio pastore"); Gerstenberger, *Psalms I,* 114 ("may be").

[91] For this almost universally accepted understanding, which is suggested by the intertextual context, it is thought to be necessary to amend the MT (by appeal to the LXX, Targum and Syriac version) of 23:6 from וְשַׁבְתִּי, at least to וְשִׁבְתִּי. Yet apparently not even this is necessary, as legitimate as it might be. It appears that the root ישׁב, "take a seat, sit, abide, dwell," could occasionally slip into forms of the root שׁוב, "to convert." Jewish exegesis in the Middle Ages still knew this, the early versions presumably as well. In modern lexicographical style one would have to indicate this by inserting into the lexicon a root "II. שׁוב" with the meaning of ישׁב. A discussion and documentation is expected in vol. 4—in preparation—of Barthélemy, *Critique textuelle.* A textual correction is, then, superflous.

[92] Norbert Lohfink, "Lexeme und Lexemgruppen in Ps 25: Ein Beitrag zur Technik der Gattungsbestimmung und der Feststellung literarischer Abhängigkeiten," in *Text, Methode und Grammatik: Wolfgang Richter zum 65. Geburtstag,* ed. Walter Groß, Hubert Irsigler, and Theodor Seidl (St. Ottilien: EOS, 1991) 271–95, can be consulted on estimated time, genre determination, and questions of dependence. Some of what follows, above all with respect to structure, is different from what was said in the first appearance of this essay. This is in part the result of the need for brevity there. But in part I have also changed my mind. In my new considerations I was stimulated especially by observations in a seminar paper by Susanne Degen (Hochschule Sankt Georgen, Frankfurt, winter semester 1993/94).

4. A Linguistically-oriented Presentation of Psalm 25

We begin by setting out a working translation of the psalm, which also indicates its structure. Notes and considerations of the structure and genre of the psalm follow.

First Prayer-domain, I

1 בא To you, O LORD, I lift up my throat,
2 O my God,[a] in you I trust;[b] do not let me be put to shame;
do not let my enemies exult over me.
3 ג Do not let those who wait for you be put to shame;
let them be ashamed who are wantonly treacherous.

First Prayer-domain, II

4 ד Make me to know your ways, O LORD;
teach me your paths.
5 ה Lead me in your truth, and teach me,
for you are the God of my salvation;
for you I[c] wait all day long.
6 ו Be mindful of your mercy, O LORD,
and of your steadfast love,[d] for they have been from of old.
7 ח Do not remember the sins of my youth or my transgressions;
according to your steadfast love remember me,
for your goodness' sake, O LORD!

Reflection-domain, I

8 ט Good and upright is the LORD;
therefore he instructs sinners in the way.
9 י He leads the humble in what is right,[e]
and teaches the humble his way.
10 כ All the paths of the LORD are steadfast love
and faithfulness,[f] for those who keep his covenant and his decrees.
11 ל For your name's sake, O LORD,
you will pardon my guilt,[g] for it is great.

Reflection-domain, II

12 מ Who are they that fear the LORD?
He will teach them the way that they should choose.

13 נ They will abide in prosperity,
and their children shall possess the land.
14 ס The [assembly] of the LORD is open to those who fear him,
and his covenant to those he grants knowledge (of his ways).[h]
15 ע My eyes are ever toward the LORD,
for he will pluck my feet out of the net.

Second Prayer-domain, I

16 פ Turn to me and be gracious to me,
for I am lonely and afflicted.
17 צ Relieve the troubles of my heart,
and[i] bring me out of my distress.
18 ר Consider[j] my affliction and my trouble,
and forgive all my sins.

Second Prayer-domain, II

19 ר Consider how many are my foes,
and with what violent hatred they hate me.
20 ש O guard my life, and deliver me;
do not let me be put to shame, for I take refuge in you.
21 ת May integrity and uprightness preserve me,
for I wait for you.
22 פ Redeem Israel, O God,
out of all its troubles.

Notes

[a] It is commonly assumed that there was a word omission (קויתי after אליך) and a haplography (the omission of אל in an original אל־אלהי). Thereby one obtains for the first verse a parallelism, to which the אלהי still belongs, and at the beginning of a second parallelism a ב occurs, as the acrostic requires.[93] But that is pure conjecture. The verbal connection to Ps 24:4 is brought out more clearly in the transmitted text. To achieve this effect it could have been totally intentional to forgo the parallel line as well as to have the repeated em-

[93] So most recently Craigie, *Psalms 1–50,* 216; even David N. Freedman, who has now become very conservative in text-critical matters, reckons with a textual corruption here and in v. 18: "Patterns in Psalms 25 and 34," in *Priests, Prophets and Scribes: Essays on the Formation and Heritage of Second Temple Judaism in Honour of Joseph Blenkinsopp,* ed. Eugene Ulrich et al., JSOT.SS 149 (Sheffield: JSOT Press, 1992) 125–26.

phasis on the resulting one-line verse through the assonance אלהי—אליך יהוה, which suppresses the expected ב in the second word after the beginning with א. Perhaps we have before us an even more artful wordplay with seven א-word beginnings into which, at a strategic point, two beginnings with ב are embedded. There emerges the following scheme of initial sounds (enlarged through several observations about inner sounds):

1:	'L..	J...	N...	'...
2aα:	'L..	B...	B...	
2aβ:	'L	'B..		
2b:	'L	J...	'.B.	L...

Through the varied position of the address to God (second position in 1, opening position in 2aα) there emerges a varied, and yet structurally clear parallelism between אשא . . . אליך, "to you I lift up" (a twofold beginning with א), and בך בטחתי, "in you I trust" (a twofold beginning with ב). The also prominent ל-sound points to the central verse of the psalm, as is still to be demonstrated. Speaking in musical terms, we have here a variation on the basic acrostic theme. In the correspondingly structured Psalm 34, probably used as a model, there already were those kinds of baroque acrostic variations.[94]

[b] Performative statement.
[c] Performative statement.

[d] וחסדיך is probably a word in parallelism with רחמיך, and the divine name separates the conceptual pair—therefore a displacement of the center of the verse in comparison with the MT. Cf. the similar situation in v. 10. For longer second cola in this psalm cf. 25:15 and 20.

[e] Or, "through a (saving) verdict," or, "to (their) rights."

[f] In contrast to the Masoretic verse division ואמת has been transferred to the second colon; otherwise the parallelism would lose its linguistic effect.

[g] Normally this is read as a plea, which is not impossible. Thus Franz Delitzsch writes: "The consecutive perfect attaches to the יהי, which, according to the sense, is contained within למען שמך just as it also elsewhere follows on deliberately pre-positioned adverbial sentence units that look to the future."[95] But it is not at all certain that the motivation introduced by למען implies a wish or a plea. Indeed the context offers no signal for that. That speaks in favor of the motivation providing a sufficient grounding.

[94] Cf. Anthony R. Ceresko, "The ABCs of Wisdom in Ps xxxiv," *VT* 35 (1985) 99–104.
[95] Delitzsch, *Biblischer Kommentar über die Psalmen*, 4th ed., BC 4.1 (Leipzig: Dörffling & Franke, 1894) 232.

Then the appended main clause would contain a statement of hope or confidence. This is also favored by the fact that the real plea for forgiveness occurs later in the psalm (v. 18b). This is clearly expressed by means of an imperative. This would have been just as possible in v. 11 if the verse had already been meant as the plea.

[h] ל + a relative clause connected by asyndeton; abbreviated allusion to v. 4 (formulation) and v. 8 (last corresponding statement of the case). The usual view that it is an infinitive construction does not make much sense and destroys the parallelism (see below for further discussion).

[i] Conjecture: הַרְחִיב וּמִמְּצוּקוֹתַי. MT would be translated, "The troubles of my heart have increased." That would be strangely inconsistent with the way the image is used. Everywhere else the two roots are together in the same verse, they express contrasts (Pss 4:1 [MT 2]; 118:5; Job 36:16). Starting with Hensler,[96] therefore, the suggested conjecture is frequently made; in the consonantal text it only requires moving a ו from the end of one word to the beginning of the next.

[j] רְאֵה could perhaps be a debasing of קראה (imperative of II קרא, "meet, come to," + accusative). So for the first time Charles Augustus and Emilie Grace Briggs.[97] If one wants to conjecture, that is the simplest solution. Supporting a conjecture is the fact that the absence of ק is not one of the irregularities that Psalm 25 shares with Psalm 34. It would be translated, "Confront my affliction and my trouble." Nevertheless, a double ראה, violating the rules for the acrostic, could be an intentional deviation from the rule in order to emphasize a change in theme—an issue to be taken up at once in the structure analysis.

We have not exhausted all there is to say about the psalm's formal structure by mentioning the alphabetical arrangement of the verse openings (which is violated on more than one occasion), even if well-known interpreters like Hermann Gunkel talk as though we had.[98] Already in 1932 Hans Möller, as a supplement to a rather general article on the structure of the psalms, carried out a masterful analysis of the structure of Psalm

[96] Mentioned, but not documented, by Ernst F. C. Rosenmüller, *Psalmi annotatione perpetua illustrati,* 3 vols., Scholia in Vetus Testamentum IV/1–3 (Leipzig: Barth, 1821–1823) 2:702.

[97] Briggs, *A Critical and Exegetical Commentary on the Book of the Psalms,* 2 vols., ICC (Edinburgh: Clark, 1906 and 1907) 1:229. They point to Ps 59:4 [MT 5] for the meaning "to meet in helpfulness."

[98] Hermann Gunkel, *Die Psalmen,* HK 2.2 (Göttingen: Vandenhoeck & Ruprecht, 1926) 106: "lacks a clear arrangement," "entire lines fit loosely into groups."

25,[99] on which the structural analysis laid out in what follows will be especially dependent.[100] Of course Möller's theory of strophes of quantitatively equal lengths cannot be sustained. In addition there is the central position of v. 11 (ל), which is in tension with his main point of departure. It tempts one to adopt a palindromic structure, which certainly is also still present, around this center. Yet that is probably not an alternative set before the present interpreter but a formal tension consciously placed in the text itself. This particular central structure has been described for the first time by Lothar Ruppert. He arrived at it, it is true, from a hypothetical prior stage of the present text. In his reconstructed text there are not actually strophes of equal length, but rather qualitative correspondences between parts of the text related to one another.[101] In view of the interpretive method used in this book, this kind of recourse to an earlier stage cannot be drawn upon, however much it could perhaps help to make the present linguistic form of the text understandable from a genetic perspective as well.

According to Ruppert the structure he has observed is not recognizable by someone speaking or hearing the text but only by someone reading it.[102] From this he concludes that Psalm 25 is pure "prayer literature."[103]

[99] Hans Möller, "Strophenbau der Psalmen," *ZAW* 50 (1932) 252–56. Without mention of Möller's article the following propose the same structure: Évode Beaucamp, *Le Psautier: Ps 1–72,* Sbi (Paris: Gabalda, 1976); Ravasi, *Salmi I.*

[100] More recent attempts that challenge this one offer me no real alternatives, with the exception of the one by Lothar Ruppert, which will be mentioned directly. Nicolaas H. Ridderbos, *Die Psalmen: Stilistische Verfahren und Aufbau: Mit besonderer Berücksichtigung von Ps 1–41,* BZAW 117 (Berlin: de Gruyter, 1972) 200–206, simplifies Möller's arrangement by drawing 25:16-21 together into a single unit, because a number of Möller's observations are not convincing to him. But by doing this he leaves unexplained several phenomena seen by Möller. Jacques Trublet and Jean-Noël Aletti, *Approche poétique et théologique des Psaumes: Analyses et Méthodes,* "Initiations" (Paris: Cerf, 1983) 47–48, vacillate between two different proposals, which are both exclusively focused on word repetitions and bring in other levels too infrequently. They appear to be unaware of Möller's work. Gerstenberger, *Psalms I,* 120, identifies Möller's strophes (by gathering 25:16-22 together into a single strophe) with different assumptions about the genre, with the result that the unique form of the text is cooked up into a genre stew. Hossfeld, in Hossfeld and Zenger, *Psalmen I,* 165–66, organizes the text more in keeping with recognizable typical elements of the genre. Möller's essay is not mentioned.

[101] Lothar Ruppert, "Psalm 25 und die Grenze kultorientierter Psalmenexegese," *ZAW* 84 (1972) 578–79. Above all Ruppert expands v. 1 and omits v. 22. That then yields the following structure: A (1-3), B (4-7), C (8-10), center (11), C' (12-14), B' (15-18), A' (19-21). In v. 11, at the center, he sees a "plea for the forgiveness of sins" (579). On this cf. above in note [g] on the text.

[102] Ruppert, "Psalm 25," 578. This structure is such that it could have been created "neither for the one reading it aloud nor for the ear of the listener but only for the sharp eye of the reader."

[103] Ibid., 582.

That presupposes that there cannot be, in addition to liturgical song and "literature," a third option, for example, the repeated recitation of memorized texts. Yet even for liturgical texts a subtle shaping of the text could be considered. Just as one can by no means comprehend the total structure of our musical works simply by listening to them, especially not for the first time, but much emerges only by frequent hearing or playing, and as a study of the score must be added throughout in order to be able to get a handle on what is only intuitively imagined, so also it is certain that much about the structure of psalms is perceived only by reflective study of the written text or at least of one committed to memory. Nevertheless, there are also initial perceptions on first hearing and a good text, even if it is an old liturgical standby, is constructed to be understood in a corresponding fashion. Therefore it is important, even in a reflective analysis, to begin with structural signals that can be perceived on first reading or hearing. They lead, even with reference to formal tensions consciously carried through in texts, more or less to the basic structures, on which then others are built and with which these compete. In this connection it is far too uncommon to pursue analytically the structural perception of the hearer or speaker in its slow development. If one chooses to do that, then the textual analysis must stick to the direction reading takes. That will be the procedure in what follows.

In Psalm 25 a threefold division, at least, must emerge clearly at first hearing or speaking. It results from fundamentally different linguistic directions and actions. It can be observed in stages as the text goes along. The opening statement of intention in 25:1, 25:2-7 is followed by a series of petitions addressed to God. Verses 8-15 distinguish themselves from this "through [their] more reflective tone." Concrete statements pointing more in the direction of the third division are made, mostly with the claim of general validity. Then in 25:16-21 there is again "one petition, in the real sense of that term, after the other," directed to God.[104]

This threefold division of the psalm is a necessary basis for any more far-reaching conjectures about structure on the part of the reader or hearer. If one looks more closely and remains with the verse's unit of measure as pre-determined by the acrostic, the division is defined by the classical number seven, insofar as that is possible, given the total number twenty-two.

1-7	prayer	7 verses
8-15	reflection	8 verses
16-22	prayer	7 verses

[104] These are the formulations of Ridderbos, *Psalmen,* 201–202. But Gunkel, *Psalmen,* 106–107, has already seen that.

Yet one presumably notices other details with greater precision in going through the text, if not at once then very soon.

In v. 4, connected with a second address to God and still within the first petition section, a new theme begins that is characterized principally by the motif of the way. The decisive keyword דרך, "way," placed at the start of the sentence, opens the verse.

In the middle of the reflective central section a question in v. 12 is set off to mark a new beginning. If up to this point in the central section the subject was the action of YHWH, from now on it is about the people on whom YHWH acts. The new beginning is emphasized by the fact that directly before it, in v. 11, the third-person statements have suddenly climaxed in an "I" statement turning briefly to YHWH. Similarly the end of the reflective section in 25:15 is indicated by a new "I" statement, from which then develops the new beginning of the petition addressed to God in 25:16.

These petitions reach a high point and a turning point in the two verses (18 and 19) that, violating the order of the alphabet, each begin with ראה, "Consider." The plea for the forgiveness of sins is connected with the first call on God to give heed. That concludes the theme "sin" (15-18). With the second call to give heed pleas for help against enemies begin. That defines the following verse. Thus the two verses that in parallel begin with ר serve as a boundary line between two sections.

This becomes even clearer through the return, from v. 19 on, of vocabulary from vv. 1-3: איבי, "my foes" (19), נפשי, "my throat = voice, soul" (20a), אל־אבוש(ה), "do not let me be put to shame" (20b), קוה Piel, "wait for" (21), אלהים, "O God"[105] (21).[106] Moreover, to the schooled ear of that period's literary culture the concentrated return of terms from the beginning heralds the approaching conclusion.[107] This is added to the fact that the end of the alphabet is approaching.

[105] Even אלהים is a relevant repetition (which, in addition, is vocative in both cases), for aside from the expression אלהי ישעי, "God of my salvation," in verse 5, the only thing that appears outside of 2 and 22 is God's name, YHWH, (nine times).

[106] To be precise, the reuse of vocabulary from the beginning already begins in 18 with the verb נשא, "lift up." But it occurs in 1 and 18 in stock phrases that are quite different from one another.

[107] The technique of signaling relationships between sections by concentrated repetitions of terms is present only in these outer sections of Psalm 25. Within the psalm vocabulary repetitions serve other functions. They either link statements standing directly next to one another or function as key terms that characterize more restricted statement segments. As signals for chiastic section correspondences one could at most still mention חטאות, "sins," in 7 and 18 (but cf. חטאים, "sinners" in 8) and, in the two segments in the middle, ירה בדרך, "instructs in the way" (8 and 12), and ברית, "covenant" (10 and 14). They stand in segments that correspond to one another in the chiastic structure of the psalm as a whole.

Thus a chiastic structure of six parts emerges, with a midline between vv. 11 and 12:

1-3	prayer (enemies)	3 verses
4-7	prayer (sin)	4 verses
8-11	reflection (God)	4 verses
12-15	reflection (humanity)	4 verses
16-18	prayer (sin)	3 verses
19-22	prayer (enemies)	4 verses

The lengths of the sections do not correspond exactly to the chiastic arrangement. Within the prayer sections at the beginning and the end there is in each case first a section with three verses and then one with four. The structural midline of the verses (between 11 and 12) also lies exactly in the middle numerically.

This structural hypothesis slowly builds up for the reader in the process of reading itself and becomes more or less evident toward the end of reading or hearing the text. Right at the end, however, the reader finds it once again called into question.

The final verse, although it is still recognizable as a part of the frame through the address, "O Elohim," contrasts with what preceded it. And that is true not only because the alphabet has already ended and the verse overshoots what the form leads the reader to expect. The content is also new. The verse does continue to be a prayer. But the suppliant is no longer, as before, praying for him- or herself, but for Israel. Moreover the prayer is no longer about enemies. The theme of sin returns. For Israel is to be redeemed from כל צרותיו, "all its troubles." It is true that in other contexts this could also designate trouble from enemies, but within this psalm the word is given a more precise definition by its use in v. 17. The picture of distress from enemies is already transferred there to the distress from sin, along with the whole allusion to the Exodus (הוציאני, "bring me out"). Moreover the Exodus motif returns in v. 22 with the verb פדה, "Redeem." So there is no doubt that the plea for Israel here must not be understood as

But there are also too many other repetitions of relevant words in segments that do not correspond to one another in the overall structure, and so these few, if important, correspondences could not serve as clear signals for determining this structure: cf., for example, למד Piel, "teach," in 4, 5, and 9 or the derivatives of the root ענה, "poor, afflicted," in 9a and b, 16, 18.

a plea for freeing Israel from distress caused by enemies but as a plea for freeing Israel from the distress of sin.

What are the consequences of this for our perception of the structure? No doubt this, that right at the end, together with the redirection of the suppliant's attention to Israel, a connection with the theme at the middle of the psalm is reestablished. That shows what the principal issue is: the forgiveness of sins.

But the reference actually points to a particular verse. Whether that is really evident by simply listening can be doubted. Perhaps we have now reached the point at which it is necessary to study the score. The verse that supplements the acrostic begins with פ. The first letter of the alphabet is called אלף, *ʾaleph.* The middle consonant of this name for the letter, namely ל, had already been highlighted in the subtle play on word-beginnings in vv. 1 and 2.[108] Now the psalm ends with a פ, the final consonant of the name. The varied acrostic thus explicitly serves notice that it is structured alphabetically. That is at least one of the functions of supplemental v. 22. The whole phenomenon points, then, to a special position for the ל verse, v. 11. As already noted, this interrupts the objective presentation of the two middle sections at the end of the first of them, not only with a return to the "I" of the psalm's speaker but also with a turning to God. It is clearly to be regarded as the center of the psalm. It also speaks of the forgiveness of sins. So the essential theme is brought out once again.

If one highlights it, then the chiastic overall structure is transformed into a palindrome that moves up to a center and then moves away from it again. The qualitative relationships between the parts, as long as one reckons with the verses as they are clearly marked off through the acrostic, become less regular but also do not lose their force:

1-3	prayer (enemies)	3 verses	א
4-7	prayer (sin)	4 verses	
8-10	reflection (God)	3 verses	
11	center (forgiveness)	1 verse	ל
12-15	reflection (humanity)	4 verses	
16-18	prayer (sin)	3 verses	
19-22	prayer (enemies)	4 verses	ף

[108] See above, textual note a.

If one contrasts v. 22 because it is directed to Israel and no longer in the alphabet with the rest of the psalm, as an entity of its own, then one actually has before and after the center of this entity the same number of verses, ten each.[109] If one counts not verses but cola, then v. 11, actually without excluding v. 22, is found in the quantitative center, since there is a tricolon in vv. 5 and 7. Then, depending on how the cola in v. 1 are counted, the ל-verse as a whole or its second colon (the statement about the forgiveness of sins) occupies a central position, with 22 cola before and 22 cola after it.[110]

It is not at all necessary to choose between a chiastic or palindromic view of the psalm's design. The body of the psalm inherited genes from both parents. In their tension they make it interesting. Probably the chiastic structure is perceived first. Yet both structures, purely from the level of content, are thwarted once again by the linear dynamic of the way the issues are stated. This will be discussed below in the interpretation of the psalm.

The question about genre in the usual sense can hardly be asked about this text. The psalm is clearly more recent than, or comes out of a life situation different from that of those psalms for which one can presuppose an original use as a text in a particular liturgical rite in an early worship context, small or large. On the basis of comparative analysis of linguistic fields it can perhaps be said that with respect to genre it is a further development of what was present at an earlier stage of the Israelite Lament.[111] That is, it gives evidence of the distinct linguistic domains of the original laments and songs of thanksgiving, augmented by verbal material about poverty and piety that later on made their way into the lament and song of thanksgiving. Beyond that it adds cumulatively some word groups that occur only sporadically and never together in the context of laments and songs of thanksgiving, such as "way and knowledge," "law," "sin and forgiveness." In that respect it resembles only the lengthy Psalm 119. It is totally unique, however, in its use of the word ברית, "covenant."[112] Since this investigation

[109] That would correspond to the situation in Psalm 34, where the ו-verse has been omitted, perhaps for the sake of the central position of the ל-verse. But this also holds true only if the concluding פ-verse 23 is not counted. Psalm 34 could actually have served as a model for Psalm 25. On the connection between the two psalms, cf. now Freedman, "Patterns" (see his p. 126 on the lack of the ו-verse in both psalms) and Frank-Lothar Hossfeld and Erich Zenger, "'Von seinem Thronsitz schaut er nieder auf alle Bewohner der Erde' (Ps 33, 14): Redaktionsgeschichte und Kompositionskritik der Psalmengruppe 25–34," in *"Wer ist wie du, Herr, unter den Göttern?": Studien zur Theologie und Religionsgeschichte Israels. Für Otto Kaiser zum 70. Geburtstag,* ed. Ingo Kottsieper et al. (Göttingen: Vandenhoeck & Ruprecht, 1994) 375–88.

[110] Well observed by Freedman, "Patterns," 128–30.

[111] On what follows cf. Lohfink, "Lexeme und Lexemgruppen in Ps 25," 293–94.

[112] Cf. Frank-Lothar Hossfeld, "Bund und Tora in den Psalmen," in *Bibel in jüdischer und christlicher Tradition: Festschrift für Johann Maier zum 60. Geburtstag,* ed. Helmut

was undertaken with reference to the word ברית, this finding is, of course, relevant. It is thoroughly conceivable, even if never demonstrable, that Psalm 25 was composed only in the context of the present collection.[113]

5. The Language-Event in Psalm 25

The direction of the entire psalm as a speech-act is determined by what frames it at the beginning: a cry for help in distress from enemies, founded on confidence (2-3). But in 25:4 this plea reenters in another plea out of a much deeper need: in the plea for instruction in the ways of YHWH and for forgiveness of the sins of youth (4-7). This deep plea, once arrived at and expressed, apparently offers the calmness to think objectively, and thereby to speak more objectively about what actually makes this confident prayer possible. The first of the two sections that speak objectively, if not actually in hymnic praise, deal with God's action (8-11): God teaches the erring and poor God's ways. Thus, at the end, the section can again become an address to God:[114] for the sake of the "name" = nature of God described in this way the person who is praying hopes for the forgiveness of sins (11).

This calls forth, at the turning point in the course of the psalm, the second objective-hymnic part, which describes the same thing from the perspective of the person who "fears" YHWH (12-15). Ever deeper forms of blessing will come upon the person. At the end of the section, as in the one preceding it, the suppliant speaks personally about the rescue that can be counted on (15). This calls forth the next part, which, in conformity with 25:4-7, is once more a pure plea (16-18). Here the prayer begins in the depths into which the corresponding section (4-7) had descended. The framework at the end (19-21), by taking up motifs from the framework at the beginning (1-3), again encompasses pleas for help in distress from enemies.

So much for a quick analysis of the psalm, still without giving any consideration to the level of meaning of the pilgrimage of the nations, to which the opening verse raises it by connecting it with the preceding Psalm 24.[115] Now it is time to show what new light falls on the statements

---

Merklein et al., BBB 88 (Frankfurt am Main: Hain, 1993) 70: "In terms of covenant theology it is a rare bird in the first Psalter of David."

[113] Hossfeld and Zenger, "Thronsitz," 384–86, do not expressly advocate this, but several of the observations they have gathered suggest the idea. Their assumption that v. 22 has been added secondarily would speak against it. But that could be debated, in the event Psalm 34 served as a model.

[114] The second colon probably expresses a hope more than a plea. Cf. above, note [g] on the text.

[115] Since the question of whether Psalm 25 had an earlier existence, independent of the present compositional context, was not clarified (and perhaps never can be clarified), it

of the psalm as soon as one reads it as a prayer of a person from the nations—or actually as the prayer of the nations coming to Zion.

6. Psalm 25 as a Prayer of the Nations on Zion

Still to be added by way of introduction is the fact that Psalm 25 recalls Psalm 24 not only in its first clause but also in two further places:

25:5 אתה אלהי ישעי, "you are the God of my salvation"
cf. 24:5, ישא . . . צדקה מאלהי ישעו, "they will receive . . . vindication from the God of their salvation"
25:12 מי־זה האיש ירא יהוה, "Who are they that fear the Lord?"
cf. 24:6, זה דור דרשיו, "Such is the company of those who seek him,"[116]
and probably also 24:8, 10, מי (הוא) זה מלך הכבוד, "Who is (this) King of glory?"[117]

But then Psalm 25 also reaches back beyond Psalm 24 to the foundational texts about the pilgrimage of the nations to Zion in Isa 2:2-5 and Mic 4:1-5. Naturally one only becomes aware of that by reading Psalm 25 within this frame of reference. When read in its own right it rather functions in independence from Zion, since, in contrast to its neighboring psalm, its vocabulary "evidences no reference to the temple."[118]

After the suppliant in 25:1, by taking up once more a statement of Psalm 24, is shown to belong to those from the nations of the world who were able to come to Zion, this suppliant comes at once to a theme that is also the primary theme of the pilgrimage-of-the-nations texts: hostility and enmity in the human world. In Isaiah 2[119] that theme comes out only

---

can also not be decided whether the interpretation given could have perhaps been all there was to say already for an earlier stage.

[116] Perhaps it should still be observed that the first lines of Ps 24:3-6 begin with מי, the last ones with זה.

[117] This echo would take on added importance if the interpretation of Ps 24:7-10 alluded to above should prove true, according to which here as well the nations coming to Jerusalem are in view, in whose midst YHWH is entering the Temple anew.

[118] Thus Hossfeld, "Bund und Tora," 70. Naturally the text, taken in itself, has just as little really convincing evidence to offer for a kind of early Jewish grass-roots community as its Sitz-im-Leben (thus Gerstenberger, *Psalms I,* 121: "The forms and contents of Psalm 25 indicate congregational worship. The community visible here is no longer a clan or family group but the local assembly of faithful Jews. This confessional group nonetheless functions in many ways as a primary or face-to-face group. The afflictions and hopes of the individual can be addressed even in the worship services of the congregation.").

[119] Unless there are particular reasons not to do so, only Isaiah 2 will be cited in what follows. The parallel in Micah 4 is of course meant to be included.

at the end of the oracle, in the climax of its message ("swords into plowshares . . ."). In Psalm 25, in the opening frame, this theme is immediately clothed in Israel's traditional forms, lament and psalm of trust (25:2-3). In this way, one may understand, the nations of Isaiah 2 could also pray when they reach Zion and turn to the God of Jacob.

And yet these nations, according to Isa 2:3, are aware that it is not only a matter of help needed at a moment of dire threat from enemies, but of radical re-education:

> ירנו מדרכיו ונלכה בארחתיו
> that he may teach us his ways
> and that we may walk in his paths.

Correspondingly, the plea in Ps 25:2-3, arising out of actual trouble from enemies, is changed into the broadly developed plea for instruction in YHWH's ways (4-5). The hope that this plea will be heard is grounded in the confession developed later, in vv. 8-11, in which the corresponding keywords reappear. Indeed they also define the third part of the psalm (12-15).[120] Actually, the concentration—surprising even for the Psalter—with which the theme "way" is discussed only becomes understandable through the connection with the pilgrimage-of-the-nations texts.

And a second theme is added in vv. 6 and 7: "the sins of my youth." On the basis of the open-ended phrase that flashes by in 25:3 without being explained there, הבוגדים ריקם, "who are wantonly treacherous," and then on the basis of 25:1 and 24:4, one probably has to say: for the nations coming to Zion these sins of youth consist in the worship of other gods with no real existence. A glance at Mic 4:5 strengthens this impression. For according to this verse the pilgrimage of the nations to Zion has not yet happened because the nations continue to call upon their gods. The theme of sin will also frame the section in 8-11 (8 and 11) and return once more in the penultimate plea, mirroring the verse in which it first appeared (18; cf. 6-7).[121]

The two themes of the section in 4-7, knowledge of the way and forgiveness of sins, merge for the suppliant from the nations at the beginning of the next section in 8-11. For it is precisely the sinners whom YHWH instructs in the way (v. 8).[122]

[120] The words or roots shared with Isaiah 2 are דרך, "way," ארח, "path," למד, "learn," ירה Hifil, "teach," שׁפט, "judge," שׁם, "name."

[121] The end of the section in 4–7 is marked in 6-7 by the threefold use of the word זכר, "remember," and, correspondingly, the end of the section in 16–18, in 18 and in the parallel new beginning in 19, is marked by the twofold ראה, "consider," that frames the plea for the forgiveness of sins: ושׂא לכל־חטאותי, "and forgive all my sins."

[122] The phrase יורה . . . בדרך, "instruct in the way," is quite rare. It occurs only in 1 Sam 12:23; Pss 25:8, 12; 32:8; Prov 4:11. As far as the spiritual climate is concerned Ps 32:8

It appears as though the nations in this part of the text are now taking over the experience of Israel, to whose holy place they have indeed come. The Israelites of the post-exilic period know themselves as the "poor." In the Hodayot from Qumran it can be seen that the self-designation as "poor" fits primarily in the teaching about the justification of sinners. Actually, the word is not even used about the sinners as such, but only when it appears in the context of God justifying the sinners by grace and setting them on a new way.[123] It is similar here (v. 9). The sinners, who have missed the mark, become the poor when God has brought them through the judgment. In this way they learn God's way along with God's own people. This way is a dialogical process. From the perspective of God it is חסד ואמת, "steadfast love and faithfulness," from Israel's it is the keeping of בריתו ועדתיו, "his covenant and his decrees" (v. 10).

In today's theological terms one would designate this entire reciprocal activity and relationship as "covenant," and in other passages in the Hebrew Bible that is also the case. Here the word ברית, normally translated as "covenant," occurs in a position that belongs to one of the two sides in the relationship, that of Israel's behavior. Now as to what it here designates, without delay! In any case, in the process which is described, the sinner is led on the way, through judgment, out of the poverty that has now become manifest into a context in which the word ברית can also be used.

If one knows from the experiences of Israel that God acts in this way, then one knows God's "name." For the sake of this name the suppliant from the nations now also hopes to experience personally the forgiveness of sins, analogous to justification (v. 11).

That leads to the corresponding second objectively formulated passage (12-15). It describes in positive terms what the suppliant from the nations, on the basis of Israel's experience of God's name, dares to hope for. The new point of view is clearly formulated at once, actually in the form of a question. The suppliant is described as ירא יהוה, which one might almost translate as a "God-fearer" (v. 12). Could it be that this later designation for the people from the nations who attach themselves to Israel is already present here?[124] In

---

is the closest parallel. But the word group טוב וישר, "good and upright," (said about YHWH) in the parallel phrase favors seeing here a direct reference to the passage in which Samuel, after the introduction of kingship, outlines the new function of the Israelite prophet: to pray for Israel and to instruct the people of Israel (והוריתי אתכם), precisely בדרך הטובה והישרה, "in the good and the right way." In the mind of the deuteronomistic author of this passage the prophetic actualization of the torah is doubtless in view.

[123] Cf. Norbert Lohfink, *Lobgesänge der Armen,* 99–100.

[124] Cf. Bernhard Duhm, *Die Psalmen,* KHC 14 (Freiburg: Mohr, 1899) 79: "It is possible, but not very likely, that the 'God-fearer' here is already a proselyte, in keeping with the later terminology."

any case Israelites are not being spoken of here. For the way in which God is instructing is "chosen" (דרך יבחר)[125] by the God-fearing person. Israel is hardly in a position to choose this way, to which it has long since been subject.[126] But now the people from the nations, after they have decided to follow YHWH's way, have a share in Israel's blessings.

In a clear allusion to a central theme of the Pentateuch, especially of Deuteronomy, the "children" of the suppliant are promised that they shall possess the land (v. 13). In this way the suppliant is to be compared to Abraham, being granted personally—this is not just for the children—a share in God's סוד, "assembly," or "secrets" (which are revealed to Israel alone), indeed in God's "covenant" as well (v. 14).

This is the passage for which this entire study has been undertaken. It merits, then, even closer attention. It forms the climax here. A circle is closed, for in 25:4 the suppliant had prayed for knowledge of the way (הודיעני), and here the covenant is now open to those to whom YHWH has granted knowledge (of the way—להודיעם). The only thing still to come, at the end of the section, is the return of the suppliant from objective observation to a personal stance and, at the same time, the transition to the part that follows, which again is made up of petitions (v. 15).

In the section in vv. 16-18 the supplications first sound forth for clarity in the realm of what is essential. In the previously investigated transition of the two ר-verses the supplications then turn again to the real trouble that set off the pilgrimage of the nations, the discord in human society. The plea for

[125] On the fact that יבחר is a relative clause without a relative pronoun there is almost unanimous agreement. In the baroque era there was still disagreement about whether the subject of יבחר was YHWH or the God-fearing person. With justification today the God-fearing person is generally preferred, but the evidence should be supplied. בחר, "choose," has דרך, "way," as its object only in Isa 66:3; Pss 25:12; 119:30; Job 29:25; Prov 3:31. That God chooses a way for a person does not occur using these terms in the entire Tanach. Perhaps it could at most be pointed out that Job, during his times of prosperity, chose (בחר) for other members of the assembly, as its most prominent member, which way they should go. But such a concept could hardly be applied to God here, since in the context no individual concrete ways of behavior are in view, but simply life in general under the guidance of God. Isaiah 66:3; Ps 119:30; Prov 3:31 point in the same direction.

[126] If as an object for בחר one requires a word for "way," only Ps 119:30 can be named as a parallel. Proverbs 3:31 and Isa 66:3 refer to a decision to go a false way. If one forgoes the word "way," then there are isolated references: the parenthetical statement that Israel in Shechem once "chose" YHWH and YHWH's service (Josh 24:15, 22) and the call to Israel to "choose" life, with which the ritual texts of the establishment of the covenant at Moab (Deuteronomy 29 and 30) conclude in Deut 30:19. On the basis of this linguistic evidence the statement that the suppliant should chose the way in which God is providing instruction applies more easily to a person from the nations than to an Israelite, even if the latter cannot be completely ruled out.

deliverance from enemies characterizes the closing frame (aside from the concluding verse), vv. 19-21. This section breathes confident certainty.

At the same time it brings up the final point: the suppliant from the nations, who has entered into Israel's experience and now lives from it, speaks a prayer for the deliverance of Israel from its troubles (v. 22). The name "Israel" occurs here in the psalm for the first and only time, but in such a moving way, when one reads the psalm as a prayer of people from the nations! And all the more when one sees that Israel's need is no different from that of the nations, the oppression caused by its own sins.

One can without doubt read the psalm in the way it has just been interpreted, even if it was not composed with this interpretation in view. Yet essentially the text really begins to speak only through this interpretation. In this way it would be the only text in the whole Old Testament in which, for the end of history, a share in Israel's "covenant" would have been promised also to people from the nations.

7. The Absence of the Word "Torah"

If one takes a closer look at all of that, then one is first of all struck by the fact that the complementary word to ברית, namely תורה, does not occur in Psalm 25. In view of the large number of words that allude to Isaiah 2 this is surprising. There the nations are indeed given torah on Zion. In Psalm 25 only the root that is present in the word תורה has been picked up, ירה, "instruct." For that very reason, of course, the absence of תורה must be regarded as relevant. The subject matter with which "torah" is concerned is, indeed, constantly present within Psalm 25 through the picture of the way and of walking. Nevertheless the psalm avoids asking God to instruct the suppliant in the torah, and a formulation of this kind is apparently not even seen as necessary.

Now it can be said that already in Psalm 1 the theme of "torah" has been tied to the image of the way (1:1, 2, 6) in such a manner that after that this image can no longer be heard in the Psalter without any reference to Israel's torah. Besides, the word תורה is not used frequently; before Psalm 25 it occurs only one other time (Ps 19:8). The Hifil of the verb ירה occurs for the very first time in the Psalter in Psalm 25. So the word, so closely tied with the image of the way, may actually introduce the idea of Israel's torah. But the fact remains that the word תורה itself is absent.

Perhaps one must reckon with a hesitation to impose on the nations the entire torah in the form in which it was given to Israel. As Ps 24:4 has drawn back in comparison with Ps 15:2-5, so also here it may be intentionally left open which form the ways of God will now actually take for the nations.

8. *The Use of the Word* ברית, *"Covenant"*

But whatever course these ways will take, they lead the nations into the "covenant." The word ברית, which occurs a total of twenty-one times in the Psalter, had not yet been used before Psalm 25. Here it occurs twice and each time in different and unexpected contexts.

In 25:10 it is followed by עדתיו, "his decrees." The only other places this word combination occurs are 2 Kgs 17:15 and Ps 132:12.[127] In the two passages in that late period, in which the redaction of the Psalter occurred, no specific designation for a certain literary-institutional entity had to have been detected any longer. The double expression was an indication of the will of YHWH embodied in Israel's torah. But why was precisely this rare word combination chosen? Solely the desire to avoid the word תורה cannot have been determinative.

The matter is even more complicated. The divine ways that are entrusted to those who "keep the covenant and decrees" are חסד ואמת, "steadfast love and faithfulness."[128] Such a close connection of this word pair with ברית ועדות is unique.

If one searches for a text in which all four expressions occur relatively near one another and also topically connected with one another, then the search will likely yield only one: the chapter about the renewal of the covenant after the sin at Sinai, Exodus 34, and what lies around it.[129] Here YHWH, in forgiving the people, offers this self-designation: אל . . . רב־חסד ואמת, "El . . . abounding in steadfast love and faithfulness," and establishes a new ברית, whose stipulations are written on the tablets of the ברית, which are then at once also called tablets of the עדות (Exod 34:6, 10, 27, 28, 29).

That by its uncommon formulations Ps 25:10 actually wishes to place before the reader's eyes the scene of forgiveness and covenant renewal on Sinai is shown also by the verse that follows immediately, v. 11, the center of the psalm. Exodus 34:5-8 is about the revelation of the divine name. The suppliant in Ps 25:11a appeals to the divine name. In the book of Exodus, after the revelation of God's name, Moses pleads for forgiveness. He says: וסלחת לעוננו, "and forgive our sins" (34:9). Ps 25:11b takes up this precise formulation.

Once this reference to Exodus 34 in Ps 25:10f. is recognized, then other formulations in the psalm are perhaps also revealed to be shaped by

[127] Here with the normal verb שמר, "keep, observe," which corresponds to the less common נצר. Otherwise נצר occurs with ברית only in Deut 33:9, with עדות only in Ps 119:2, 22, 129.

[128] In the sense of "true, constant faithfulness."

[129] On this text complex cf. now above all Christoph Dohmen, "Der Sinaibund als Neuer Bund nach Ex 19–34," in *Der Neue Bund im Alten*. Additional literature is given there.

this background. In Exod 33:13, in the conversations in which Moses fights for God's forgiveness of Israel, he pleads: הודעני נא את־דרכיך, "show me your ways"—this is the way the section of Psalm 25 in 4-7 begins. In Ps 25:6-7 the plea for forgiveness built around the word זכר, "remember," contains many keywords that are also important in Exodus 32–34.[130] Even the talk of the "children" who "shall possess the land" (Ps 25:13) plays a role in Exod 32:13 and 33:6. The last great series of petitions is opened in Ps 25:13 with פנה־אלי וחנני, "Turn to me and be gracious to me." That is like an echo of Exod 33:19: חנתי את־אשר אחן, "I will be gracious to whom I will be gracious." But above all Ps 25:18b, ושׂא לכל־חטאותי, "forgive all my sins," is the short form, turned into a petition, of the self-designation of YHWH in Exod 34:7 as the compassionate one who forgives (נשׂא עון ופשע וחטאה, "forgiving iniquity and transgression and sin").

So the word ברית first occurs in Psalm 25 in the context of statements related to Exodus 34.[131] Now Exodus 32–34 is not about the original establishment of the covenant at Sinai but about its breach through idolatry and its renewal on the basis of divine forgiveness. A parallel is thus established between the distinctive sin of the nations, idolatry, and the primal sin of Israel, the worship of the golden calf, between YHWH's forgiveness of Israel and YHWH's forgiveness of the nations coming to Zion, between Israel's renewed covenant and the incorporation of the nations—freed from the sins of their youth—into Israel's covenant. The final point is expressly made in v. 14.

But first to linguistic problems with this verse. If we think in terms of pure parallelism, then both clauses have to be noun clauses. The phrases introduced by Lamed, ליראיו and להודיעם, need to have the same function. This is also possible if in the second colon הודיעם is understood as a relative clause without a relative pronoun.[132] Because of the laws of parallelism this explanation is superior to any other from the start.[133] The

[130] Cf. Exod 32:13, זכר; 33:19, רחם; 34:6, אל רחום; 34:7, פשע.

[131] So now also Frank-Lothar Hossfeld: "Proximity to Exodus 34, at least at the level of its deuteronomistic reworking, also suggests itself for Psalm 25. Favoring this are the use in Ps 25:7, 11 of the three most important concepts for sin in Exod 34:7; the allusions in Ps 25:6, 10 to the grace formula in Exod 34:6; and the mention of covenant or law in Ps 25:10, 14 and Exod 34:10, 27ff." (Hossfeld and Zenger, *Psalmen I,* 165–66).

[132] Quite literally: "And his covenant (is open) to those of whom it is true: he has let them know." The problem of the unstated object of "know" is there for most of the syntactical solutions that are discussed, and so it cannot be used to argue against this one in particular.

[133] The most important, clarified in translation, are: (1) "His friendship belongs to those who fear him; (to them belongs also) his covenant, (which he grants,) to let them know"; (2) "his friendship belongs to those who fear him; his covenant he will let them know" (*coniugatio periphrastica*); (3) "his friendship belongs to those who fear him; his

unexpressed object of the knowledge is presumably the "way" of YHWH. In the two descriptions introduced by *lamed* there is a combining of the first and last characterizations, from the material in 25:4-14, of the person who is going to God.[134]

סוד is a poetic word that gained importance rather late.[135] It designates the heavenly assembly of God, which is present in the Israelite congregation gathered for worship. Into this congregation the person on the pilgrimage of the nations to Zion is now received. It is to be observed that this congregation was indeed founded in the book of Exodus. Thus it is only logical that the parallel clause speaks of the reception into that relationship with God that can be called "covenant" and at Sinai was established and renewed by forgiveness.

The fact that what is discussed in the background texts, in Exodus 33–34, is not the initial establishment of the covenant at Sinai but its renewal finally directs attention to Jer 31:31-34, the foundational text about the "new covenant." Indeed it will not be by chance that the expression סלח לעון, "to forgive sin," which is, in fact, quite rare,[136] connects Exod 34:9 with Jer 31:34. In Exodus 34 Israel is always reading within the torah itself of the possibility it offers of the "new covenant." If Psalm 25 now promises the nations a future share in the archetypal events of Exodus 34, then that is connected with the promise of a new covenant for Judah and Israel in the future. The theme of a torah taught in the new covenant by God, no longer by humanity and of a knowledge of YHWH imparted by God and not by humanity is central in Jer 31:31-34. Perhaps the prominence of the theme of divine instruction in Psalm 25 shows that this psalm will remind the reader who meditates on it not only of Exodus 34 but also of the promise of the new covenant.

---

covenant, truly, he will let them know (it)" (*lamed emphaticum*). In all three cases there is no longer any precise parallelism. In the first case the object of the "knowing" becomes a real puzzle. In the second and third cases one is committed to the idea of "knowing" the covenant. This idea is attested nowhere else and does not suggest itself from the context, unless "covenant" here would be completely synonymous with "way." But in that case the statement would also be coming somewhat too late.

[134] Chiastically, of course: on the person who fears God, cf. v. 12; on instruction in the way, cf. v. 4.

[135] Cf. Heinz-Josef Fabry, "סוד *sôd*," *ThWAT* 5 (1986) 775–82. He writes on Ps 25:14: here "every restriction" was "removed and YHWH's divine council so thoroughly democratized that everyone 'who fears YHWH' can participate in the *sôd*. This democratization is an important step in the semantic transition by which *sôd* became the designation of the Old Testament worshiping community" (778).

[136] Here is a list of all the occurrences: Exod 34:9; Num 14:19; Jer 31:34; 33:8; 36:3; 50:20; Pss 25:11; 103:3.

9. Summary

The promise of Israel's covenant also for the nations, which thus embraces Psalm 25, is apparently unique in the entire Hebrew Bible. In the interpretation we have undertaken, it was left open whether the psalm presupposes as suppliant the nations from Isaiah 2 as a whole or individual people from the nations. This will also have to be left up in the air. In the psalm itself a singular subject speaks. But on the basis of Psalm 24 a plural subject is to be considered. That one must leave the issue up in the air here is, however, relevant and distinguishes this text from Isa 56:1-7, for example, where it is clearly individuals who join Israel.

This promise of the new covenant for the nations is woven into a statement that only becomes clear on the redactional level of meaning, woven in such a way that modern biblical interpretation has apparently still not seen it at all. Even in this investigation it could be made visible only with great effort. But if the decisive steps on the path of knowledge we have presented have been set down in the right places, Psalm 25 could become an important text in Jewish-Christian dialogue: precisely for this reason as well, that with reference to the nations it leaves the talk about the torah in the realm of allusion in such a way that it remains open whether one needs to think right off about the highly specific laws of the Pentateuch and their regulative details or even about the *halacha* that already at that time had for a long time been constructed around these laws. That the nations receive instruction in the way that they have chosen, and that this instruction may in a real sense be designated torah has been shown. Yet at the same time the content of this instruction is apparently not simply identical with the torah given to Israel. For this reason our psalm prefers to avoid this word. Nevertheless, the nations become sharers of Israel's "covenant" and can pray for Israel.

If one accepts this understanding of Psalm 25, then it is probably also easier to acquire an eye that is open to recognize an endtime connection of the nations and covenant also in other sections of the Psalter. With this in mind, to begin with, the allusion to the so-called covenant formula in Psalm 33 will be discussed in the chapter that follows.

CHAPTER 4

The Covenant Formula in Psalm 33[1]

When Israel spoke of the "covenant" it often used a specific formula that described the essence of the covenant with aptness and brevity—at least as far as the divine side is concerned. One speaks of the "covenant formula." Perhaps it would be better to give this formula another name, "departure formula," for example (because of the frequent connection with the exodus motif) or "election formula" (since it is about God's elective activity). In any case it expresses only one side of the covenant relationship, for it speaks only about the "activity" of God in the establishment of the covenant relationship and not about Israel's obligation to the torah that resulted from this. Naturally, the first and crucial act is God's. But only when both are named together does one really have what a term like "covenant formula," taken strictly, would require. But the designation has been adopted in biblical study for the narrower formula, which speaks only from God's perspective, and for this reason it will be used this way also in what follows.

The basic form of the covenant formula is:

> I will be your God,
> And you shall be my people.[2]

[1] This chapter is previously unpublished. It should also be regarded as my further work on the theme of Norbert Lohfink, "Die Universalisierung der 'Bundesformel' in Ps 100,3," *ThPh* 65 (1990) 172–83. I thank especially Walter Groß for a conversation about the syntax of the verbs (though I, of course, bear full responsibility for my interpretations) and Georg Braulik for important suggestions.

[2] For the list of examples, cf. Norbert Lohfink, "Dt 26:17-19 und die 'Bundesformel,'" *ZKTh* 91 (1969) 517, reprinted in idem, *Studien zum Deuteronomium und zur deuteronomistischen Literatur I,* SBAB 8 (Stuttgart: Verlag Katolisches Bibelwerk, 1990).

It is thus a two-part formula, and the fact that in both parts God's "covenant activity" is defined both from God's side and from Israel's side has likely been the reason that one has already seen in it a full description of the covenant relationship. Each of its two parts also frequently occurs separately, of course, but what follows deals only with its two-part expression.

To be in force the covenant formula has to have been spoken by God as its originator. It is most readily comparable, among the life-events in Israelite society, to the *verba solemnia* surmised for the acknowledgment of a child (of which adoption is a specific example) and to the marriage ceremony: "I am his father, and he is my son" and "You are my wife, and I am your husband." In the Deuteronomistic understanding of the covenant between YHWH and Israel it expresses the promise of the divine partner, while the human partner makes a commitment to the torah of YHWH. The key text and most developed example is Deut 26:17-19. In the priestly source in the Pentateuch it is found in the crucial passage Exod 6:7.

On the question whether in Israel's Scriptures the covenant is promised not only to Israel but also to the nations, the covenant formula naturally serves as an especially important touchstone, for it explicitly states that in the covenant God makes the commitment to be in relationship to one people. In all the examples of its full form in torah and prophets the reference to Israel is clear. On the other hand, in Isa 19:25 we find this sentence, undoubtedly formulated by allusion to one of its elements:

> Blessed be Egypt my people,
> and Assyria the work of my hands
> and Israel my heritage.

That a reminiscence of the covenant formula is really intended here is also shown by the fact that earlier (19:20-22) there is talk about YHWH's activity on Egypt's behalf that corresponds to YHWH's activity at and after Israel's exodus from Egypt. The covenant formula thus appears to be transferable to people outside of Israel.

To be sure, the problem with such a transfer is seen at once: this text sounds as if in days to come there will be several peoples of God.[3] Or is the covenant formula transferable also in another form? Indeed also in

[3] At least that is the view of Walter Groß, "Wer soll YHWH verehren? Der Streit um die Aufgabe und die Identität Israels in der Spannung zwischen Abgrenzung und Öffnung," in *Kirche in der Zeit: Walter Kasper zur Bischofsweihe: Gabe der Katholisch-Theologischen Fakultät Tübingen,* ed. Hermann J. Vogt (Munich: Wewel, 1990) 17–22. A somewhat different view is found in Ernst Haag, "'Gesegnet sei mein Volk Ägypten' (Jes 19,25): Ein Zeugnis alttestamentlicher Eschatologie," in *Aspekte spätägyptischer Kultur: Festschrift für Erich Winter zum 65. Geburtstag,* ed. Martina Minas and Jürgen Zeidler, Aegyptiaca Treverensia 7 (Mainz: Verlag Philipp von Zabern, 1994) 147, n. 20.

Psalm 25 there was no talk of a covenant of YHWH with the nations that would have been different from the covenant with Israel. Rather, what was in view there was the pilgrimage of the nations to Zion and, in connection with that, a share for the nations in the one covenant of God with Israel, which, through the compassion of God, continued as a covenant even after the sin of idolatry. In what follows we would like to address the question to the Psalter. In the process attention will quickly focus on Ps 33:12.

In the Psalter there are no examples of the covenant formula in its basic form. On the other hand, formulations that remind one of it and that with a high degree of certainty allude to it are found in three places: in Pss 33:12; 95:7; and 100:3.

Psalm 95 is a confession by Israel of its creator God who is at the same time its covenant God.[4] The double hymn in 95:1-7a first treats the creator and then the God of the covenant. It ends in 7a with the covenant formula. Then, after a call to listen, the voice of God that fills the rest of the psalm (8-11) comes in, exhorting obedience to the voice of the God of the covenant and calling to remembrance stories about sin during the wandering in the wilderness.

It is different in Psalm 100.[5] Here the covenant formula is found in the mouth of the nations entering the temple on Zion. They confess the God enthroned there as follows in v. 3:

> Know that the LORD (alone) is God;
> It is he that made us, and we are his;
> we are his people, and the sheep of his pasture.

Presumably Ps 95:7 and Ps 100:3 are joined to one another in the final redaction of Psalm Book IV, as several formulational connections show. Psalm 100 is the climax of psalm series 93–100, which culminates in the theme about the nations. But all of that will be treated later, in chapter 6 of this book.

On reaching Psalms 95 and 100, at least in a synchronic reading of the Psalter, one will be reminded of the first allusion to the covenant formula

[4] From the literature cf. especially Georg Braulik, "Gottes Ruhe—das Land oder der Tempel? Zu Psalm 95.11," in *Freude an der Weisung des Herrn: Beiträge zur Theologie der Psalmen: Festgabe zum 70. Geburtstag von Heinrich Groß,* ed. Ernst Haag and Frank-Lothar Hossfeld (Stuttgart: Katholisches Bibelwerk, 1986) 33–44, and Frank-Lothar Hossfeld, "Psalm 95: Gattungsgeschichtliche, Kompositionskritische und bibeltheologische Anfragen," in *Neue Wege der Psalmenforschung: Für Walter Beyerlin,* ed. Klaus Seybold and Erich Zenger, HBS 1 (Freiburg: Herder, 1994) 29–44.

[5] On what follows cf. Lohfink, "Ps 100:3"; Erich Zenger, "Israel und Kirche im gemeinsamen Gottesbund: Beobachtungen zum theologischen Programm des 4. Psalmenbuchs (Ps 90–106)," in *Israel und Kirche heute: Beiträge zum christlich-jüdischen Dialog: Für Ernst Ludwig Ehrlich,* ed. Marcel Marcus et al. (Freiburg: Herder, 1991) 246–50.

in the Psalter, in Ps 33:12, and perhaps in retrospect regard it as a kind of proleptic announcement of the system of statements in Psalm Book IV. Did it have to prepare for something here or to indicate the building of a bridge? Was it still speaking only of Israel or was there already here a reference to the nations?

Such questions must be asked in the light of what happens with the covenant formula in Pss 95:7 and 100:3. They suggest a closer look at Psalm 33,[6] which is not interpreted all that frequently. For without an analysis of the entire psalm, also including its connections to the preceding and following psalm complexes, the questions we have raised cannot be answered.

I. Psalm 33 as a Whole

1. Translation and Notes

The translation that now follows is, where possible, concordant with the psalm's determinative structure, as the way it is printed already indicates. Yet be aware from the start that in the main part of the psalm the structure we have indicated, with its orientation to the center, stands in tension with a more linear competing structure. Only in the interplay between these two structures do we have the full structure of the psalm. More later in the structural analysis!

Introduction

1 Rejoice in the LORD, O you righteous.
    (for) praise befits the upright.[a]
2 Praise the LORD with the lyre;
    make melody to him with the harp of ten strings.
3 Sing to him a new song;
    play skillfully on the strings, with loud shouts.

[6] Here are all the works we can name that are substantially devoted to Psalm 33 alone: Alfons Deissler, "Der anthologische Charakter des Psalmes 33 (32)," in *Mélanges bibliques rédigés en l'honneur de André Robert,* TICP 4 (Paris: Bloud & Gay, 1957) 225–33; Klaus Koch, "Wort und Einheit des Schöpfergottes in Memphis und Jerusalem," *ZThK* 62 (1965), reprinted, with additions and corrections in idem, *Studien zur alttestamentlichen und altorientalischen Religionsgeschichte* (Göttingen: Vandenhoeck & Ruprecht, 1988) 61–105; Jean M. Vincent, "Recherches exégétiques sur le psaume xxxiii," *VT* 28 (1979) 442–54; Pierre Auffret, "'Les pensées de son coeur': Étude structurelle du Ps 33," *ScEs* 39 (1987) 47–69; idem, "'Allez, fils, entendez-moi!': Étude structurelle du psaume 34 et son rapport au psaume 33," *EeT* 19 (1988) 5–31.

Main Section I

4 For the word of the LORD is upright,
and all his[b] work is done in faithfulness.[c]
5 Whose—the one who loves righteousness and justice—[d]
the LORD's steadfast love—of it the earth is full.[e]
6 By the word of the LORD the heavens were made,
and all their host[f] by the (Spirit-)breath of his mouth.
7 (Before him,) who (constantly) gathers the waters of the sea as if they were a mound,[g]
forces the deeps into storehouses,[h]
8 Before the LORD let all the earth fear,[i]
before him let all the inhabitants of the world stand in awe.
9 For he spoke, he alone,[j] and it came to be;
he, he alone, commanded, and it[k] stood firm.

Central Section

10 The LORD has overthrown[l] the counsel of the nations;
he has stood on its head[m] the plan[n] of the peoples.[o]
11 The counsel of the LORD stands forever,
the plan[p] of his heart to all generations.
12 Happy is the nation whose God is the LORD,
the people whom he has chosen as his heritage.

Main Section II

13 The LORD has looked down from heaven;
he has seen all individual[q] people.[r]
14 From where he sits enthroned he has watched
all the inhabitants of the earth—
15 (he,) who has (both)[s] fashioned the hearts of them all,
(and) observed all their deeds.
16 It is not true that the king was saved by his great army,[t]
nor will even a hero be delivered by his great strength.
17 It is vain to count on the horse for rescue,[u]
and despite his great army he (the hero) will not escape.
18 Truly the eye of the LORD is[v] on those who fear him,
on those who hope in his steadfast love.
19 to deliver their soul from death,
and to keep them alive[w] in famine.

Conclusion

20 Our soul (thus)[x] waits for the LORD,
who (alone) is our help and shield.[y]
21 For[z] our heart shall be glad in him,
because we (will) have trusted in his holy name.
22 Let your steadfast love, O LORD, be upon us,
even as we (will) have hoped in you.

Notes

[a] The nominal clause in the second half of the verse could equally well be a parallel main clause, in this case to be understood as an imperative ("Let praise befit the upright"), or also a subordinate clause, in this case causal ("for praise befits the upright"). The initial, emphatic position of the indirect object in the predicate (לישׁרים), which is actually a parallel designation for the צדיקים called upon in the vocative in the first half of the verse, supports the idea that a reason is to be given why precisely this group is called to give praise. An interpretation as an imperative main clause, in the midst of the many calls to praise in the context, would rob the clause of its formal, clearly recognizable specificity. In fact a hymnic appeal to the "righteous/upright" in the context of the Psalter requires a justification. The only examples of such an appeal to the "righteous" are Ps 32:11 (the immediately preceding intimation of Ps 33:1); Ps 97:12 (for parallelism with "upright in heart" cf. the prior verse). Beyond that we could still call attention to the confirmatory conclusion of Psalm 140 in v. 13 [MT 14] (// "upright"). That makes the appeal to the righteous/upright to offer praise practically unique. In English "upright," as the word on which the clause is dependent, must come at its end.

[b] According to Klaus Koch,[7] the suffix does not refer back to YHWH but to the word of YHWH, and this also holds true of the elliptical subject in v. 5a. But a different explanation is called for in this latter case (see below). Here it is more likely that the reference is back to YHWH and that "YHWH's work" and not "the work of YHWH's word" must be supplied. The context shows that YHWH's work is accomplished by the word. There is no evidence of a desire to hypostatize the divine word.

[c] [German: "Wirklichkeitsdichte," "solid reality"] Or "reliability." The contrasting concept שׁקר then occurs in v. 17.

[7] Koch, "Wort und Einheit," 274, n. 74.

[d] To speak here of a "hymnic participle," as Gunkel's *Introduction* does,[8] for example, and to simply translate with a present-tense main clause, as normally happens,[9] ought not be possible any longer after the form-critical analysis of the so-called "hymnic participles" by Frank Crüsemann.[10] Regardless of whether, perhaps, a formulation is used that is assumed for hymns of a different type, we must ask about the syntax that is operative now. This is true in v. 5a as well as in vv. 7 and 15. It is unlikely that v. 5a is an independent clause, since a participial clause requires a subject. A deletion of יהוה is unlikely, since the subjects of the preceding clauses were not יהוה but דבר־יהוה and מעשׂהו. It is best to understand the participial group in v. 5a as a characterization, given in advance, of יהוה, who is mentioned in the expression that follows, חסד יהוה. The translation tries to be faithful to the construction.[11]

[e] After the nominal clauses in v. 4, which express general statements of fact, v. 5b might be seeking to offer a perfective, if not general statement. It does not yet direct attention to the past, indeed to the primal period, as v. 6 then does, making a new start with a repeated דבר יהוה.

[f] It is surely the stars that are in view. According to Klaus Koch all meteorological phenomena, like wind, thunder, and lightning, are to be included.[12]

[g] Instead of the Masoretic *kannēd,* "as in a pile of grain/a wall," several early translations presuppose *kannō(ʾ)d,* "as in a (goatskin) pouch." On the imagery, cf. Job 38:37. There the subject is the heavenly water containers from which the rain comes. If *kannō(ʾ)d* is the original reading, then the subject here as well would be the heavenly water supplies from which the rain flows, while v. 7b would be speaking of the watery depths that come forth in the sea and in springs. Then there would be a clear parallelism, and

[8] Hermann Gunkel, *Introduction to Psalms. The Genres of the Religious Lyric of Israel.* Completed by Joachim Begrich, tr. James D. Nogalski. Mercer Library of Biblical Studies (Macon, Ga.: Mercer Univ. Press, 1998) 31.

[9] Cf., for example, Hans-Joachim Kraus, *Psalmen,* 5th rev. ed., 2 vols., BK 15/1 and 15/2 (Neukirchen-Vluyn: Neukirchener Verlag, 1978) 1:408: "He it is, then, who loves righteousness and justice," or the *Einheitsübersetzung,* "He loves righteousness and justice."

[10] Frank Crüsemann, *Studien zur Formgeschichte von Hymnus und Danklied in Israel,* WMANT 32 (Neukirchen-Vluyn: Neukirchener Verlag, 1969) 83–154, particularly 129–31.

[11] Since Hermann Gunkel, *Die Psalmen,* HK 2.2 (Göttingen: Vandenhoeck & Ruprecht, 1926) 138, does not use a period (cf. his translation in vv. 7 and 15) after v. 5a, but a comma, one can actually read his text in the sense of this interpretation: "He, who loves righteousness and justice, of YHWH's grace is the earth full." Similarly (without further justification), Hermann Spieckermann, "'Die ganze Erde ist seiner Herrlichkeit voll:' Pantheismus im Alten Testament?" *ZThK* 87 (1990) 415–36, at 426.

[12] Koch, "Wort und Einheit," 276.

at the same time the descent from above to below in the description of creation. The reading in the Masoretic text would come from a secondary inner-biblical harmonization. Then it might be pointing to the heaped-up waters of the Reed Sea and of the Jordan during the crossing of that river (cf. the word נֵד, "wall," in Exod 15:8; Josh 3:13, 16; Ps 78:13; also the verb that soon becomes important in the psalm, עמד, "stand," in Josh 3:13, 16). But the talk about the "waters of the sea" speaks for the originality of the Masoretic reading. That hardly permits thinking about water that is enclosed in heavenly containers or even in clouds, which are to be thought of as waterskins. So perhaps already in v. 7a we have come down from heaven, and the sea, which originally covered the earth, in this colon was driven to the margin of the dry land and there more or less heaped up or made into a delimiting wall. This imagery can be independent of any Exodus connotation. The choice between the two readings is not easy. It could actually be the case that *nōd* was the original reading but that, because of the echo of *nēd*, the passage through the Reed Sea and the Jordan were also meant to be heard from the beginning. Since this similarity of sounds cannot be reproduced in English, the translation above presumes that *nēd* is the original reading. Then more of the possible sense comes across.[13]

[h] As in v. 5a we have neither a participial main clause (there is no subject, not even one that has been deleted) nor an attributive expansion of a preceding word for God. Once again יהוה, from the main clause (ייראו מיְהוה) that then follows, may be anticipated. The discontinuity with v. 6 also means that the time perspective can change. Verse 6 has started out as a past-tense statement about creation. Now creation is also traversed in a descent moving from top to bottom through the cosmic system (heaven, water, earth). But that does not mean that a past-tense creation report is continuing. It may be surmised in the background. At the same time, however, the temporal stage changes. When the object "earth" is reached in v. 8, a jussive form is already moving forward into the future. Only with the supporting argument summarized in v. 9 does the past tense surface again. In this passage through the stages of time within vv. 6-8, the participles in v. 7 could indicate the middle stage between the past in v. 6 and the jussive future alignment in v. 8. The verse should viewed as a description of ongoing action that explodes the bounds of time. YHWH is constantly keeping the earth and its inhabitants safe from water that by nature wants to

[13] The recent advocates of the respective readings are listed by Claus Petersen, *Mythos im Alten Testament: Bestimmung des Mythosbegriffs und Untersuchung der mythischen Elemente in den Psalmen*, BZAW 157 (Berlin: de Gruyter, 1982) 102, n. 1 and 103, n. 3. On 108–109 there is detailed argumentation against the assumption of a reference to the Exodus (although Petersen reads *nēd*).

flood them. That would then also be the reason the earth and its inhabitants must have fear and awe before YHWH, who is constantly keeping them safe. Whether they can continue to exist depends on YHWH alone, moment by moment, ever anew. With that in view, v. 7 would also have a foundational nuance for the main clause that then follows. The supporting argument introduced with כי in v. 9 refers to the passage as a whole and thus has a different function.

Overall the understanding developed here is similar to that of the old interpreters. They often concluded from the change of form that v. 6 spoke of the creation while v. 7, by contrast, spoke of the preservation of the world.

[i] A jussive translation, "since what follows still speaks of the diversity of humanity's basic attitudes."[14]

[j] An emphatic הוא, also in the colon that follows.

[k] Namely what was commanded. In the preceding clauses there is no masculine word that could serve as an antecedent, so here and in the prior colon only the content of what was said and commanded can itself be the subject. Perhaps the first colon speaks of the creation of the heaven and its host through the divine word, the second of the subduing of the sea by a divine command.

[l] For הפיר, according to the practices of modern lexicography, one must postulate a secondary root *pwr,* "break," to a main root *prr*. It would occur only two or three times. The main root *prr* itself then divides once more (I "break," II "shake"). Normally one includes our passage under *prr I,* "break," a choice that already suggests itself because several, and precisely the oldest, examples classified under *prr I* are connected with the object עצה, "intention."[15] But nothing keeps us from questioning the sharp division between *prr I* and *II.*[16] At that time it all was probably viewed as a single verb with different meanings. But then the basic concept of shaking and overthrowing—now contrary to the direction that Ruppert's arguments take—would be conceivable also for the examples using עצה. It actually fits well in all these passages. Since explicit statements about radical upheaval occur later in the psalm, the meaning "cause to shake, overthrow" seems the most appropriate to me. Ernst Kutsch has called attention to the fact that *prr* Hifil, with reference to its objects, is clearly different from *šbr,* "shatter," and *šḥt,* "destroy."[17]

[14] Henning Graf Reventlow, *Gebet im Alten Testament* (Stuttgart: Kohlhammer, 1986) 133, n. 78.

[15] 2 Samuel 15:34; 17:14; Isa 8:10; 14:27 (implicitly); Ezra 4:5; Neh 4:9—for מחשבה, "plan," cf. Job 5:12 (עדה also occurs in the context); Prov 15:22.

[16] Cf. the arguments of Lothar Ruppert, "פרר," *ThWAT* 6 (1989) 774–75.

[17] Ernst Kutsch, Art. "פרר," *THAT* 2 (1976) 487.

[m] The verb *nwʾ* is also a very rare word whose basic meaning is hard to comprehend. The corresponding Akkadian word *nêʾu* has the meaning "overturn." I consider it possible that it makes a statement about overthrowing here as well and translate accordingly.

[n] Reading the singular, with 4QPs^{q} (*lectio difficilior*).

[o] The past tense, which returned in v. 9 with the rationale that concluded the statements about creation in vv. 6-9, applies also to v. 10. The *qatal*-clauses express throughout an individual statement of the issue in past tense; at most they have a perfective nuance. The frustration of the plans of the nations is in any case God's doing from of old. Then the time perspective is overturned once more in v. 11, just as happened in v. 7. Verse 11 speaks of the unlimited future. That is shown not only by the *yiqtol* form of the verbs but especially by the time references לעולם, "forever," and לדר ודר, "to all generations." There follows in v. 12 a doubly stated nominal clause that, through what precedes, naturally also comes to stand in a future, trans-temporal sphere. The past tense (*qatal*) statement about election it contains is found in a relative clause (without a relative pronoun) and therefore does not define the time of the main clause. YHWH's own activity in history is thus not viewed from the perspective of its establishment in the ancient past but with respect to what is still expected in the future.

[p] Reading the singular with 4QPs^{q} (*lectio difficilior*).

[q] בני (literally "sons of") individualizes the generic concept אדם, "humanity."

[r] The *qatal* form at the end of v. 12, even if, strictly speaking, it must perhaps be translated as a *futurum exactum,* enables the part of the psalm that is making a new beginning, as earlier with the new start in v. 10, to simply continue with the same verb form and thereby to be in the primal period once more. There the text stays up to and including v. 15. The judging and electing action of God also is grounded in creation—which is also expressed by the content of v. 15. The two participles in v. 15, each supplied with an article (היצר, "the one fashioning," and המבין, "the one observing"), are not predicates, but the key pieces of two parallel subject groups, held together by יחד, for the predicate groups in v. 14. The key piece of these latter groups is השגיח, "he has watched," a *qatal* verb. Verse 15 thus contains subordinate elements of a sentence that as a whole relates to the past.[18]

[18] So already Heinrich Ewald, *Die Dichter des alten Bundes: Zweiter Theil: Die Psalmen* (Göttingen: Vandenhoeck & Ruprecht, ^{2}1840) 423. In his translation as a whole Ewald has perhaps the clearest grasp of the psalm's syntax and temporal relationships.

[s] יחד, "in one, together, with one another," in a somewhat unusual word order controlled by the poetic parallelism, binds the two subject definitions for the entire sentence in vv. 14-15 into a unity in v. 15a and b.[19]

[t] Here we have a nominal clause whose predicate is אין, "nothingness"—translated freely here with "It is not true that," since the subject is an entire verb clause that makes an assertion about something that happened at a given point in the past.

[u] A noun clause constructed by analogy to v. 16a. It is assumed here that with הסוס לתשועה, "The horse to the rescue!" we are dealing with an idiomatic way of speaking.

[v] Or, in view of v. 13, the content of which is taken up once more, "was." But as a whole the noun clauses at the beginning of vv. 16-18 appear to make universally applicable fundamental statements, even if they are grounded in the primal time at creation. In vv. 16b and 17b the *yiqtol* forms, and in v. 19 the infinitive constructions, show that the universally valid statements are important for the suppliant especially with respect to the impending future. That leads to the future perspective that controls the conclusion of the psalm in vv. 20-22.

[w] On this translation of חיה Piel cf. Deut 6:24; 2 Sam 12:3; Jer 49:11; Eccl 7:12; Neh 9:6.[20]

[x] Verse 20 wants in any case to say that the speakers of the psalm are to be set in the context of what is said in vv. 18-19. The statement is made by means of a *qatal* form. That can point to a decision made in the past or to a performative statement that thus happens in the moment of speaking. I accept the latter, since only statements about the future follow in vv. 21a and 22a. The petitionary character of v. 22a also supports the fact that v. 20a is to be understood as performative. The two clauses in vv. 21b and 22c are dependent on the statements that precede them and for that reason have no influence on the prevailing sphere of time. From the standpoint of the future that is in view in the main clause they reach back into a time period that, seen from the future, is in the past.

[y] Verse 20b is a noun clause (הוא!). In the context we must expect "YHWH (and no other)" as the predicate. Since הוא, serving a deictic function in

[19] So already correctly Hermann Hupfeld, *Die Psalmen,* 2d. ed. by Eduard Riehm, 4 vols. (Gotha: Perthes, 1867–1871) 2:246.

[20] Norbert Lohfink, "Deuteronomy 6:24: לְחַיֹּתֵנוּ 'to maintain us,'" in *"Shaʿarei Talmon": Studies in the Bible, Qumran, and the Ancient Near East Presented to Shemaryahu Talmon,* ed. Michael Fishbane and Emanuel Tov (Winona Lake: Eisenbrauns, 1992) 115–16.

reference to YHWH, occupies the final position, the clause must be a subordinate clause, according to the (still unpublished) positional rules of Diethelm Michel. Therefore it is to be regarded as a relative clause, in apposition to ליהוה at the end of v. 20a.

z There is no reason that the כי that opens v. 21 should not express purpose.[21] The hope in YHWH expressed in v. 20 has its "motivating" basis in the expectation of finding, through YHWH, joy of heart in the future. This expectation itself is again given an "objective" basis (כי in v. 21b) by virtue of confidence in YHWH's name. Thus everything is put in YHWH's hands. Therefore the psalm concludes in v. 22 with a plea that steps out into the future, a plea that is based on thoughts of reciprocity: God's coming action should correspond to the human confidence that goes before it.

2. *Psalm 33 as a Poetic Structure Oriented to Its Center*[22]

In its overall structure the psalm certainly is "precisely a prime example of a *Hymn*."[23] With relative ease the main outline can be divided as follows:

1-3	Introduction	Calls for praise: plural imperatives
4-19	Main section	Beginning with כי; objective statements in third person
20-22	Conclusion	"We" and "you (singular)": confidence and petition

[21] In contrast to the *Einheitsübersetzung,* which has "indeed" here and completely overlooks the כי that follows.

[22] Detailed analyses of the structure of the text have been systematically carried out only in the recent period. I make reference to the various studies here in one place: Nicholaas Ridderbos, *Die Psalmen: Stilistische Verfahren und Aufbau: Mit besonderer Berücksichtigung von Ps 1–41,* BZAW 117 (Berlin: de Gruyter, 1972) 236–45; Vincent, "Recherches," 447–51; Pierre Auffret, *Hymnes d'Égypte et d'Israël: Etudes de structures littéraires,* OBO 34 (Fribourg: Éditions Universitaires; Göttingen: Vandenhoeck & Ruprecht, 1981) 55–73; Marc Girard, *Les psaumes: Analyse structurelle et interprétation: 1–50.* Recherches, NS 2 (Montréal: Editions Bellarmin; Paris: Cerf, 1984) 260–66; Auffret, "Pensées." Almost all crucial observations have been assembled in these works, even if with diverse results. By no means are all the observations enumerated in what follows. Some of the works are probably too strictly confined to a literary analysis of the surface structure and barely pay attention to syntax and content. What is offered here tries above all to open new paths through its reader-oriented analysis.

[23] Frank-Lothar Hossfeld and Erich Zenger, *Die Psalmen I: Psalm 1–50,* NEB 29 (Würzburg: Echter, 1993) 205; this recognition is old and is already found in Ernst F. C.

This main outline can be clearly recognized in the very formal characteristics given in the third column, and it also becomes apparent on reading or hearing the psalm for the first time. The you (plural) address in the introduction does not return in the entire psalm. The we statements in the conclusion, and especially the accompanying turning of this "we" to God as "you" in the final verse, are, it is true, already prepared for secretly in the middle of the psalm ("Happy the people . . ."), but they still appear as something completely new and are certainly relevant for the form as a whole.

It is important to observe the quantitative regularity that is shown in this overall structure. The psalm has twenty-two verses in all, each with two cola. The number twenty-two corresponds to the letters of the alphabet. The psalm is not an acrostic. But simply the number of verses is in itself an allusion to the alphabet. This signals comprehensiveness, completeness, a small but closed literary "world." This is strengthened by the fact that the introduction and conclusion are of equal length.

1-3	Introduction	3 verses
4-19	Main section	16 verses
20-22	Conclusion	3 verses

Everything now depends on precisely how the sixteen verses in the main section are arranged. In what follows the intention is to analyze them as the reader experiences them on a first reading. That is to say, the text and its divisional signs are followed from the perspective of the reader. In doing this we shall establish at each point what the reader, on the basis of information thus far obtained, already knows and what new information is acquired. This way of considering the text enables us to expect that along the way the reader is going to have to revise general hypotheses set out earlier. In many cases how things actually are finally becomes obvious only in retrospect. That the number of verses in the psalm corresponds to

Rosenmüller, *Psalmi annotatione perpetua illustrati,* 3 vols., Scholia in Vetus Testamentum IV/1–3 (Leipzig: Barth, 1821–23) 2:826. For hymns that conclude with petitions, Ridderbos, *Psalmen,* 236, points to Pss 19:12-13 [MT 13-14]; 104:31-35; 139:19-24. It is true that Gunkel and Begrich restrict this: such petitions are more typical of Babylonia and Egypt than of Israel (*Introduction,* 40). Crüsemann, *Studien,* 129–30, shows that the psalm is anything but an example of an originally pure form of the genre. In his view it contains first of all, in vv. 1-4, a "complete imperatival hymn," to which the "long main part of the psalm in vv. 5-19" has "been added, in which, in an apparently quite free and masterful way, entirely different elements of form and style have been juxtaposed." Finally he says that vv. 20-21 and 22 are to be regarded as independent entities. In principle that is certainly correct, even if it is impossible to separate vv. 4-5 from one another. With a text this late it is no longer adequate to see it as a crystal-clear example of a genre.

the number of letters in the alphabet, for example, will become clear to the reader only at the end, indeed perhaps only after working with the text for a long time.

The transition from the hymnic call to the hymnic main section, as a transition from appeals to statements, pointedly marked at the beginning of v. 4 through the word כי, "for,"[24] will doubtless be clearly perceived, given the background of the presupposed familiarity with the genre of the imperative hymn. The new beginning is more strongly perceived in that the groups addressed in v. 1 at the beginning of the introduction (the "righteous" and "upright") now mark, in chiastic correspondence, the statements about God in the first two lines: the word of the LORD is ישר, "upright" (v. 4), and he loves צדקה ומשפט, "righteousness and justice" (v. 5). This is the way the statements about God one expects in the hymn have their beginning. Theoretically they could continue to the end of the psalm. But already in vv. 8-9 a sense of conclusion occurs for the first time.

Hymns can be concluded with a short reprise of the introduction or of the entire basic form of a hymn.[25] One now experiences in vv. 8-9 something like a return of the basic model of the hymn. It is true that there is not a call to praise in v. 8. But the call for fear and awe before YHWH spills out of the linguistic world of the hymnic confession[26] and is an elocutionary speech act, namely one that issues a call. If there then follows in v. 9, introduced by the hymnic transitional particle כי, a new hymnic reason for the call, summarizing the statements about the word of God and creation in the hymnic reason for praise that precedes it, one has the clear impression that the hymn that starts at the beginning of the psalm, and therewith possibly the entire psalm, is at an end. The statement about creation has indeed also run its course through the path on which it had set out. From heaven with its stars, by way of the waters located at various places in the cosmos, it has finally reached—already, in fact, within the call to fear YHWH in v. 8—the earth and the people living thereon. Heaven + the heavenly host on one side, the earth + the world's inhabitants on the other, frame the entire statement about creation. The conclusion appears to have come. That v. 5 is an announcement that extends still further is not yet

[24] Against the translation "indeed, truly," advocated primarily by Crüsemann, *Studien*; cf. the new plea for the old rendering of "for" by Patrick D. Miller, *They Cried to the Lord: The Form and Theology of Biblical Prayer* (Minneapolis: Augsburg Fortress, 1994) 358–62.

[25] Gunkel and Begrich, *Introduction,* 40: "Even the *conclusion* of the whole frequently manifests the forms of the introduction." For an entire brief hymn as conclusion, cf. Ps 99:9, for example.

[26] On the rarity of an interruptive admonition in the hymn cf. Gunkel and Begrich, *Introduction,* 39.

known at this point in the text. The fact that in v. 8 the keyword ארץ, "earth," from v. 5 reappears rather obscures this possibility.

In any case, the text then goes further. But the text that continues in v. 10 immediately appears to confirm the impression that the hymn, at least, has ended. It speaks of something other than the previously discussed creation. There are also formal observations. Verse 10 begins with its subject "YHWH" placed in first position for emphasis. Up to this point the name of God had, of course, occurred frequently, but always as a designation for the object or in the genitive, never for the subject of the statement. That it now for the first time stands as a designation for the subject is all the more striking, since already in the preceding v. 9 YHWH was also a doubly-stressed subject, but with the pronoun הוא, "he," in place of the divine name. At a completely analogous place (at the beginning of a verb clause, before a *qatal* verb) we now have suddenly not הוא, but יהוה. That suggests a new beginning.

An entirely new theme also begins, namely that of the plan of history, indicated through the two keywords עצה, "counsel," and מחשבת, "plan," in v. 10. The two words are repeated right away in v. 11 and in the same order. The contrast between the many nations and the one chosen people that connects vv. 10 and 12 over v. 11 is also not something one would naturally expect on the basis of the creation theme that precedes it. So the section of the text in vv. 10-12 presents itself as something new and different.

But then this section also clearly ends in v. 12. For with v. 13 the dimension "heaven—earth" is present again. As v. 6 had begun with the keyword "heaven," so now also v. 13. The entity "all the inhabitants of the earth," developed in parallelism in v. 8, is paralleled in vv. 13 and 14 in a new way:

8a	all the earth	8b	all the inhabitants of the world
13b	all individual people	14b	all the inhabitants of the earth

The new theme is God's creative look into hearts. It is also not at all clear right away in v. 13 that v. 5 was a hidden advance notice of the part of the psalm that begins here, for the keyword that makes the connection, חסד, "steadfast love," does not sound until v. 18. The impression persists that vv. 10-12 are an insertion of a different kind, put in consciously, after which the psalm then continues as it had before this intermezzo. On the other hand, from v. 13 on an unbroken line runs through the psalm to the end. At most the jump from all humanity to the kings and war heroes in v. 16 serves as a small new beginning, but really not an actual break. Through word repetitions vv. 12 and 22 have the effect of being two corresponding concluding sections: cf. the name for God, יהוה, אשר, and לך/לו.

On the other hand the transition from the "he" to the "we" statement in v. 20 is certainly striking. The supposition that arises at this shift to the personal is soon confirmed: namely, that the concluding section of the hymn has been reached. Now at least it is also clear that, to use an architectural image, we have a building constructed around a center. Verses 10-12 form the central dome. Here we already find the covenant formula.

In the end it actually becomes clear that even outwardly, in a quantitative way, vv. 10-12 stand almost exactly at the center of the psalm.

> Naturally with twenty-two verses, determined by the number of letters in the alphabet, something with three lines cannot precisely form the midpoint. The midline as far as verses are concerned runs between vv. 11 and 12. Two lines of the central part precede it and one follows. But as soon as one moves from counting lines to counting words, the assumption that the block forms the somewhat isolated center of the psalm becomes more convincing. The psalm contains (if we ignore the use of the *maqqeph* by the Masoretes) 161 words in all. The middle word, number 81, is the word אשרי, "blessed," with which v. 12 begins. Before it there are eighty words and after it eighty words as well.

Here we need to ask about the consequences that such a central structure has for what is being said. When a block with a different subject matter is inserted in a text, in the center and strictly isolated, splitting the surrounding text into two parts like a wedge, then it usually has special connections to the beginning and end of the text as a whole. How these connections are to be defined depends on the particular text. Theoretically anything is possible, by no means only that the statements are identical. Statements that contradict one another are also conceivable. This alone stands: there are connections.

Now the block vv. 10-12 undoubtedly aims toward the beatitude that forms its third line. Its subject, which is clearly recognizable by its allusion to the so-called "covenant formula," is the chosen people of God as the goal of YHWH's plan for history—whereby, it is true, the name Israel does not occur.

The absence of the word "Israel" must still be given further consideration later. Here we only mention the problem. Are the people of the covenant no longer simply identical with Israel? In the introduction there was in v. 1 a restriction of those addressed that we had already found striking: in a way quite uncharacteristic of the psalms the "righteous" and the "upright" were summoned to praise. A restriction that somehow corresponds to this can also be observed in the conclusion. Here a "we" emerges that is defined on the basis of trust in YHWH in contrast to trust in one's own might. This contrast had been clearly elaborated earlier, in vv.

16-19. In that case as well it had not been connected with the keyword "Israel." Was this shared limitation of a group, paralleling a non-mention of the entity "Israel," supposed to be the aspect that, focused on the right relationship to YHWH, connected introduction, central section, and conclusion with one another? This suggestion is meant to guide the arguments that follow, yet it still leaves open many possibilities for a more precise interpretation.

For the present we offer only a diagram for the structure of the psalm arrived at from the process of reading, in which the middle section, vv. 10-12, especially stands out:

1-3	Introduction	Hymnic calls to צדיקים and ישרים	3 verses
4-9	Main section I	Creation through the word	6 verses
10-12	*Central section*	YHWH and the nations/YHWH's people	3 verses
13-19	Main section II	God and human freedom	7 verses
20-22	Conclusion	Those who have decided to hope in YHWH speak	3 verses

The quantitative harmony is astonishingly large. The only irregularity, the one-verse difference in length between the second and fourth parts, is determined by the fact that the three parts of greatest interest, at the beginning, in the middle, and at the end, each contain three verses, and ultimately the even number of twenty-two verses had to be reached because of the number of letters in the alphabet.

3. *The Central Section as a Linear Sequence of Announcements and Two Strophes*

If readers have reached the end of main section II, then, as much as they feel that a poetic central section has just now been traversed, they can at the same time actually have an experience such as one has with an image that is meant to be ambiguous: the perception of the structure shifts and another, more dynamic and forward-moving linear structure of the entire main section of the psalm is revealed.

The occasion for that, first of all, is that vv. 4-5 are now recognized, in looking back, as a statement of the outline. They are a focal point of the text. They not only take up the motifs of the actual beginning of the psalm (as discussed above), but they also make preliminary verbal references to what is to come. Verse 4, with its keywords "word of the LORD" and "his work" (root עשׂה), is immediately taken up in v. 6. That could still be a simple connection. But then in v. 18, thus right at the end of main section II, when the keyword "steadfast love of the LORD" from v. 5 recurs, it can be clear to the reader that vv. 4-5 must have been annunciatory in character. They have anticipated the beginning and end motif of the entire body of the psalm. That is in keeping with the perception already described that vv. 4-5 make general statements about God, while only v. 6 reaches back into the past to the act of creation. Verses 4-5 are not only the beginning of the hymnic praise but at the same time a preliminary sketch of the whole. While this "statement of the outline" contains the framing motifs, this is certainly not to say that an inner arrangement of the subject matter of the text thus circumscribed has as yet automatically been given with it.

But this is revealed precisely in v. 18, where the reader, pursuing a reader-oriented interpretation, can actually recognize the annunciatory function of vv. 4-5 for the first time. For there, in v. 18, the עין יהוה, the "eye of the LORD," is related to hoping in חסדו, "his steadfast love." But the eye of YHWH embraces a theme that has shaped the text beginning with v. 13, "The LORD has looked down from heaven; he has seen all individual people."

Since the keyword "heaven" marks v. 6 and v. 13, vv. 6 and 13 are clearly the starting points of the two parts announced in vv. 4-5 through the naming of their outer motifs. We can construct the following diagram:

4-5 Statement of the outline

4 The word of YHWH (דבר־יהוה) / YHWH's work (מעשׂהו)
5 YHWH's steadfast love (חסד יהוה)

6-12 Strophe I: the word of YHWH — 6 Heaven (שׁמים)

6 The word of YHWH (בדבר יהוה) / 7 made (נעשׂו)
9 YHWH spoke / commanded (verbs speaking about the word)

13-19 Strophe II: the look /steadfast love of YHWH — 13 Heaven (שׁמים)

13 Looked / seen / 14 watched (verbs speaking about seeing)
18 The eye of YHWH (עין יהוה) / YHWH's steadfast love (חסדו)

In strophe II the term "steadfast love" is thus not picked up right away at the beginning. Rather the reader is led to this theme through the thought, not formally announced in vv. 4-5, about seeing, which emerges at once in a threefold treatment (vv. 13-14). After the word of YHWH created the universe (strophe I), YHWH is enthroned in heaven. There YHWH's eye becomes crucial, penetrating the creation in judgment and election (strophe II). It is only from YHWH's looking that the motif of YHWH's "steadfast love" is developed, the term only recurring toward the end of the second part, as a framing element equivalent to "word" at the beginning of strophe I. Verbs can also be used to speak of YHWH's word and YHWH's eye. Noun and verb statements are also chiastically related in the two parts.

Now to the extent of the two strophes. Since the second extends at least from vv. 13-18, indeed also still includes v. 19, which is not independent, it encompasses seven lines. So, looking back, one will also suppose that the first strophe has a corresponding length. Although there is in vv. 10-12 no keyword from v. 4, that is no indication that these verses do not belong to the first strophe. Then it encompasses vv. 6-12, thus seven lines as well. That vv. 10-12 are to be read closely with the preceding verses is also shown by the connection through the repeated root עמד, "stand" (vv. 9b, 11a). There is no room in this strophic system for a special central section.

There are a number of parallels between the two strophes. In strophe I we can observe a line of creative works by the divine word that descends from above to below: heaven (v. 6), water (v. 7), earth (vv. 8-9).[27] By analogy in strophe II we have the movement of the divine look, expressed in two parallel statements: from heaven to humanity (v. 13), from the throne to the inhabitants of the earth (vv. 14-15).

The final parts of the strophes are also interesting. In strophe I all the nations of the world stand over against the one people whom God has chosen (vv. 10 and 12). But strophe II also closes with a contrast. It is a contrast between confidence in military might, characteristic of all states, and confidence and hope in the steadfast love of God (vv. 18-19), to whom the "we" that speaks in the conclusion will then make confession. At the end of both strophes it is also clearly said that God wants nothing to do with one of the things named and desires the other. So these ending sections of the strophes—vv. 10-12 and 16-19—correspond to one another. One could draw up the following structural diagram:

[27] Strictly speaking, the setting up and populating of heaven (with the stars) is followed by the relocation of the waters, in part also in the subterranean realm, and then attention is turned to the land surface that has thereby emerged and its inhabitants.

I	A	6-9	YHWH's word has created the cosmos	4 verses
	B	10-12	YHWH's plan for history is directed to a chosen people	3 verses
II	A'	13-15	YHWH's look has created freedom for all people	3 verses
	B'	16-19	A choice: confidence in one's own might or in YHWH	4 verses

Quantitatively the distribution of blocks, which are arranged rather in parallels with respect to content and time periods, is chiastic: 4 + 3 / 3 + 4 verse lines.

This structure of the hymnic main section, which can only be recognized from v. 18 on, and which calls into question the central structure observed earlier, is dynamic and linear. In the process of reading it can in any case actually be seen only when one has come to the final verses of the main section. Earlier the structure emphasizing the center suggested itself. This, then, has also shown itself not to be superceded and absent. For precisely at the place at which the linear structure is perceptible it also combines with the center-oriented structure, which up to that point had alone been perceptible. Verses 10-12, the center of the one structure, are now, as section IB of the first strophe, associated with section IIB' of the second strophe. This in turn, precisely in the dynamic that is related to the content, is the indispensable presupposition for what then is given voice in the framing conclusion of the entire psalm. Without the disclosure in vv. 16-18 that people are saved solely by hope in YHWH's steadfast love, the confession about hoping in YHWH's steadfast love in vv. 20-22 would be unthinkable.

4. On the Theology of the Body of the Psalm

First, in order to dispense with an interpretation that is sometimes encountered: in all probability one can hardly characterize the two strophes of the main section in such a way that the one deals with "YHWH the creator" and the other with "YHWH the controller of history."[28] For history is also treated already in IB, and in II things are under discussion that relate heavily to the individual, less to society and thereby to history. Something

[28] Thus, for example, Koch, "Wort und Einheit," 278, sees in v. 12 a "second thematic phrase" and, from there on, "to the work of Yahweh's word in creation is added the work in the history of Israel."

in the public arena comes up in v. 16 at the earliest, and a "we" does not occur until the conclusion in vv. 20-22.

But it also does not help to latch onto the structure-indicating keywords from vv. 4-5, "the word of the LORD" and "the steadfast love (or, if one prefers, grace) of the LORD." If interpretation is what is intended, these words need to be broken down, especially the second, which only appears at the end of the part of the text to which it belongs and is prepared for in advance by the motif of the eye of YHWH. The statement of the outline in vv. 4-5, as has been shown, indicates the starting and ending points of the main section, not two themes that dominate everything. Keywords of that kind do not necessarily have to indicate the themes of the parts that are announced.

Since at the beginning of the second strophe YHWH is pictured as sitting on the throne in heaven, it is natural to think of YHWH here as ruler and judge. The hymn, at least from this point on, would become a covert song to YHWH as king. This deserves further attention.

The announcement in v. 5a speaks of צדקה ומשפט, "righteousness and justice," that YHWH loves. On the surface of the text that seems to remain a dead motif. The words do not occur again. But it should be asked what subject matter is evoked here. What does this word group have to say?

On the concordance data: The word group צדקה ומשפט (in this order) is only found in Gen 18:9; Ps 33:5; Prov 21:3; on that cf. the separation of the terms in parallels (again in the order given here) in Deut 33:21; Isa 58:2; Pss 36:6 [MT 7]; 103:6; Prov 8:20; 16:18. The double expression צדק ומשפט (again in this order) appears in Hos 2:21 (followed by חסד); Pss 37:6; 89:14 [MT 15]; 97:2; 119:75 (followed by אמונה); Prov 1:3 (followed by מישרים); 2:9 (ditto); in addition, separated in parallels in Isa 32:1; Jer 22:13; Ps 72:2; Job 29:14. The complete verbal group אהב צדקה ומשפט occurs nowhere else. Of the words under discussion here, אהב has as object elsewhere only משפט (Isa 61:8; Pss 37:28; 99:4); Ps 11:7 and Prov 15:9, the two passages that one would perhaps like to draw upon for צדקה, are both, on closer examination, somewhat different; there is not a single example of אהב with צדק.

If one analyzes more closely this group of passages that are more or less closely related to one another, the suspicion arises that especially Pss 89:14 [MT 15]; 97:2; 99:4 can be drawn upon to explain our psalm. In all three passages there are also other words and motifs that occur in Psalm 33. Psalm 33:5 appears to be dealing with a connection of the statement about God, also found elsewhere, אהב משפט, with the image of justice, righteousness, steadfast love and truth as the foundation of the divine throne or as things that accompany God.

But that means that the image of the divine throne was already present in v. 5a, in terms of that subject matter. In that case it is, of course, interesting that according to v. 5b, in contrast to the entities belonging to the divine throne, צדקה ומשפט, the entity חסד is found below, on earth. It fills the sphere under heaven. On the other hand, the juxtaposition of the two statements in v. 5a and 5b shows that the entities צדקה ומשפט apparently supply the heavenly standard for the divine חסד that holds sway in the sub-solar world.[29] This bridge that has already been set up here between heaven and earth allows the following consideration of the connection between v. 5 and the text from v. 13 on.

The second strophe of the main section is cryptically controlled by the conviction that people are in distress and have to be saved, rescued, protected. The focus of royal judging (and therewith also of judging by the king as god) in the ancient orient was in fact not simply the punishment of crime and the establishment of an abstract correspondence between guilt and penalty, but the (re-)establishment of a just order through help for the poor and disadvantaged, who are themselves no longer able to battle for their own interests in the world. "Righteousness and justice" are actually only established in that manner. Apparently those who, as the disadvantaged of the world, allow God to give them חסד, that is God's royal steadfast love and favor, are the true "righteous." We would have here something like a doctrine of justification.

That would mean that we must identify the "we" speaking in the conclusion in vv. 20-22 with the "righteous" who at the beginning of the psalm are called to offer a hymn of praise—even though the word "righteous/righteousness" is not taken up again at the end. That the "righteous/upright" from v. 1 and the "we" speaking in vv. 20-22 are one and the same is all the more likely since the beginning and conclusion of a text are often related to one another, especially in a palindromic structure, and the specific summons to the "righteous" to praise God that stands at the beginning of the psalm is so totally unusual. All of this has already been discussed earlier as a possibility.

The Hebrew Bible is well acquainted with a doctrine of justification that precedes Paul's; an example is the Deuteronomic statement that Israel obtained the divine gift of the land not on the basis of its "own righteousness" but—despite being a rebellious and stiff-necked people—solely on the basis of God's promise to their ancestors.[30] In this material as well as in Paul the concept of sin plays a decisive role. But apparently here in Psalm 33 a different doctrine of justification is developed. It does without sin as a leading concept. It works only with the contrast between human autonomy that goes its own way and relies on might, on the one hand, and

[29] Cf. Koch, "Wort und Einheit." 274–75.

[30] Deuteronomy 9:1-7. Cf. Georg Braulik, "Die Entstehung der Rechtfertigungslehre in den Bearbeitungsschichten des Buches Deuteronomium: Ein Beitrag zur Klärung der Voraussetzungen paulinischer Theologie," *ThPh* 64 (1989) 321–33.

human poverty and openness for divine activity on the other. Here trust and hope correspond to faith in Paul.

That is especially striking because the psalm that precedes it, Psalm 32, which Psalm 33 continues, is heavily stamped with the theme of "sin" and "forgiveness." We do not have to conclude that a theology counter to that in Psalm 32 is developed here. It could also deal with something like a justification in accordance with the forgiveness of sins.

That can and must be left open, for unfortunately, in this context, no comprehensive interpretation of the psalm can be offered. But this psalm has not yet received the attention it deserves, also and especially by systematic theologians.

II. The Covenant Formula in Ps 33:12

The covenant formula in v. 12 is important for evaluating the psalm's doctrine of justification. Even if in the second strophe it becomes clear that God's determination of human freedom, stemming from the creation events, is specifically directed to individuals, so also, speaking on the basis of the psalm's center-oriented structure, precisely the beginning, middle, and end of the psalm show that God's will to justify is in the last analysis directed toward a "we," toward a "people," not to individual souls. That is also precisely what is expressed by the beatitude that stands at the center of the psalm, the beatitude in whose service the covenant formula functions. Which "people" is in view here? Israel? Ordinarily the psalm is interpreted in this way without a moment's hesitation. But the question must be pursued analytically. For even the form of the covenant formula in Ps 33:12 is already rather different.

1. The Augmentation of the Covenant Formula

In comparison with the basic form of the covenant formula, the version in Ps 33:12 exhibits a whole series of variations. First, the formula is embedded in a beatitude. With respect to the covenant formula in its full form this is unique. The only passage that can be compared with it is Ps 144:15b, where, at the end of a beatitude that first of all carries that particular psalm forward, one half of the covenant formula appears, which at the same time brings the whole psalm to an end. In Ps 33:12 the form of the beatitude might well be most easily explained as a reference to the beginning of the psalm that precedes it, Psalm 32. That psalm opens with two beatitudes about the sinner who has found forgiveness. In contrast to that, here in the center of Psalm 33 another vision is put in the foreground, intentionally it appears. Here the question about sin plays no role. As much as the form of the beatitude signals a climax in the course of the text, it thus also, above all, provides a transverse reference in the context of the Psalter.

It is also contrary to the normal form that in both its members the covenant formula is formulated from the perspective of the human partner in the covenant. But that is also easy to explain. It is made necessary by the decision to use the macarism as the surrounding form. A macarism has to make the ones blessed the subject of the statement.

Since the covenant formula is stated in both of its members from the perspective of the human partner, the parallelism, in addition to the word עם, "people," customarily used in the covenant formula, also is compelled to use the poetic parallel word גוי, "nation." But it is nevertheless surprising that the uncommon word גוי stands in first position. That loosens the close connection to Israel, which normally appears as עם, and strengthens the statement's connection to the totality of the nations of world, which had been spoken of in v. 10, also in the order גוים—עמים, "nations—peoples." A chiastic return of the word-pair would have been completely possible.

Also unnecessary, and in that respect deliberate and significant, is the placement of the asyndetic relative clause בחר לנחלה לו, "(the people whom) he has chosen as his heritage," which is attached to the word עם in the second colon. Here, with reference to the people named in the covenant formula, we have the introduction first of the leading word for "election," and second of the qualification of the people intended as "heritage/inheritance" of the divinity. This combination of words and motifs is unique in the entire Hebrew Bible. That speaks not only for the late origin of the psalm but also for the express desire to bring together diverse traditional Israel-statements, each of which is regarded as characteristic.[31]

The expression בחר לו לנחלה, "to choose something as heritage," occurs in the Hebrew Bible here alone. That already points to the fact that elements of the tradition are connected with one another here that otherwise only exist separately.

[31] One will therefore hardly agree with Horst Seebaß, "בחר," *TDOT* 2 (1977) 73–87, when he offers Ps 33:8-15 (sic!) as the decisive and, strictly speaking, only evidence for his assumption that the statement about the election of Israel originates in the "hymnic tradition." For the only other passage he cites is Psalm 117, but the word בחר does not occur there. Psalm 135:4, likewise a late psalm, he incredibly brushes aside, because only the "servants of YHWH in the outer courts" are addressed. Despite that, however, v. 4 does speak of Israel. But even this text could not support the hypothesis. There are no other examples in hymns.

The statement about the election of Israel (using the term בחר) is found frequently in, and is thus likely typical for, both Deuteronomistic language and Deutero-Isaiah. Beyond that it only occurs in a few other isolated passages.[32]

The designation of Israel as YHWH's "portion, inheritance" could be older. It is also more widely scattered and is frequently found in prayers of supplication. Again it is typical in Deuteronomistic language as well as in the language of the psalms.[33] The references do not overlap with those having statements about election.[34] A formulation that recalls one of the halves of the covenant formula occurs once.[35] In addition, it is striking that a statement about being brought out of Egypt often occurs in the context. In Ps 33:12 that is not the case. Words that are typical of the Exodus tradition, like "bring out" (יצא Hifil) or "redeem" (פדה), are totally absent from Psalm 33, although they certainly could have appeared.[36]

On the whole it can be said that the covenant formula introduced into Ps 33:12 was augmented with statements that traditionally express the special relationship between Israel and YHWH. On the other hand, despite all the enrichment the topic receives, the name Israel does not occur, and there is no mention of historical events that could be spoken of with reference to Israel alone, such as the Exodus. That is at least striking. That the theme of "sin and forgiveness" does not occur in Psalm 33 is, on the other hand, much easier to explain. It was the theme of the preceding psalm. The intention was apparently to expand this psalm by the conscious use of a different aspect of the matter. Even this assumption is confirmed once again by the supplementing of the covenant formula through the

[32] The references are: Deut 4:37; 7:6; 10:15; 14:2; 1 Kgs 3:8; Isa 14:1; 41:8-9; 43:10; 44:1-2; 49:7; Jer 33:24; Ezek 20:5; Pss 33:12; 135:4. Since the Deuteronomic examples are all in late strata, at most 1 Kgs 3:8 could already come from an earlier, pre-exilic Deuteronomistic stratum. Perhaps because of 1 Kgs 3:6 this passage is especially close to Psalm 33.

[33] The references for עם in parallels or in another connection with נחלה are: Deut 4:20; 9:26, 29; 32:9; 1 Kgs 8:51, 53; Isa 19:25; 47:6; 63:17; Joel 2:17; 4:2; Pss 28:9; 33:12; 78:62, 71; 94:5, 14; 106:40. Additional references to the topic but without the word עם are: 1 Sam 10:1; 2 Sam 21:3; 2 Kgs 21:14; Jer 10:16; 12:8-9; 51:19; Mic 7:14, 18; Pss 74:2; 106:5. Particularly some of the narrative texts could be older. On נחלה in the Nagid formula (1 Sam 10:1), cf. Norbert Lohfink, "Beobachtungen zur Geschichte des Ausdrucks עם יהוה," in *Probleme biblischer Theologie: Gerhard von Rad um 70. Geburtstag,* ed. Hans W. Wolff (Munich: Kaiser, 1971) 283–85.

[34] Unless one uses other vocabulary. For statements on election that use other verbs, cf. Deut 32:9; 1 Kgs 8:53. Another word for "possession" (סגלה) is found in Deut 7:6; 14:2; Ps 135:4.

[35] Deut 4:20.

[36] Cf. the occurrences of roots from the same verbal domain that are less typical for the Exodus: ישע, "save" (33:16, 17); נצל, "deliver" (vv. 16, 19); and מלט, "escape" (v. 17).

motif "Israel the inheritance of God." For in the chapter that is central to covenant theology and the theology of the forgiveness of sins, Exodus 34, Moses' plea in v. 9 that the people's sin be forgiven ends with the plea to take the people as an inheritance:

אם־נא מצאתי חן בעיניך אדני
ילך־נא אדני בקרבנו
כי עם־קשה־ערף הוא
וסלחת לעוננו ולחטאתנו
ונחלתנו

"If now I have found favor in your sight, O LORD,
I pray, let the LORD go with us.
Although this is a stiff-necked people,
pardon our iniquity and our sin,
and take us for your inheritance."[37]

So the theme of the "forgiveness of sins" may well be missing in Psalm 33—yet the foundational canonical passage for covenant and forgiveness of sins in Exodus 34 shows that it is near at hand. The absence of the name of Israel and of any reference to Israel's history, on the other hand, requires an explanation.

But first still another suggestion! The statement about the people in the covenant formula is also expanded in Psalms 95 and 100. But the expansion looks different. It goes:

Ps 95:7 עם מרעיתו וצאן ידו
the people of his pasture, and the sheep of his hand
Ps 100:3 עמו וצאן מרעיתו
his people, and the sheep of his pasture

Here the people have become the sheep tended by God. That is an ancient royal metaphor. Thus the metaphor of YHWH as king is introduced into the covenant formula. That is a process analogous to the one that can be seen in Ps 33:12 with the election- and heritage concept. In the light of the assumption, already referred to and to be taken up again later, that the references to the covenant formula in the Psalter possess a redactional connection, the question arises, of course, why a different supplementation of the basic formula was chosen here. One can, of course, answer that a fact of this kind is simply to be accepted by the interpreter. But at least two observations can be made that could show where the explanation lies.

[37] The verb נחל is used here. Therefore the passage does not appear in the list of references given above.

First, the only occurrence of the parallelism of עם and נחלה *prior to* Psalm 33, namely in Ps 28:9 (well known from the *Te Deum*), also contains the verb רעה, "to shepherd."

> הושיעה את־עמך וברך את־נחלתך
>
> ורעם ונשאם עד־העולם
>
> O save your people, and bless your heritage;
> be their shepherd, and carry them forever.

One can thus observe a doling out of the final motifs of Psalm 28 to the different occurrences of the covenant formula.

Secondly, the precise formulation with which the covenant formula in Psalms 95 and 100 is enlarged does not occur until Psalm Book III, but there it becomes a leitmotif.[38] Thus Ps 95:7 could easily pick it up. There could certainly also be the awareness here that in Psalm Book III this terminology is also paired with talk about God's people as God's נחלה, "heritage."[39] Moreover, the talk about YHWH's heritage also plays a role in Psalm 94, which directly precedes Psalm 95 (94:5, 14). Closer inspection thus strengthens rather than weakens the idea that the examples of the covenant formula in the Psalter are connected.

2. *The Detachment of the Covenant Formula from Actual Israel and Its History*

By so massive a recourse to Israel's central traditions as the one that appears in Ps 33:12 in the augmentation of the covenant formula, it is truly astonishing to have to observe the omissions we have mentioned. One sees them more clearly, perhaps, when one observes how interpreters fill them in, by introducing the word "Israel," for example, into the interpretation. Bernhard Duhm does it in an elegantly indirect manner: "V. 12 recalls Deut 33:29."[40] For Deut 33:29 is an explicit beatitude on Israel. Hans-Joachim Kraus is much more explicit:

> Because the "word" and "counsel" of YHWH are known[41] (Ps 76:2), the people that God has chosen are therefore blessed.[42]

Gianfranco Ravasi writes:

> The historical plan of salvation runs its course with reference to a specific people, on whom verse 12 pronounces a blessing (Ps 1:1). And the basis for

[38] Pss 74:1; 77:20 [MT 21]; 78:52, 71-72; 79:13; 80:1 [MT 2].

[39] Cf. Ps 74:1-2; also 78:71-2.

[40] *Die Psalmen,* KHC 14 (Freiburg: Mohr, 1899) 96.

[41] Probably what is meant is: spoken in confessions of faith.

[42] *Psalmen,* 1:413.

> the beatitude is the election *(bḳr)* through which Israel becomes the precious "heritage" of God.[43]

Frank-Lothar Hossfeld and Erich Zenger, who see in the psalm a witness to a more widely developed theology of the poor, also appeal to "the varied covenant formula in 33:12" in order to read a "specific concern for the poor people Israel" in the psalm. They acknowledge, it is true, beyond the usual interpretation, a limit to this orientation to Israel in the psalm, when they immediately add:

> But there is also the possibility that those among the inhabitants of the world who fear God (33:8, 13f.) are included among those who fear God and look to YHWH.[44]

Is that really only a possibility that *also* exists as some kind of addition to the rule? Is the psalm aware of such a distinction between the rule and a marginal addition? It is really astonishing that even where one finds in the psalm one of the latest sections of the Psalter the thought has not grabbed people's attention that the Israel that actually exists is no longer spoken of naïvely. This fact now needs to be looked into.

Signals of the comprehensive, the universal are heard throughout the psalm. Seven times the word כל, "all, entire," occurs.[45] Spatially, the full dimensions of the creation are repeatedly paced off, and not only that, but also temporally the world of the psalm extends from creation's primal past, evoked again and again, to the farthest cosmic (לעולם) and historical human future (לדר ודר—both in v. 11). The negative statements of vv. 10 and 16-17 are all-embracing in their negativity. Even the fact that the number of verses corresponds to the letters of the alphabet contributes to this impression.

Even more interesting is the transformed return of the word חסד, "steadfast love," and the repetition, likewise belonging to this context, of ירא, "fear," and יחל, "hope." According to v. 5 the "earth," that is the entire subsolar realm of the universe, is "full" (מלאה) of YHWH's steadfast love—not only the land of Israel.[46] But how is that actually spelled out? Accord-

[43] *Il libro dei Salmi: Commento e attualizzazione,* 3 vols. (Bologna: Ediioni Dehoniane, 1986) 3:605 (Ravasi's words were translated into German by Lohfink).

[44] Frank-Lothar Hossfeld and Erich Zenger, "'Von seinem Thronsitz schaut er nieder auf alle Bewohner der Erde' (Ps 33:14): Redaktionsgeschichte und Kompositionskritik der Psalmengruppe 25–34, in *"Wer ist wie du, Herr, unter den Göttern?": Studien zur Theologie und Religionsgeschichte Israels für Otto Kaiser zum 70. Geburtstag,* ed. Ingo Kottsieper et al. (Göttingen: Vandenhoeck & Ruprecht, 1994) 387.

[45] Ps 33:4b, 6b, 8a,b, 13b, 14b, 15. The two outer references, by using the same noun, מעשה, form a frame for the sevenfold use.

[46] The commentaries often point to Isa 6:3 as background. That may not be false. But texts such as Gen 6:13; Isa 11:9; Ps 104:24 are even closer, and in these the whole of humanity is even more explicitly in view.

ing to v. 18, those who hope in YHWH's steadfast love are identical with those who fear YHWH. But according to v. 8, once again, it is not the Israelites who are called upon to fear YHWH but "all the earth," "all the inhabitants of the world." At the end of the psalm a "we" takes linguistic form. It is explicitly defined (v. 22b) through hope in YHWH (cf. v. 18) and not, by contrast, through membership in historic Israel. Its prayer is about the enjoyment of YHWH's steadfast love (v. 22a). The entire psalm is given definition through this complex of statements that get by without the name Israel and are clarified through frequent word repetitions.

A widening of perspective might also be created by the verbal phrase שׁיר שׁיר חדשׁ, "sing a new song," right at the beginning of the psalm (Ps 33:3). It was apparently formulated for the first time in Isa 42:10 and belongs already there, beyond the return from Babylon, to the worldwide context of the new message about YHWH's activity among all the nations of the world.[47] That is the full dimension of the "new" that is to be sung. What is the meaning of the phrase in the Psalter? It occurs for the first time in Ps 33:3. Then it is used again in Ps 40:3 [MT 4]. This psalm is found in the concluding section of Psalm Book I, where it recapitulates important statements from that book.[48] Verses 4-5 are full of word and statement connections to Psalm 33, so that in the talk about a new song we probably only have a reference back to Ps 33:3.[49] Then the only references that follow are solely within psalm groups that can be identified with precision. The second of these is the conclusion of the entire Psalter. Here we have the expression in the next-to-last psalm of the final David-Psalter and in the next-to-last psalm of the great concluding Hallel, namely in Pss 144:9 and 149:1. This psalm complex is still later and clearly takes up again the existing motif of the "new song," at least in Ps 149:1 in the fixed frame of the motif about the connection to the nations of the world. That leaves

[47] Cf. now Frank Matheus, *Singt dem Herrn ein neues Lied: Die Hymnen Deuterojesajas,* SBS 141 (Stuttgart: Katholisches Bibelwerk, 1990) 133–42.

[48] Cf. Frank-Lothar Hossfeld and Erich Zenger, "'Selig, wer auf die Armen achtet' (Ps 41:2): Beobachtungen zur Gottesvolk-Theologie des ersten Davidpsalters," *JBTh* 7 (1992) 29–33. The basic monograph on Psalm 40 is Georg Braulik, *Psalm 40 und der Gottesknecht,* FzB 18 (Würzburg: Echter, 1975).

[49] One should also note the past-tense statements found in 40:3 [MT 4]. It is thus directly stated that this is a quotation. Braulik, *Psalm 40,* 109, has already called attention to the fact that this is the only example in which the phrase is not used in a (hymnic) summons. Hossfeld and Zenger, "Selig," 30, n. 19, explain the passage about the "new song" as a redactional contrast to "being silent" in Ps 38:13 [MT 14] and Ps 39:9 [10] (probably that instead of 39:13 [14]): "With the 'new song' YHWH himself has overcome this condition." But can this characteristic phrase be explained simply by appeal to contextual contrasts? The two authors themselves actually say that 40:3a [4a] "could also go back only to the final redaction of the Psalter."

only the group of Psalms 93–100. In this group Psalms 96 and 98 form the innermost circle around the center, Psalm 97, which sings of the revelation of the reign of YHWH before all nations.[50] They both begin with the summons to sing a new song (96:1; 98:1). They both end with the theme of the coming of YHWH to a judgment with צדק, "righteousness," and אמונה, "truth," or מישרים, "equity" (cf. the two almost identical concluding sections 96:11-13 and 98:7-9)—all of this is full of reminiscences of Psalm 33. These connections are specific. They are not explainable on the basis of generally available formal language. The motif of the reordering of the relationship between Israel and the nations stands at the center.

In Ps 33:10 the overthrow of the historical projects of the nations is discussed in the past tense, but when in v. 11 the realization of God's plans is spoken of, the psalm looks into the future. The beatitude spoken over the people chosen by God in v. 12 does, it is true, look back at their being chosen by God in the past. But, precisely also in view of the next three verses, that has more to do with the primal election tied to the creation than with historical events like the Exodus or, especially, the post-exilic rebuilding of the Temple.[51] So there is no backward glance at an election that has already taken place in history, at the departure from Egypt, for example.

A historical event could come into view in v. 16—if the interpretation is correct that this is the negation of a quoted statement. But the alleged rescue of a king (or every conceivable king) is not in any way described as the rescue of a king of Israel. In the light of v. 10, once again it is the nations of the world in general that are more likely in view.

There is another issue. Why is the conceptual pair "righteousness and justice" or the concept of the "fear of God" in Psalm 33 never explained with reference to the Law? In other psalms, including some that precede Psalm 33, that is precisely what happens.

[50] On the layout of this psalm group cf. Erich Zenger, "Israel und Kirche im gemeinsamen Gottesbund: Beobachtungen zum theologischen Programm des 4. Psalmenbuchs (Ps 90–106)," in *Israel und Kirche Heute: Beiträge zum christlichen-jüdischen Dialog: Für Ernst Ludwig Ehrlich,* ed. Marcel Marcus et al. (Freiburg: Herder, 1991) 240–42. There is more on this in chapter 6 of this book.

[51] Without any basis in the text Heinrich Graetz, *Kritischer Commentar zu den Psalmen nebst Text und Uebersetzung,* 2 vols. (Breslau: Schottlaender, 1882–1883) 1:264, writes with reference to Ps 33:10: "Which plans destructive to Israel and which nations has God thwarted? Or, putting it objectively, which plans have been destroyed for Israel's sake and from which side had they come? Probably the reference is to the plans '*of the enemies of Judah and Benjamin,*' who had interrupted the building of the temple and the fortification of the colony that had returned after the Babylonian exile, until Darius issued the permission for these activities, continuing Cyrus' favorable attitude toward the Jewish people. A different time period for this historical presupposition cannot be found."

Nor does an Israel-oriented piety favoring the poor emerge.[52] At the very least the psalm has distanced itself from a possible origin in a theology favoring the poor and ended up in what is much more general and abstract. According to this psalm everyone in the realm of the whole creation needs rescue, even the country that is powerful. The psalm is *not* oriented to an equation of the poor and Israel or the poor and a "true Israel." It would also be completely open to a statement about nations who in the context of the pilgrimage of the nations come to hope in YHWH.

On this basis certain suppositions can now be developed. The psalm frees itself from the concept of a sovereign historical will of God that with certainty favors historical Israel, and it places those who want to share in the "steadfast love of YHWH," which actually fills the whole creation (v. 5), under one norm, namely that of giving up reliance on one's own might and of full hope in YHWH. If one simply applies the statement of the covenant formula in v. 12 in a naïve and unreflective way to actual Israel, then the thesis stated by v. 11, namely, that YHWH's intention and plan are never thwarted, is ultimately called into question. For is the creator so sure of the trust of his actual people Israel? The entire history of Israel contradicts that. On this basis one dare not without further ado presuppose an identity of the "righteous" in this psalm with the actual historical people of Israel.

No other identification is offered. On the contrary, the question remains open who the people of God are that are now associated with the covenant formula. It is not even simply denied that Israel on the one side and the "people of God," "righteous," and "we" on the other are one and the same. It is left up in the air whether the two are the same or not. All that is certain is that YHWH will prepare for himself a people whose God he is and that represents YHWH's heritage in the world. What YHWH intends will happen. That is what the psalm says precisely at its center. And it says it on the basis of Israel's experience and vocabulary. But at the same time the realization of God's goals has its conditions. So the question is with whom YHWH at the end will realize the intended goals, who the people of YHWH's covenant will be. It is the old question that was present already at Sinai as YHWH revealed to Moses the desire to destroy this people and to allow a new and better people to emerge from him, Moses (Exod 32:10;

[52] That is the assumption of Zenger in Hossfeld and Zenger, *Psalmen,* 1:206: The psalm could be "a 'literary' composition of the post-exilic 'piety favoring the poor.'" To support that one could only adduce v. 19, "to keep them alive in famine." Now it is true that the mention of hunger can point to poverty, but here the text sounds as though it is speaking rather about a famine that can strike poor and rich equally. In a psalm that is also so strongly shaped by creation motifs we more likely have a reference to the dependence of all people on the fruitfulness of the earth. In any case, the psalm contains no socio-economic contrast with an opposing group, "the rich." The opposing group is defined differently.

Deut 9:14; cf. Num 14:12). In our psalm the condition for the formation of the covenant people is stated. It is not the observance of the law. The condition is—stated in New Testament terms—"faith": to depend solely on God's steadfast love rather than one's own plan or one's own might.

So the possibility remains open that the chosen people of God is, in the final analysis, not at all identical with the tangible existing Israel. That in turn can be developed in two directions: the first is the idea of a "true Israel" within actual, historical Israel. This is, indeed, the direction of the "theology favoring the poor," which can be developed from many texts, especially also from the psalms. The other direction (which probably presupposes and supplements the first) is in the sense of a participation of the nations (or of people from the nations) in the chosen people of God. The second idea is a theme that, at the level of the redactional linking of the psalms, begins with the concluding section of Psalm 22. It can probably be seen for the last time prior to Psalm 33 in Psalms 25 and 26.[53] Is the theme of the "pilgrimage" of the nations meant to return once more in Psalm 33 as well?

If YHWH, according to Ps 33:10, has overthrown and stood on their heads the counsel and plan of the nations, that does not, of course, mean that YHWH could not prepare new possibilities for them, lying in the direction of his own counsel and his own plan—precisely in the context of the people chosen by YHWH. And on the other hand, when vv. 16-17 say that trusting in might and military power is doomed to fail, that does not, of course, mean that that was done only by the other nations and never within actual Israel. Insofar as people do this, even if outwardly they belong to Israel, they cannot actually belong to the "we" who speak at the end of the psalm.

Since the covenant formula is used for this indeterminative statement, one must conclude that also in Psalm 33 Israel's "covenant" is left open for the nations. It should be noted how this differs from Psalm 25. There (at the level of the final text) a different people, or a suppliant from the nations, prays. The suppliant speaks of Israel's covenant and of being taken up into it. Here in Psalm 33 we have a psalm whose suppliant is by no means so clearly established. The suppliant speaks of a plan of God that is meant for a covenant people that is not simply identical with Israel and that knows a covenant formula that is at least open to participation by non-Israelites.

[53] Cf. chapter 3 above.

3. *Psalm 33 and the Preceding Psalms*

In a thorough analysis of the compositional relationships operative within Psalms 25–34, Frank-Lothar Hossfeld and Erich Zenger have defended the thesis that Psalm 33 occupies a "special position" therein.[54] They say that within the palindromic composition framed by Psalms 25 and 34 and centered in Psalm 29 and already present within the first Psalter of David, Psalm 33 was "inserted after Psalm 32" as a "supplemental commentary,"[55] in the Hellenistic period, perhaps only by "a macro-redaction of the book of Psalms."[56]

There is much in the psalm that favors a post-exilic origin.[57] Observations already made above and the strikingly strong points of contact with Psalm 32 assembled by Hossfeld and Zenger, but also the connections with more distant sections of the Psalter,[58] let it appear at least possible that the psalm was only composed for its insertion into the Psalter, precisely at this location. Erich Zenger, however, cites as evidence that it was originally composed for "use in the official worship in the Temple": (1) the calls for praise in vv. 1-3 that include notations about the use of instruments; (2) the fact that the "hymn" genre, which embraces "teaching," if not actual "dogmatic instruction," also originally requires the worshiping congregation as "Sitz im Leben."[59] But both arguments only allow consequences to be drawn about the origin of the genre, but not the designation of the original purpose of each particular text that conforms to the model of that genre. The character of the psalm as a commentary on much that precedes it, but also the remote points of contact with what is to follow, remain unexplained by such an assumption.

[54] Hossfeld and Zenger, "Thronsitz," 386 (section title).

[55] Ibid., 386.

[56] Ibid., 388. They find support for this in "the similarities with Pss 146–150, but also the points of contact with Ps 90:17 (the beginning of Psalm Book IV) and with Ps 107:41-43 (the beginning of Psalm Book V)" (ibid., n. 44).

[57] Petersen, *Mythos,* 114–15, assembles arguments based on content and terminology.

[58] For the data consult Hossfeld and Zenger, "Thronsitz," 386–87. For the relationships with Psalm 34 see also Auffret, "Allez, fils," 22–27. The psalm also picks up motifs from preceding psalms more strongly than is evident from Hossfeld and Zenger, "Thronsitz," 387, n. 40. Compare, for example, on the keywords "righteousness" and "uprightness" (33:1, 4-5) Ps 11:7; on the purposes of the nations (33:10) Pss 1:1; 20:4 [MT 5]; on God's looking down from heaven (33:13-15) Pss 11:4-7 and 14:2; on the testing of hearts (33:15) Pss 11:4-5; 26:2; on the failure of displays of military might (33:16-17) Ps 20:7-8 [MT 8-9]; on YHWH as "shield" (33:20) Pss 7:10 [MT 11]; 18:2, 30, 35 [MT 3, 31, 36]; 28:7. In all these cases, however, the perspectives are new; indeed, denials are issued for the expectations that have arisen on the basis of similar earlier passages.

[59] Hossfeld and Zenger, *Psalmen,* 1:206.

However, for our synchronic look at the psalm such questions about origin are not to be determinative. On the other hand, it is an urgent question whether the contrast with actual, historical Israel that has been pointed out for the entire psalm, but especially also for the covenant formula in Ps 33:12, represents an extraneous element in the structure of the composition or whether it fits into a larger arc. With regard to this question there are still some things to add in order to supplement the statements by Hossfeld and Zenger.

First of all, since Israel's post-exilic piety favoring the poor normally also implied a relationship to Israel of one kind or another, let it be emphasized again that Psalm 33, although it is probably more recent than the witnesses for the piety favoring the poor that surround it, does not itself belong to these witnesses. A short summary can clarify that.

The psalms about the poor are not distributed equally in the Psalter. This is especially true about Psalm Book I. Terms for poverty are totally absent until Psalm 8, that is, up to the middle of the first compositional unit of Book I (Psalms 3–14).[60] With Psalm 9/10 they begin all of a sudden right in their center and then, with a certain regularity, they also appear in the second compositional unit (Psalms 15–24).[61] The third compositional unit (Psalms 25–34) is then characterized by the fact that the framing psalms (25 and 34) clearly contain the theme about the poor. The terminology about the poor is particularly rich in them, and that is certainly also intended as a hermeneutical presupposition for the interpretation of the final text of the whole psalm group they frame. In the group, that is, within the frame, on the contrary, the orientation of the text to the poor is almost completely absent. The two individual passages that one could name are Ps 31:7 [MT 8] (ראית את־עניי, "you have seen my affliction"—but that is fully explained as a allusion to the Exodus credo) and our passage, Ps 33:19, where only the motif of hunger appears, which also, as explained above, does not necessarily point to a spirituality favorable to the poor. For a synchronic, canonical reading the framing theme about the poor naturally illuminates the whole section within the frame. But then it nevertheless remains that in Psalm 33 the poor—and from that a "poor Israel"—do not become thematic. Insofar as the light of a theology favoring the poor falls on Psalm 33 from the structure in which it is contained, the source of the light is Psalm 25 rather than Psalm 34 that follows it. But in Psalm 25, at

[60] On this layout, cf. Hossfeld and Zenger, "Selig."

[61] Frank-Lothar Hossfeld and Erich Zenger, "'Wer darf hinaufziehn zum Berg JHWHs?': Zur Redaktionsgeschichte und Theologie der Psalmengruppe 15–24," in *Biblische Theologie und gesellschaftlicher Wandel: Für Norbert Lohfink,* ed. Georg Braulik et al. (Freiburg: Herder, 1993) 166–82.

the level of the final text that interests us, the suppliant who belongs to the "nations" finds a place within the propositions about the poor that belong to Israel's piety favoring the poor. Thus, through the possible presence of a theology favoring the poor nothing stands in the way of the psalm's openness to a statement about the covenant relating also to the nations.

But now the decisive question: Has not the theme of the pilgrimage of the nations, which, at the level of the final text was a distinctive feature of the psalms from Psalm 22 on, long since become submerged again after Psalm 26, so that we are dealing once more with prayers solely oriented to Israel? Therefore does not Psalm 33, on this level, project into the Psalter like an extraneous object after all, in the event that it once again breaks the bounds of the long-regained "Israel perspective"? This question needs to be addressed with care precisely with reference to the aspects that have here been placed in the foreground.

For an "Israel perspective" (already brought into the psalm group by an earlier redactional reworking) the only passages that can be cited are the following: Pss 25:22; 28:9; 29:11; 34:22 [MT 23].[62] But if one looks closely, the name "Israel" is found only in Ps 25:22. At the end of the prayer the suppliant from the nations prays also for Israel, to which the suppliant has been drawn. The other passages speak of YHWH's "people" and "heritage" (28:9), of YHWH's "people" (29:11), of YHWH's "servants" (34:22 [23])—all designations that, when theology favoring the poor or the thought about the pilgrimage of the nations are in the air, can be understood in a more restricted or more open manner than we get with a precise focus on the actual people Israel. So one has to ask in what sense, at least on the level of the final text, an "Israel perspective" is present here at all.

In order to set the phenomenon against the proper background, let us give a brief overview of the distribution of the names Israel, Zion, and Jerusalem, as well as of the use of עם, "people," for Israel in the entire Psalter. In order to make the comparison possible, let the Psalter be divided into fifteen groups of ten psalms each:

Psalms	*Israel*	*Zion*	*Jerusalem*	*People*
Pss 1–10	—	3x	—	1x
Pss 11–20	2x	2x	—	2x
Pss 21–30	3x[63]	—	—	4x[64]

[62] That is the formulation of Hossfeld and Zenger, "Thronsitz," 386.

[63] For the last time in Ps 25:22.

[64] References: Pss 22:32 (?); 28:9; 29:11 (2x). Further details have already been given above in the main text.

Psalms	*Israel*	*Zion*	*Jerusalem*	*People-Cont'd*
Pss 31–40	—	—	—	1x[65]
Pss 41–50	2x	4x	—	4x
Pss 51–60	3x	2x	1x	4x
Pss 61–70	5x	2x	1x	3x
Pss 71–80	12x	3x	2x	12x
Pss 81–90	6x	3x	—	9x
Pss 91–100	1x	2x	—	6x
Pss 101–110	4x	3x	1x	9x
Pss 111–120	5x	—	1x	5x
Pss 121–130	8x	4x	5x	1x
Pss 131–140	7x	6x	4x	3x
Pss 141–150	5x	3x	2x	6x

The overview would have to go into much greater detail if one wanted to draw more extensive conclusions. Other names would need to be added: Jacob, Ephraim, Judah, for example. Perhaps Zion and Jerusalem should be taken together. But for the purposes of the questions posed here, the picture that emerges is sufficient. Psalm Book I (Psalms 1–41), as far as an "Israel perspective" is concerned, is clearly different from the rest of the Psalter. And that is true especially of the section that is of interest here, Psalms 25–34. Here we find no clear and tangible "Israel perspective" (not even one produced by redactional supplements alone), supported by appropriate markers, of the kind we find in the rest of the Psalter.

Now there is an obvious explanation for that. We could be dealing here with the earliest collection in the Psalter, onto which the rest crystallized, and this collection came from a core cluster of liturgies of lament and thanksgiving that possibly did not originate in highly structured public worship. They were not concerned with Israel and Jerusalem but with individuals, often also with the king, and with their troubles. But under conditions of this kind the linguistic elements we are looking for are not to be expected.

The information is presumably correct. Nevertheless the question remains why the redactional reworking that undoubtedly occurred here as elsewhere in the Psalter, and by which the prayers of individuals were taken out of their original private context (insofar as there was one), has not introduced also in Psalm Book I a clearer Israel marker.

But the data, at least between Psalms 25 and 33, appear to hold together in that previously the theme of the "pilgrimage of the nations" stood

[65] This one reference is the covenant formula discussed here in 33:12.

in the foreground. From the fact that Psalms 25 and 26, by their connection with Psalm 24, whose keywords they take up, have to be understood as prayers by people from the nations, it does not, of course, follow that all succeeding psalms are assigned the same subject. For that to be the case we would probably require in every case a clearer connection to the immediately preceding psalm or to Psalm 24, lying further and further behind. The sequence of psalms is already going to sink back again to the normal subject, namely praying Israel. Only now it is the case that this Israel no longer consists of Israel alone. The nations that have come to Zion are present or at least they can always be present. They join in the prayer. That is the origin of an openness in these psalms, which shows itself in the fact that there are no markers of an explicit Israel perspective.

But then in a macro-context of this kind the openness of the statements about God's people and the covenant in Ps 33:12 are not only completely understandable but actually required. The psalm merely brings out more clearly what was always potentially present in the preceding series of psalms. Only the concluding doxology of Psalm Book I will bring the people's name "Israel" back once again with emphasis (Ps 41:13 [MT 14]), and that allows Psalm Book II to begin anew, in a sense with a new naïveté about Israel. In this respect, then, for the statement about the taking up of the nations into Israel's covenant with its God, Psalm 33 is a kind of bridge statement to the domain in which the theme is to be treated broadly once more: the psalm group that runs up to Psalm 100.

The perspective developed here for Psalms 25–34 is probably confirmed once more by the fact that the missing Israel perspective is not paralleled by a missing Temple perspective. The Temple plays, as Hossfeld and Zenger correctly emphasize, a major role. It is "the location of the prayed-for or experienced deliverance, because YHWH, the king of the gods and of the world, is present in it (Psalm 29)."[66] But the pilgrimage of the nations leads precisely to the Temple on Zion, and without the Temple this theologoumenon would not exist.

If in Psalms 27 and 28 the theme of "kingship" also maintains its strength, then it is fully possible for Psalm 27 to be spoken also by a king from the nations,[67] or by a Messiah who resides on a Zion visited also by the nations. In Psalm 28 the speaker himself hardly emerges as a king. Only at the end is a prayer for people and "anointed" added (Ps 28:8-9). That, in another form, is a conclusion, with a turning to Israel, similar to the one to be seen already in Ps 25:22.

[66] Hossfeld and Zenger, "Thronsitz," 283.

[67] Would not v. 10a, which, despite existing parallels, makes many interpreters squirm, then acquire an entirely new and profound meaning?

Thus the statement about the possible access of the nations to Israel's covenant with God, which Psalm 25 contains at the level of the final text, is carried forward as something of an open possibility through the strange phrasing of the covenant formula in Ps 33:12. The following chapters will turn to two sections of the Psalter in which the theme is expressly developed once more.

CHAPTER 5

Zion as Mother of the Nations in Psalm 87[1]

With "Zion" and "Jerusalem" important concepts for the religion of Israel are combined, concepts whose roots go back into the pre-Israelite period.[2] As the "mountain of God" and the "city of God," Jerusalem is the place where the most high God resides and is enthroned. It is from here that God keeps cosmic chaos in check. On God's mountain the cosmic assault of the nations comes to naught. Above all Zion is YHWH's "place of appearing" and the "sun of righteousness." The God enthroned on Zion gives the people dwelling in the city of God protection and salvation. In the two preceding chapters it became evident that these qualities of Zion were sought by the nations in the "pilgrimage of the nations." This chapter is intended to develop more fully the theological quality of Zion. In an important study in 1989 Odil Hannes Steck called attention to the fact

> that the city of Jerusalem not infrequently stands in the texts as an entity *sui generis* between YHWH and the inhabitants. . . . Jerusalem/Zion . . . in these texts of the Old Testament . . . is not simply a collective concept for

[1] This chapter is in part dependent on: Erich Zenger, "Zur redaktionsgeschichtlichen Bedeutung der Korachpsalmen," in *Neue Wege der Psalmenforschung: Für Walter Beyerlin,* ed. Klaus Seybold and Erich Zenger, HBS 1 (Freiburg: Herder, 1994) 175–98, and "Die Gotteszeugenschaft des 83. Psalms. Anmerkungen zur pseudotheologischen Ablehnung der sogenannten Fluchpsalmen," in *Und dennoch ist von Gott zu reden. Festchrift für Herbert Vorgrimler,* ed. Matthias Lutz-Bachmann (Freiburg: Herder, 1994) 11–37.

[2] Cf. most recently Othmar Keel, "Fern von Jerusalem. Frühe Jerusalemer Kulttraditionen und ihre Trägerinnen," in *Ort der Begegnung: Festchrift für Laurentius Klein zur Vollendung des 65. Lebensjahres,* ed. Ferdinand Hahn et al., BBB 90 (Bodenheim: Athenäum Hain Hanstein Verlagsgesellschaft, 1993) 439–502.

> the inhabitants, thus an expression for which "population, Israel, people" could be used, but also not simply an expression only for the inanimate land and its buildings. The city as a place surprisingly also has here an active function, acting on and for people. And still more: this quality of having an active function apparently actually increases in that Zion is presented as—and not only by way of comparison like!—a person, as a female person with a two-fold personal relationship: toward YHWH and toward people.[3]

In Psalm 87, read synchronically and contextually, this quality of Zion is opened to the nations of the world: Zion/Jerusalem is YHWH's "beloved" *and* "mother of the nations."

I. YHWH, Zion, and the Nations in Psalm 87

1. A Difficult Psalm—"Audacious to the Point of Incomprehensibility" (Hermann Gunkel)?

That Psalm 87 is relevant for our theme does not go unchallenged. First, this is connected with the Hebrew text of the psalm, which in the opinion of many exegetes is virtually incomprehensible. The ancient versions already document the difficulties through their divergences from their "original."[4] Modern translators and commentators have often tried, by textual transpositions and conjectures, to produce a "readable" text. The great psalm interpreter Hermann Gunkel made a "sleeping copyist" responsible for the difficulties he sees in the transmitted text: "One will have to assume

[3] Odil H. Steck, "Zion als Gelände und Gestalt. Überlegungen zur Wahrnehmung Jerusalems als Stadt und Frau im Alten Testament," *ZThK* 86 (1989) 261–81 (reprint, idem, *Gottesknecht und Zion,* 126–45); cf. also the sketches rich in material about the conceptual connections in the ancient Orient between divinity—city—inhabitants of the city as "children" of the city/divinity by Hermann Spieckermann, "Stadtgott und Gottesstadt. Beobachtungen im Alten Orient und im Alten Testament," *Bib* 73 (1992) 1–31.

[4] The ancient Greek versions (Septuagint, Aquila, Theodotion and Symmachus) already exhibit here for the comparatively short psalm an unusual number of differences that merit a separate discussion. The three most important are: (1) The versions use different time frames in connection with the theme of the psalm (a statement about the present? a vision of the future?); (2) The Septuagint [in which the psalm is Psalm 86] expressly reads in v. 5: μήτηρ Σιων, ἐρεῖ ἄνθρωπος, "Mother Zion, a person (= one) will say," from which many exegetes reconstruct a corresponding Hebrew text, in which the title "mother" was explicitly used: "And to Zion one says, Mother!" In the opinion of other exegetes, whom I join, the reading in the Septuagint is an "interpretation" of the text or a later misreading of an original μὴ τῇ (MH THI) Σιων ἐρεῖ; (3) In v. 7 the Greek versions read "dwelling" (κατοικία) instead of "springs" (Hebrew text). A short but good discussion is offered by Thijs Booij, "Some observations on Psalm LXXXVII," *VT* 37 (1987) 16–25; cf. also Georg Schmuttermayr, "Um Psalm 87 (86):5," *BZ* 7 (1963) 104–10.

that the copyist had first omitted vv. 5c, 6, 7, which were then written in the margin and added in the wrong place, and that, in addition, 1b ended up after 2 and 4ab after 4c." Gunkel therefore transposes and reconstructs as original a psalm with the sequence vv. 2, 1b, 5c, 7, 3, 6, 4c, 4ab, 5ab—with the following evaluation: "Naturally an interpreter decides to shake up the lines like that only with a heavy heart; but the splendid result bears witness to the correctness of the conjecture; in place of the confusion that a sleeping copyist created, we have a thoroughly unified and coherent text."[5]

Already before Gunkel and also after him there were numerous other "shakeups of the text" in order to make Psalm 87 comprehensible.[6] But even after such transpositions, for many the text remains strange and puzzling. Thus Artur Weiser, who postulates the textual sequence vv. 1b, 5b, 2-3, 6, 4, 5a, 7, is of the opinion that the psalm "presents difficulties of exposition as a result of its peculiar character." For the

> language of the poet is anything but flowing. He moulds his brief sentences in such a daring and abrupt manner that only a few characteristic features are thrown into bold relief while their inner connection is left in the dark. The thoughts of the psalm, too, match the peculiar character of its language. It is not possible at first glance to see a consistent thought-sequence. It is left to the reader to find out how the thoughts are related to each other. In my opinion the lack of a visible connection of thought and the peculiar stylistic character of the piece have to be explained in the light of the special

[5] Hermann Gunkel, *Die Psalmen,* HK 2.2 (Göttingen: Vandenhoeck & Ruprecht, 1926) 378.

[6] Cf. the compilation of positions by Booij, "Psalm LXXXVII," 16, n 2. In 1986 (which was prior, of course, to the "new period" of synchronic and canonical exegesis of the psalms) Klaus Seybold recommended the following form of the text in his beautiful introduction, *Die Psalmen. Eine Einführung,* Urban-Taschenbücher 382 (Stuttgart: Kolhammer, 1986):

V. 2 YHWH loves the gates of Zion more than all the dwelling places of Jacob.
V. 1 Its foundation lies upon holy mountains;
V. 5b he himself has established it, the Most High.
V. 4a "I count Rahab and Babylon among my acquaintances,
Philistia and Tyre as well, along with Cush;
V. 5a but to Zion I say: ('Mother'),
and: 'a man was born in it!'"
V. 3 Glorious things are spoken of you, O city of God! Selah.
V. 7 Singers and dancers, all who (sing of) you.
V. 6 YHWH, it is said (among) the nations:
"'This one was born there!' Selah."

He comments on this "shaking up of the text," like Gunkel (see above), as follows: "A reconstruction that has to speak for itself. The mosaic of this psalm of Zion, which has been put together in a new way (and improved partially in accord with the LXX) has an especially beautiful form" (*Die Psalmen,* 68).

> situation to which the psalm presumably owes its origin. The poet finds himself in the Temple of Jerusalem on the occasion of a great pilgrimage-festival. The festal throng moves along in solemn procession, in step with the rhythm of the hymns. People from all over the world pass by before the eyes of the singer. It is as if the whole world had arranged to meet in this place. They have come from the Nile and the Euphrates, from the lands of the Philistines and of the Phoenicians, and even black figures from distant Ethiopia are not absent from this gathering of nations in the house of God on Mount Zion. However much they may differ from each other in language and appearance, they are all united in *one* faith, believing in the *one* God whom they jointly profess. The hymn which they sing (v. 7) impresses itself deeply on the poet's memory; for all of them the Temple of Jerusalem is their home, though cradled in some remote country. In an imaginative picture of almost visionary power, which at a single stroke embraces things near and far, the poet portrays the thoughts which that vision has awaked in him and around which his song has crystallized, thoughts of the majesty of God, who is worshiped by the whole world, and of Jerusalem's importance as the spiritual centre of the world. It must have been an experience of this kind that led to the composition of the psalm. Such a situation would explain equally well the exultation expressed in the hymn of praise, the prophetic element and the link between the descriptive element and the cult; it also makes understandable why the various thoughts, images and stylistic forms are placed side by side without connection.[7]

Today exegesis is correct to view massive textual transpositions of that kind with attitudes that run from skeptical to dismissive. There are actually new studies that to a very large degree preserve the transmitted text and interpret it as meaningful in its entirety.[8] We also want to proceed in this way and likewise examine the psalm, in keeping with the methodological approach employed in our study, in the compositional context of its neighboring psalms. It will be seen that the psalm neither originates from a surge of emotions at a temple festival in Jerusalem nor puts together scraps of thought that are difficult to comprehend. The psalm is rather a post-cultic psalm[9] that programmatically summarizes the theme

[7] Artur Weiser, *The Psalms. A Commentary,* The Old Testament Library (Philadelphia: Westminster, 1962) 579–80.

[8] Booij, "Psalm LXXXVII"; Mark S. Smith, "The Structure of Psalm LXXXVII," *VT* 38 (1988) 357–58; Johanna W. H. Bos, "Psalm 87," *Int* 47 (1993) 281–85.

[9] On this concept, which signals "farewell" to the dominance of genre-historical exegesis of the psalms, cf. Fritz Stolz, *Psalmen im nachkultischen Raum,* ThSt 129 (Zürich: Theologischer Verlag, 1983); Jürgen van Oorschot, "Nachkultische Psalmen und spätbiblische Rollendichtung," *ZAW* 106 (1994) 69–86; on the topic see as well Hans-Peter Mathys, *Dichter und Beter. Theologen aus spätalttestamentlicher Zeit,* OBO 132 (Fribourg: Universitätsverlag; Göttingen: Vandenhoeck & Ruprecht, 1994) 231–51.

"Israel and the nations"; possibly it was actually composed for the "literary" context in which it is now found.

The discussion about the understanding of the psalm as a whole, a controversial issue in research, also has to be decided here on the basis of the contextual connections. Whether the psalm imputes a "theological" citizenship on Zion to the diaspora Jews, individual proselytes, or the nations remains to this day open and contested. Out of the colorful multiplicity of exegetical opinions only a few can be referred to—these also serving to sharpen the problem for our own interpretation.

In the way "critical of the Jews" that was typical of him, Bernhard Duhm writes about our psalm:

> The Jews are totally settled in abroad, everywhere, but they still feel like foreigners there. God pays attention to the nations only insofar as they have Jews in their midst. On the other hand, the diaspora Jews do not have the slightest intention of moving to Palestine and have no need to do that. For them it is sufficient to feel that they are citizens of Zion and of the Temple, and YHWH is also satisfied with that.

Especially since he translates in v. 4 not, "I boast of/number Rahab . . . *among* those who know me," but "I boast of Rahab . . . *on account of/because of* my confessors," he comments on vv. 4-5 as follows: "The countries that are named shelter large Jewish colonies, and that is why YHWH boasts of them or remembers them; of them he says: here, in Tyre, Babylon, etc., this or that Jew was born, which then gives those lands and cities a certain worth. Naturally there is no talk of proselytes."[10]

A classical advocate of the position that *also* enables the proselytes to be included is Hermann Gunkel:

> With a vivid and surprising phrase the second strophe transfers us to heaven, to YHWH himself. God possesses, as the poet envisions it, a "writing" about the peoples, that is, a heavenly register, like those the kings of the earth keep of their subjects (Ezek 13:9) . . . Here it is presupposed that all individuals are entered in God's book, together with a notation about their place of birth. The Israelite religion, which explains this conception in its own way, naturally envisions the pious ones of YHWH who are recorded in this way and thereby expresses the consoling thought that the Most High knows his own.
>
> The author of this poem envisions YHWH making entries in the book; in a sense the author is looking over YHWH's shoulder and overhearing the words YHWH speaks to himself during the writing . . . "This one was born here, and that one over there." God himself must be astounded how many different places God needs to note for those who are his; there are plenty of

[10] Bernhard Duhm, *Die Psalmen,* KHC 14 (Freiburg: Mohr, 1899) 218–19.

> Jews who were born in Babylon and in Egypt! . . . And with proud joy God sees how many faithful ones God has everywhere . . . What the poet actually sees is that in all lands there is a multitude of Jews and proselytes. The poet's boldness . . . concludes that these people "know" YHWH . . . But when Rahab and Babylon receive the honorary title "confessors of Yahweh" in this way, then Zion also dare not be without a name. And this name can be none other than "mother of all"; Zion is the "mother city" (2 Sam 20:19) of all who are hers: "Every single one of them is at home therein": here everyone who holds to YHWH, wherever his or her cradle may have stood, has citizenship, a true home; here the birth is noted once again.

That Psalm 87 is setting forth an eschatological vision is, to be sure, strongly denied by Gunkel: "The idea of the conversion of the Gentiles at the endtime, which many interpreters have brought in here, is quite remote from the psalm, which speaks not about a hope but about the present."[11]

With decisiveness Rudolf Kittel interprets the psalm with reference to proselytes from all over the world:

> The more YHWH found confessors among the Gentiles, the more numerous the children became who were born of those long barren (Isa 55:1; cf. 44:4-5), and the more Jerusalem became the spiritual mother of all nations. The proselytes from among the Gentiles call themselves Zion's children, because they have found here the very best, the knowledge of the true God and community with God as the spiritual midpoint of the world (Isa 2:2ff.). It is quite possible that we have here a pilgrimage song of the proselytes, which they began to sing as they journeyed at festival time to the place of their longing and spiritual new birth.[12]

Friedrich Nötscher at least wants to leave open the universal, eschatological perspective. According to him "it is a question of whether the poet celebrated Jerusalem only as the spiritual home of Israelites and proselytes living in the diaspora at that time, perhaps in the Persian period, or whether the poet wants to announce the conversion of Gentiles in the messianic or eschatological time of salvation. With the known lack of prophetic perspective, perhaps the two are not to be kept apart."[13]

In contrast to this, Alfons Deissler sees the universal line drawn out clearly in this psalm:

> Psalm 87 is a song of Zion (cf. Psalms 46; 48; 132) with an eschatological outlook and with a remarkable universal breadth . . . The people from Egypt and Babylon, from West and East, those from nearby Canaan and from far-

[11] Gunkel, *Psalmen,* 379–80.

[12] Rudolf Kittel, *Die Psalmen, übersetzt und erklärt,* KAT XIII (Leipzig: Deichert-Scholl, 1929) 289.

[13] Friedrich Nötscher, *Das Buch der Psalmen,* EB 4 (Würzburg: Echter, 1959) 192.

> off Ethiopia, have the same place of birth written in their birth certificate—Jerusalem. That is true first of all of diaspora Jews, who make up entire colonies in foreign lands (for example, Elephantine near Aswan in Upper Egypt), as well as proselytes in the narrower as well as the wider senses (= the God-fearers), with whom we may reckon ever more strongly in the post-exilic period. For them all Jerusalem is the city of YHWH, their covenant God. The solemn word from God, however, surely reaches out more widely and into the future. It becomes an echo of Zech 2:11 [MT 15]: "Many nations shall join themselves to the LORD on that day, and shall be my people; and I will dwell in your midst" (cf. Isa 2:2ff. and 60:1ff.) and of Isa. 19:23ff.: "the Egyptians will worship with the Assyrians. On that day Israel will be the third with Egypt and Assyria, a blessing in the midst of the earth, whom the LORD of hosts has blessed, saying, 'Blessed be Egypt my people, and Assyria the work of my hands, and Israel my heritage.'"
>
> . . . Verse 6 expresses the same thing in a new, if related image: As in Isa 4:3 and Ezek 13:9 YHWH draws up a list of citizens for Jerusalem in the time of salvation, which is also the "book of life" (cf. Isa 4:3; Ps 69:28 [MT 29]; Exod 32:32; Dan 12:1; Mal 3:16), and enters therein the nations, or their remnant rescued from the catastrophes (cf. Zech 9:7). The concluding verse views them at worship as singers (cf. 2 Chr 5:12) and dancers (cf. 2 Sam 6:14 . . .). Here Jer 31:4 finds a universal fulfillment: "O virgin Israel! Again you shall take your tambourines, and go forth in the dance of the merrymakers" (cf. Jer 31:13).[14]

Against universalistic interpretations of that kind, which, incidentally, have been advocated more frequently in recent years,[15] there have also been sharp protests—not least in the name of an alleged Proprium Christianum *and* of the special call of Israel. This is what Évode Beaucamp thinks in his commentary on the psalms: Whoever brings the perspective on the nations into Psalm 87 forgets that it is only Jesus' death on the cross that has actually brought about the universality of salvation: "It is therefore wrong in this regard to look for any kind of anticipation already in the Old Testament. Israel did not have the possibility or the right to renounce the (singular) privilege that its covenant God had imposed on it."[16]

[14] Alfons Deissler, *Die Psalmen. II. Teil (Ps 42–89),* KK1/2 (Düsseldorf: Patmos, 1964) 171–72.

[15] Most recently, and especially impressive: Luis Alonso-Schökel and Cecilia Carniti, *Salmos II (Salmos 73–150). Traducción, introducciones y comentario,* Nueva biblia Española (Estella: Editorial Verbo Divino, 1993) 1121–29 (with an ecclesiological "rereading," unfortunately without reference to Jewish-Christian relations); James L. Mays, *Psalms,* Interpretation. A Bible Commentary for Preaching and Teaching (Louisville: John Knox, 1994) 280–82.

[16] Évode Beaucamp, *Le Psautier: Ps 73–150,* SBi (Paris: Gabalda, 1979) 76 (German translation by Erich Zenger).

Also, according to Beaucamp, the universalistic vision that makes Zion into God's center for all nations cannot find any support from the text of Psalm 87. He divides the psalm into two sections, vv. 1-4 and vv. 5-7. The section vv. 1-4 contains the divine oracle in v. 4, which YHWH proclaims to the faithful from among YHWH's people. This oracle has its explosiveness precisely in the face of the overthrow of Jerusalem announced in the deuteronomistic theology of judgment, against which Psalm 87 affirms: YHWH remains faithful to the election, in that YHWH loves Zion (cf. Ps 78:68-69). In v. 4a YHWH reminds "the worshipers" of the two great proofs of YHWH's love: "I remind those who know me of Egypt and Babylon," that is, of the first and second Exodus! And YHWH proclaims, by taking up images of salvation from Deutero-Isaiah, that "the nations" are coming to Zion to pay homage and bring gifts to YHWH or to YHWH's people dwelling on Zion (cf. Isa 45:14-16). This homage by the nations is not an acknowledgment of YHWH as God of the nations but the other side of that coin that is meant to bring the people of Zion salvation and peace.

Even the most recent extensive study of Psalm 87 by Andreas Stadelmann pleads for a "narrow," downright particularistic interpretation. Stadelmann first surprises us with a "universalistic" interpretation of the places of Jacob named in v. 2: "There is no doubt that v. 2 is envisioning places for authentic worship of YHWH outside of Jerusalem. But these no longer exist at the time of the Korahites within the borders of the ancient tribal territories. What do exist are living congregations of YHWH living more or less distant from Zion-Jerusalem. The poet evidently has such worshipers of YHWH in mind; wherever they live and gather in houses of prayer, there is *Jacob* (in a national and religious sense)." That "Jacob" at the time of the Korahites had settled down in Egypt and in Babylon, in Philistia and in Phoenicia is, according to Stadelmann, the first important message of our psalm, which it proclaims in v. 4: "*Jacob* as a national and religious entity has taken up residence as far as the end of the world (Cush)." The theme of Psalm 87 is not the relationship of Israel to the nations, but the relationship of this entity "Jacob" to God's city Jerusalem or Zion: "It is about . . . the actual presence of YHWH in Zion-Jerusalem and about those faithful to YHWH who are scattered to the four winds." That is shown in Stadelmann's view precisely by a comparison of our psalm with the prophetic texts that arose at the same time as Psalm 87. He summarizes the results of his study as follows:

> If one examines Psalm 87 with the Persian period as the background, when prophetic eschatology and early apocalypticism played a significant role, one must classify this psalm, probably the purest song of Zion in the Psalter, as decidedly unprophetic and uneschatological, even as anti-eschatological

in orientation. H. Gunkel's understanding, according to which the idea of the conversion of the Gentiles at the endtime is thoroughly foreign to the psalm, since it does not speak about a hope but talks about the present, is still to be given full assent. Psalm 87 is about pilgrims who are true to YHWH, who are already there, staying precisely in Zion-Jerusalem or still going to come (back). The Korahites are not interested in the nations, but continue to advocate a nationalistically and confessionally oriented theology. There is no trace of missionary zeal or of a special regard for proselytes. . . . One can also scarcely agree with the view of R. Sorg, that the psalm represents a spirit that bursts the bounds of the exclusive and monolithic narrowness of the restoration under Ezra; rather it is the opposite view that is correct. This praise for Zion reproduces the feelings that diaspora Jews entertain toward Zion-Jerusalem . . . Psalm 87 bears a nationalistic stamp and it is basically intended for the adherents of the religion of YHWH.[17]

2. *The Plan of Psalm 87*

It is true that the ancient versions apparently already had difficulties in understanding the psalm, as is shown by their divergences from one another and especially their differences from the Masoretic text document. But it is completely possible to preserve, to a large extent, the transmitted Hebrew text—and to make good sense of it. If one becomes free of genre criticism's postulates—which hold that the psalm has to have a liturgical Sitz-im-Leben and be structured accordingly—an astonishingly artful structure emerges for the text and its images, as the following diagram can show:[18]

Psalm 87

1a Of the Korahites. A Psalm. A Song

1b Its foundation on holy mountains

2a is loved by YHWH,

[17] Andreas Stadelmann, "Psalm 87 (86)—Theologischer Gehalt und gesellschaftliche Wirkung," in *Ein Gott, eine Offenbarung: Beiträge zur biblischen Exegese, Theologie und Spiritualität: Festschrift für Notker Füglister OSB zum 60. Geburtstag,* ed. Friedrich V. Reiterer (Würzburg: Echter, 1991) 333–56; Sorg's essay cited by Stadelmann is Rembert Sorg, *Ecumenic Psalm 87. Original Form and Two Rereadings,* with an Appendix of Psalm 110,3 (Fifield, Wis.: King of Martyrs Priory, 1969).

[18] On this structure cf. Gianfranco Ravasi, *Il libro dei Salmi: Commento e attualizzazione,* 3 vols. (Bologna: Edizioni Dehoniane, 1986) 796–97; Booij, "Psalm LXXXVII," 22–25 (divided, it is true, 1-2, 3-5, 6-7); Smith, "Psalm LXXXVII" (divided 1-2, 3-7).

2b the gates of Zion
2c more than all the dwellings of Jacob.

3a Glorious things are said *in/by you,*
3b city of God. [*Selah*]

4a "I list Rahab and Babylon among those who know me,
4b behold, Philistia also, and Tyre, along with Cush:
4c *this one was born there.*"
5a Yes, to Zion is said:
5b "*Every single one was born in/of it.*
5c Yes, he has equipped it, the Most High."
6a YHWH counts them off,
6b when he registers the nations:
6c "*This one was born there.*" [*Selah*]

7a They sing and dance:
7b "All my springs are *in/from you.*"

If one reads this psalm in accord with the directions to the reader offered at its start, the psalm wants to present poetically YHWH's special love for Zion.[19] But in that case the controversial exegetical question of the identity of the speaker of the birth proclamations quoted in direct address in vv. 4-6 has essentially been already answered: it is YHWH himself, as v. 6 indeed also says unmistakably. Thus vv. 4-6 are shown to be the central section of the psalm. It is organized concentrically, to which two structural forms point:

1) The order of the three birth proclamations is organized according to the scheme ABA:

A	This one	was born there (v. 4)
B	Every single one	was born in it (v. 5)
A	This one	was born there (v. 6)

2) With respect to the motif, v. 4 and v. 6 form a frame *(inclusio)*; in both verses the image of YHWH who registers the nations stands in the background.

[19] It is debated in the commentaries whether one should read v. 1b as an independent noun clause ("Its foundation rests on holy mountains"); in that case, of course, the pronominal suffix is at first indefinite. I prefer understanding 1b to be a "*casus-pendens* construction" or as having its emphasis on the object placed at the beginning.

Around this middle section lie the two sections vv. 1b-3b and v. 7. They are related to one another through the words "in you" (vv. 3a and 7b); through these words they are also interwoven with the center of the psalm in v. 5b. This division of Psalm 87 into three parts that we have sketched is also indicated and confirmed by the verbal signal "Selah" (סלה) that stands at the end of vv. 3 and 6.

It can be considered whether in the first section vv. 1b-2c are again structurally separated from v. 3ab, since v. 3 addresses the city of God in the second person while vv. 1b-2 speak about Zion in the third person. Then vv. 1b-2 would present the theme of the psalm, which is then developed in the actual body of the psalm, vv. 3-7.

The two outer sections (vv. 1-3 and v. 7) agree in their pictorial and conceptual world, which is typical of Zion theology. Zion is the city of God located on the "holy mountain," which is both the cosmic mountain of the world and the mountain of paradise, in which YHWH is enthroned and dwells as king of the world and God of all-encompassing *shalom*. That in the midst of this city, or in the midst of the palace/temple of the God who dwells within it, the "springs of life" gush forth, belongs constitutively to this conception.[20]

When v. 2b mentions "the gates of Zion," several connotations can be present. As demonstrated by ancient oriental iconography and many comparable texts, the city gates are peculiar to a city, to whose characteristics, in contrast to a village, the city wall, with its gate or gates, specifically belongs.[21] By metonymy "the gates of Zion" can, of course, also call the Temple precincts to mind. The ordering of justice and life established and proclaimed by YHWH is connected with "the gates" of the Temple.[22] The two outer sections, then, sing about the significance of Zion as location and source of universal righteousness. On the basis of the surface structure of the psalm it is hard to decide who the speaker of the section in vv. 1b-3 is.

[20] Cf. especially Ps 46:4 [MT 5]; Ezek 47:1-12; Joel 4:18; Zech 13:1; 14:8, but also Gen 2:10-14. Whether we have here an allusion to the early Jewish topos of Sinai/Horeb as the "fountainhead" of the torah (cf. only Exod 17:6) cannot be discussed further here.

[21] Cf. Christoph Uehlinger, "'Zeichne eine Stadt . . . und belagere sie!' Bild und Wort in einer Zeichenhandlung Ezechiels gegen Jerusalem (Ez 4f)," in *Jerusalem. Texte—Bilder—Steine. Zum 100. Geburtstag von Hildi und Othmar Keel-Leu,* ed. Max Küchler and Christoph Uehlinger, NTOA 6 (Fribourg: Universitätsverlag; Göttingen: Vandenhoeck & Ruprecht, 1987) 153–72.

[22] On the Temple gates as "gates of righteousness" and the "conditions for entrance"/"entrance liturgies" cf., among others, Sigurdur Ö. Steingrimsson, *Tor der Gerechtigkeit: Eine literaturwissenschaftliche Untersuchung der sogenannten Einzugsliturgien im AT: Ps 15; 24:3-5 und Jes 33:14-16,* ATSAT 22 (St. Ottilien: EOS, 1984) 134–39; Walter Beyerlin, *Weisheitlich-kultische Heilsordnung. Studien zum 15. Psalm,* BThSt 9 (Neukirchen-Vluyn: Neukirchener Verlag, 1985) 90–97; as well as chapter 3 on Psalm 24 above.

The speaker of the quote in v. 7b is "the nations" who are referred to in the middle section, vv. 4-6.

The middle section (vv. 4-6) is thoroughly stamped by the image that YHWH confers citizenship in the city of God on the members of the many nations, in that YHWH enters them in the "citizenship rolls." Whether the conception of the heavenly book of life and fate, attested elsewhere in the ancient Near East, stands in the background here,[23] or whether the registration of the members' names that comes up in connection with the institution of the citizen-temple-congregation[24] supplied the idea (more likely in my view) is of secondary importance. More important is the determination that YHWH here accords to those who belong to the two great traditional enemy powers Egypt (Rahab) and Babylon, as well as to the lands of Philistia, Phoenicia, and Cush, in a legally binding way (with rights and obligations), a personal connection to Zion.

The enumeration of the five names is not meant exclusively. Rather the whole earth is in view, as Zion is proclaimed as its midpoint ("navel"). The four names that are mentioned mark the four compass points, West (Egypt), East (Babylon), North (Philistia and Tyre), and South (Cush). In this geographical/spatial perspective Zion is a place. On the other hand, in the middle of the psalm thoroughly personal notes are sounded, which view Zion as woman and mother. This multivalence of Zion as place and Zion as woman corresponds to the metamorphosis of Zion from territory to person or from the city as place to the city as woman in Isaiah.[25] While Zion is depicted as mother of the Israelites in Isa 54:1-10 and 66:7-14, this metaphor is expanded here to Zion as mother of the nations—not, of course, through "natural" birth, but through YHWH's own determination and election. On the basis of the themes stated in vv. 1-2 it is important to note that YHWH gives the nations to Zion as "children" because YHWH loves Zion.

The vision of a rootage of the nations in Zion sketched in Psalm 87 comes close to the eschatological vision depicted in Zech 2:10-12 [MT

[23] Cf. Erich Zenger, "Ps 87:6 und die Tafeln vom Sinai," in *Wort, Lied und Gottesspruch, II: Beiträge zu Psalmen und Propheten. Festschrift für Joseph Ziegler,* ed. Josef Schreiner, fzb 2 (Würzburg: Echter, 1972).

[24] On this cf. Isa 4:3 and Ezek 13:9, but also Ezek 32:32. Basic on citizen-temple-congregation are the numerous works by Joel P. Weinberg; cf. especially "Demographische Notizen zur Geschichte der nachexilischen Gemeinde in Juda," *Klio* 54 (1972) 45–49; "Das Beit ʾAbot im 6.-4. Jahrhundert v.u.Z.," *VT* 23 (1973) 400–14; "Die Agrarverhältnisse in der Bürger-Tempel-Gemeinde der Achämenidenzeit," *AAH* 22 (1974) 473–86.

[25] Cf. Steck, "Zion als Gebäude und Gestalt," 133–44; on Zion as a mother who bears, raises, and cares for children see especially Isa 49:22; 51:18; 54:1, as well as the entire textual context of Isaiah 60–61 and the book of Lamentations. The topos of Zion as mother, in my opinion, also lies in the background of Ps 8:2 [MT 3]; cf. Frank-Lothar Hossfeld and Erich Zenger, *Die Psalmen I: Psalm 1–50,* Die Neue Echter Bibel 29 (Würzburg: Echter, 1993) 79.

14-16]; the order of the thematic elements runs counter to each other in the two texts, as our diagram shows:

Zech 2:10-12 [MT 14-16]		Psalm 87
V. 10 [14]	Sing and rejoice, O daughter Zion! For lo, I will come and dwell in your midst, says the LORD.	V. 7
V. 11 [15]	Many nations shall join themselves to the LORD on that day, and shall be my people; and I will dwell in your midst. . . .	Vv. 4-6
V. 12 [16]	The LORD will inherit Judah as his portion in the holy land, and will again choose Jerusalem.	V. 2

The plan sketched in Psalm 87 in multi-perspective imagery only obtains its specific profile from the context for which it was created. On the basis of this context the question of its (epochal) time of origin can also be addressed. The context of Psalm 87 is, first, the group of Korah psalms; second, Psalm 87 must be read from the perspective of Psalm 83 (or of the group of Asaph psalms, 73–83, which concludes with Psalm 83), since it is drawn up as a psalm of contrast to it. Looking at the other Korah psalms will help us to understand the structurally difficult colon Ps 87:5c. Looking at Psalm 83 can make it clear that the five nations or place names presented in Ps 87:4 are by no means meant to designate the diaspora Jews living there but emblemtically designate the totality of the (enemy) nations.

II. Psalm 87 in the Context of the Korah Psalms

The Korah psalms are located together in two groups in the book of Psalms: Psalms 42–49 and 84–85, 87–88. It is uncertain whether Psalm 89 should also be regarded as a Korah psalm; it is true that the notation "of the Korahites" is lacking in the title, but it has in common with its predecessor, Psalm 88, which is identified as a Korah psalm, the attribution "A Maskil of . . . the Ezrahite." On the level of the composition of the book of Psalms, the Korah psalms occupy a significant place: Psalms 42–49 open Psalm Book II (42–72); Psalms 84–88, 89 close Psalm Book III (73–89).

1. Classifying the Psalm Titles

Even if the (secondary) psalm titles as a whole still present a problem investigators have not resolved, a classification scheme can be observed with respect to these psalms, as a look at the following table of the titles of the Korah psalms shows:[26]

Psalm 42	To the leader. A Maskil of the Korahites.
Psalm 43	
Psalm 44	To the leader. Of the Korahites. A Maskil.
Psalm 45	To the leader: according to Lilies. Of the Korahites. A Maskil. A Love Song.
Psalm 46	To the leader. Of the Korahites. According to Alamoth. A Song.
Psalm 47	To the leader. Of the Korahites. A Psalm.
Psalm 48	A Song. A Psalm of the Korahites.
Psalm 49	To the leader. Of the Korahites. A Psalm.
Psalm 84	To the leader: according to the Gittith. Of the Korahites. A Psalm.
Psalm 85	To the leader. Of the Korahites. A Psalm.
[Psalm 86]	A Prayer of David.
Psalm 87	Of the Korahites. A Psalm. A Song.
Psalm 88	A Song. A Psalm of the Korahites. To the leader: according to Mahalath Leannoth. A Maskil of Heman the Ezrahite.
Psalm 89A	Maskil of Ethan the Ezrahite.

[26] On the hermeneutical relevance of the psalm titles cf. also Erich Zenger, "Kanonische Psalmenauslegung," 407–409. The titles are as a rule not only a reflection of the process of composition of the component parts of the book of Psalms, often corroborating the results gained through redaction-critical analyses with respect to the stages of growth of the component parts or the Psalter as a whole (a simple example: the diverse title systems in the Psalm Books, 3–41, 42–72, 73–89 and 90–106, 107–150, as well as the diverse "classification" in comparison with the two "David collections," 3–41, 51–72), but they often also provide important information for the interpretation of a particular individual psalm in the context of what the redaction process envisions as its "neighboring psalms" (for example, Psalm 30 in its relationship to Psalm 29; the small group 65–68 in its location with respect to the small groups 52–55, 56–60, 61–64, etc.).

The titles, varied in details, on a purely statistical basis permit the recognition of a form that intends a numerical symbolism. "Psalm" (מזמור) occurs seven times, "song" (שׁיר) five times, "Maskil" (משׂכיל) three times. If the tradition attested by the greater number of manuscripts is respected, according to which Psalms 42 and 43—read by critical exegesis as a unity—were originally to be read as two psalms (actually as "twin psalms"),[27] there are a total of twelve Korah psalms—corresponding to the twelve Asaph psalms, 50, 73–83.[28] In the event Psalm 89 is regarded as a Korah psalm, we also have the number twelve on the level of the existing text. It is possible that the title over Psalm 43 was omitted when Psalm 89 was added to the composition.[29]

On the basis of the title, Psalms 42 and 44 belong together, since in them alone the three elements appear, "To the leader. A Maskil. Of the Korahites." It is true that these three elements also occur in Psalm 45, which thereby, on the one hand, presents itself as an addition to Psalms 42–44. On the other hand, the title of Psalm 45 contains additional elements that place it in the group 45–48.

First, the four Psalms 45–48 are to be arranged in pairs. Psalms 45 and 46 are connected through designations containing the word "Song," שׁיר, and through a musical direction introduced by "according to," על. Psalms 47 and 48 belong together on the basis of the shared designation "Psalm," מזמור. That a break is intended at 48 is indicated by the special form of its title. For one thing, in distinction to 47 it has in addition to "Psalm," מזמור, the notation "Song," שׁיר. In addition, Psalm 48 does not have the phrase "To the leader," למנצח.

It is true that Psalm 49 has a title identical with that in Psalm 47, but it is set apart from the group 45–48 because of the unique title in Psalm 48 that designates Psalms 45–48 as a group.

Psalms 84 and 85, 86 and 87 are again arranged in pairs: 84 and 85 have in common the designation "Psalm." Psalms 84–85 and 87–88 are put into a group that belongs together by the technical musical direction given in the two bracketing Psalms, 84 and 88: "According to . . . ," על + x.

[27] A compilation of arguments that Psalms 42 and 43 belong together compositionally is found in Hossfeld and Zenger, *Psalmen I,* 265. A counterview is, to be sure, offered by Matthias Millard, *Die Komposition des Psalters. Ein formgeschichtlicher Ansatz,* FAT 9 (Tübingen: Mohr, 1994) 12: "Since the majority of manuscripts understand Psalm 43 to be separate from Psalm 42, despite the nearness of the two psalms, and since this, from a text-critical perspective, is the more difficult reading, it appears to me that the more likely solution is that Psalm 42 was originally independent of Psalm 43."

[28] Is the rivalry of the two groups transmitting these psalms (whoever they are) mirrored in the number twelve shared by both collections?

[29] During the formulation of the "messianic Psalter," Psalms 2–89; on this, see below.

Psalm 88 is oriented back to the beginning of the first series of the Korah psalms with the supplementary designation "Maskil," מַשְׂכִּיל, in its title. In addition, the element "Maskil," מַשְׂכִּיל, and the notation "of the Ezrahite," הָאֶזְרָחִי, point to Psalm 89.

2. A Common Linguistic and Theological Profile

That the Korah psalms, analogously to the Asaph psalms, have a common linguistic profile and shared motifs, which point to their origin and to transmission in a common spiritual home, is a widely shared scholarly consensus. In taking up and extending observations of earlier exegesis we can list the following characteristics by which the Korah psalms are distinguished from other psalms in the Psalter:[30]

God is called the "living God," אֵל־חָי, only in Pss 42:2 [MT 3] and 84:2 [MT 3] in the entire Psalter. In the rest of the Old Testament the term occurs only in Hos 2:1 and Jos 3:1.

It is true that the concept of the face of YHWH, connected with cultic connotations, is found many times also in the rest of the Psalter, but it is found in the Korah psalms in a striking or even unique manner. Text-critically difficult is the concept of the "saving face" of God[31] that is possibly intended in the refrain of Psalm(s) 42/43 (42:5, 11 [MT 6, 12]; 43:5). Here we have a connection of the face of God with the conceptual field of the root "rescue/salvation," ישׁע, frequently found in the Korah psalms. Strikingly we find in Pss 44:24 and 88:14 [MT 25 and 15] the reproach to God, "you hide your face." Rare in the Psalter is the combination attested in 42:2 [3] "to appear before God's face" (ראה Niphal + face of God), which other-

[30] Cf. especially Gunther Wanke, *Die Zionstheologie der Korachiten in ihrem traditionsgeschichtlichen Zusammenhang,* BZAW 97 (Berlin: de Gruyter, 1966) 1–38; Michael D. Goulder, *The Psalms of the Sons of Korah,* JSOT.SS 20 (Sheffield: JSOT Press, 1982) 3–7; Uwe Sperling, *Das theophanische Jahwe-Überlegenheitslied. Forschungsbericht und gattungskritische Untersuchung der sogenannten Zionlieder,* EHS XXIII.426 (Frankfurt: Peter Lang, 1993) 309–81; Sidney Kelly, "The Zion-Victory Songs: Psalms 46, 48, and 76. A Critical Study of Modern Methods of Psalmic Interpretation" (Dissertation Vanderbilt University, Nashville, 1968) studies only Psalms 46, 48, and 76; the question about the difference between the two Korah psalms, 46 and 48, and the Asaph psalm, 76, receives too brief a treatment. John Goldingay, *Songs from a Strange Land. Psalms 42–54,* The Bible Speaks Today (Downers Grove, Ill.: InterVarsity Press, 1978) offers (almost) nothing for the question we are discussing.

[31] For one thing, this reading adds אלהי (from 42:6 [MT 7]) to 42:5 [6], in 42:5 [6] changes פניו (from 42:11 [MT 12] and 43:5) into פני, and eliminates the syndetic ואלהי (from 42:6 [7]) in 42:11 [12] and 43:5. Peter Craigie, *Psalms 1–50,* WBC 19 (Waco, Tex.: Word Books, 1983) 324, for example, also sees it this way.

wise occurs in the context of cultic stipulations (for example, Exod 23:15, 17; 34:20, 23 and frequently); it is taken up once again in Ps 84:7 [MT 8].

The word "soul" (נפש) with the connotation of urgent longing is also quite typical of the language of the psalms, but in the Korah psalms there is a heaping up of "soul" references (42/43 frequently; 44:25 [26]; 49:8, 15, 18 [9, 15, (19)]; 84:2 [3]; 88:3, 14 [4, 15]).

The noun לחץ as a designation of "oppression" by enemies occurs in the Psalter only in 42:9 [MT 10]; 43:2; 44:24 [25].

"Dwelling places/dwellings," משכנות, as a designation of God's dwelling occurs in 43:3; 56:4 [5]; 84:1 [2]; 87:2; by contrast the graves of the dead are also called "dwelling places," משכנות, in 49:11 [12].

As a designation for the people of God the proper name Israel is never used in the Korah psalms; what is found is only the proper name Jacob (cf. Jacob: 44:4; 47:4; 85:1 [MT 5, 5, 2]; 87:2; the God of Jacob: 46:7, 11 [MT 8, 12]; 84:8 [9]. In contrast to this the Asaph psalms use Israel, Jacob, and Joseph.[32] The self-designation of Israel as the "people of YHWH," עם יהוה, quite typical for the Asaph psalms, occurs in the Korah psalms only in 44:12 [13]; 85:2, 6 [3, 7]—in passages that are dependent redactionally on the Asaph psalms.[33]

The divine name "YHWH Sabaoth/LORD of hosts," יהוה צבאות, is found in the Psalter only eight times, six of them in the Korah psalms: 46:7, 11 [MT 8, 12]; 48:8 [9]; 84:1, 3, 12 [2, 4, 13]. The other two occurrences are 24:10 and 69:6 [7]. The long form "LORD God of hosts," יהוה אלהים צבאות, appears in 84:8 [9] and outside the Korah collection also in 59:5 [6]; 80:4, 19 [5, 20]; 89:8 [9]. In addition, in 80:7, 14 [8, 15] one finds the combination "God of hosts," אלהים צבאות.

Characteristic, though not typical for the Korah psalms are the designations for God "El/God," אל (42:1, 8, 9 [MT 2, 9, 10]; 43:4; 44:20 [21]; 84:3; 85:8 [9]) and "Most High," עליון (46:4 [5]; 47:2 [3]; 87:5).

[32] Israel: 50:7; 73:1; 76:1 [2]; 78:5; 80:1 [2]; 81:4, 8, 11, 13 [5, 9, 12, 14]; 83:4 [5]. Jacob: 75:9 [10]; 76:6 [7]; 77:15 [16]; 78:5, 21, 71; 79:7; 81:1, 4 [2, 5]; Joseph: 77:15 [16]; 78:67; 80:1 [2]; 81:5 [6]. The proper names Ephraim (78:9, 67; 80:2 [3]), Benjamin, and Manasseh (80:2 [3]) also do not occur in the Korah psalms.

[33] Israel as the "people of YHWH" in the Asaph psalms: 50:4, 7; 77:15, 20 [16, 21]; 78:20, 52, 62, 71; 79:13; 80:4 [5]; 81:8, 11, 13 [9, 12, 14]. On 44:12 [13] as a part of the post-exilic continuation of the pre-exilic basic Psalm 44:1-8 [2-9] cf. Hossfeld and Zenger, *Psalmen 1*, 271–72. The theological proximity of the continuation, 44:9-26 [10-27], to the Asaph psalms is shown especially in 44:13 [14] (cf. 79:4; 80:6 [7]); 44:17 [18] (cf. 50:5); 44:20 [21] (cf. 50:7, 22; 81:9-10 [10-11]); 44:23 [24] (cf. 74:1; 77:7 [8]; 80:2 [3]); 44:26 [27] (cf. 82:8). On Psalm 85 as a "more recent" Korah psalm, which belongs to the "continuation" of the Elohist Psalter, 42–83, see below.

The word combination "city of Elohim," עיר־(ה)אלהים, occurs in the Old Testament only in 46:4 [5]; 48:1, 8 [MT 2, 9]; 87:3. In addition, "city of YHWH Sabaoth/city of the LORD of hosts," עיר־יהוה צבאות, occurs in 48:8 [9]. The combination "city of YHWH/city of the LORD," עיר־יהוה, is used only Ps 101:8 and Isa 60:14.

"Shield," מגן, as a metonym for king, is found in the Old Testament only in the Korah psalms 47:9 and 84:9 [10, 10] (and, dependent thereon, 89:18 [19]).

The relatively infrequent examples of being "cast off" (זנח) by God are also concentrated in the Asaph and Korah psalms (43:2; 44:9, 23 [10, 24]; 88:14 [15] or 74:1; 77:7 [8]; dependent thereon is the reference in 89:38 [39]. Beyond that the concept is found only in Ps 60:1, 10 [MT 3, 12] (= 108:11 [12]), in which case the relationship of literary dependence existing between Psalm 60 and Psalm 44 can remain open here.[34]

As a group the Korah psalms, which of course differ from one another in details, bear the strong mark of the concepts and individual motifs typical of Zion theology (chaos-cosmos; world mountain; city of God; assault by the nations; sanctuary concepts; God as saving light and refuge; the whole earth as the stage for the events, among others).

Finally, every one of the Korah psalms has been shaped by means of similar poetic techniques.[35] In most of the Korah psalms there are structural signals for the arrangement of the strophes by means of which the structural forms of the psalms are shown not to correspond, as a rule, to the so-called basic forms genre research has developed for lament and/or supplication or hymn and/or song of thanksgiving. Functioning as structural signals are verbally similar refrains, set phrases, motif variations such as repetitions or significantly placed syntactical particles.

3. The Compositional Structure of the Korah Psalms 84–85, 87–88

Psalm 87 must be read, in the first place, as one of the four Korah psalms 84–85, 87–88. Their compositional sequence is oriented to the sequence of Korah psalms 42–49 that preceded them. That the two subgroups were not put together by the same hand is shown by three observations:

a) The two psalm groups appear in different books in the Psalter.

[34] Psalm 60 occupies a special place with respect to composition and redaction as the only "community lament" among the individual psalms of lament or supplication 51–64; since 60:10-12 [12-14] "works together with" both 44:5 [6] (pre-exilic) *and* 44:9 [10] (post-exilic), 60 must depend on 44.

[35] Cf. the summary by Erich Zenger, "Zur redaktionsgeschichtlichen Bedeutung der Korachpsalmen," in *Neue Wege der Psalmenforschung*, 175–98, at 179–82.

b) While the group 42–49 is an "Elohist" redaction and a part of the so-called Elohist Psalter 42–83 (on this see below), this redaction is not in evidence in Psalms 84–88*.

c) The Korah psalms 84–88* are connected redactionally with the Asaph psalms that precede them, which is not true in the same way of the Korah psalms 42–49.

The compositional pattern shaping Korah psalms 42–49, which Psalms 84–85, 87–88 then imitate, is the thematic sequence lament—answer (from God)—lament.[36]

The composition 42–49 begins with Psalm 42/43 as an individual song of longing for an encounter with the God of Zion, whose hiddenness or acts of rejection are lamented. This individual lament is intensified in the succeeding Psalm, 44, into the collective accusation against the God who has rejected the people. Then the four Psalms 45–48 answer this repeated lament with the proclamation about the God of Zion who rescues the inhabitants of the city of God and the "daughters of Judah" who dwell around it and brings peace to the whole earth or to the nations of the world. The hymnically intensifying proclamation of the reign of the God of Zion, which is underscored in Psalms 45 and 46 with quotations of direct address by God,[37] then changes abruptly into the individual wisdom-impregnated lament about mortality in Psalm 49, which, of course, is to be read compositionally as the intentional concluding psalm (no address to God!) of the subgroup 42–49. This compositional function of Psalm 49 can be recognized first of all by the fact that with its universal call to listen at the beginning (v. 1 [MT 2]) it takes up the perspective about the nations in Psalms 44–48.[38]

The Masoretic (but perhaps already an early Jewish) tradition has in any case expressly connected Psalm 48 at the end with Psalm 49 through the reading "against death/until death/beyond death," על מות. Second, the individual Psalm 49 is intended to be an answer to the individual Psalm(s) 42/43; in particular, the statement of hope woven into the lament about mortality and

[36] That in the compositional combining of individual psalms *(iuxtapositio)* "form critical" models also stand in the background has been brought out by Millard, *Komposition;* even if I cannot follow all his compositional turns, his understanding really makes a fundamental contribution to future exegesis on the Psalms. For Psalms 42–49 and 84–85, 87–88 we also find in his work the threefold pattern given above, even if the details differ.

[37] 45:10-12 [11-13]; 46:10 [11]. That direct address by God can be inserted into the Psalms without being introduced as such is also shown by 14:4 [5]; 75:2-3 [3-4]; 91:14-16. That in the address by God in 45:10-12 [11-13] God uses a self-designation in the third person ("the king") is indeed unusual, but it is not impossible, as can be seen from 50:14, 22; 75:7 [8]; 81:15 [16].

[38] Millard, *Komposition,* 77–78, now also points to this.

death in 49:15 [MT 16], that God "will ransom" the "soul," נפש, from the power of death, is to be related to the encouragement to hope directed to the "soul" in the thrice-repeated refrain 42:5, 11 [MT 6, 12]; 43:5.

The Korah psalms 84–85, 87–88 in their compositional sequence are oriented to the subgroup of Psalms 42–49, a position that Eckart Otto, among others, had already advocated. He writes:

> Psalms 84; 85; 87; 88 repeat this structure. Psalm 84 presupposes Psalm 42/43 . . . and actualizes it for the pilgrimage situation. With Psalm 85, corresponding to Psalm 44, there follows a thematically closely related community lament, with Psalm 87 a post-exilic hymn of Zion corresponding to Psalms 46 and 48. Psalm 88 corresponds to the death motif in Psalm 49.[39]

This thesis was recently supported by Mattias Millard with the following form-critical observations:

> Both groups of Korah psalms are divided into singular and plural psalms. The plural psalms form the core of the collections, while the singular psalms occupy . . . the framing position. The basic form-critical pattern of the plural psalms at the core of the two Korah psalm groups can be understood by analogy to the lament as a transition from lament to praise. . . . Especially with respect to the second Korah psalm collection it can . . . be presumed that from the start this is laid out in imitation of the first and is also to be located originally in a wisdom/post-cultic context.[40]

Psalm 87 is the theological midpoint of the composition 84–85, 87–88. At the same time it ties together the program that is broadly developed in the Korah psalms 45–48 as the midpoint of the composition 42–49.

The two beginning psalms of the subgroup 84 and 85 form a compositional or redactional unity. Psalm 84, interspersed with hymnic motifs and traditionally designated as a song of Zion, is a song of longing for the God of Zion and the blessing that flows from this God. By means of the juxtapositon of Psalm 85 precisely this motif of God blessing the people and the land from Zion is carried further and supplemented with an entire collage of technical theological concepts. The lament that is barely suggested in Psalm 84 becomes intensified in Psalm 85 as a lament over the wrath of God.

Both in the structural sequence of increasing and expanding laments and also by taking up important keywords Psalms 84–85 parallel Psalms

[39] Eckart Otto, "ציון, *ṣijjôn*," *ThWAT* 6, 1015.

[40] Millard, *Komposition,* 78–79. If this position is accepted, the thesis formulated by Wanke, *Zionstheologie,* 3 (and since then unhesitatingly presupposed by many) can no longer be maintained: "We can . . . assume that Psalms 84, 85, 87, 88 were unknown to the 'Elohistic' redactor, but nevertheless belonged to the original Korah collection but were separated from it at a later stage."

42–44. In 84 as in 42/43 it is the “soul,” נפש, that is full of longing for the “dwelling places,” משכנות, and for the “house,” בית, of the God of Zion (cf. 84:1 [MT 2] with 43:3 and 84:4 [5] with 42:4 [5]), who both in 84:2 [3] and in 42:2, 8 [3, 9] receives the epithet “living God,” אל־חי. And the salvation-historical survey in Psalms 85 and 44 in both cases sums up YHWH’s turning to the land with the verb “be favorable to, delight in,” רצה (cf. 85:1 [2]; 44:3 [4]) and awaits, as a renewed gift, YHWH’s “steadfast love,” חסד (cf. 85:10 [11]; 44:26 [27]), through which YHWH’s wrath, under which the people are suffering, comes to an end (cf. 85:4-7 [5-8] and 44:17-22 [18-23]). In all probability it is hardly by chance that the address to God “my king,” מלכי, occurs in 84:3 [4]; it is also used in 44:4 [5].

The section Ps 85:8-13 [9-14], shaped in the style of a prophetic oracle that announces the comprehensive saving gift of peace for YHWH’s people, presents this salvation, on the one hand, precisely as cosmic renewal (cf. Ps 85:11-12 [MT 12-13]) and, on the other hand, views it as the coming of YHWH to Zion, as the allusions to the book of Isaiah suggest.

This is appropriately followed by Psalm 87, which at the compositional level is to be read as the answer, given from Zion by the God of Zion, to the yearning lament of Psalms 84–85. This response character emerges first from the two outer sections of the psalm, in which the city of God is lauded as the institution for which the God of Zion has special love (vv. 1-3 [MT 1b-3]) and as the source of all life (v. 7). These two outer sections are oriented to Psalms 84–85 by key words (on “dwellings of Jacob” in 87:2, cf. 84:1 [2]; 85:1 [2]; on “glorious” in 87:3, cf. 84:11 [12]; 85:9 [10]; on “all springs” in 87:7, cf. 84:6 [7]). In the middle section (vv. 4-6) God’s answer is given repeatedly as direct address by God in which Zion, the city of God, assumes the form of the mother of the nations.

That Psalm 87 in the composition of the Korah psalm group 85–88* corresponds structurally to Psalms 45–48 in the first Korah psalm group is underscored by numerous allusions to these four psalms through keywords, so that one must designate and interpret Psalm 87 as the summation of Psalms 45–48.

The points of contact and allusions are unmistakable:

	[MT in brackets]
“on the holy mount” בהררי־קדש	v. 1 [1b]: cf. 48:1 [2]
“dwellings of Jacob” משכנות יעקב	v. 2b: cf. 46:4 [5]
“city of God” עיר האלהים	v. 3b: cf. 46:4 [5]; 48:1, 8 [2, 9]
“who know me” לידעי	v. 4a: cf. 46:10 [11]
“he has established” והוא יכוננה	(v. 5b: cf. 48:8 [9])

"the Most High" עליון	(v. 5b: cf. 46:4 [5]; 47:2 [3])
"my springs in you" מעיני בך	(v. 7b: cf. 46:4 [5])

In the light of this strong keyword linking with Psalms 46–48, which is also plausible with respect to the theme as a whole (Zion as the place and "source" of life for "Jacob" and the previously hostile nations of the world), it does not seem to me to be out of the question to connect Zion's role as mother, proclaimed in Psalm 87 by YHWH, with the role of the beloved queen and bride,[41] also proclaimed by YHWH in Psalm 45. The suppliants offering laments in Psalms 84–85 are confronted in Psalm 87 with the vision of Zion as YHWH's beloved wife, who becomes the mother of the nations.

The perspective that connects Psalm 87 back to Psalms 45–48 gives it a surprisingly deep profile:

1) While Psalms 45–48, with the motif of the assault of the nations—which comes to naught in the face of terror before the God going forth from Zion (Psalms 46 and 48), with the willing or forced homage by the nations in Zion and with the pilgrimage of the nations to Zion (Psalms 45 and 47), celebrate the special role of Zion as the city of God and as "beloved" by Zion's king, the line of sight is turned around in Psalm 87. Now the rescue of Zion is no longer in view, but rather the rescue of the nations through Zion/out of Zion: "*all* the springs" of life are to be found in Zion. The life-giving function of Zion that Psalm 87 proclaims is the result, one could say, of the event depicted or presented as a vision in Psalms 45–48. It is precisely this composite view of these five Korah psalms that makes it clear that a picture of the future is drawn here that comes very close to the one in Isa 2:1-5 and 11:1-10.[42]

2) When viewed from the perspective of Psalms 45–48, the colon 87:5c, considered awkward by many exegetes (and therefore usually relocated or removed), becomes understandable. It is not only a citation from Ps 48:8 [MT 9], but in a certain sense it works together with Psalm 48 as a whole (as the high point of the compositional group 45–48). The verb used in 48:8 [9]; 87:5, כון Hifil/Polel, "establish, equip," has a very broad spec-

[41] On this view, according to which the "daughter" addressed in Ps 45:10-15 [11-16] is the daughter of Zion, whose love the king of Zion desires, see Hossfeld and Zenger, *Psalmen 1,* 283; cf. now also Millard, *Komposition,* 75–76; in support of an "allegorical interpretation of Psalm 45 as the wedding of God with the people," Millard, ibid., points to "the allusion to a marriage contract between God and Israel, for example, in the prophetic acts of Hosea (Hosea 1–3: Israel's idolatry is adultery) and Ezekiel's surveys of biblical history (Ezekiel 16 and 23)."

[42] On this cf. chapter 3 above.

trum of meaning and use encompassing various aspects of YHWH's creative, life-giving, and preserving activity. Klaus Koch summarizes the meaning of the verb in the Psalter (כון Hifil = *hēkîn;* כון Polel = *kônēn*) this way:

> Hymnic sections of the Psalter and late wisdom praise YHWH for what he establishes in creation, . . . The verb *hēkîn* is never used of creation as a whole but of extraordinary works that bring beneficent order to the rest of creation, such as the heavens (Ps 89:2 [3]; Prov 3:19; 8:27), the light of the sun and moon (Ps 8:3 [4]; 74:16), the mountains (Ps 65:6 [7]), and above all the earth as *tēbēl,* arable land moistened by rainfall (Ps 24:2; 68:9 [10]; Jer 10:12; etc.). Strictly speaking, *hēkîn* does not denote an act of creation as such but the shaping and establishing of an entity already present. . . . The positive aspect of *kûn (hiphil* and *polel),* implying the preservation and enhancement of life, explains why the passages under discussion often cite the myth of God's battle with the primeval sea in antithesis to God's *hēkîn.* God established the earth above the tumultuous seas (Ps 24:1f.; cf. Jer 10:12f. par. 51:15f.). Having slain Leviathan and related monsters, YHWH established light and the sun as forces of order (Ps 74:12-16) or the mountains to maintain the cosmos (Ps 65:6-7 [7-8]). He brought into being *ṣedeq* and *mišpāt* as "guarantors" *(mākôn)* of his throne (Ps 89:9-14 [10-15]).[43]

This life-sustaining "equipping" of Zion, of which Ps 87:5c speaks by alluding to or taking up Ps 89:8 [9], is the second act, which follows the first act of the "founding/establishing" of Zion mentioned in 87:1.

3) It is possible that in 87:5c there is also a reminder of the manner in which YHWH "equips" Zion to be source of life for the nations. In Ps 48:9-11 [10-12] the equipping of Zion spoken of in 48:8 [9] is explicitly seen in the saving gifts of "righteousness and justice" that are present there or go forth from there; with these YHWH as king of the world "deprives" the enemy nations "of their power." This legal aspect is also found in Psalm 87: from the seat of power YHWH, the king of the world, takes the nations into YHWH's realm in a legal and binding way and obligates them from that time on to follow the laws of this realm. That YHWH declares in 87:4a that Rahab and Babylon are among "those who (ac)know(ledge) me," from the perspective of Ps 46:10 [11] ("Be still, and know that I am YHWH") means precisely this: the nations are prepared to take instructions from YHWH in his ordering of world peace. On the level of the book of Psalms, 87:4a has to be read from the perspective of Ps 25:14: Egypt and Babylon belong to those who acknowledge YHWH—because YHWH has given them knowledge about himself and the covenant.[44]

[43] Klaus Koch, Art. "כון, *kūn,*" *Theological Dictionary of the Old Testament,* ed. J. Johannes Botterwick and Helmer Ringgren (Grand Rapids: Eerdmans, 1977–) 7:97–98.

[44] On the interpretation of Ps 25:14 cf. chapter 3 above. If one reads 87:4 from the perspective of Ps 25:14, Psalm 87 comes very close to Isa 19:25; on this see the recent work

To be sure, the historical and political reality of the world in which Psalm 87 arose is a far cry from the vision sketched in Psalm 87. That is driven home by Psalm 88, which is connected compositionally to Psalm 87. With the sharpness of its theological accusation this psalm is a massive open conclusion not only to the little collection Psalms 84–88*, but also to the entire sub-collection Psalms 42–88(89), which is framed by the Korah psalms. Compositionally Psalm 88 takes up several motifs of lament/accusation of Psalms 84 and 85; above all, however, with respect to motif and structure it corresponds to the lament about death in Psalm 49. The middle of Psalm 88 (vv. 10-12 [11-13]), in which the lamenting "I" of the psalm abandons the "I"-perspective, stakes a claim on precisely the gifts that in Psalms 45–48 and 87, as "life-principles," are explicitly or implicitly to have deep root in Zion, namely, the steadfast love (חסד), faithfulness (אמונה) and righteousness (צדקה) of YHWH.[45]

The compositional pattern employed by both partial collections of Korah psalms, 42–49 and 84–88, lament—God's answer—lament, is also found twice in the sequence of Asaph psalms 73–83. This twofold sequence opens in each case, in Psalms 73 and 78, with a wisdom teaching.[46]

"teaching"	lament →		God's answer →	lament
73	74	("we")	75 + 76	77 ("I")
78	79 + 88	("we")	81 + 82	83 ("I")

This structural analogy of the Asaph psalms to Psalms 84–85, 87, 88 (which are older!) supports the idea that the psalm series 84–85, 87–88 goes back to a redaction inspired not only by the collection Psalms 42–49 but also by the Asaph collection, as the borrowing of several keywords from the Asaph psalms indicates.[47]

of Ernst Haag, "'Gesegnet sei mein Volk Ägypten' (Jes 19:25): Ein Zeugnis alttestamentlicher Eschatologie," in *Aspekte spätägyptischer Kultur: Festschrift für Erich Winter zum 65. Geburtstag,* ed. Martina Minas and Jürgen Zeidler, Aegyptiaca Treverensia 7 (Mainz: Verlag Philipp von Zabern, 1994), and chapter 4 above. Moreover, a perspective on Ps 100:3 is also opened up here (on this see below, chapter 6).

[45] On the composition of Psalm 88 and the lines along which its statements flow cf. Walter Groß and Karl-Josef Kuschel, *"Ich schaffe Finsternis und Unheil!" Ist Gott verantwortlich für das Übel?* (Mainz: Matthias Grünewald, 1992) 51–52, as well as Zenger, "Korachpsalmen," 180–81.

[46] Cf. also the pattern in Millard, *Komposition,* 46, 95.

[47] For example, for the "people of YHWH concept," atypical for the Korah psalms, in 85:6, 8 [MT 7, 9] and on the "Zion theology" of 85:5-6, cf. Asaph psalms 77:7 [8]; 79:5; 80:3-4 [4-5]; on the Zion theology of 87:2, cf. 76:2 [3]; 78:68.

From these (perhaps somewhat bewildering) compositional and redaction-critical connections it is now possible to determine the time of origin of Psalm 87 and of the partial composition Psalms 84–85, 87–88.

1) Since the partial psalm composition 84–85, 87–88 presupposes both Psalm sequence 42–49 and Psalm sequence 73–83 it must be more recent than they, and they in turn, on the basis of their theological conception, can be dated in the fifth century at the earliest.[48]

2) The Korah psalms 42–49 and the Asaph psalms 73–83 form the frame for the so-called Elohistic Psalter, Psalms 42–83. What characterizes it, by common consent, is that to a large extent it replaces the divine name YHWH for God with the designation Elohim. *This* theological "universalization" of Psalms 42–83 is closely connected, in my opinion, with the theme of the nations, which, with Korah psalms 42–49, stands at the beginning of the Elohistic Psalter. The importation of the "nations psalm" 67 into its present context, for example, also goes back to this Elohistic redaction. The Elohistic redaction is usually dated in the second half of the fourth century.[49]

3) Since Psalms 84–85, 87–88 are *no longer* "Elohistic" in redaction or concept, they must have been connected to the Elohistic Psalter at a later time. The time of Alexander the Great is conceivable, or, because of the lament character of Psalms 84–85, 87–88, with which the vision of Psalm 87 is imbued, precisely the period of the collapse of Alexander's empire. In that case Psalm 87 is to be read as a utopian counter-conception.

III. Psalm 87 as a Contrast to Psalm 83

1. The Connection with Asaph Psalms 73–83

The Korah psalm group 84–85, 87–88, as we have seen, takes the inspiration for its structure *also* from the group of Asaph psalms that preceded it,

[48] On the in any case post-exilic dating of the final form of Psalms 42–49 cf. Hossfeld and Zenger, *Psalms 1;* on the Asaph psalms cf. Karl-Johan Illmann, *Thema und Tradition in den Asaf-Psalmen,* Publications of the Research Institute of the Abo Akademi Foundation 13 (Abo: Research Institute of the AAF, 1976); Harry P. Nasuti, *Tradition History and the Psalms of Asaph,* SBL.DS 88 (Atlanta: Scholars, 1988); Pieter Schelling, *De Asafpsalmen. Hun Samenhang en Achtergrond,* Dissertationes Neerlandicae: Series Theologica (Kampen: Kok, 1985); Klaus Seybold, "Das 'Wir' in den Asaph-Psalmen. Spezifische Probleme einer Psalmgruppe," in *Neue Wege der Psalmenforschung,* 143–55; Erich Zenger, "Asaf/Asifiten," *Lexicon für Theologie und Kirche* (1993) 1:1052–53.

[49] Cf., for example, the recent work of Walter Beyerlin, *Im Licht der Traditionen. Psalm LXVII und CXV. Ein Entwicklungszusammenhang,* VTS XLV (Leiden : Brill, 1992) 41–42.

73–83. This group has a thoroughly distinctive character through which it is set apart from the (in many ways related) Korah psalms. As a whole they are strongly marked by the experience of the devastation of Zion and reflect this experience in lament, with theological topics about judgment and, by contrast, with invocations of YHWH as the Protector-God of Zion. They appropriate and use in rich variety the "classical" traditions of Israel about creation, exodus, and conquest of the land. They are stongly marked by the demands of YHWH in the decalogue, especially the first commandment. From a literary perspective they frequently employ direct address by God. Psalm 83 is intentionally located as the concluding psalm of the partial composition of Asaph psalms 73–83. Together with the Asaph psalm 50, which can be regarded as a "new edition" of Psalm 81,[50] the twelve (!) Asaph psalms now form a frame around the collection of Davidic psalms 51–72.

Psalm 87 is connected with the concluding Psalm 83 through three appropriations of important key words:

a) The two geographical designations "Philistia and Tyre" occur in 83:7 [8] and 87:4.

b) Psalm 83 culminates with a statement that YHWH should show the nations through a theophany that YHWH alone is the "Most High" (83:18 [19]). According to 87:5 YHWH is shown to be the "Most High" by "equipping" Zion as the "center" and "source of life" for the nations.

c) The goal of YHWH's intervention against the assault of the nations intent on annihilating Israel is, according to 83:18 [19], that the nations (ac)know(ledge) YHWH and YHWH's name; in Ps 87:4 YHWH lists the great powers as those "who (ac)know(ledge) me."

What the two psalms have in common above all is the theme YHWH and the nations. Psalm 83 reflects on it with a "theology of judgment," while Psalm 87 employs a "pacifistic" vision. In Psalm 83 the nations are thwarted, as it were, because of Israel and come by means of YHWH's judgment to an acknowledgment of YHWH. In Psalm 87 the nations are gathered on Zion where they dance and sing, "All my springs are in you." On this basis one can read Psalm 87 as a contrast to Psalm 83 in every sense.

[50] The theological and redaction-critical relationship of the three interrelated Psalms 50, 81, and 95 cannot be discussed here. Frank-Lothar Hossfeld, "Psalm 95: Gattungsgeschichtliche, kompositionskritische und bibeltheologische Anfragen," in *Neue Wege der Psalmenforschung,* 29–44, assumes the sequence 81 → 95 → 50. By contrast, Hermann Spieckermann, "Rede Gottes und Wort Gottes in den Psalmen," in *Neue Wege der Psalmenforschung,* 157–73, argues for the sequence 50 → 95 → 81. I myself think in terms of the sequence 81 → 50 → 95:7b-11 (on vv. 7b-11 as a compositionally determined expansion of Psalm 95, cf. the next chapter).

2. *The Speech-event in Psalm 83*

Psalm 83 [the verse numbers in the MT are higher by one; the title is numbered as v. 1 in the MT]

A Song. A Psalm of/for Asaph

1a Elohim, do not keep silence;
do not hold your peace or be still, El!

2a Even now your enemies are in tumult;
2b those who hate you have raised their heads.
3a They lay crafty plans against your people;
3b they consult together against those you protect.
4a They say, "Come, let us wipe them out as a nation;
4b let the name of Israel be remembered no more."
5a They conspire with one accord;
5b against you they make a covenant—

6a the tents of Edom and the Ishmaelites,
6b Moab and the Hagrites,
7a Gebal and Ammon and Amalek,
7b Philistia with the inhabitants of Tyre;
8a Assyria also has joined them;
8b they are the strong arm of the children of Lot. *Selah*

9a Do to them as you did to Midian
9b as to Sisera and Jabin at the Wadi Kishon,
10a who were destroyed at En-dor,
10b who became dung for the ground.
11a Make their nobles like Oreb and Zeeb,
11b all their princes like Zebah and Zalmunna,
12a who said, "Let us take the pastures of God
12b for our own possession."

13a My Elohim, make them like a tumbleweed,
13b like chaff before the wind.
14a As fire consumes the forest
14b as the flame sets the mountains ablaze,
15a so pursue them with your tempest
15b and terrify them with your hurricane.

16a	Fill their faces with shame
16b	so that they may seek your name, O LORD.
17a	Let them be put to shame and dismayed forever;
17b	let them perish in disgrace.
18a	Let them know that you alone, whose name is the LORD,
18b	are the Most High over all the earth.

The psalm[51] is (explicitly or implicitly) shaped throughout as an appelative direct address to God, in which the three negative commands at the beginning in v. 1 [2] and the four imperatives in vv. 9, 11, 13, 17 [10, 12, 14, 17] of the direct address plainly convey a militant and demanding urgency: it is a battle with God for proof that God is God in and for Israel—before the forum of the nations of the world. Israel here makes itself the attorney in the case against God, and that on the basis of the experience that Israel and God belong together like two sides of a medal. If Israel is threatened, YHWH, as Israel's God, is threatened. If Israel's name disappears, YHWH, the God of Israel, "disappears."

To overstate the case: in the psalm Israel shouts at God finally to do something for God's own "survival." The "theo-dramatic" dynamics of the psalm is given strong linguistic emphasis through its opening and closing lines. While the two cola of v. 1 [2] are formed in such a way that they are framed by the designations for God Elohim and El, the two cola of v. 18 [19] collide in the middle with the divine name YHWH and the designation of God as "the Most High" *(Elyōn).*

[51] The date of the psalm is debated by scholars. The specific arguments are usually derived from the "historical" constellation sketched in vv. 6-8 [7-9]; sometimes linguistic observations are also employed. On the scholarly opinions, which extend from the early monarchy to the Maccabean period, cf. the overview in Ravasi, *Psalmi,* 725–27. For the option, adopted by numerous commentators, of assigning the psalm to the pre-exilic period the mention of Assyria in v. 8 [9] or the absence of a reference to Egypt and Babylon plays a decisive role.

This problem cannot be discussed here in more detail. Five observations must suffice: (1) Assyria or "the king of Assyria" is in post-exilic texts often emblematic for the world power hostile to God or Israel *par excellence*. (2) Because of the compositional structure of the "list of nations" (9 + 1) only a single great power can be named. (3) The system for the "list of nations" worked out by us above speaks against all attempts to seek a unique historical event behind vv. 5-8 [6-9]. (4) It is true that the theme of a united "attack by the nations" against Israel/Zion is conceivable in the pre-exilic period (cf. Psalms 46 and 48), but it is primarily taken up and developed in the post-exilic period (cf. Psalm 76; Ezekiel 38–39; Joel 4; Zechariah 14). (5) At least for the "wholistic" reading of Psalm 83 as the conclusion of the group 50, 73–83, Ps 83:2-8 [3-9] is to be understood "in general terms" (cf. Psalm 2).

Only in these two examples of parallelism do we encounter the express naming of God in each line, whereby the process of the divine proof that is demanded is very cleverly put together: as the one who is silent, God is called "Elohim" and "El," in a sense a "distant God," a "divinity" without name or face who, one might say, has "gone underground" in the world of the gods of the nations. Worse still: the nations are already in the process of doing away with God, annihilating God, in fact. Therefore Israel threatens God in this psalm, with extreme images of its fears and with reminders of its constitutive history with God, finally to give up the divine remoteness and weariness and to reveal himself in "his name" YHWH, which simultaneously names both the particularity and universality of God's being (v. 18 [19]).

The psalm is clearly divided into two parts, to which the *Selah* at the end of v. 8 [9] calls attention. The *first part* (vv. 1-8 [2-9]) is a lament and protest against a God who unmoved, untouched, or indeed powerlessly puts up with the attack of the nations of the world directed against God and the people. The lament begins with the series of three intensifying negative commands in which Israel's whole relationship to God has blackened into total darkness: that YHWH speaks, acts, feels concern, in short, is a living God, who lives in and with the people, that is a core assertion of the faith transmitted in Israel—and precisely that has been and is being shown to be untrue and irrelevant by Israel's history, as this is developed in the complex sentence that graphically makes that case in vv. 2-8 [3-9]. This complex sentence in turn consists of two sections, vv. 2-5 and 6-8 [3-6 and 7-9].

The section vv. 2-5 [3-6] laments in chiastic form the plans hostile nations are directing against YHWH and the people (v. 2 [3]: against YHWH; vv. 3-4 [4-5]: against YHWH's people; v. 5 [6]: against YHWH). The enemy acts are described, on the one hand, with metaphors from the human sphere: the enemies "hate," "raise their heads," "consult," speak to one another, have a "heart" and an "arm." Correspondingly, the transcendent YHWH is also presented in such an immanent form that YHWH appears just like a person who is threatened and in danger: "*against you* they make a covenant" (v. 5b [6b]).

On the other hand, the first verb, "are in tumult," which comes from the language of the battle against chaos,[52] gives the entire action a mythical dimension, with which the elemental and basic significance of the conflict depicted here is expressed. That we are not dealing with a battle

[52] Cf. especially Pss 46:3, 6 [4, 7]; 65:7 [8]; Isa 17:12; Jer 6:23 = 50:42; 51:55; on the noun המון cf., among others, Judg 4:7 (!); Isa 29:5-8; Jer 47:3; 51:42; Ezek 7:7-11; Joel 4:14. On the relationship between Psalm 83 and Isa 17:1-14, cf. Bernhard Gosse, "Le Psaume 83, Isaïe 62:6-7 et la tradition des Oracles contre les Naions des livres d'Isaïe et d'Ezéchiel," *BN* 70 (1993) 9–12.

focused against Israel but with the mythical attack of the nations against YHWH and against God's existence as a God in relation to Israel finds expression both in the words of conspiracy put in the mouths of the nations in v. 4 [5] and in the formulation that summarizes the account, "they make a covenant" (v. 5b [6b]), which is chosen in pointed opposition to the covenantal relationship between YHWH and Israel it presupposes.

How radically our psalm feels and indicates the calling into question of YHWH's existence as God by means of the history can also be inferred from the artfully constructed tableau of enemy nations that is attached as the second section, vv. 6-8 [7-9], which names the actors in the conspiracy lamented in vv. 2-5 [3-6]. Against the repeated attempts of exegetes to interpret this section with reference to a unique historic constellation, the following must be maintained: it is already shown simply by the poetic and symbolic configuration of the section that the catastrophic side of Israel's history in general is in view here. The names of the nations and tribes given here stand emblematically for the nations of the world experienced as enemies *and* feared by Israel during its history, in whose midst it is living.

With respect to form this "tableau of nations" exhibits five characteristics that are relevant for its interpretation:[53] (1) Ten nations are named, already making it clear that we are dealing with a sum total here, with a kind of "historical review." (2) Linguistically and stylistically the series of ten names is arranged in the sequence 9 + 1. After the series of names listed in vv. 6-7 [7-8] Assyria is syntactically set off as the tenth member in v. 8 [9]. This "historical summation" thus knows about two levels of history; there are the "small" actors, who in turn are supported and driven by a "great" actor. (3) The order of the nine "small" nations follows a geographical pattern that evokes Israel's threatening encirclement from East and West.[54] (4) The choice of names is clearly an allusion to the traditions that tell of Israel's route into the promised land and of the settlement in the land.[55] (5) That exactly nine nations are bundled together into a group is probably connected with the notion—frequently attested in Egyptian

[53] On this compositional technique in vv. 6-8 [7-9] cf. also Bruna Costacurta, "L'aggressione contro Dio. Studio del Salmo 83," *Bib* 64 (1983) 518–41, and Marvin E. Tate, *Psalms 51–100*, WBC 20 (Dallas: Word Books, 1990) 347.

[54] If one follows the "movement" that is indicated by the names, which are easy to locate, there emerges a double movement from South to North. In the East: Edom, Moab, Ammon; in the West/along the coast: Philistia, Tyre. The other (tribal) names are to be attached to these "great" names.

[55] On Edom, Moab, and Ammon with respect to this issue cf. especially: Num 20:14-21; Numbers 22–24; Judg 11:12-28; 2 Chr 20:10-12; on Philistia, cf. Judges 13–16; 1 Samuel 4–6; 17–19; 27–31; 2 Sam 5:17-25; on Tyre, cf. Isa 23:1-18; Jer 25:22; Ezekiel 26–28.

iconography and "national theology"—of the "nineness" of the nations and of the "nine bows" that symbolize *all* the hostile nations subject to the Egyptian king.[56] Thus when our psalm deplores the revolt of this group of nine nations, Israel is thereby invoking YHWH's roll as the subduer of chaos for the sake of the cosmos.

Launching out three separate times, the *second section* (vv. 9-18 [10-19]) demands that YHWH act, with the intensity of the sought-after evidence of God's response increasing both in imagery and in the designations used for God: vv. 9-12 [10-13], alluding to Judges 4–8, recall the "primal" acts of God against the enemies of Israel,[57] with an explicit reference to God coming only in the quotation of the words of the enemies; the images used do not point to the acts of YHWH but to the fate of the enemies.

By contrast, the next section, vv. 13-15 [14-16], which begins with the emphatic address to God, "my Elohim," brings images from the language used in a (nature) theophany,[58] with the enclitic second person singular suffix in v. 15 [16] setting the stage for the personal aspect of the coming of God that we then encounter in the concluding section (vv. 16-18 [17-19]) with the explicit double reference to YHWH's name. The images in these final sections, which take up the stylized language of the psalms,[59] picture the confrontation between YHWH and the enemy nations as a personal encounter that will lead to (ac)knowledge(ment) of YHWH by the nations and thereby to an end of the history of Israel's suffering lamented in the psalm.

Israel's passionate adherence to the truth about God in their quest for new experiences of God comes to expression in the "montage" of metaphors about God that is set forth in the three sections: vv. 9-12, 13-15, 16-18 [10-13, 14-16, 17-19]. They are metaphors about God in a double sense: first, they name the experiences of God "gathered" in collective memory,

[56] Cf. Walter Wifall, "The Foreign Nations. Israel's 'Nine Bows,'" *Bulletin of Egyptological Seminar* 3 (1981) 122, and Othmar Keel, *Die Welt der altorientalischen Bildsymbolik und das Alte Testament. Am Beispiel der Psalmen* (Neukirchen-Vluyn: Neukirchener Verlag; Zürich: Benziger, [4]1984) 233.

[57] On the threats to Israel in the "primal history" by the "Canaanites," cf. Judges 4–5, by the Midianites, cf. Judges 6–8 (especially Judg 7:23-25; 8:21). The sequence given in the text, Midian-Canaanites-Midian, follows an ABA pattern and must not be destroyed by striking "Midian" at the beginning, as many commentators propose. It is possible that Midian is explicitly put first in view of Judg 7:2, as suggested by Petrus Nowack, "Psalm 83 in der Feier der Liturgie," *Dienender Glaube* 68 (1992) 55.

[58] Since what we have here is a montage of epiphany and theophany metaphors, they must not be interpreted one-sidedly as images of destruction.

[59] On v. 16 [17]: cf. 44:15 [16]; 69:7 [8]; on v. 17 [18]: 6:10 [11]; 35:4, 26; 40:14 [15] = 70:2 [3]; 69:6 [7]; 71:13, 24; on v. 18 [19]: 46:10 [11]; 97:9; 109:27; Sir 36:5.

wanting to grasp their "truth" anew; with them Israel, in a manner of speaking, takes on for itself the task of "reconstructing" and learning anew the creative coming of YHWH and YHWH's righteousness, which to that point lies in a metaphorical state of collapse. And, second, they are images held up to YHWH to plead that YHWH exhaust anew the "divine potential" that is evoked in them—for the sake of God's own "truth." Therefore the tensions and contradictions between the individual elements we find in the montage of metaphors in vv. 9-18 [10-19] must not be resolved by literary criticism or theological leveling that conforms to any particular statement.[60]

Above all, the third section may not be understood as an "orthodox" softening. It urgently presses YHWH, as the God of Israel, for self-disclosure at once and at last as the Most High, that is the battler against chaos who comes from Zion—in accord with God's "name," YHWH, whose protecting-saving power the psalm claims, with its metaphorical evocation of YHWH as the warrior God from the beginning of Israel's history. The metaphorical "working in" of accounts of the rescue of Israel from the Canaanites and Midianites, who wanted to take away its "land from God," is certainly not a plea for the naive "repetition" of these wars (that would take away YHWH's "historical dimension" and make YHWH into a mythical idol!). The metaphor field with which the psalm operates is, rather, the combination of epiphany (vv. 9-15 [10-16]) and theophany (vv. 16-18 [17-19]), which has as its intention the acknowledgment of YHWH by "all" nations—and thereby the rescue of Israel.

[60] In the commentaries we find three models for producing a "coherent" statement in vv. 9-18 [10-19]. (1) Alterations of the text (usually the "positive" statement in 16b [17b] is changed since it does not agree with the "negative" statements in the context; for example, Hermann Gunkel, *Die Psalmen,* ad loc.: "'so that they may seek your name' is in this context very strange . . . The simplest solution is that of Ehrlich, in the commentary of Rudolf Kittel, *š^{e}lom^{e}ka*, 'in order that they seek peace with you,' that is, have to surrender"; cf. also Mitchell Dahood and Willy Staerk, ad loc. (2) Textual transpositions (for example, Bernard Duhm, *Die Psalmen,* KHC 14 (Freiburg: Mohr, 1899) ad loc., "V. 13 [14] appears to belong before v. 16 [17] . . . V. 16b [17b] has turned out to be a variant of v. 18a [19a], which has *yēd^{e}ʿû* for *j^{e}baq^{e}šû* and thereby the better text, for that those nations whose destruction the author desires should seek YHWH's name contradicts the context; they are to learn the name of YHWH, that is, experience how strong YHWH is." (3) There are literary-critical expositions of various layers in the text (for example, Charles Augustus Briggs and Emilie Grace Briggs, *A Critical and Exegetical Commentary on the Book of the Psalms,* 2 vols. ICC [Edinburgh: Clark, 1906 and 1904] ad loc.: "Glosses make the Ps. more appropriate for public worship by softening the imprecation, making its final purpose the conversion of the nations and the recognition of the God of Israel as the God of all the earth [vv. 16b, 18]"; cf. also *The Interpreter's Bible*, ad loc.).

3. *The Synchronic Correlation with the Other Asaph Psalms*

Psalm 83 acquires a significant interpretive context as the final psalm of the twelve Asaph psalms, 50, 73–83, which wrap around the David Psalter as a frame. This canonical integration of the psalm gives it the following additional connotations:

a) In the canonical reading, "do not keep silence," one of the appeals opening Psalm 83, goes back to the first Asaph psalm, 50:3: "Our God comes and does not keep silence."[61] The theophany of YHWH announced in Psalm 50, which proclaims God's law to the people and sets it up and implements it in judgment in their midst—and this on a global stage (Ps 50:1)—is actualized in our final Asaph psalm as an event also proclaimed to the nations living on this stage. The arc spanning from Psalm 50 to Psalm 83 then also interprets the meaning of the knowledge of YHWH by the nations called for in Ps 83:16, 18 [17, 19]: acceptance of God's law revealed on Sinai and going forth from Zion.

b) For a canonical reading the nations' plan of destruction, which is designated in Ps 83:5 [6] as "making a covenant," is in opposition to the "covenant making" of the faithful ones of Ps 50:5, who submit themselves to YHWH.

c) The "attack by the nations" depicted in Psalm 83 acquires, as a "canonical" summary of the threat to and devastation of Zion lamented in Psalms 74, 76, 79, and 80, that deep drama that finds expression in the "wishes for destruction" in Psalm 83.

d) The theology of the "name of YHWH" that is indicated in Ps 83:16, 18 [17, 19] is anticipated in the "theology of the name" in Ps 74:18; 75:1 [2]; 76:1 [2]; 80:18 [19].

e) The designation for God that concludes the Asaph collection—YHWH the Most High *(Elyôn)*—envisages the role that belongs to the God of Israel, the role of judge as the universal guarantor of justice and righteousness. That is indicated first by the repeated use of *Elyôn* as the title for God in the Asaph collection (50:14; 73:11; 77:10 [11]; 78:17; 82:6; 83:18 [19]; second, the metaphor "YHWH as judge" is expressly taken up and developed in Psalms 50 (especially in vv. 4-6), 75 (especially vv. 2, 7 [3, 8]), 76 (especially vv. 8-9 [9-10]), and 82 (especially 1, 8).

[61] In Psalm 50 the element "and does not keep silence" is secondary, that is, the element must go back to the "Asaph redaction," which thereby describes an arc spanning from Psalm 50 to Psalm 83; on the function of Psalm 50 as the "opening" of the composition 50–83, cf. Frank-Lothar Hossfeld, "Ps 50 und die Verkündigung des Gottesrechts," in *Ein Gott, Eine Offenbarung,* 100–101. On the connection between Ps 83:1 [2] and Isa 62:6-7, cf. Gosse, "Le Psaume 83."

f) The "monotheistic" confession of YHWH hoped for from the nations in Ps 83:18 [19] is anticipated in Psalm 82 through YHWH's own announcement of the "death" of all gods.

g) That Psalm 83 dare not be misunderstood as an expression of nationalistic or triumphalistic lust for power is impressed on us by repeated keyword contacts Psalm 83 has with Psalm 73, which is a sensitive testimony to Israel's suffering under God—and to the longing for God which—despite that—is alive in Israel.[62]

h) Read as the concluding psalm of the twelve (!) Asaph psalms, Psalm 83 is seen to be a "theodicy psalm" in a very direct sense. This does not, of course, happen by the psalm "justifying" God; rather it happens as the psalm demands God's righteousness by crying out against YHWH over the unjustice that threatens YHWH's very existence as God—and this screaming at God happens as a metaphor for the hope that YHWH also will not tolerate and accept this injustice.[63]

To be sure, Psalm 83 portrays the triangular relationship God-Israel-nations with the imagery of war and of the courtroom. In a dialectical tension with this Psalm 87 sketches the vision of YHWH who from Zion permits the nations to share in the river of life, along paths of peace in the reign of God. That Psalm 87, with its five geographical designations, does not have in view the diaspora Jews but all the nations of the world is shown precisely by this dialectic between Psalms 83 and 87. That Psalm 83, with its "tableau of the nations," is about the hostile environment confronting Israel is uncontested. So why should it be different in Psalm 87? Also in Ps 87:4 the enumeration is determined by a system of strong statements: in the sayings about the foreign nations in the books of Isaiah and Jeremiah, Rahab and Babylon are plainly mythical figures of violence and war. That they are now named in first position is connected with this symbolism, as well as with the fact that they were the two great forces of destruction for Zion. With their "conversion" to YHWH, which YHWH personally "decides" and announces (Ps 87:4), the renewal of all the nations of the world begins. That is the message of Psalm 87, when it is read as a counter-text to Psalm 83.

[62] Points of contact through keywords and motifs: "El-Elyôn": 73:11; 83:1, 18 [2, 19]; "disappear, perish": 73:27; 83:17 [18]; quotes from the enemy: 73:11; 83:4, 12 [5, 13]; interdependence of YHWH and Israel: 73:1; 83:2-5 [3-6]; knowledge of YHWH: 73:16; 83:18 [19].

[63] On accusation against God as the only appropriate articulation of the theodicy question, cf., among others, Hans-Peter Müller, "Theodizee? Anschlußerörterungen zum Buch Hiob," *ZThK* 89 (1992) 271, 278–79; Groß and Kuschel, *"Ich schaffe Finsternis,"* 53–59, 197–218.

IV. The Messianic Perspective

1. The Significance of Psalm 86 for Its Successor Psalm 87

Psalm 86 has been inserted into the middle of the group of Korah psalms 84–85, 87–88 (at the time these Korah psalms were put together or somewhat later, along with the creation of the "Messianic Psalter," Psalms 2–89; see below). On the one hand, in the context of its immediate neighboring psalms it occupies a recognizably unique position:

a) According to its title, Psalm 86 is not a Korah psalm but a psalm of David.

b) As a clear "I"-Psalm (individual psalm) it is located between the collective Psalm 85 and Psalm 87, the "Zion-nations-psalm."

c) Psalm 86 is strongly marked by a "theology of the poor" that is absent in Psalms 84–85, 87–88.

On the other hand, the psalm is not out of place in the composition. It shares motifs with Psalm 85 (cf. 86:5 with 85:2, 7 [3, 8]; 86:15 with 85:10 [11]) and with Psalm 87 (cf. 86:9 with 87:4-6).

Psalm 86 is also related in a striking way to Psalm 72, the "messianic" concluding psalm of the second Psalter of David, 51–72, and of Psalm Book IV, 42–72. Psalm 86 is connected with Psalm 72 especially through the "theology of the poor," but also through thematic reminiscences (cf. 86:1-2 with 72:12-13; 86:10 with 72:18) and through verbal borrowing (cf. 86:9 with 72:11).

Whether Psalm 86 was created only for incorporation into the Korah psalms 84–85, 87–88, as many exegetes assume,[64] need not be decided here. Important for us is the following: as the prayer of a poor and persecuted person whom the title identifies as "David," the psalm is the urgent appeal for YHWH to let the vision laid out in Psalm 87—of the universal liberation of the nations by the actualization of YHWH's royal reign (cf. Ps 86:8-10)—at long last become reality. In its cry of lament for YHWH's royal reign, Psalm 86 intersects with Psalm 25, discussed above, and with Psalm 103, interpreted in the next chapter. Like these psalms, Psalm 86 also looks forward to the decisive eschatological turning when the God of the Sinai covenant is revealed, as it states with a citation of Psalm 34:

> For you, O LORD, are good and forgiving,
> abounding in steadfast love to all who call on you.

[64] Cf. the observations in Tate, *Psalms 51–100*, 380, and those in Leslie C. Allen, *Psalms 101–150*, WBC 21 (Waco, Tex.: Word Books, 1983) 15.

> But you, O LORD, are a God merciful and gracious,
> slow to anger and abounding in steadfast love and faithfulness
> (Ps 86:5, 15).

That the "Davidic" suppliant of the psalm also slips into the role of the "servant" of YHWH (cf. Ps 86:2, 4, 16) indicates that the praying "I" is actually Israel, asking for gracious deliverance, so that at long last all nations come to acknowledge YHWH, of whom indeed it is true:

> There is none like you among the gods, O LORD,
> nor are there any works like yours.
> *All the nations you have made shall come and bow down before you,*
> and shall glorify *your name.*
> For you are (indeed?) great and do wondrous things;
> you alone are God (Ps 86:8-10).

For those who arrive at this text by way of a reading of the psalms that precede it, Ps 86:9 will not be merely a reminder of the vision, sketched in Psalm 72, of the pilgrimage of the nations brought about "through the messiah." Above all the reader will of necessity be struck by the connection with Psalms 22–26 (described above in chapter 3). Psalm 86:8-11 is actually full of allusions to this group of psalms. The pilgrimage of the nations and their homage to YHWH corresponds to the movement opened in Ps 22:27 [28]ff., which solidifies in Ps 25:4-5 in the plea:

> Make me to know your ways, O LORD,
> teach me your paths.
> Lead me (on the way) in your truth, and teach me.

If it still remains open in the textual context of Psalms 22–26, on the surface of the text, whether *the nations* (join in) speak(ing) this plea for instruction in the Torah and a share in the covenant, it is clear in Psalm 86: it is the nations who, together with Israel, speak this prayer that is cited in Ps 86:11 (in words almost identical to Ps 25:4-5). The exegetical justification for this way of reading Ps 86:11 is supplied by the text of the psalm itself. In Ps 86:9 it is announced that the nations shall *glorify the name of YHWH*. This is precisely what happens in the "prayer" of Ps 86:12:

> I give thanks to you, O LORD my God, with my whole heart,
> and I will *glorify your name* forever.

The secret of this name that the nations will praise is then summarized in Ps 86:15 with the "Sinai formula" from Exod 34:6. We are then surprised that this "citation" is followed by the citation of the plea that introduces the fourth strophe of Psalm 25:

Turn to me and be gracious to me (25:16).[65]

To be sure, Psalm 86 is and remains first of all a "prayer for David," for the messianic king and for his messianic people, as the references to royal Psalm 72, but also to royal Psalm 89, which closes Psalm Book III, emphasize.

2. The "Messianic Psalter"

What this "messianic" perspective means for the understanding of Psalm 87 would have to be discussed more extensively, particularly since the two Royal psalms 72 and 89 are, for their part, part of a reading program that already begins with royal Psalm 2. That will have to happen somewhere else. Here we can only summarize some of the points: Psalms 2, 72, and 89 are located, on the level of the book of Psalms, at a compositionally striking place: Psalm 2 stands at the head of Psalm Book I (Psalms 3–41) or at the head of the "Elohistic Psalter of David" (to put it in redaction-critical terms) that concludes with Psalm 72 (Ps 72:20: "The prayers of David son of Jesse are ended"). In macrostructural terms Psalm 89 is the conclusion of Psalm Book III (Psalms 73–89). From a redaction-critical perspective Psalm 89 forms the conclusion of the "Messianic Psalter" (Psalms 2–89),[66] which arose about 300 B.C.E.

In this "Messianic" Psalter, on the one hand, there is a meditative review of Israel's ambivalent experiences with its historic monarchy: from David (Psalms 3ff.) through Solomon (Psalm 72 is a prayer of the aged David for his son Solomon) to the end of the monarchy in the year 587 (Psalm 89). But in contrast to this trajectory of the monarchy the "Messianic" Psalter holds fast to the promise given in the covenant with David: the opening programmatic text, Psalm 2, recapitulates the promise given through Nathan in 2 Sam 7:14 (cf. Ps 2:7) in the context of the threatening nations. The concluding Psalm 89, in accord with its "historical" location, works in 2 Sam 7:14-16 both as an interpretation of the situation and as the plea that opens up the future (cf. Ps 89:26, 29, 32 [27, 30, 33]). Then, in its concluding section, Psalm 89—in a "democratizing" manner—enlarges the messianic perspective to include Israel as a people.[67]

[65] Between Psalms 86 and 25 there are still additional points of contact that would have to be discussed: 86:2, cf. 25:20; 86:4b, cf. 25:1; 86:11d, cf. 25:14a; 86:17a, cf. 25:2a.

[66] For now cf. on this view Erich Zenger, "'So betete David für seinen Sohn Salomo und für den König Messias.' Überlegungen sur holistischen und kanonischen Lektüre des 72. Psalms," *JBTh* 8 (1993) 57–72.

[67] The expansion of Psalm 89, vv. 46-51 [47-52] is connected with the attachment of Psalm Book IV, as is indicated not only by the strikingly numerous points of contact

The faithfulness of God promised to "David" with respect to his "son" applies to a "messianc" Israel[68]—precisely with a view toward the nations, as Ps 72:17 (with a citation of the perspective on the nations that opens Israel's history, Gen 12:1-3) indicates:

> May all nations be blessed in him;
> may they pronounce him happy.

So the Messianic Psalter bathes Zion in an eschatological light as the mother of the nations, which accords Israel a messianic role as mediator—and this, all experiences to the contrary notwithstanding, rooted in the grace of the "God of Zion," as YHWH's own proclamation in Ps 2:6-7 shows:

> "I have set my king on *Zion, my holy hill"* (cf. Ps 87:2):
> . . . You are my son;
> today *I have given birth to you (in Zion)* (cf. Ps 87:5, 6).[69]

The "world revolution" pictured in Psalm 2 is transformed in Psalm 87 into a great "world family,"[70] when Zion as the mother of messianic Israel (Psalm 2) and as the mother of all humanity (Psalm 87) becomes the "capitol" of the king of the world, YHWH himself. That is the great theme of Psalm Book IV, at which we plan to look in the next chapter.

---

through motifs and keywords in 89:46-51 [47-52] both with Psalm 90 and with Psalm 102 (on this cf. our next chapter); on the analysis of Psalm 89, cf. Timo Vejola, *Verheißung in der Krise. Studien zur Literatur und Theologie der Exilszeit anhand des 89. Psalms,* AASF B 220 (Helsinki: Academia Scientiarum Fennica, 1982).

[68] In Ps 89:50 [51] the Masoretic text must be preserved: "your servants" (the Einheitsübersetzung has a different reading). Ps 89:49 [50] cites Isa 55:3, where the Davidic promises are also "democratized." In the self-designation "your servants" one can see the self-understanding of the group(s) in which the psalm books arose and were transmitted; the addressees of the book of Isaiah were also defined as "servants of YHWH," above all in Isaiah 65–66 (cf. also the expansion beyond Israel in Isa 56:6!).

[69] On the translation "give birth to" (instead of "beget") cf. also Manfred Görg, *Mythos, Glaube und Geschichte. Die Bilder des christlichen Credo und ihre Wurzeln im alten Ägypten* (Düsseldorf: Patmos, 1992) 119–21.

[70] On the connection of Psalm 2 with the prophetic oracles against the nations, cf., among others, Bernard Gosse, "Le Psaume 2 et l'usage rédactionnel des Oracles contre les Nations à l'époque post-exilique," *BN* 62 (1992) 18–24.

CHAPTER 6

The God of Israel's Reign over the World (Psalms 90–106)[1]

As we saw at the conclusion of the previous chapter, the sequence of Royal psalms 2, 72, and 89 trace the dialectic of Israel's messianic hopes. It is the dialectic of restoration and utopia. By recourse to the time of David, seen as "ideal," the vow is made to restore that primal time. At the same time, however, out of the experience of a catastrophic present arises the vision of a future that goes beyond what had once been. This tension between restoration and utopian tendencies increases in Psalm Book IV, partly in contrast to the "messianic" program in Psalms 2–89, to give way to a "theocratic" program that characterizes the last two psalm books, 90–106 and 107–148, (149–50).[2] In Psalm Book IV this leads to the largely

[1] In what follows I take up my study "Israel und Kirche im gemeinsamen Gottesbund: Beobachtungen zum theologischen Programm des 4. Psalmenbuchs (Ps 90–106)," in *Israel und Kirche heute: Beiträge zum christlich-jüdischen Dialog: Für Ernst Ludwig Ehrlich,* ed. Marcel Marcus et al. (Freiburg: Herder, 1991) 236–54, on the one hand making it more precise from a diachronic perspective and reading Psalm Book IV as a whole with a synchronic interest and with greater discrimination. I am indebted for important suggestions to the now completed Münster dissertation of Gunild Brunert, *Ps 102 im Kontext des Vierten Psalmenbuchs* (Dissertation, Münster, 1994). Several important impulses to my additional work also came from the questions of Frank Crüsemann; on this cf. Frank Crüsemann, "'Ihnen gehören . . . die Bundesschlüsse' (Röm 9:4). Die alttestamentliche Bundestheologie und der christlich-jüdische Dialog," *KuI* 9 (1994) 21–38, as well as Erich Zenger, "Juden und Christen doch nicht im gemeinsamen Gottesbund? Antwort auf Frank Crüsemann," *KuI* 9 (1994) 39–52.

[2] This development from the messianic to the theocratic program is also found in the expansion of Ps 2:1-9 through Ps 2:10-12. The contrastive tension between Psalm Books 1–3 and 4–5 was first seen with this degree of clarity, as far as I know, by Gerald H. Wilson, *The Editing of the Hebrew Psalter,* SBL.DS 76 (Chico: Scholars, 1985)—although he exaggerates it when he reads Psalms 2–89 as "a documentation of failure": "As such this grouping

hymnic (though framed by lament; see below) sketch of the universal royal reign of YHWH, which YHWH brings about in a grandiose theophany on Zion. Israel with these psalms once again invites the nations to experience this theophany of YHWH, the ruler of the world, who will bring to fruition YHWH's system of justice against all chaos. That Judaism sings a portion of these psalms (together with Psalm 29) precisely on the Sabbath, the day the world was finished and the day of redemption, is, therefore, not surprising. On the contrary: these psalms are the program for a world-sabbath, without which no reign of universal righteousness begins.

I. The Profile of Psalm Book IV

1. The Specific Shape of the Collection 90–106

Psalm Book IV, Psalms 90–106, marked off at the level of the final composition by the concluding doxologies, Ps 89:52 [MT 53] (the end of Psalm Book III, Psalms 73–89) and Ps 106:48, has its own distinctive literary and theological profile, through which it is clearly distinguished from the remaining books:[3]

1) In contrast to the previous psalm books, in which, through their titles, almost all psalms are assigned to an "author" (usually David, otherwise the Korahites or Asaph), the psalms of Psalm Book IV are predominantly anonymous or even without titles. Psalm 90 is the only psalm of Moses in the entire Psalter. Psalms 101 and 103 are psalms of David.

2) While in Psalm Books I–III (3–41, 42–72, 73–89) laments and prayers predominate, now hymns or a basic hymnic tone prevail.

3) At least Psalms 93 and 95–99, as one can already see at first glance, are so strongly connected and linguistically related to one another

stands as the 'answer' to the problem posed in Ps. 89 as to the apparent failure of the Davidic covenant with which Books One–Three are primarily concerned. Briefly summarized the answer given is: 1) YHWH is king; 2) He has been our 'refuge' in the past, long before the monarchy existed (i.e., in the Mosaic period); 3) He will continue to be our refuge now that the monarchy is gone; 4) Blessed are they that trust him!" (*Editing,* 215). Cf. also idem, "Shaping the Psalter: A Consideration of the Editorial Linkage in the Book of Psalms," in *The Shape and Shaping of the Psalter,* ed. J. Clinton McCann, JSOT.SS 159 (Shefield: JSOT Press, 1993) 72–82, though the compositional structure of Psalm Book IV that he there proposes is not fully convincing.

[3] On this profile cf. especially Klaus Koch, "Der Psalter und seine Redaktionsgeschichte," in *Neue Wege der Psalmenforschung: Für Walter Beyerlin,* ed. Klaus Seybold and Erich Zenger, HBS 1 (Freiburg: Herder, 1994) 259–62. The study of Michael D. Goulder, "The Fourth Book of the Psalter," *JTS* 26 (1975) 269–89, yields nothing for our investigation; it reconstructs a rather unlikely cultic Sitz-im-Leben for Psalm Book IV.

through the theme of YHWH's universal reign that their being put together cannot be by chance.

2. *The Framing through Psalms 90 and 106*

The two psalms on the ends, Psalms 90 and 106, form a frame (inclusio) around the collection. As a diachronic analysis of Psalm 90 can show, this frame was deliberately constructed when Psalm 90 was put at the beginning of Psalm Book IV.

The keyword connections between the two psalms are obvious:

> 90:13-14:
> Turn, O LORD! How long?
> Have compassion on your servants.
> Satisfy us in the morning with your steadfast love,
> so that we may rejoice and be glad all our days.
>
> 106:45:
> For their sake he remembered his covenant,
> and he showed compassion according to the abundance of his steadfast love.

These keyword connections are to be regarded as an intentional frame because, according to a broad scholarly consensus, vv. 13-17 represent an expansion of the original psalm, 90:(1), 2-12, whose statements have a field of vision open both to the concluding psalm of the prior Psalm Book III, Psalm 89, and to Psalm Book IV that follows. Only the most important observations supporting that can be given here, especially because our interest is focused on a synchronic reading.

That Psalm 90 was not a unity from the start suggests itself on the basis of the following observations:[4]

a) Verses 13-14 are seen as a new beginning over against v. 12 by virtue of the fact that the imperative request in v. 12 already states the goal of God's intervention and thereby arrives at a certain conclusion. Verses

[4] That Ps 90:13-17 represents an expansion is accepted by most recent works; cf. only Hans-Peter Müller, "Der 90. Psalm. Ein Paradigma exegetischer Aufgaben," *ZThK* 81 (1984) 265–85; Werner H. Schmidt, "'Der du die Menschen lässest sterben!' Exegetische Anmerkungen zu Ps 90," in *Was ist der Mensch. . . ? Beiträge zur Anthropologie des Alten Testaments. Hans Walter Wolff zum 80. Geburtstag,* ed. Frank Crüsemann, Christof Hardmeier and Rainer Kessler (Munich: Kaiser, 1992) 115–30; Erich Zenger, "'Dem vergänglichen Werk unserer Hände gib Du Bestand!' Ein theologisches Gespräch mit dem 90. Psalm," in *Die Verantwortung des Menschen für eine bewohnbare Welt,* ed. Raimon Panikkar and Walter Strolz (Freiburg: Herder, 1985) 11–36 (the repeated layering of Ps 90:13-17 suggested by me in that work I today regard as an exaggeration, not least from a redaction-critical and wholistic perspective!).

13-14 begin anew with imperatives that are intended to lead to the goal envisioned in vv. 14-15. Compared with the perspective on humanity as a whole in vv. 2-12 and the non-Israel-specific understanding of God, developed using the divine name אל, "God," from v. 13 on the Israel-specific relationship YHWH-servants of YHWH or the phrase "our God" steps into the foreground.

b) While in vv. 2-12 the lifespans of (many) individual lives are in view, vv. 13-17 are about the days and years of a historical context that spans generations.

c) Verses 1 [1b] and 17 agree in the designation of God as אדני, "Adonai—Ruler of all"; at the same time, v. 1 [1b] formulates the historical, generation-spanning experience that YHWH has been shown to be מעון, "hiding-place/refuge."[5] Thus v. 16, as an expansion of the basic psalm, vv. 2-12, must be seen as a "lament about morality."

The "expansion" of Psalm 90 goes back to Psalm 89, the concluding psalm of Psalm Book III that precedes it. With the designation for God "Ruler of all" YHWH is summoned in Ps 89:50-51 [MT 51-52] to remember and intervene on behalf of YHWH's "servants," who suffer the insults of "all of the many nations." The theological connection opened with Psalm 90 will, as we shall see, give a direct answer to this—the vision of a different relationship between Israel and the nations. That YHWH is addressed as "refuge" in 90:1 is inspired terminologically by Ps 91:9; the generation-spanning perspective "in all generations" is a prelude to Ps 100:5, the concluding verse of the "composition about the pilgrimage of the nations," Psalms 93–100, which we shall still interpret in greater detail. If in Psalm 90 the tension is built up between universal mortality under God's "wrath" and the full life of "the servants of YHWH," which comes from YHWH's steadfast love and favor, this happens especially by reference to Psalm 102 (cf. especially Ps 102:24-28 [25-29]); probably also resonating here is the call of Israel as "servant of YHWH" (developed in Isaiah) who has a special task of moving the nations to an acknowledgment of YHWH's reign.[6]

The concluding doxology that brings Psalm Book IV to a close in Ps 106:48 is quite similar to the concluding doxology of Psalm Book I, Ps

[5] Against the conjectures undertaken again and again, cf. the correct observations of Werner H. Schmidt, "Psalm 90," 119, n. 14: "*mā‘ōn,* 'residence, dwelling place, hiding place,' can be used in the sense of 'refuge' (Ps 71:3; 91:9), so that the frequently undertaken change into *mā‘ōz,* 'stronghold, place of refuge' (cf. Ps 27:1; 31:3, among others) is unnecessary. Moreover, on the one hand, Deut 33:27 serves to dissuade us from it; on the other hand, the agreement with Ps 91:9 appears to be a reason for these two psalms to be put together." If 90:1 [1b] was added by a redactor as is assumed above, the word actually comes from the "source," 91:9.

[6] On this cf. chapter 3 above.

41:13 [14]. To be sure, the unique, concluding appeal, "And let everything/all the people say, 'Amen,'" gives an imploring urgency to the vision of a "new" relationship of Israel to the nations sketched in Psalms 90–106.[7]

3. The Moses Dimension

Psalm Book IV has a Moses dimension that distinguishes it from the other psalm books. As the first psalm in the composition Psalm 90 begins with the creation of the world and of humanity described in Genesis (Ps 90:3 alludes to Gen 3:19), and Psalm 106 as the last psalm recapitulates the conquest and life in the land, with the latter being evaluated under the perspective of Deut 7:1-5, 16; 29:26; 31:17; 32:17. To that extent the composition Psalms 90–106 is Pentateuch-oriented, that is, Moses-oriented. Moreover, Moses is named seven times in the collection! (90 [title, MT 1]; 99:6; 103:7; 105:26; 106:16, 23, 32), while he is mentioned elsewhere in the Psalter only a single time (77:20 [21]). Above all, notice is to be taken of the function of Moses indicated by the (secondary) title[8] of Psalm 90 [MT v. 1], which is emphasized through the suggestive references to the Moses tradition in the Pentateuch.

Precisely when one takes seriously the nadir of Israel's history lamented in Psalm 89, which means the dispersal among the nations and their scorn,

[7] That Psalm Book IV closes with Psalm 106 and not with Psalm 107 is to be maintained despite the objections of Hartmut Gese. Gese, "Die Entstehung der Büchereinteilung des Psalters," in *Wort, Lied und Gottesspruch, II: Beiträge zu Psalmen und Propheten. Festschrift für Joseph Ziegler,* ed. Joseph Schreiner; fzb 2 (Würzburg: Echter, 1972) 62, argues for his position: 1. Psalms 105–107 form a "small group" that belongs together. 2. "The doxology in Psalm 106 is surely not added for the closing of a psalm collection . . . , but is connected with the liturgical petition in Ps 106:47; it has no redactional function as do Pss 41:13 [14]; 72:18; 89:52 [53]." The following should be said about his specific points: (1) Gese's argument that Psalms 105–107 are defined as a unit through identically worded hymnic introductory formulas is not entirely correct even on the level of the text itself; their function in the individual psalms is also varied. (2) The relationship of dependency between Psalm 106 and 1 Chronicles 16 is actually rather to be described in such a way that "the present ending of Psalm 106, together with the concluding formula of Psalm Book IV, . . . (is) presupposed by 1 Chr 16:8-36, . . . for the transfer of a doxological summons into an account about its being carried out is more likely than the expansion of a fixed poetic utterance by a single long line taken from a prose narrative. Other differences in the comparison also speak for a reformulation in Chronicles, above all a tendency to assimilation to the exemplary Davidic period. For that very reason it is reported that the people at that time really responded to the doxological summons"—Klaus Koch, "Der Psalter," 268. On the theological program of Psalm 106 in the context of Chronicles cf. Hans-Peter Mathys, *Dichter und Beter. Theologen aus spätalttestamentlicher Zeit,* OBO 132 (Fribourg: Universitätsverlag; Göttingen: Vandenhoeck & Ruprecht, 1994) 201–17.

[8] Even the title תפלה, "Prayer," could be an allusion to Deut 9:26.

and when this catastrophe is evaluated from the perspective of the (Deuteronomistic) "theology of God's wrath," what is needed is the prophetic suppliant *par excellence* of the "primal beginning," if the history of God with Israel is to continue. Therefore it is not by chance that Ps 90:13 alludes to Moses' successful prayer after the sin with the golden calf (Exod 32:12-13):

> "Turn from your fierce wrath; change your mind and do not bring disaster on your people. Remember Abraham, Isaac, and Israel, your servants . . ." And the LORD changed his mind about the disaster that he planned to bring on his people.

The great "theodicy poem" of Moses in Deuteronomy 32, with which Israel interpreted the crisis of exile, is also remembered verbally in Ps 90:13 (cf. Deut 32:36); Psalm 90 as a whole has a strikingly strong relationship with Deuteronomy 32.[9]

Probably even the secondary address to God that opens Psalm 90, "you have been our dwelling place . . ." (90:1 [1b]) alludes to the blessing of Moses in Deuteronomy 33 (cf. Deut 33:27 [the connection can be seen in the NRSV marginal reading, "The eternal God is a dwelling place." Trans.]), which like Psalm 90 is ascribed to the (prophetic) "man of God" (איש האלהים) by its title.

The vision sketched in Psalms 90–106, therefore, stands under Mosaic authority. "Moses" legitimates, as we shall see, precisely by recourse to the "canonical" pentateuchal traditions, the bringing together of the history of Israel and of the nations of the world.

[9] The essentially unified "song of Moses" in Deuteronomy 32, whose origin during the exile or in the early post-exilic period still appears most plausible, is a "theodicy with a consolatory ending" (Karl Budde) which, as the proem in vv. 1-3, brings out, as pedagogic wisdom "teaching" is meant to confer on the addressees new life, strength, and consolation. Above all the "song" has the intention of making Israel capable—precisely in the face of the catastrophic experiences of its history—of falling prostrate before YHWH alone as the king of the world (cf. Deut 32:43). Thus in vv. 4-5 its theme proclaims the trustworthiness and righteousness of YHWH (YHWH is the saving "rock" *par excellence:* this divine name, coming from Zion/Jerusalem theology, occurs in Deuteronomy 32 seven times!) in contrast to the unfaithfulness/guilt of Israel. This is precisely the perspective of Psalm Book IV as well; the universalistic perspective developed in that book, which brings Israel and the nations together in the acknowledgment of YHWH, is probably also given in one of the textual variants of Deut 32:43 (secondarily?): "Praise, you nations, his people!"

II. The Opening: Psalms 90–92

1. The Compositional Arc (iuxtapositio)

The three psalms with which Psalm Book IV opens, Psalms 90–92, are in their sequence intended as a thematic unity; they trace an arc that moves forward by what is done or said.[10] Psalm 90 begins as a lament over humanity's subjection to death and to God's wrath and intensifies into a prayer for YHWH's gracious turning to his servants. To this lament and prayer Psalm 91 answers with a double assurance or promise. In the style of a wisdom teaching, a fictitious/anonymous speaker (a wisdom teacher or, on the compositional level of Psalms 90–92, "Moses") first imparts to a "you" that is not more closely defined (the "student of wisdom" or, on the compositional level, Israel) the certainty that YHWH is the saving refuge of those who entrust themselves to YHWH. Psalm 91 then culminates in the assurance, in the form of direct address by God, of long life and salvation (ישועה) given by God. That this assurance is no empty word but finds fulfilment in those who entrust themselves to it is emphasized in the psalm of thanksgiving that follows, Psalm 92, which with its opening is closely linked with the divine oracle in Psalm 91 (91:14: "I will protect those who know my name"; 92:1: "It is good . . . to sing praises to your name").

2. Common Motifs (concatenatio)

The sequence of the three psalms according to the scheme *lament—word of encouragement from God—thanksgiving* is underscored by common/related motifs. To the metaphor of the dried up grass in 90:5-6, Psalm 92:12-15 [13-16] contrasts the metaphor of the fruit-bearing palm tree and the firmly rooted and tall cedar of Lebanon. The motif of confidence and protection with which Ps 90:1 is opened is frequently worked in and varied in Psalms 91 and 92. Especially the prayers spoken in 90:13-17 are taken up, partly verbally and partly by contrast, in the Thanksgiving Psalm 92 in such a way that the thesis suggests itself that these prayers (which are redactional; see above) in Psalm 90 are formulated on the basis of Psalm

[10] Cf. also Joseph Reindl, "Weisheitliche Bearbeitung von Psalmen. Ein Beitrag zum Verständnis des Psalters," *VTS* 32 (1981) 350–54; Matthias Millard, *Die Komposition des Psalters. Ein formgeschichtlicher Ansatz,* FAT 9 (Tübingen: Mohr, 1994) 148–49. Less convincing is David Howard's attempt to prove that Psalms 90–94 trace an (actually original?) compositional arc—David Howard, "A Contextual Reading of Psalms 90–94," in *The Shape and Shaping of the Psalter,* ed. J. Clinton McCann, JSOT.SS 159 (Sheffield: JSOT Press, 1993) 108–23.

92. To the prayer in 90:14, “Satisfy us in the morning with your steadfast love, so that we may rejoice and be glad,” 92:2, 4 [3, 5] looks back: “to declare your steadfast love in the morning . . . [You] have made me glad . . . I sing for joy.” The prayer in 90:16, “Let your work be manifest to your servants,” is fulfilled in 92:4 [5]: “For you . . . have made me glad by your work.” The concluding prayer in 90:17b, “and prosper . . . the work of our hands,” it is given, by way of contrast, its theological foundation in 92:4-5 [MT 5-6]: “at the works of your hands I sing for joy. How great are your works, O LORD!”

3. The Mosaic Conclusion

The conclusion of the compositional unit Psalms 90–92 with 92:15 [16] once again alludes to the great theodicy poem of Moses in Deuteronomy 32:

> Ps 92:15 [16]:
> showing that the LORD is upright (ישׁר);
> he is my rock, and there is no unrighteousness (עולה) in him.
>
> Deut 32:4:
> The Rock, his work is perfect,
> and all his ways are just.
> A faithful God, there is no unrighteousness (עול) (in him),
> just and upright (ישׁר) is he.

With this “Mosaic” conclusion the composition Psalms 90–92 opens to the composition that follows, Psalms 93–100, in which YHWH is praised as “rock” (94:22; 95:1). From Deuteronomy 32 is introduced, at the same time, how YHWH’s “uprightness” is shown: by the rescue of Israel from the threat of enemy nations by the world’s king, YHWH, who will reconcile Israel and the nations under YHWH’s reign (Psalms 93–100). The Temple or Zion perspective dominating Psalms 93–100 is already heard many times in the composition Psalms 90–92, whereby (in accord with the technique of directing the reader) Psalms 93–100 are shown to be a continuation of Psalms 90–92.

III. The Center: Psalms 93–100

That Psalms 93–100 were put together because of their semantic and theological affinity is not a new insight.[11] There probably is also a consensus

[11] For basic work on these psalms cf. Jörg Jeremias, *Das Königtum Gottes in den Psalmen. Israels Begegnung mit dem kanaanäischen Mythos in den Jahwe-König-Psalmen*, FRLANT 141 (Göttingen: Vandenhoeck & Ruprecht, 1987); David M. Howard, *The Structure of Psalms 93–100* (Ann Arbor: University Microfilms, 1986).

that not all these psalms originate in the same period. It is true that in all of them the universal reign of YHWH is in view, which consists primarily in the realization of justice (משפט) in the sense of a just and life-affirming world order.[12] With respect to the realization of this ordering of the world and of life three divergent perspectives can be seen in Psalms 93–100, giving rise to a diachronic stratification within the psalm group. The stratification corresponds at the same time to an analogous layering in the book of Isaiah, from which, in many respects, these psalms take their inspiration, as the numerous semantic borrowings and allusions testify.

1. A First Line of Testimony: Psalms 93, 95, 96, 98, 99, 100*

The six Psalms 93, 95*, 96, 98, 99, 100, which are on the same diachronic (redactional) level, affirm the reign of YHWH over the world as a reality that can (at least partially) be experienced now.

1) Psalm 93, with the proclamation formula "YHWH has become king/YHWH rules as king" (יהוה מלך), gives the theme of the composition that follows. In the "stylistic form of the 'crisis that has been overcome'" there is a celebration of YHWH's eternal kingship, which is effected as the enduring triumph over chaos "from of old" (v. 2) to eternity (v. 5). The historical implementation of this chaos-subduing reign of God happens through the law *and* through the Temple in Jerusalem or through the law of YHWH that proceeds from this Temple (cf. Isa 2:1-5).[13] On the one hand,

[12] In this regard this group of psalms has a strikingly strong connection with Psalm 33, discussed above in chapter 4.

[13] On a "primal" understanding of Psalm 93, cf. above all Hermann Spieckermann, *Heilsgegenwart: Eine Theologie der Psalmen,* FRLANT 148 (Göttingen: Vandenhoeck & Ruprecht, 1989) 180–86; Bernd Janowski, "Das Königtum Gottes in den Psalmen. Bemerkungen zu einem neuen Gesamtentwurf," *ZThK* 86 (1989) 389–454; reprinted in idem, *Gottes Gegenwart in Israel. Beiträge zur Theologie des Alten Testaments* (Neukirchen-Vluyn: Neukirchener Verlag, 1993) 148–213; Eckart Otto, "Mythos und Geschichte im Alten Testament. Zur Diskussion einer neuen Arbeit von J. Jeremias," *BN* 42 (1988) 93–102; Thomas Podella, "Der 'Chaoskampfmythos' im Alten Testament. Eine Problemanzeige," in *Mesopotamica—Ugaritica—Biblica. Festschrift für Kurt Bergerhof zur Vollendung seines 70. Lebensjahres am 7. Mai 1992,* ed. Manfried Dietrich and Oswald Loretz; AOAT 232 (Neukirchen-Vluyn: Neukirchener Verlag; Kevelaer: Butzon & Bercker, 1993) 313–19; Hubert Irsigler, "Thronbesteigung in Psalm 93? Der Textverlauf als Prozeß syntaktischer und semantischer Interpretation," in *Text, Methode und Grammatik: Wolfgang Richter zum 65. Geburtstag,* ed. Walter Groß, Hubert Irsigler and Theodor Seidl (St. Ottlien: EOS, 1991) 151–90.

The structure proposed in Rudolf Mosis, "'Ströme erheben, Jahwe, ihr Tosen . . .' Beobachtungen zu Ps 93," in *Ein Gott, eine Offenbarung: Beiträge zur biblischen Exegese, Theologie und Spiritualität: Festschrift für Notker Füglister OSB zum 60. Geburtstag,* ed. Friedrich V. Reiterer (Würzburg: Echter, 1991), is problematic for many reasons: (1) The colometric division of the "thematic statement" in v. 1 is very unlikely. (2) התאזר, "he is

Psalm 93, through the (redactional) "You are from everlasting" (v. 2b) traces the arc back to Ps 90:2, the beginning of Psalm Book IV. On the other hand, important thematic words are heard that are taken up and developed in the composition that follows. The theme עז, "strength," (of YHWH the king) mentioned in 93:1 is explicitly connected in 96:6-7 with the Temple (in Jerusalem) in such a way that YHWH's strength is said to be present there and can be experienced there—precisely with reference to the nations, who are called to come there on pilgrimage.

That the "strength" of this king consists in the justice and righteousness that the king has revealed in Israel ("Jacob") is explained in 99:4.[14] Indeed, there can be an allusion to the decalogue proclaimed on Sinai in Ps 99:7 through the keyword עדותיו, "his commands." Support for this connection could come from the fact that the redactional verse Ps 93:5 pointedly uses the expression עדות it finds in 99:7.[15] This connection is also underscored by the statement, redactionally inserted into 96:10 from 93:1b: "The world is (or he has) firmly established; it shall never be

girded," is too short to be a colon. (3) Seeing that vv. 2 and 5 are closely related is, of course, important, but is this an *inclusio*? (4) Can vv. 3-4 really be read as lament → confession?

[14] How Ps 99:4 is to be understood is, of course, a source of considerable scholarly debate; cf. the overview of the various possible interpretations in Ruth Scoralick, *Trishagion und Gottesherrschaft. Psalm 99 als Neuinterpretation von Tora und Propheten,* SBS 138 (Stuttgart: Katholiches Bibelwerk, 1989) 62–73.

[15] Once again the understanding of Ps 99:7 is controversial. Here I join Scoralick, *Trishagion,* who translates: "In the pillar of cloud he spoke to them; they kept his commands and the statute that he gave them." Because of the motif of the pillar of cloud and its connection with Moses, Aaron, and Samuel given in Ps 99:6, one could think that "commands and statute" in 99:7 are " general expressions for the concrete instructions that YHWH gave on Sinai and from the tabernacle. Whether perhaps *ʿedotâw* is to be read in the sense of 'covenantal statutes, commands' and whether *ḥoq* possibly recalls the repeated *hoq ʿôlām* of the priestly code, can in any case be surmised here, though it cannot be proven" (Scoralick, *Trishagion,* 101–102).

Even more disputed is the understanding of עדתיך, "your commands (?), your testimonies (?)," in Ps 93:5. On this cf. the summary by Janowski, "Das Königtum Gottes," 415 (= idem, *Gottes Gegenwart in Israel. Beiträge zur Theologie des Alten Testaments* [Neukirchen-Vluyn: Neukirchener Verlag, 1993] 174), n. 94: "With Spieckermann, *Heilsgegenwart,* 171 with n. 10 we understand *ʿedotækā,* 'your testimonies,' not as divine covenental statutes or stipulations of the law or agreement, but as 'Yahweh's testamonies in the word (probably transmitted in the priestly tradition), as command, prayer (formula) or oracle' (171) . . . To the interpretive suggestion of Jeremias—which he himself characterizes as speculative (loc. cit. 25–26: 'statutes,' a new interpretation of an older concept or interpretation of a concept occurring in the post-exilic period), we cannot give assent any more than to the proposal of Otto ("Mythos und Geschichte," 101) . . . to connect *ʿdwt* with the new Assyrian *adê* (pl. of *adû,* 'oath, defense'), taken from the Aramaic, since—despite partial similarity in subject matter ('reliability' of the *adê*)—the conception- and institution-historical background is different."

moved," because in 96:10 it has been inserted between the message to be proclaimed to the nations, "YHWH is king" and "He will judge the nations with equity" (במישרים).[16] Of course the texts leave strangely up in the air how YHWH's "reign over the world" and YHWH's rule over Israel more precisely relate to one another.

2) Psalms 95 and 99, interwoven in manifold ways, unfold the meaning of YHWH's reign for Israel. Psalm 95 is a two-part (vv. 1-5, 6-7a) hymn and a (redactionally appended) warning speech by YHWH (vv. 7b-11).[17] The psalm invites Israel to pay homage to the "great" (v. 3) king of the world, YHWH, who is greater than all the gods, as *its* king, and as the covenant people to listen to *YHWH's* voice (v. 7), to acknowledge and walk in "YHWH's ways" of Torah (v. 10). That and how the king of the world, YHWH, has been revealed as king of the covenant people in its "canonical" history is explained by the three-part (vv. 1-3, 4-5, 6-9) thematic Psalm 99.[18] It takes its inspiration from the vision sketched in Isa 6:1-11 of YHWH, the king of the world and of the gods enthroned on Zion, with the important difference that the *trishagion* is now no longer to be shouted/sung by the seraphim but by Israel and the nations.

The network of relationships between Psalms 95 and 99 is very close: as Psalm 95 summons Israel, so now Psalm 99 summons Israel and the nations to praise YHWH, the God of Israel, and to prostrate themselves before YHWH (95:6; 99:5), the "great" God (95:3; 99:2) of whom the speakers of the psalm say: he is "our God" (95:7; 99:5, 8, 9). In three ways Psalm 99 explains and deepens the "covenant formula" (YHWH our God—we YHWH's people) used in Ps 95:7 for the relationship between YHWH and Israel: (a) by the reference to Moses, Aaron and Samuel as "foundational figures" for the people of God (a reference to "torah" and "prophets"); (b) by the reference to the gift of the Law; (c) by citing the central Sinai confession in Exod 34:6-7.

3) The psalms standing at the center of the composition 93, 95*, 96, 98, 99, 100, Psalms 96 and 98, are imperative hymns (each having two parts, 96:1-6, 7-13; 98:1-3, 4-9), which explicitly develop the theme of the

[16] A different literary-critical decision is made by Jeremias, *Königtum Gottes,* 122, with respect to v. 10, which "is overfilled"with three lines; looking to 1 Chronicles does not bring us any further, since the text is unclear precisely at that place. If one reads Pss 96:10 and 98:9 in synchronic association with Ps 99:4, במשרים, "with equity," (96:10; 98:9) possibly receives the connotation "world order" which is given in Ps 99:4 in משרים.

[17] The original unity of Psalm 95 is defended by Frank-Lothar Hossfeld, "Psalm 95: Gattungsgeschichtliche, kompositionskritische und bibeltheologische Anfragen," in *Neue Wege der Psalmenforschung,* 30–32.

[18] On the division of Psalm 99 into the three strophes, vv. 1-3, 4-5, and 6-9, as well as on its interpretation, cf. especially Scoralick, *Trishagion.*

relationship of the nations to the God of Israel in the light of God's dealings with Israel. The two psalms are semantically interwoven in so many ways "that they can only be interpreted together."[19] These psalms are about nothing less than that the nations and their families (cf. Gen 12:3) are summoned to come to Zion in order to accept in that way YHWH's universal rule over the world and YHWH's justice. In this regard Psalm 98 is once again a heightening compared to Psalm 96. First, at the beginning of both psalms all the nations of the world are summoned to join in singing the "new song":

> 96:1:
> O sing to the LORD a new song,
> sing to the LORD, all the earth.
>
> 98:1, 4:
> O sing to the LORD a new song,
> . . . .
> Make a joyful noise to the LORD, all the earth,
> break forth into joyous song and sing praises.

Psalm 96:7-9 explicitly says that this summons to "all the earth" has in view the nations of the world. The psalm explicitly summons the nations to undertake the "pilgrimage of the nations" and to join in the worship in the Temple:

> 96:7-9:
> Ascribe to the LORD, O families of the nations,
> Ascribe to the LORD glory and strength.
> Ascribe to the LORD the glory due his name;
> Bring an offering, and come into his courts.
> Worship the LORD in holy splendor;
> tremble before him, all the earth.

That then suddenly in 96:10 "the families of the nations" are no longer meant to be included, but only Israel, as many interpreters assume,[20] appears to me to contradict the entire statement scheme of the two Psalms 96 and 98. These psalms are not about a "missionary task" for Israel but about the attainment of understanding by and among the nations:

> 96:10:
> Say (to one another) among the nations, "The LORD is king!

[19] Jeremias, *Königtum Gottes*, 131.

[20] Thus, most recently, Crüsemann, "Bundestheologie," in explicit contradiction to this position, already advocated by me in "Israel und Kirche im einen Gottesbund? Auf die Suche nach einer für beide akzeptablen Verhältnisbestimmung," *KuI* 6 (1991) 99–114.

The world is firmly established; it shall never be moved.
He will judge the nations with equity."

Both psalms, in dependence on the book of Isaiah, explicitly and in similar language establish *how* the nations come to this understanding.[21] It is YHWH's saving activity for Israel:

96:2-3:
Sing to the LORD, bless his name;
  tell of his salvation from day to day.
Declare his glory among the nations,
  his marvelous works among all the peoples.
98:1-3:
O sing to the LORD a new song,
  for he has done marvelous things.
. . . .
YHWH has made known his victory;
  he has revealed his vindication in the sight of the nations.
He has remembered his steadfast love and faithfulness
  to the house of Israel.
All the ends of the earth have seen
  the salvation/deliverance given by our God.

The renewed turning of YHWH to Israel after and in the midst of judgment has revealed the depth dimension of YHWH's reign: YHWH is not interested in annihilation and death but in deliverance and life. Therefore the nations should and can acknowledge YHWH's reign and submit to it. If this happens the world will at the same time be wonderfully transformed, as the cosmic imagery of the two psalms, which once again draws upon the book of Isaiah (cf. Isa 44:23; 49:13; 55:12), indicates:

96:11-13:
Let the heavens be glad, and let the earth rejoice;
  let the sea roar, and all that fills it;
  let the field exult, and everything in it.
Then shall all the trees of the forest sing for joy
  before the LORD, for he is coming,
  for he is coming to judge the earth.
He will judge the world with righteousness,
  and the peoples with his truth.
98:7-9
Let the sea roar, and all that fills it;
  the world and those who live in it.

[21] Cf. especially Ps 98:1-3 with Isa 51:4-5; 52:10, as well as Pss 96:13; 98:9 with Isa 2:4.

Let the floods clap their hands;
let the hills sing together for joy
at the presence of the LORD, for he is coming
to judge the earth.
He will judge/reconcile the world with righteousness,
and the peoples with equity.

The summons of these psalms to "all the earth" or "all nations/peoples" is neither rhetorical window-dressing nor a reference to some proselytes, and certainly not a reference to the Jewish diaspora streaming in from all over the world. The "new song" ringing out here is the message about YHWH, the "judge" of the whole earth, who by the deliverance of Israel reestablishes the disrupted world order—before the eyes of all nations. "The act of deliverance that Deutero-Isaiah had proclaimed is so self-evident for Psalm 98 that the nations, "seeing it," have taken part in it, and it is now up to them to draw the consequences."[22] Psalm 100, as the concluding psalm of the composition 93–100, sings of these consequences for the nations.

4) Psalm 100 shares with Psalms 93, 95*, 96, 98, 99 the perspective that YHWH's reign over the world can be experienced in the present. It is true that it lacks the term "king," but the imperative that opens the psalm, "Make a joyful noise to the LORD," is a technical term for the shouts of joy accorded a king. Above all, however, the psalm takes up the vocabulary and the conceptual world of the preceding psalms so thoroughly that these, as we want to show below, provide the frame of reference for interpreting it, unless one is methodologically closed to the plan of looking at the material wholistically. Rabbi Samson Raphael Hirsch has summarized this succinctly: "This psalm of thanksgiving is put here as a finale, as it were, to the preceding psalms which sang of the advent of the new era on earth."[23]

The six-part composition Psalms 93, 95*, 96, 98, 99, 100, because of its theological proximity to Isa 2:1-4; 51:4-5 and the vision sketched there of a peaceful world order that is already at work in the present, can well be imagined in the time between 500 and 400 B.C.E., that is, in the Persian period; possibly it is even to be situated in the context of the "canonization" of the Torah under Ezra.[24]

[22] Jeremias, *Königtum Gottes,* 135.

[23] Samson R. Hirsch, *The Psalms* (Jerusalem/New York: Feldheim Publishers, 1978; first appeared in German in 1882) 125.

[24] On this chronological estimate cf. also Odil H. Steck, *Der Abschluß der Prophetie im Alten Testament. Ein Versuch zur Frage der Vorgeschichte des Kanons,* BThSt 17 (Neukirchen-Vluyn: Neukirchener Verlag, 1991) 108–109. That the "canonization" of the Torah took place from the Jerusalem Temple is no side issue here!

2. *A Further Line of Testimony: Psalm 97*

At the center of this composition, presumably in the Hellenistic period after the collapse of Alexander's kingdom,[25] Psalm 97 found its place. This psalm sees the universal reign of YHWH coming only at the eschatological turning and in/after an imminent judgment of the world. On the one hand, the psalm draws from its neighboring psalms, as the following outline shows:

v. 1	The LORD is king (cf. 93:1; 96:10; 99:1).
	Let the earth rejoice (cf. 96:11).
	let . . . be glad (cf. 96:11).
v. 2	righteousness and justice (cf. 96:13; 98:9; 99:4).
	are the foundation of his throne (cf. 93:2).
v. 4	the world (cf. 93:1; 96:10, 13; 98:9).
v. 6	all nations behold his glory (cf. 96:3; 98:3).
v. 7	all gods bow down before him (cf. 95:6; 96:9; 99:5, 9).
v. 9	exalted far above all gods (cf. 95:3).

On the other hand, the psalm has a striking similarity with the eschatological vision of Isaiah 65–66:[26]

v. 1:	Isa 66:19
v. 3:	Isa 66:14-15
v. 6:	Isa 66:18
v. 7:	Isa 65:3-5; 66:3, 17

Jörg Jeremias characterizes how Psalm 97 differs from the psalms of the compositional unit 93, 95*, 96, 98, 99, 100 as follows: "The expectation of a linear end to the present, as we learned to know of it in the Persian period, makes room for the hope of a sudden, world-shaking intervention of YHWH, through which God's justice is realized in such a way that the heathen, idolatrous powers are humbled once and for all."[27] The judgment theophany of YHWH, at which YHWH will bring about justice and righteousness through the annihilation of the wicked, is the appearance of the

[25] On the dating of the psalm in the Hellenistic period, cf. Jeremias, *Königtum Gottes,* 142–43; Steck, *Abschluß der Prophetie,* 108–109. Into temporal and theological proximity with Psalm 97 Jeremias also puts Psalms 9/10 and 145, as well as Ps 22:27-30 [28-31]. On the relationship of Psalm 97 to Psalm 33, cf. chapter 4 above.

[26] On this cf. Steck, *Abschluß der Prophetie,* 109; in the redaction-critical model of O. H. Steck we are dealing with "reassessment III in the Book of Isaiah," which he locates between 302/1 and 270 B.C.E. (302/1 B.C.E. : the capture of Jerusalem by Ptolomy I).

[27] Jeremias, *Königtum Gottes*, 136–37.

God of Sinai (cf. the metaphors of vv. 2-3); at the same time it is the dawning of the "sun of righteousness" (cf. v. 11).

Whether Psalm 97 was written for the context in which it now stands is difficult to decide. Much, of course, speaks in favor of the idea that this psalm, particularly in light of its numerous points of contact with the neighboring psalms, belongs "in the framework of a literary practice of reading psalms in the service of a piety seeking assurance."[28] But then the question is raised whether the psalm does not go back to the redaction that created Psalm Book IV as a whole. In any case, speaking for this assumption are several references from Psalm 97 to Psalm 104 as well as the observation that the reworking of Psalm 102, by which Psalm 102 was inserted into the context, is strongly inspired by Isaiah 65–66 (just like Psalm 97).[29]

3. A Third Line of Testimony: Psalm 94

Psalm 94, once again, has to be more recent, with its urgent demand that YHWH at long last appear as the "God of vengeance" (אל־נקמות) in order to put an end to the work of "the evildoers" and save "the righteous." This psalm is in concert with an apocalyptic tendency in the Psalter, which finds expression in Psalm 1 and Ps 2:10-12, among others, but also in Psalm 109.[30] The psalm probably goes back to a redaction that has the entire Psalm Book in view. Psalm 94 is also inspired semantically by its neighboring psalms. It is true that the concept of "king" is lacking in Psalm 94, but there are several statements that belong to the topic of royal rule, especially since they appear in neighboring psalms as statements about the king. This is true, first, of the title "judge of the earth" (v. 2; cf. 96:13; 98:9) and, second, of the verbal combination "righteousness and justice" (v. 15), which we encounter in Psalms 96, 97, 98, 99 as marks of YHWH's reign.

[28] Steck, *Abschluß der Prophetie,* 109.

[29] Cf. 97:2-3 with 104:3-4; 97:5 with 104:32; 97:10 with 104:35. For evidence of a "reassessment" within Psalm 102 (vv. 12-23, 24a, 26, 27a, 28 [MT 13-24, 25a, 27, 28a, 29]), cf. now Brunert, "Psalm 102," which also discusses the dependence of the "reassessment" on the book of Isaiah; this is already noticed also by Steck, "Zu Eigenart und Herkunft von Ps 102," *ZAW* 102 (1990) 357–72, who, to be sure, declares the psalm as a whole to be a unity and created as such for its present literary context.

[30] On the relationship of Psalm 94 to Psalms 1, 2:10-12 and 149, cf. 94:1 with 149:7; 94:3 with 1:5-6; 94:8 with 2:10; 94:10 with 2:11; 94:12 with 1:2; 94:15 with 1:5-6. On the points of contact between Psalms 93 and 94 in the light of Isa 59:15b-20, cf. also Bernard Gosse, "Les introductions des Psaumes 93–94 et Isaïe 59:15b-20," *ZAW* 106 (1994) 303–306.

Important observations about this apocalypticizing final redaction of the Psalter are now offered (even if in a way that is too sweeping and literary critically exaggerated) by

Above all, the lament about the destruction of widows, strangers, and orphans formulated in 94:5-6 has as its background the concept (in the ancient Near East and in ancient Israel) of the king as the protector of these wretched ones. As a lament and supplication that, in the face of the threat to the existence of the people of God through the evildoers within the people itself and in the nations of the world, summons the "appearance" of the God of vengeance (cf. Ps 99:8), Psalm 94 gives an unprecedented urgency to the "spiritual" pilgrimage of Israel and of the nations to the Temple, the place from which YHWH will rule over the world. The confession of confidence in YHWH, the rock, in 94:22 both traces the arc back to 92:16 and leads over to the following Psalm 95, which opens with the summons to royal rejoicing before YHWH, "the rock of our salvation."

4. The High Point of the Composition: Psalm 100

Psalm 100, as the concluding psalm of the group 93–100, is the high point of the composition in which—read synchronically—several layers are superimposed. Psalms 93 and 94 form the dialectic opening of the composition. Psalm 93 gives the theme of the composition: YHWH's universal rule over the world, carried out from Zion by means of YHWH's covenant law. Psalm 94 contrasts this "lofty" agenda with the opposing historic reality that holds sway in Israel itself, in the relationship between Israel and the nations, as well as among the nations. There evildoers dominate, bending justice, killing widows, strangers, and orphans, destroying the life of the righteous—and saying thereby, "The LORD does not see; the God of Jacob does not perceive" (94:7). To a certain extent Psalm 94 guarantees that the reign of YHWH is sure to be realized in the everyday lives of the little people and of individuals, and at the same time it maintains that YHWH's reign with YHWH's people and heritage (94:5, 14) must begin and become visible if the nations are to be attracted and convinced by its world-pacifying and world-changing "strength" (93:1; 96:4; 99:4).

Psalm 95, read synchronically, ties in closely with Psalm 94. It makes clear why YHWH's reign has not yet unfolded its full form and especially its power to change the nations: because Israel is not living in accord with the covenant (cf. the covenant formula in 95:7) and is not listening "today" to the voice of YHWH's Torah. The hortatory appeal in first person plural which which Psalm 95 begins is, therefore, the invitation for Israel to walk

---

Christoph Levin, "Das Gebetbuch der Gerechten. Literargeschichtliche Beobachtungen am Psalter," *ZThK* 90 (1993) 355–81; on the connection between Psalm 2 and Psalm 149, cf. finally Gosse, "Le Psaume CXLIX et la reinterprétation post-exilique de la tradition prophétique," *VT* 54 (1994) 259–63.

in the ways of its king, YHWH—in order, *in this way,* to motivate the nations to that pilgrimage to Zion to which Psalms 96–100 call. Linguistically Psalm 95 has the closest connections with the concluding Psalm 100 and, together with Psalm 100, creates a frame around Psalms 96–99, the "imperative" group addressed to the nations.

Within the group Psalms 96–99, Psalms 96–98 form a concentric triad, the theme supplied by Psalm 97 at the center. Now while Psalms 96 and 98 envision the carrying out of God's reign in a basically peaceful way, Psalm 97 portrays it as an event of (punitive) judgment. Psalms 96–98, which, when they are read on the level of the final text of the Psalm Book, are full of reminiscences of Psalm 33 (interpreted above in chapter 4), sing of the "coming" of YHWH to a judgment in "righteousness" and "equity" as a revelation of YHWH's reign before all nations. Psalm 99 then joins in, in harmony with this scene, by presenting YHWH enthroned on the cherubim on holy Mount Zion.

Now, with Psalm 100, the scenic and theological high point of the entire composition can follow.[31] It calls Israel and the nations to the *common* acknowledgment of YHWH's reign over the world. Thereby the prerogative of Israel named in Ps 95:6-7 is extended to the nations who acknowledge YHWH. Even if this is not unique (cf. already Ps 47:9 [10]: "The princes of the peoples gather as the people of the God of Abraham,"[32] but also Isa 19:25), it is still true that Psalm 100 offers one of the most spectacular theological statements in the Hebrew Bible in that it now places the covenant formula also in the mouth of the nations as a confession of their "new" relationship with God. So that no misunderstanding remains: in this psalm "the nations" do not take the place of Israel, and the differences between Israel and the nations are also not removed—the structure of the composition Psalms 93–100* indeed maintains the differences, as sketched above. All the same: the composition outlines the vision that YHWH's saving activity for Israel, which is becoming visible "before the eyes of the nations," leads the nations to join the "service" of Israel under and for the universal reign of the God YHWH.

[31] On Psalm 100 as the high point of the Royal YHWH Psalms, cf. especially Howard, *Structure,* 213–15; Norbert Lohfink, "Die Universalisierung der 'Bundesformel' in Ps 100,3," *ThPh* 65 (1990) 172–83; on the theological relevance cf. also James L. Mays, "Worship, World and Power: An Interpretation of Psalm 100," *Int* 23 (1969) 315–30; Walter Brueggemann, "Psalm 100," *Int* 39 (1985) 65–69; J. Clinton McCann, *A Theological Introduction to the Book of Psalms. The Psalms as Torah* (Nashville: Abingdon, 1993) 64–70.

[32] On the interpretation cf. Erich Zenger, "Der Gott Abrahams und die Völker. Beobachtungen zu Psalm 47," in *Die Väter Israels. Beiträge zur Theologie der Patriarchenüberlieferungen im Alten Testament. Festschrift für Josef Scharbert zum 70. Geburtstag,* ed. Manfred Görg and A. R. Müller (Stuttgart: Katholisches Bibelwerk, 1989) 413–30.

This "bringing together" of Israel and the nations is underscored in Psalm 100 as the final psalm of the composition 93–100* by Psalm 100 taking up verbatim elements both from the "Israel Psalm" 95 and from the "nations psalms" 96, 98 (and from Psalm 99), as the following chart shows:

Psalm 100		Psalms 95, 96, 98, 99
A Psalm of Thanks(giving) [MT 1a]		
1	[1b] Make a joyful noise to the LORD, all the earth.	verbatim: 98:4; cf. 95:1-2; 96:1, 9
2a	Worship the LORD with gladness;	correlate: YHWH as king
2b	come into his presence with singing	cf. 95:6; 96:4, 8
3a	Know that the LORD (alone) is God	cf. 98:2; verbatim: 95:7
3b	It is he that made us, and we are his;	verbatim: 95:6, 7
3c	we are his people, and the sheep of his pasture.	verbatim: 95:7
4a	Enter his gates with thanksgiving,	cf. 96:8; 99:3; 95:2
4b	and his courts with praise.	cf. 96:4
4c	Give thanks to him, bless his name	verbatim: 96:2; cf. 99:3
5a	For the LORD is good	
5b	his steadfast love endures forever,	cf. 98:3
5c	and his faithfulness to all generations.	cf. 96:13; 98:3

The first three imperatives are a summons to render worshipful acclaim to YHWH as king,[33] to offer YHWH exclusive service as king,[34] and to appear before YHWH in order to receive his instructions.[35] Those to whom these appeals are addressed are not, as most newer commentaries suppose, the Israelites who have come from all over the world on a pilgrimage to Jerusalem and who are now summoning one another to serve YHWH.[36] If one pays attention

[33] On "acclaim for the king" as a reaction to an enthronement, cf. 1 Sam 10:24; 2 Kgs 11:12; transferred to YHWH: Pss 47:1-2 [MT 2-3]; 98:6.

[34] On this meaning of עבד את יהוה, "to serve YHWH," cf. Exod 8:1 [MT 7:26]; 8:20 [16]; 9:1, 13; 10:3; Josh 24:14-15, 18; Isa 19:23; Mal 3:14.

[35] On this meaning of בוא לפני, "to come/go before the face," cf. 1 Kgs 1:28, 32.

[36] Hermann Gunkel, *Die Psalmen,* HK 2.2 (Göttingen: Vandenhoeck & Ruprecht, 1926) 432, draws the circle even smaller: the summons goes "to the whole land (that is to

to the connections Psalm 100 has with Psalms 93–99 and particularly to the fact that Ps 100:1 quotes Ps 98:4a verbatim, where the imperative of Psalm 98 as a whole unquestionably turns to all the nations living on the whole earth, it is natural to assume also for Ps 100:1: Here through Israel as the speaker of the psalm all the nations of the world are summoned, at a great "pilgrimage of the nations" to Zion, to accept YHWH as their king. Thereby Psalm 100 is a fitting sequel to Psalm 99, which actually begins with the enthronement cry: "The LORD is king: let the peoples tremble! . . . let the earth quake!" What is actually intended with this is unfolded by the appeals in Psalm 100.

That these appeals ring out as a reaction to a prior action of YHWH's is underscored by the fourth imperative, which is shaped by the recognition formula. This formula, attested above all in prophetic (especially Ezekiel) and priestly (the Exodus narrative in P) theology—for which the non-reversible order of, first, the action of YHWH and, second, the human recognition is constitutive—finally summarizes the process through which YHWH and the secret of YHWH's name are revealed in specific historical events: "By this you will/should recognize that I, YHWH am your God . . ."[37] The (ac)knowledge(ment) of this self-revelation of YHWH in Israel's history before the tribunal of the nations is what this fourth imperative is about. That which describes the special honor of Israel as YHWH's covenant people in Ps 95:6-7 is here expanded, with appropriate changes, to include all nations: YHWH, the God of Israel (95:7: "our God") now simply becomes YHWH, God, the one God of all nations, which YHWH has *created* just like Israel (cf. 95:6), who therefore belong to YHWH just like Israel (cf. Isa 43:1)—and all this with an honor up to that point reserved for Israel: Because YHWH is king of all nations, the nations are also "YHWH's people" and "the sheep of YHWH's pasture." With the nations in view, the "covenant formula" is formulated, of course, only from a creation theology perspective;[38] on the other hand, it is the covenant people Israel who invite the nations to participate in the covenant relationship.

---

say, to all the citizens of the land of YHWH who have found themselves assembled for the festival of thanksgiving at the Temple)."

[37] Cf. the two studies by Walther Zimmerli that continue to be basic on this, *Erkenntnis Gottes nach dem Buch Ezechiel. Eine theologische Studie,* AThANT 27 (Zürich: Theologischer Verlag, 1954), reprinted in idem, *Gottes Offenbarung: Gesammelte Aufsätze zum Alten Testament,* ThB 19 (Munich: Kaiser, 1963) 41–119, and "Das Wort des göttlichen Selbsterweises (Erweiswort), eine prophetische Gattung," in idem, *Gottes Offenbarung,* 120–32.

[38] Just two examples of the creation-theological use in the Ancient East of the imagery of humanity as the flock of the creator deity:

1) In the Enuma Elish, as the assembly of the gods hands over to the creator god Marduk reign over the whole cosmos, the speaker of the divine assembly says:

The theological explosiveness of the knowledge formulated in Ps 100:3, to which Israel is to lead "the nations," does not really dawn on the reader until one sees that Ps 100:3 is making direct reference to the thematically unified Psalm group 46–48.[39] In Psalm 46 Israel states its conviction that YHWH shows himself to be the source of life not in war but precisely by removing war as a political mode of action, and summons the nations of the world: "Come, behold the works of the LORD; . . . He makes wars cease to the end of the earth" (46:8-9 [MT 9-10]). The psalm reaches its highpoint in the invitation from God to the nations: "Be still (setting aside your politics of power and war) and know that I am God!" (46:10 [11]).[40] This address by God is cited in Ps 100:3 and put in the mouths of the nations: "Know that the LORD (alone) is God."

Psalm 47 then depicts the vision of the representatives of the nations listening to this invitation and coming to pay homage to the king: "The princes of the peoples gather as the people of the God of Abraham. For the

---

> May his rule be supreme, may he have no rivals. May he shepherd the black-headed ones, his creatures (Enuma Elish, 6.106-7).

2) In the Egyptian "Teaching for Merikare" a lament in the face of catastrophic experiences receives this answer:

> Well cared for is humanity, the cattle of God.
> God has repelled on their behalf the chaos-monster.

Especially important with reference to our Psalm 100 is the imagery of Shamash, the god of justice, who is sung of as a shepherd in his justice-creating luminous power:

> The people of the world, all of them, thou dost watch over.
> Whatever Ea, the counselor-king, has willed to create, thou art guarding altogether.
> Those endowed with life, thou likewise dost tend;
> Thou indeed art their shepherd both above and below.
> Faithfully thou dost continue to pass through the heavens;
> The broad earth thou dost visit daily.
> . . . the sea, the mountains, the earth, and the heavens.
> Like a . . . steadfastly thou goest every day.
> The lower region, belonging to the prince Kubu and the Anunnaki, thou dost guard;
> The upper world, consisting of all inhabited places, thou dost lead aright.
> Shepherd of the lower world, guardian of the upper,
> Guide, light of everything, O Shamash, art thou.

> ("Hymn to the Sun-God," *Ancient Near Eastern Texts,* ed. James B. Pritchard, 2d ed. [Princeton, N.J.: Princeton University Press, 1955] 387–88).

[39] On the interpretation of Psalm group 46–48 which follows, cf. my interpretation in Frank-Lothar Hossfeld and Erich Zenger, *Die Psalmen I: Psalm 1–50,* NEB 29 (Würzburg: Echter, 1993) 284–99.

[40] On interpreting the address in Ps 46:8-10 [9-11] with reference to the nations, cf. Norbert Lohfink, "'Der den Kriegen einen Sabbat bereitet.' Psalm 46—ein Beispiel alttestamentlicher Friedenslyrik," *BiKi* 44 (1989) 148–53.

shields (that is the rulers) of the earth belong to (this) God" (47:9 [10]). As Abraham, according to the tradition, once separated himself from the false gods of his ancestors, so the nations renounce their former gods in order to become "people of YHWH the divine king," for "to God they belong."[41] The confession in Ps 100:3, "we are his; we are his people," alludes to this vision in Psalm 47. Finally, Psalm 48 celebrates YHWH as the divine king enthroned on Zion, whose "righteousness" consists in "steadfast love" (48:9-11 [10-12]) and whom the kings and nations choose as their royal shepherd: "this is God, our God forever and ever. He will be our guide forever" (48:14 [15]).[42]

This perspective sounds forth in Psalm 100 both in the phrase "and (we are) the sheep of his pasture" (100:3) and in the word of praise in 100:5, "his steadfast love endures forever." The allusions in Psalm 100 to Psalms 46–48, which celebrate YHWH as the "king of peace,"[43] actually imitate the sequence of these psalms, so that there is no question: with Psalm 100 a vision is sketched according to which the reign of God as a universal reign of peace and of righteousness becomes a reality in that "the earth will be full of the knowledge of the LORD as the waters cover the sea" (Isa 11:9).

In the face of this vision of a peaceful homage of the nations before YHWH, the second strophe of Psalm 100 actually intensifies. With the three imperatives in v. 4 the nations are invited, like the Israelites, indeed like the priests of Israel, to walk through the gates in the walls of the Temple compound and in the courts of the Temple compound to join in singing (cf. Psalm 117)[44] the traditional songs of praise to YHWH[45] and the prayers of thanksgiving and praise ("the blessings") of his name (cf. Ps 99:3, 6-8).

[41] On the renunciation of false gods as a presupposition for the pilgrimage of the nations, cf. the discussion of Psalm 25 above in chapter 3.

[42] The summons in Ps 48:12-14 [13-15] does not have as its object what is usually seen there, a cultic procession of the congregation on Zion or an inspection of the walls to look for possible damage by the inhabitants of Jerusalem. Rather it is directed—by analogy to the linguistic structure of the neighboring psalms—to the kings to accept YHWH as the God present in the city of Zion, whom they "saw" and before whom they were "astounded" (cf. 48:5 [6]).

[43] Cf. the connections between 46:8-9 [MT 9-10] and 48:4-7 [5-8], but also the statement in 47:4, which is in no sense intended militaristically.

[44] Ps 117:2 is meant to be inclusive: YHWH's steadfast love and faithfulness hold sway powerfully "over us," that is, over Israel *and* the nations. That is to be maintained against the majority of interpreters, also against Mathys, *Dichter*, 292–97. That Psalm 117 was created for the Hallel, Psalms 113–118, precisely with a "theology of the nations" in mind is shown by the Münster dissertation of Jutta Schröten, *Entstehung, Komposition und Wirkungsgeschichte des 118. Psalms*, BBB 95 (Weinheim: Beltz Athenaeum, 1995).

[45] Cf. especially Pss 96:2, 8; 116:17-19; 134:2; 135:19.

Verse 5 summarizes these songs of praise in a hymnic confession that apparently draws on a body of liturgical formulas[46] often used at that time. That YHWH is "good" (cf. also the word of Jesus in Mark 10:18) is the central statement with which the experiences of deliverance of the people Israel (cf. Psalms 106 and 136) and of individuals (cf. Psalms 107 and 119) are answered.

That this goodness of YHWH is rooted in his חסד ("steadfast love"), which is reliable and true—true in fact for as long as history endures ("forever and to all generations"), became visible, as Psalms 96, 98, and 99 emphasize, precisely in YHWH's gracious turning to the "suffering servant" Israel. That YHWH has saved and saves the covenant people in and from judgment is grounded in his being God, which is proclaimed in the name YHWH and in the interpretation of this name given on Sinai: "The LORD passed before [Moses], and proclaimed, 'The LORD, the LORD, a God merciful and gracious, slow to anger, and abounding in steadfast love and faithfulness'" (Exod 34:6). With the confession of v. 5, which they are to speak together with Israel, the nations thus not only acknowledge YHWH as their king (cf. Ps 100:5 making use of Pss 96:13 and 98:3), but also take up the fundamental principle of YHWH's just order, which Israel is to proclaim "to the nations and kingdoms" when they, as those who "fear God" (cf. Ps 102:15 [16]), "gather together" (Ps 102:22 [23]) on Zion, in order to carry out that to which Ps 100:2 summons them, to "Worship the LORD" (cf. Ps 102:22 [23]).

IV. The Concluding Psalm Group 101–106

The six psalms that follow the Royal YHWH Psalms 93–100 are always arranged in pairs. At the same time they form a compositional unity that, together with the compositional unit Psalms 90–92, serves as a frame around the Royal YHWH Psalms at the center of Psalm Book IV.

1. Psalm-Pair 101–102

Psalms 101 and 102 have the redactional titles "Of/For David" (101) and "A prayer of one afflicted, when faint and pleading before the LORD" (102). The title in 102 is inspired by the Davidic psalm 142:2 [3]. That favors also reading Psalm 102 as "Davidic," especially since the expansion of Psalm 102, by which the psalm was incorporated into the composition 101–106 and into Psalm Book IV at all, reaches back to "David's lament" Ps 89:46

[46] Cf. Jer 33:11; 1 Chr 16:34; 2 Chr 5:13; 7:3; Ezra 3:11.

[47] with v. 2 [2b] ("Do not hide your face from me") and with v. 23 [24] ("he has shortened my days") to Ps 89:45 [46].[47] Both psalms have in common the concern of the "Davidic/royal" suppliant for "the city of YHWH" (101:8) and for "Zion/Jerusalem" (102:13, 14, 16, 21 [14, 15, 17, 22]). Both psalms fit in with the perspective sketched in Psalms 93–100.

Psalm 101 is inspired by the flow/format of the entrance liturgy.[48] Because of this it is an apt sequel to Psalm 100, in which the nations are summoned to enter "the gates" of YHWH's Temple, in order to meet there YHWH as the God of steadfast love and justice. It is precisely this "program" that the Davidic/royal suppliant proclaims in Psalm 101. Read scenically it stands more or less at the gates of the Temple and formulates the conditions for entrance. And more: this king presents himself as a person who will use force to bring about justice and righteousness and to preserve Jerusalem as a "city of YHWH"—by destroying all evildoers.

In many ways Psalm 102 forms a contrast to this.[49] The "royal" suppliant of this psalm is not the violent fighter for justice and righteousness but bears traits of the suffering servant of the book of Isaiah. Zion/Jerusalem is destroyed and its inhabitants are carted off and imprisoned. The "renewal" does not depend now on the powerful attainment of justice and righteousness, but on the mercy and grace of YHWH, the king of the world, who hears the lamentation and cry for help "of the poor king" and in turning to Israel, despised, mocked, and fallen under the wrathful judgment of YHWH, reveals the fundamental principle of YHWH's justice: helping the weak to find justice, granting the prisoners freedom, and life to those doomed to die (102:21). In a sense *these* are the "conditions for entrance" into the Temple of YHWH, the king of Zion and of the world. When this "reestablishment" of Zion happens by grace the pilgrimage of the nations viewed eschatologically in Psalms 93–100 will be set in motion, as the redactional expansion of Psalm 102 proclaims by frequent references to Psalms 93–100, but also by taking up Isaiah 65–66 (see above).

2. *Psalm-Pair 103 and 104*

First, Psalms 103 and 104, which are tied together and designated by the title in Psalm 103 (redactionally) as a "psalm of David," are the continua-

[47] On Psalm 89 as the concluding psalm of the "Messianic Psalter," 2–89, cf. the preceding chapter; on the thesis that Psalm Book IV as a whole is conceived as a theocratic development of the "Messianic Psalter" see above, 161–65.

[48] On this view see already (to be sure with a different emphasis) Sigurdur Ö. Steingrimsson, *Tor der Gerechtigkeit: Eine literaturwissenschaftliche Untersuchung der sogenannten Einzugsliturgien im AT: Ps 15; 24:3-5 und Jes 33:14-16,* ATSAT 22 (St. Ottilien: EOS, 1984) 138–39; Millard, *Komposition,* 147.

[49] This is elaborated well by Brunert, "Psalm 102."

tion of Psalms 101–102. Psalm 103 heightens the theme sounded in Psalm 102 of YHWH's mercy as the fundamental power of YHWH's reign. It is interwoven with Psalm 104 in so many ways that the two psalms can simply be read as "twin psalms." The Midrash Tehillim also regards Psalms 103 and 104 as an overlapping composition when it explicitly compares the summons that occurs five times in the two psalms combined, "Bless the LORD, O my soul" (103:1, 2, 22; 104:1, 35), with the five books of the Torah.[50] Actually the appeals in Ps 103:22 and 104:35 are redactional interpolations, intended to link the two psalms together into a unified composition.[51]

The two psalms are linked to one another by motif at their "seams." Psalm 103 closes in 103:19-22 with the image of YHWH who has erected the royal throne in heaven and is there surrounded by YHWH's "messengers" and "ministers" (מְשָׁרְתָיו). With precisely this image Ps 104:2-4 then begins anew, and in this connection it cannot be by chance that "the ministers" of YHWH appear only in these two psalms in the entire psalm book. Also, the secondary[52] colon Ps 104:29b ("and return to their dust") traces an arc to Ps 103:14b ("he remembers that we are dust"). Important keyword connections between the two psalms, which possibly were only created redactionally,[53] are the motifs of "satisfying with good" (Pss 103:5; 104:28) and of the "renewal" of life by YHWH (Pss 103:5; 104:30).

Finally, the two psalms are connected to one another by the designation "works of YHWH" (מַעֲשִׂים) for the creation (Pss 103:22; 104:24). The two psalms sing of YHWH's royal works and in this way fit into the perspective of Psalms 93–100: Psalm 103, as our thematic interpretation below will make clear, calls for praise for YHWH's steadfast love and mercy, which YHWH promised the people in the covenant at Sinai as a

[50] Moreover, the midrash arranges these five appeals into a connected mystical biography of David: as David was in the womb he spoke Ps 103:1; as he was born he prayed Ps 103:2; as he traveled widely during his life he spoke Ps 103:22; as he died and beheld God's glory he spoke Ps 104:1; at the eschatological consumation he will cry out Ps 104:35.

[51] The summons is in 103:1-2 connected "in a substantial way" with the "introduction" (vv. 1-5); "here the entire psalm unfolds from it," as Frank Crüsemann, *Studien zur Formgeschichte von Hymnus und Danklied in Israel,* WMANT 32 (Neukirchen-Vluyn: Neukirchener Verlag, 1969) 302, correctly observes. In 103:22; 104:1, 35 it is a supplementary frame or redactional linking.

[52] 104:29b is a third colon. Stylistically it deviates so obviously from the conditional structure that, in the same way in each case, characterizes vv. 28-30—with a second singular Qal perfect protasis and a third plural Qal perfect apodosis, attached by asyndeton—that its supplementary character is highly probable.

[53] The keywords are firmly entrenched in the context of Psalm 104; in Psalm 103 they could be a "continuation" emphasizing the composition, to the extent that v. 4 is already a climax (death-life), especially since the motif "satisfies with good" is also important in Pss 91:16; 105:40.

"covenant for the forgiveness of sins"; Psalm 104 calls for praise for YHWH's steadfast love, with which YHWH rules and enlivens the entire creation. In connection with Psalms 93–100 it is significant that in Psalm 103 the "just order" of YHWH the king of the world is explicitly characterized as deliverance of the oppressed and despised (Ps 103:6). As the "place of revelation" *of this* just order the covenant history of YHWH with the people is described in Psalms 103–104. Psalm-pair 105–106 is attached precisely at this point and reconciles it with the painful present of "little" Israel that nevertheless is able to count on the promise of the covenant God—and on the fact that the vision sketched in Psalms 90–106 as a whole, of the universal reign of YHWH that will bring Israel and the nations together in peace, will be realized.

3. Twin Psalms 105 and 106

That Psalms 105 and 106 are "twin psalms," that stand side by side not simply by chance or merely by a superficial keyword association, but that the redactor who put them side by side intended a double statement that will be heard in their connection to one another, was already emphasized by Walther Zimmerli in 1972.[54] The two psalms, which particularly at their "seams" also have semantic interconnections,[55] are "historical psalms" that tell Israel's primal canonical history. Even if the historical arc partly overlaps in the telling, the two psalms are in the "right" order in the sequence 105–106 in the sense that Psalm 106 only briefly at its beginning recapitulates the historical arc described in Psalm 105, in order then to describe the time of the Exodus, the wandering in the wilderness, and especially the conquest as a time of sin and infidelity.

Both psalms present the history of Israel as a "covenant history" by means of which the reality of the covenant is shown, in the first place, by YHWH's remembering of the holy covenant word to *Abraham* and leading Israel out of slavery in Egypt and into "the lands of the nations" (cf. Ps 105:8-10, 42-44). In the second place the reality of the covenant is shown, in the midst of YHWH's (justifiable) wrath over the sins of the people, not least on account of the supplication of *Moses* (106:23; on this cf. the discussion of Psalm 90 above!), by the covenant God's remembering "the covenant" and letting the people experience "compassion according to the

[54] Walther Zimmerli, "Zwillingspsalmen," in *Wort, Lied und Gottesspruch, II: Beiträge zu Psalmen und Propheten. Festschrift für Joseph Ziegler,* ed. Joseph Schreiner, fzb 2 (Würzburg: Echter, 1972) 109.

[55] זכר, "remember": 105:42; 106:4; עם יהוה, "the people of YHWH": 105:43; 106:4; בחירי יהוה, "YHWH's chosen ones": 105:43; 106:5; שמר, observe, keep": 105:45; 106:3; "Praise the LORD": 105:45; 106:1.

abundance of his steadfast love" (cf. Ps 106:45-46).[56] Both historical accounts, from the way each opens (summons to praise: Pss 105:1-6; 106:1-5) but also from the concluding phrase of the composition (Ps 106:47b), are in the final analysis praise for YHWH's fidelity to the covenant in the face of oppression by enemies (Psalm 105) and under the burden of Israel's own sin. The redactor, who put the psalms side by side and placed them at the conclusion of Psalm Book IV, here wants

> to express that in praise to God the two statements fundamentally belong together: praise for YHWH's unshakable fidelity to the covenant and the open confession of the sinful history of God's people, in which its individual members also know themselves to be included. This sinfulness leads into depths beyond which only the miracle of God's fidelity to the covenant promise can effect deliverance. The one has no desire to be heard without the other. By means of the two, however, the praise to God occurs to which Israel knows itself called.[57]

As the concluding psalms of Psalm Book IV the two psalms reflect the catastrophic situation of the exile and the dangerous situation that broke out anew for Israel in the time of the formation of Psalm Book IV, after the collapse of Alexander's empire. And more: this catastrophic situation for Israel appears to rule out the coming of the universal reign of YHWH, which indeed according to Psalms 93–100 (and also the other texts from the psalms and Isaiah treated in this investigation) is very closely tied to Israel's fate. This is contradicted by Psalms 105 and 106 as the conclusion of Psalm Book IV insofar as they powerfully invoke the promises to Abraham and the covenant with Moses. With this they trace the arc back to the beginning of Psalm Book IV: "LORD, you have been our dwelling place in all generations" (Ps 90:1).

4. *Psalm 103*

For the question guiding our study, how the relationship between Israel and the nations is seen in the Bible, within Psalm group 101–106 Psalm 103 is illuminating in that it expands the covenant perspective connecting Israel and the nations that is heard already in Psalm 100.

Psalm 103[58] is praise for the God of the Sinai covenant. The much discussed question whether the psalm is a song of thanksgiving for deliverance

[56] By contrast, Ps 106:6-7 sees the sin of Israel precisely in the fact that "they did not remember the abundance of your steadfast love."

[57] Zimmerli, "Zwillingspsalmen," 111.

[58] On this psalm, in addition to the commentaries, cf. especially Crüsemann, *Studien*, 302–304; Klaus Seybold, *Das Gebet des Kranken im Alten Testament*, BWANT 5, 19

received or a hymn can be decided both from the "introduction" (103:1-5)[59] and from the main section (103:6-18)[60] but also from the formal relationship with the neighboring creation hymn, Psalm 104.[61] These all indicate that the psalm is a hymn that wishes to praise YHWH's "holy name" (103:1) in accord with the revelation that, according to Exodus 33–34, was made known to Moses and Israel at Sinai. The psalm makes frequent use of Exodus 33–34, which the author of the psalm probably knew in its final form. It is especially the main section of the psalm that offers an exegesis of Exodus 33–34, which presents the Sinai covenant as a "covenant renewal," just as this is developed on the level of the final text with the sequence Exod 34:9 (plea for forgiveness) and Exod 34:10 (covenant promise as an answer to this plea).[62]

(Stuttgart: Kohlhammer, 1973) 142–46; Hermann Spieckermann, "'Barmherzig und gnädig ist der Herr . . . ,'" *ZAW* 102 (1990) 1–18; on the influence of Psalm 103 on the Jesus tradition and on the "Eighteen Benedictions," cf. Otto Betz, "Jesu Lieblingspsalm. Die Bedeutung von Psalm 103 für das Werk Jesu," in idem, *Jesus. Der Messias Israels. Aufsätze zur biblischen Theologie,* WUNT 42 (Tübingen: Mohr, 1987) 185–201.

[59] The summons to one's own soul that occurs in vv. 1-2 extends syntactically to v. 5: the string of participles in vv. 3-5a is closely tied to the Tetragrammaton of vv. 1-2; the string is tied to "the soul" by the archaizing feminine suffix; v. 5b also belongs to this syntactically; the colon indicates the structural end of the introduction by the change from a participle to a Qal perfect; besides, from v. 6 on the reference to "the soul" is lacking and we have the anarthrous hymnic participle.

[60] In this section statements in we-style and statements about the group of "those who fear YHWH" overlap; through this pluralistic perspective vv. 6-18 are clearly distinguished from vv. 1-5. The section is framed by three keyword connections: עשׂה "do, work" (6a, 18b), צדקה, "righteousness" (6a, 17b), בנים, "sons, children" (7b, 17b). With v. 19 the "conclusion" begins. It summons the entire heavenly court and all works of creation to praise YHWH (vv. 19-22), with vv. 19b and 22ab forming an inclusio.

[61] Psalm 104 is a "creation hymn" with "introduction" (vv. 1-2a), hymnic main section, which praises both YHWH's creative activity "at the beginning" and his continuing devotion to the creation (vv. 2b-30), and "conclusion" (vv. 31-35). Analogously, Psalm 103 is a "historical hymn," which in its main section also sings of YHWH's "primal" historical activity at Sinai (vv. 7 and 11-13 are past tenses: "he made known," "his steadfast love was great," "he removed," "he had compassion") and of his abiding devotion, made known in this historical activity, to the history of Israel (and the nations, see below). For these reasons the two psalms are not individual songs of thanksgiving.

[62] The three phases of the covenant event described in Exodus 19–34, namely, the making of the covenant on the basis of the decalogue (Exodus 19–24)—the breaking of the covenant (Exodus 32)—the renewal of the covenant (Exodus 32–34), in Exod 34:9-10 are narrowed precisely to the dialectic of forgiveness (34:9) and the covenant renewal that arises from it (Exod 34:10), along with a renewed proclamation of God's law (Exod 34:10-26). Even if in Exod 34:10 the concept "new covenant" is not used, the history of Israel that is promised in Exod 34:10 is to be seen only as a history from the perspective of the covenant "renewed" at Sinai. As Jer 31:31-34 shows, "new" covenant is an "Old Testament" category through and through. From its innermost nature God's covenant as a gift of the merciful God is always focused on renewal, as can also be demonstrated from Isa 54:7-10; 61:4-9.

The main section, Ps 103:6-18, opens in v. 6 with a generalizing hymnic statement that emphasizes YHWH's partisanship as a "demonstration of justice" for all the oppressed—more or less as a "summation" of YHWH's saving activity not only on behalf of Israel as a whole but also of groups and individuals. Then vv. 7-11 allude to the plea of Moses formulated in Exod 33:13, "Show me your ways," and the fulfilment of this plea described in Exod 34:6-7 (YHWH passed before Moses and thoroughly explained to him "YHWH's ways," calling out YHWH's own name and explaining this through a series of antithetical hymnic statements) and its realization in Exod 34:9-10 (YHWH puts this "name" into practice through forgiveness and covenant renewal).

In comparison with Exodus 34 new accents are clearly set forth, which take their inspiration from prophetic theology:[63] that which is already proclaimed pointedly in the introduction with an allusion to Exod 34:9, namely, that YHWH "forgives all (!) iniquity" (v. 3), is now developed and pondered in vv. 8-10, by citing from Exod 34:6-7 only "the formula about grace," while the aspect of the God who punishes is retracted in a fourfold (!) denial. This "new" Sinai theology is then extensively grounded in two subsections of six lines each, vv. 11-13 and 14-16, first with reference to YHWH's nature, which is fundamentally defined as "steadfast love" and "mercy,"[64] and second with reference to the nature of humanity, which is fundamentally defined by mortality.[65] Verses 17-18 then summarize the statements about God in the main section, now also introducing the important category ברית ("covenant"), which here, to be sure, has almost become a synonym for the Torah, as the noun פקדים ("commandments") used in the parallel shows, as does the verb שמר ("observe, keep") connected with ברית. That is fully consistent with the theology, also developed in Jeremiah 31, of the "new covenant" whose center is the Torah.[66]

On this subject cf. especially Erich Zenger, *Das Erste Testament. Die jüdische Bibel und die Christen* (Düsseldorf: Patmos, 1994) 108–19; Christoph Dohmen, "Der Sinaibund als Neuer Bund nach Ex 19–34," in *Der Neue Bund im Alten: Studien zur Bundestheologie der beiden Testamente,* ed. Erich Zenger, QD 146 (Freiburg: Herder, 1993) 51–83.

[63] Cf. on v. 6b: Jer 50:33; v. 7: Isa 57:16; v. 11: Isa 55:7-9; v. 12: Mic 7:19; v. 13: Isa 49:15; 63:16; Jer 31:9, 20; Hos 2:6; 11:1, 3, 4.

[64] Verses 11-13 are a composition with three comparisons. The outer two (vv. 11 and 13) are connected by the phrase "for those who fear him"; they explain the two thematic words חסד ורחמים, "steadfast love and mercy" (cf. vv. 4b, 8). In the center of this composition stands the statement about the forgiveness of sins, on which the emphasis lies.

[65] This section also has a frame; this time through the two כי-phrases in vv. 14 and 16; the section is inspired by Isa 40:6-8 or Ps 90:5-6.

[66] Cf. Jer 31:33; Deut 30:1-10 as well as especially Psalm 25, treated above in chapter 3, with which Psalm 103 shows a striking number of common semantic and thematic elements (cf. especially 103:3 with 25:11; 103:7 with 25:4; 103:8 with 25:7; 103:17-18 with 25:10, 14).

In the context of the composition of Psalm Book IV the question is now raised whether the recipients of the steadfast love and compassion of the God of Sinai, namely, "those who fear YHWH" (vv. 11, 13, 17) are to be sought only in the circle of the "children of Israel" named in 103:7 or whether in the perspective of the canonical reading "the nations" are also in view. That the "Sinai theology" proclaimed in Psalm 103 also applies to the nations is in my opinion suggested by two observations:

a) The summons that is directed to the nations in Ps 100:4, to praise "the name of YHWH," is focused on the "nature" of YHWH as it is praised in Psalm 103 by reference to Exodus 33–34. The appeals for praise in Ps 100:4 and in Ps 103:1 also use in both cases the same verb ברך, "bless/praise."

b) The pilgrimage of the nations to the renewed Zion pictured in Ps 102:16, 22-23, which is evoked by an action of YHWH that corresponds to the grace formula in Exod 34:6, is an expression of the fear of the name of YHWH (v. 16), that is to say, of the attitude that in Ps 103:11, 13, 17 draws to itself "the steadfast love" and "compassion" of the God of Sinai.

5. The Vision of Psalm Composition 90–106

From the programmatic composition of Psalm Book IV the following fascinating vision accordingly emerges for the relationship Israel—the nations: the reign of YHWH over creation, established from of old, has chosen Zion, in order, on the one hand, to work צדקות ("saving deeds") here in the midst of YHWH's people Israel and in order, on the other hand, from Zion to "lure" the nations, fascinated by the God of Sinai's palpable steadfast love for Israel, into YHWH's covenant of peace, and to let them live peacefully next to and with one another on the basis of the "truth of God" common to Israel and the nations—"Know that the LORD (alone) is God. It is he that made us, and we are his; we are his people, and the sheep of his pasture" (Ps 100:3).

Psalm Book IV holds fast to this utopia of the king's universal reign—against all catastrophic experiences in Israel's history (Psalms 102, 105–106) and against all experiences of mortality and death (Psalms 90 and 102). The vision of YHWH's reign in Psalm Book IV, as the composition indicates, is placed under the authority of Israel's two great foundational figures, Moses (Psalms 90–92) and David (Psalms 101–106). Their prayer is the theological fire that keeps alive—all doubt to the contrary notwithstanding—the vision of a new world sketched in Psalms 93–100.

CHAPTER 7

Theological Relevance: The Drama of Covenant History

In our predominantly synchronic reading of Isaiah and the Psalms we have remained on the "neutral" ground of the Hebrew Bible. Thus we have not read them from the perspective of post-biblical or even current Judaism as Tanach nor have we placed them in canon of the Christian Bible, as our First (Old) Testament. This would have been necessary, helpful, and quite interesting—precisely in light of the question outlined in the first chapter of our book, which has occupied us both for years. We wanted to describe the perspective of the Hebrew Bible at the historic moment of its canonization. We wanted to work on the prolegomena, about which Jews and Christians could agree, before the necessary discussion can be carried on about the Christian, Jewish, and common consequences on the basis of these "findings."

In this concluding chapter, however, we want in a preliminary way from a decidedly Christian perspective to indicate some consequences for a fresh perspective on the relationship between Jews and Christians. The starting point is the complex of exegetical insights resulting from our analyses:

1) In the Hebrew Bible "covenant" designates the relationship between YHWH and Israel not as something static, but as a dynamic event. "Covenant" evokes the ever-changing history of God with God's people Israel. It is true that there is talk about a covenant in diverse contexts and eras. There are also differing conceptions of "covenant," and they occur in differing systems of discourse. Despite this, however, a "canonical" discussion of covenant is also legitimate. Here, then, it is not a question of several "covenants," but of the one covenant from Sinai that unfolds and is actualized and becomes new (that is, is renewed by YHWH) again and again. Therefore covenant is an "open" category that pervades the canon.

2) This "covenant" is a prerogative of Israel. It is grounded in the election of the people Israel by God. But election means at the same time Israel's being enlisted into service by its God, service that, from the beginning, had the nations of the world in mind. The enlistment into service has the form of the Torah. The reference to the nations of the world, threaded through the entire fabric of the Hebrew Bible, was already wound onto the spool in Gen 12:1-3. It is especially evident in the book of Isaiah and in the Psalms.

3) Both in the book of Isaiah and in the Psalms the motif of the (eschatological) pilgrimage of the nations to Zion is often taken up and modified. The pilgrimage of the nations or of individuals from the nations is sparked by YHWH's gracious saving activity for Israel, which the nations observe; sparked by Israel, living on Zion, living YHWH's Torah, indeed even despite its failures at living Torah; sparked finally simply by the "election" of the nations to be sharers in YHWH's reign. What the relationship will be between the nations called by YHWH into YHWH's reign and the covenant people Israel the texts strangely leave up in the air. One could think of it as participation in the covenant reality or even as incorporation into the covenant *history*. The goal of this participation is in any case the pacification of the nations toward one another *and* peace with Israel.

4) When the nations come to Zion they will be instructed there by YHWH about YHWH's comprehensive world order: they will become acquainted with the ways YHWH has taught Moses and the people. They will experience the renewing power of the forgiveness of sins. And they will hear YHWH's reconciling judgments and the revelation of YHWH's will about justice and righteousness. How these words of YHWH to and for the nations of the world are related in a more detailed way to Israel's Torah the texts (apparently intentionally) leave undetermined. That YHWH's Torah comes to the nations through God's servant Israel is often said by the book of Isaiah (42:1-4; 51:4, 7).

In several psalms Israel, as mediator of God's Torah to the nations, has "messianic," that is Davidic, characteristics (cf. Psalms 2 and 86, as well as the psalm series 100–103). In the synchronically read psalm sequence 24–25 the torah of the nations is concretized with the help of the pattern of the entrance liturgy. However, the relationship of this "torah of the nations" to the Torah of Moses (in agreement and disagreement) may be specified more precisely—the *basso continuo* of the texts that we have analyzed is: without Israel and its Torah there is no universal salvation from the hand of God.[1]

[1] On the problem as a whole, cf. the volume edited by Erich Zenger, *Die Tora als Kanon für Juden und Christen,* HBS 10 (Freiburg; Herder, 1996).

If we apply these exegetical insights to the relationship between Israel and the Church,[2] one could carry the thinking further in the following direction:

1) Jews and Christians believe that they live in and from the "covenant with God." These are not two different covenants. It is one and the same covenant, in whose dynamic reality they, of course, share in different ways. The covenant at Sinai was established with Israel alone. Into *this* event between God and Israel no third party can be "included" in such a way that thereby Israel's special relationship to its God is retroactively changed. But insofar as the Sinai covenant establishes not a static but a dynamic and historically open reality, there is legitimacy to the Christian position that says: in and through Jesus, the Christ, the covenant of God with Israel *has* been opened to the nations or to all people.[3] That is

[2] This is a field that is for the most part still uncultivated by Christian theology. It is true that the more recent ecclesiological sketches (most recently that by Jürgen Werbick, *Kirche. Ekklesiologischer Entwurf für Studium und Praxis* [Freiburg: Herder, 1994]) describe and reflect on the emergence of the Church from Israel. But that there is a continuing bond between the Church and the Jews of today as people of the covenant never cancelled by God, and how this bond is to be thought out more deeply from the perspective of systematic theology, are hardly discussed. Important first steps for this, however, are found in Herbert Vorgrimler, "Israel und Kirche vor dem gemeinsamen Bundesgott," *Christen und Juden. Voraussetzungen für ein erneuertes Verhältnis. Mit Beiträgen von Edna Brocke, Peter Fiedler, Hubert Frankemölle, Klemens Richter, Herbert Vorgrimler, Erich Zenger,* ed. Siegfried Schröer (Altenberge: Oros, 1992) 104–26, in Friedrich-Wilhelm Marquardt, "Entwurf zu einer christlichen Theologie des Bundes," in *Lernen in Jerusalem—Lernen mit Jerusalem. Anstöße zur Erneuerung in Theologie und Kirche,* ed. Martin Stöhr, VIKL 20 (Berlin: Institut Kirche und Judentum, 1993) 93–109, and in the works of Paul M. Van Buren, above all in the second volume of his trilogy, *A Theology of the Jewish-Christian Reality. Part 2: A Christian Theology of the People of Israel* (New York: Seabury, 1983)—on this cf. now Wolfgang Schweitzer, *Der Jude Jesus und die Völker der Welt. Ein Gespräch mit Paul M. Van Buren. Mit Beiträgen von Paul M. Van Buren, Bertolt Klappert und Michael Wyschogrod,* VIKJ 19 (Berlin: Institut Kirche und Judentum, 1993).

The discussions of Karl-Josef Kuschel on the theme "The God of Israel and the Nations" move in the still broader perspective of the relationship Judaism—Christianity—Islam: *Streit um Abraham. Was Juden, Christen und Muslime trennt und was sie eint* (Munich: Piper, 1994). A good overview of the discussion of the relevance of the category "people of God" for determining the relationship between Jews and Christians is given by Christian Frevel, "Die gespaltene Einheit des Gottesvolkes. Volk Gottes als biblische Kategorie im Kontext des christlich-jüdischen Gesprächs," *BiLi* 66 (1993) 80–97.

The theme treated by us of the pilgrimage of the nations is taken up from a systematic theology perspective and thought about further by Bertold Klappert, "Eine Christologie der Völkerwallfahrt zum Zion," in *Jesusbekenntnis und Christusnachfolge,* eds. Bertold Klappert, Hans-Joachim Kraus, Friedrich-Wilhelm Marquardt, and Martin Stöhr (Munich: Kaiser, 1992).

[3] With these distinctions we would also like to answer the question of Frank Crüsemann, which in his critical discussion of the formulations used by the Rhineland Synod in 1980 ("We believe . . . that the Church through Jesus Christ has been included in God's

"scriptural" insofar as those promises and visions in the book of Isaiah we have interpreted in this book envision something of this kind at the end of time. The Church is that part of the nations that has accepted the call of Jesus to acknowledge the God of Israel.

Since Jews and Christians live in the single, shared covenant with God there is a kind of dialectic in the history of the covenant. In it Jews and Christians exist in an antagonistic tension, in the sense that each lives with its particular identity under the perspective of the one covenant with God: Israel is the original covenant people of God, while the Church is God's covenant people only insofar as, through Jesus, they are connected with Israel. On the other hand, the covenant history of Israel has in principle received a new dynamic quality through its "scriptural" opening to the Church, even if actually, until today, this dialectic relationship of Israel and the Church to one another has had for Israel almost nothing but negative consequences.

2) Despite the predominantly negative results of the history of the relationship between Jews and Christians up to now, it would not be "scriptural," either on the basis of the Jewish or the Christian Bible, if Jews and Christians now wanted to walk on two separate paths and avoid one another. That is frequently the naïve model for further discussion that argues "historically." There was at first, it is said, a single way. That was with the people of Israel before Jesus. Then the way forked. The two paths diverged. The one was the path of the Jews. The other, the Christian path, was that of the Gentiles. At some point, as the two paths had sufficient distance between them, they perhaps began to run parallel, and all that is also what God wanted. Until the end of the world, in accord with God's intention, they are to continue their parallel courses. The sun shines on both ways. Thus they are both paths of salvation. The one is the path that God foresaw for the ancient chosen people; the other is the path, mediated by the connecting link of a quickly obliterated and basically quite small group of Jewish Christians, that God foresaw for the other nations, the Gentiles. For the Gentiles Jesus was relevant. He is the Messiah of the Gentiles. The Jews do not need him; without him they are already with the heavenly Father.

That might sound very nice, but it involves imposing too much landscape architecture on salvation history. That is not the way history works,

covenant with his people") he also directed to our exegetical contributions. Crüsemann's principal objection runs: "The formula about inclusion in the one existing covenant, despite the intentions and hopes connected with it, specifically fails to state the continuing identity of Israel" (Crüsemann, "'Ihnen gehören . . . die Bundeschlüsse' (Röm 9, 4). Die alttestamentliche Bundestheologie und der christlich-jüdische Dialog," *KuI* 9 (1994) 21–38.

especially not salvation history. Paul certainly does not talk in this way. Whoever interprets Romans 9–11 along these lines is mistaken.

Nor, as we have shown in this book, do the book of Isaiah and the psalms allow, in the future that they sketch or yearn for in prayer, Israel and the nations to guard against any mutual contact in this way. God has a single plan of salvation, and at the end God wants there to be "one." In history there is guilt. There is freedom. There is remorse and there is reconciliation. There is the drama, and in the drama each person and their actions affect all other people and all other subsequent actions. In this sense the common covenant history of Israel and the Church is "dramatic" and remains "dramatic" until its consummation, determined by God alone. Until this consummation Jews and Christians are "on the way," "caught up in the walk." The biblical word for "way" here does not mean the unoccupied street, but the way one walks and lives ("way of life"). This way is "dramatic" in a double sense: for one thing, because it is designed for moving forward, and second because as one walks this way new landscapes are always emerging and being traversed. This common way is dramatic because Jews and Christians each walk and experience it differently. *In this sense* one can also speak of two ways or of a twofold way of salvation.

To be sure, in the twofold nature of the way there is so much suffering, guilt, and trouble; through it the praise of God in God's creation is so thoroughly stifled that the drama has to move forward. It has to lead out of this trouble. The Christians must provoke the Jews to jealousy; the Jews must provoke the Christians to jealousy.

The picture of the two "ways" has a somewhat too enlightened and self-evident effect, especially in the land of a thousand superhighways. We at least need additional pictures that show once again how shocking the history really is.

According to the imagery of the Old Testament, for God the people are actually God's beloved bride. Perhaps we should simply ask, does God want to be polygamous? Does God want two brides? The answer to this (rhetorically meant) question cannot look like the answer our forebears gave it at the portals of the gothic cathedrals: on one side the proud woman "Church," on the other the shattered, rejected woman "Synagogue," with her eyes bound, even if she did still fully bear the marks of her own beauty and worth.

At these portals the duality of the historical reality is acknowledged. It shakes us more because it is less abstract: not two ways, but two women. Yet these figures at the cathedral portal betray the fact that the "dramatic" character of the knowledge is surrendered. The transitory situation of duality is set in stone and declared to be valid for all time—at the expense of the one woman, the rejected one. Therefore it is totally appropriate that the two women from the Strasbourg cathedral are in the Diaspora Museum in

Tel Aviv as a silent commentary to the witnesses of the Jewish extermination in our land. They document a static and thereby false view of the correctly acknowledged, actually present duality.

The theory of the dramatic, double way of salvation seeks to avoid precisely the error of the cathedral portals. But all it avoids with certainty is the rejection of the one woman, not the unhistorical nature of the view. For it is resigned to the duality. Thereby it no longer takes the question about salvation in its full, this-worldly, historical seriousness, even if it talks of ways of *salvation*.

3) As Vatican Council II dealt with the issue of non-Christian religions in *Nostra aetate,* it finally came down to the question of whether God really—as earlier generations of Christians had believed—condemns to hell after their deaths all who do not affirm the Christian confession of faith. It was urgently necessary to clarify that. But is that the real question between Christians and Jews: who goes to heaven after their death and who does not? Do we dare to put that question on the table when the way of *salvation* is discussed between Christians and Jews?

God certainly denies eternal love in the life to come to none who ultimately seek God and follows their conscience. Yes, and beyond that, also in this life there is for every person always a new possibility for repentance before God. God's grace goes after everyone, be they heathen, Jew, or Christian. Those who are neither Jews nor Christians fully encounter this grace also in their own religious institutions. The Old Testament already knew that as well. We all need this grace ever anew, and—we trust—it is not denied us.

In looking at the question, it would almost be too great a waste of time and effort to formulate more special theories about the theological relationship between Judaism and Christianity. Why then once again even speak specifically about two ways of salvation? One would need from the start to speak of almost innumerable ways of salvation, and it would not be bad if Lessing's Nathan were right with his parable of the ring.

At least between Jews and Christians the issue cannot be this concept of "salvation." What this concept intends is always part of the discussion, self-evident. None of it is to be denied. But for the Bible, and indeed not only for the First but also for the New Testament, when it uses various terms to develop ideas about "salvation," the concern is not only the "eternal" salvation of individual souls but the form of this world, which is out of order and which God wants to restore.

It is about the question of whether and how God succeeds in changing this human history, so deeply marked by guilt, discord, and violence, into that which God actually had in mind at creation. It is about the question of whether harmonious songs of praise can sound again from God's creation, whether in the desecrated and empty spaces of this world God's honor can be present again. At least that is the biblical form of the question of salvation. It is the question about heaven and hell already here, about salvation *history*. If "salvation" is spoken of in this way, Jews and Christians on the one hand and the world of the many religions on the other are not at all in the same position. God works out the history of *salvation* God set in motion by creating God's people Israel and the Church of Jesus Christ. Here there is "election." It may seem to us Jews and Christians to be a burden to be "chosen." But we dare not flee it by introducing a purely otherworldly concept of salvation and being willing to let it go at that.

For this definition of the question of salvation, which is at issue here alone, it cannot continue to be a matter of indifference if the bearers and protagonists of the one salvation of God are divided. In fact that is what they are, and so there now is a "double way of salvation."

If that is the reality, then for this reason one must also speak of the "double way of salvation" so that neither denies that God uses the other as an instrument. To condemn the two actually existing paths to continue parallel for all time, and that even with the justification that there are indeed infinitely many parallel paths to salvation, would be to doubt the possibility of real salvation for this world, that salvation of which the Bible speaks. That, as hard as it sounds, amounts to unbelief over against God's biblical word.

When and how the eschatological vision of the pilgrimage of the nations to Zion is fulfilled in such a way that, in accord with Isaiah 66, "all flesh" meeting the conditions for entrance into God's reign, "God is all in all" (1 Cor 15:28) and the universal "salvation" of God's reign becomes a reality, lies in the hand of the covenant God of Israel, who is the creator of heaven and earth and the father of Jesus Christ. For Christians, until that time, it is worth taking to heart what Pesikta Rabbati, a rabbinic sermon collection, says about this:[4]

> From new moon to new moon, and from sabbath to sabbath, all flesh shall come to worship before me, says the LORD (Isa 66:23). It does not say all Israel shall come but "all flesh shall come." Rabbi Pinchas said, What does "all flesh" mean? Everyone who suppresses their base instincts in this world is worthy to see the face of the Shekinah . . . Another interpretation: "All flesh will come in order to honor me." Even the Gentiles? No, not all the Gentiles, but only those who have not enslaved Israel; the King Messiah receives them alone!

[4] On this cf. also Clemens Thoma, *Das Messiasproject. Theologie Jüdisch-christlicher Begegnung* (Würzburg: Pattloch, 1994).

Can we not read this sermon excerpt as a commentary on Jesus' eschatological vision in Matt 25:31-46? Perhaps, in the light of this perspective, the early Jewish and early Christian prayer, "Our Father, Your kingdom come!" preserves a dimension that has been forgotten—a dimension essential to the salvation of us *all*.

Bibliography

Albertz, Rainer, et al., eds. *Schöpfung und Befreiung: Für Claus Westermann zum 80. Geburtstag.* Stuttgart: Calwer, 1989.

Aletti, Jean-Noël: see Trublet, Jacques.

Allen, Leslie C. *Psalms 101–150.* WBC 21. Waco, Texas: Word, 1983.

Alonso-Schökel, Luis, and Cecilia Carniti. *Salmos II (Salmos 73–150). Traducción, introducciones y comentario.* Nueva biblia Española. Estella: Editorial Verbo Divino, 1993.

Altmann, Alexander, ed. *Biblical Motifs; Origins and Transformations.* Studies and Texts 3. Cambridge, Mass.: Harvard University Press, 1966.

Andersen, Francis I., and A. Dean Forbes. *The Vocabulary of the Old Testament.* Rome: Editrice Pontificio Istituto Biblico, 1989.

Angenendt, Arnold, and Herbert Vorgrimler, eds. *Sie wandern von Kraft zu Kraft. Aufbrüche, Wege, Begegnungen. Festgabe für Bischof Reinhard Lettmann.* Kevelaer: Butzon & Bercker, 1993.

Asselt, Willem Jan van. *The Covenant Theology of Johannes Coccejus (1603–1669): An Examination of its Structure.* SHCT 58. Leiden: Brill, 1994.

Auffret, Pierre. *Hymnes d'Egypte et d'Israël: Etudes de structures littéraires.* OBO 34. Fribourg: Editions Universitaires; Göttingen: Vandenhoeck & Ruprecht, 1981.

_____. "'Les pensées de son coeur': Etude structurelle du Ps 33," *ScEs* 39 (1987) 47–69.

_____. "'Allez, fils, entendez-moi!': Etude structurelle du psaume 34 et son rapport au psaume 33," *EeT* 19 (1988) 5–31.

Auwers, Jean-Marie. *Le psautier hébraïque et ses éditeurs: Recherches sur une forme canonique du livre des Psaumes.* Dissertation, Louvain, 1994.

Barbiero, Gianni. "*mamleket kohănîm* (Es 19,6a): I sacerdoti al potere?" *RivB* 37 (1989) 427–46.

Barré, Michael L. "Mesopotamian Light on the Idiom *nāśāʾ nepeš*," *CBQ* 52 (1990) 46–54.

Barth, Christian. "Concatenatio im ersten Buch des Psalters 4,9," in Britta Benzing, et al., eds., *Wort und Wirklichkeit: Studien zur Afrikanistik und Orientalistik*

I: Eugen Ludwig Rapp zum 70. Geburtstag. Meisenheim am Glan: Verlag Anton Hain, 1976, 30–40.

Barthélemy, Dominique. *Critique textuelle de l'Ancien Testament: 1. Josué, Juges, Ruth, Samuel, Rois, Chroniques, Esras, Néhémie, Esther: Rapport final du Comité pour l'analyse textuelle de l'Ancien Testament hébreu institué par l'Alliance Biblique Universelle, établi en coopération avec Alexander R. Hulst †, Norbert Lohfink, William D. McHardy, H. Peter Rüger, coéditeur, James A. Sanders, coéditeur.* OBO 50/1. Fribourg: Editions Universitaires; Göttingen: Vandenhoeck & Ruprecht, 1982; 2. *Isaïe, Jérémie, Lamentations.* OBO 50/2; 1986.

Beaucamp, Evode. *Le Psautier: Ps 1–72.* SBi. Paris: Gabalda, 1976.

_____. *Le Psautier: Ps 73–150.* SBi. Paris: Gabalda, 1979.

Beauchamp, Paul. "Propositions sur l'alliance de l'Ancien Testament comme structure centrale," *RSR* 58 (1970) 161–93.

Benzing, Brigitta, et al., eds. *Wort und Wirklichkeit: Studien zur Afrikanistik und Orientalistik I: Eugen Ludwig Rapp zum 70. Geburtstag.* Meisenheim am Glan: Verlag Anton Hain, 1976.

Berger, Klaus. *Theologiegeschichte des Urchristentums: Theologie des Neuen Testaments.* Tübingen and Basel: Francke, 1994.

Betz, Otto. *Jesus. Der Messias Israels. Aufsätze zur biblischen Theologie.* WUNT 42. Tübingen: Mohr, 1987.

_____. "Jesu Lieblingspsalm. Die Bedeutung von Psalm 103 für das Werk Jesu," in idem, *Jesus,* 185–201.

Beyerlin, Walter. *Weisheitlich-kultische Heilsordnung. Studien zum 15. Psalm.* BThSt 9. Neukirchen-Vluyn: Neukirchener Verlag, 1985.

_____. *Im Licht der Traditionen. Psalm LXVII und CXV. Ein Entwicklungszusammenhang.* VTS LXV. Leiden: Brill, 1992.

Blum, Erhard. "Israël à la montagne de Dieu: Remarques sur Ex 19–24; 32–34 et sur le contexte littéraire et historique de sa composition," in Albert de Pury, ed., *Le Pentateuque en question: Les origines et la composition des cinq premiers livres de la Bible à la lumière des recherches récentes.* Geneva: Labor et fides, 1989, 271–95.

_____. *Studien zur Komposition des Pentateuch.* BZAW 189. Berlin: de Gruyter, 1990.

Blum, Erhard, et al., eds. *Die hebräische Bibel und ihre zweifache Nachgeschichte: Festschrift für Rolf Rendtorff zum 65. Geburtstag.* Neukirchen-Vluyn: Neukirchener Verlag, 1990.

Booij, Thijs. "Some observations on Psalm LXXXVII," *VT* 37 (1987) 16–25.

Bos, Johanna W. H. "Psalm 87," *Int* 47 (1993) 281–85.

Braulik, Georg. "Die Ausdrücke für 'Gesetz' im Buch Deuteronomium," *Bib* 51 (1970) 39–66; reprinted in idem, *Studien zur Theologie des Deuteronomiums* (1988) 11–38.

_____. *Psalm 40 und der Gottesknecht.* FzB 18. Würzburg: Echter, 1975.

_____. *Die Mittel deuteronomischer Rhetorik erhoben aus Deuteronomium 4,1-40.* AnBib 68. Rome: Biblical Institute Press, 1978.

_____. "Gottes Ruhe—das Land oder der Tempel? Zu Psalm 95,11," in Ernst Haag and Frank-Lothar Hossfeld, eds., *Freude an der Weisung des Herrn: Beiträge zur Theologie der Psalmen: Festgabe zum 70. Geburtstag von Heinrich Groß*. Stuttgart: Katholisches Bibelwerk, 1986, 33–44.

_____. *Studien zur Theologie des Deuteronomiums*. SBAB 2. Stuttgart: Katholisches Bibelwerk, 1988.

_____. "Literarkritik und die Einrahmung von Gemälden: Zur literarkritischen und redaktionsgeschichtlichen Analyse von Dtn 4,1–6,3 und 29,1–30,10 durch D. Knapp," *RB* 96 (1989) 266–86.

_____. "Die Entstehung der Rechtfertigungslehre in den Bearbeitungsschichten des Buches Deuteronomium: Ein Beitrag zur Klärung der Voraussetzungen paulinischer Theologie," *ThPh* 64 (1989) 321–33.

_____. *Deuteronomium II: 16,18–34,12*. NEB. Würzburg: Echter, 1992.

_____. "'Weisheit' im Buch Deuteronomium," in Bernd Janowski, ed., *Weisheit außerhalb der kanonischen Weisheitsschriften*. Veröffentlichungen der Wissenschaftlichen Gesellschaft für Theologie 10. Gütersloh: Kaiser/Gütersloher Verlagshaus, 1996, 39–69.

_____. "Das Deuteronomium und die Bücher Ijob, Sprichwörter, Rut. Zur Frage früher kanonizität des Deuteronomiums," in Erich Zenger, ed., *Die Tora als Kanon für Juden und Christen*. HBS 10 (Freiburg: Herder, 1996) 61–138.

Braulik, Georg, ed. *Bundesdokument und Gesetz: Studien zum Deuteronomium*. HBS 4. Freiburg: Herder, 1995.

Braulik, Georg, Walter Groß, and Sean McEvenue, eds. *Biblische Theologie und gesellschaftlicher Wandel: Für Norbert Lohfink*. Freiburg: Herder, 1993.

Brekelmans, Christian, and Johan Lust, eds. *Pentateuchal and Deuteronomistic Studies: Papers Read at the XIIIth IOSOT Congress Leuven 1989*. BEThL 94. Louvain: University Press/Peeters, 1990.

Briggs, Charles Augustus, and Emilie Grace Briggs. *A Critical and Exegetical Commentary on the Book of the Psalms*. 2 vols. ICC. Edinburgh: T & T Clark, 1906, 1907.

Brocke, Edna. "Von den 'Schriften' zum 'Alten Testament'—und zurück? Jüdische Fragen zur christlichen Suche einer 'Mitte der Schrift,'" in Erhard Blum, ed., *Die hebräische Bibel und ihre zweifache Nachgeschichte* (1990) 581–94.

Brockelmann, Carl. *Hebräische Syntax*. Neukirchen: Erziehungsverein, 1956.

Brueggemann, Walter. *The Message of the Psalms. A Theological Commentary*. Minneapolis: Augsburg, 1984.

_____. "Psalm 100," *Int* 39 (1985) 65–69.

Brunert, Gunild. *Ps 102 im Kontext des Vierten Psalmenbuchs*. SBB 30. Stuttgart: Katholisches Bibelwerk, 1996.

Buber, Martin. *Der Jude und sein Judentum. Gesammelte Aufsätze und Reden*. bibliotheca judaica. 2nd ed. Gerlingen: Schneider, 1993.

_____. "Kirche, Staat, Volk, Judentum," in idem, *Der Jude und sein Judentum*, 544–56.

Buren, Paul M. Van. *A Theology of the Jewish Christian Reality. Part 2: A Christian Theology of the People of Israel*. New York: Seabury, 1983.

Cazelles, Henri. "'Royaume de prêtres et nation consacrée' (Ex XIX,6)," in Charles Kannengiesser and Yves Marchasson, eds., *Humanisme et foi chrétienne: Mélanges scientifiques du centenaire de l'Institut Catholique de Paris.* Paris: Beauchesne, 1976.

_____. "Alliance de Sinaï, alliance de l'Horeb et renouvellement de l'alliance," in Herbert Donner, Robert Hanhart, and Rudolf Smend, eds., *Beiträge zur alttestamentlichen Theologie: Festschrift für Walther Zimmerli zum 70. Geburtstag.* Göttingen: Vandenhoeck & Ruprecht, 1977, 69–79 (= idem, *Autour de l'Exode,* 299–309.

_____. *Autour de l'Exode.* SBi. Paris: Gabalda, 1987.

Ceresko, Anthony R. "The ABCs of Wisdom in Ps xxxiv," *VT* 35 (1985) 99–104.

Childs, Brevard S. *The Book of Exodus: A Critical Theological Commentary.* OTL. London: SCM, 1974.

Christen und Juden II. Zur theologischen Neuorientierung im Verhältnis zum Judentum. Eine Studie der Evangelischen Kirche in Deutschland. Gütersloh: Mohn, 1991.

Costacurta, Bruna. "L'aggressione contro Dio. Studio del Salmo 83," *Bib* 64 (1983) 518–41.

Craigie, Peter C. *Psalms 1–50.* WBC 19. Waco, Texas: Word, 1983.

Cross, Frank M. "The Divine Warrior in Israel's Early Cult," in Alexander Altmann, ed., *Biblical Motifs* (1966) 11–30.

Crüsemann, Frank. *Studien zur Formgeschichte von Hymnus und Danklied in Israel.* WMANT 32. Neukirchen-Vluyn: Neukirchener Verlag, 1969.

_____. "'Ihnen gehören . . . die Bundesschlüsse' (Röm 9,4). Die alttestamentliche Bundestheologie und der christlich-jüdische Dialog," *KuI* 9 (1994) 21–38.

Crüsemann, Frank, Christof Hardmeier, and Rainer Kessler, eds. *Was ist der Mensch . . . ? Beiträge zur Anthropologie des Alten Testaments. Hans Walter Wolff zum 80. Geburtstag.* Munich: Kaiser, 1992.

Davies, Graham I. "The Destiny of the Nations in the Book of Isaiah," in Jacques Vermeylen, ed., *The Book of Isaiah: Les oracles et leur relectures, unité et complexité de l'ouvrage.* BEThL 81. Louvain: University Press/Peeters, 1989, 93–120.

Deissler, Alfons. "Der anthologische Charakter des Psalmes 33 (32)," in *Mélanges bibliques rédités en l'honneur de André Robert.* TICP 4. Paris: Bloud & Gay, 1957, 225–33.

_____. *Die Psalmen. II. Teil (Ps 42–89).* KK 1/2. Düsseldorf: Patmos, 1964.

Delitzsch, Franz. *Commentar über das Buch Jesaia.* BC 3,1. 4th ed. Leipzig: Dörffling & Franke, 1889.

_____. *Biblischer Kommentar über die Psalmen.* BC 4,1. 5th ed. revised; edited by Friedrich Delitzsch. Leipzig: Dörffling & Franke, 1894.

Delsman, W. C. et al., eds. *Von Kanaan bis Kerala: Festschrift für Prof. Mag. Dr. Dr. J.P.M. van der Ploeg* O.P. *zur Vollendung des siebzigsten Lebensjahres am 4. Juli 1979: Überreicht von Kollegen, Freunden und Schülern.* AOAT 211. Kevelaer: Butzon & Bercker; Neukirchen-Vluyn: Neukirchener Verlag, 1982.

Dietrich, Manfried, and Oswald Loretz, eds. *Mesopotamica—Ugaritica—Biblica. Festschrift für Kurt Bergerhof zur Vollendung seines 70. Lebensjahres am 7. Mai 1992.* AOAT 232. Neukirchen-Vluyn: Neukirchener Verlag; Kevelaer: Butzon & Bercker, 1993.

Dion, Paul E. "L'universalisme religieux dans les différentes couches rédactionelles d'Isaïe 40–55," *Bib* 51 (1970) 161–82.

Dohmen, Christoph. "Der Sinaibund als Neuer Bund nach Ex 19–34," in Erich Zenger, ed., *Der Neue Bund im Alten: Studien zur Bundestheologie der beiden Testamente.* QD 146. Freiburg: Herder, 1993, 51–83.

Donner, Herbert. "Jesaja lvi 1-7: Ein Abrogationsfall innerhalb des Kanons—Implikationen und Konsequenzen," in John Adney Emerton, ed., *Congress Volume Salamanca 1983.* VT.S 36. Leiden: Brill, 1985, 81–95.

Donner, Herbert, Robert Hanhart, and Rudolf Smend, eds. *Beiträge zur alttestamentlichen Theologie: Festschrift für Walter Zimmerli zum 70. Geburtstag.* Göttingen: Vandenhoeck & Ruprecht, 1977.

Dozeman, Thomas B. *God on the Mountain: A Study of Redaction, Theology and Canon in Exodus 19–24.* SBLMS 37. Atlanta: Scholars, 1989.

Duhm, Bernhard. *Das Buch Jesaja.* HK 3,1. Göttingen: Vandenhoeck & Ruprecht, 1892; 5th ed. 1968.

_____. *Die Psalmen.* KHC 14. Freiburg: Mohr, 1899.

Eichrodt, Walter. *Theologie des Alten Testaments.* 2 vols. 6th ed. vol. I Stuttgart: Klotz; Göttingen: Vandenhoeck & Ruprecht, 1959; 4th ed. vol. II, 1961.

Ellis, R. R. *An Examination of the Covenant Promises of Exodus 19:5-6 and Their Theological Significance for Israel.* Dissertation Fort Worth SW Baptist Theological Seminary, n.d.

Emerton, John Adney, ed. *Congress Volume Salamanca 1983.* VT.S 36. Leiden: Brill, 1985.

Ewald, Heinrich. *Die Dichter des alten Bundes: Zweiter Theil: Die Psalmen.* 2nd ed. Göttingen: Vandenhoeck & Ruprecht, 1840.

Fabry, Heinz-Josef. "סוֹד *sôd,*" *ThWAT* 5 (1986) 775–82.

Fischer, Georg, and Norbert Lohfink. "'Diese Worte sollst du summen': Dtn 6,7 *wᵉdibbartā bām*—ein verlorener Schlüssel zur meditativen Kultur in Israel," *ThPh* 62 (1987) 59–72.

Fischer, Irmtraud. "Die Bedeutung der Tora Israels für die Völker nach dem Jesajabuch," in Erich Zenger, ed., *Die Tora als Kanon für Juden und Christen.* HBS 10. Freiburg: Herder, 1996, 139–67.

Fishbane, Michael, and Emanuel Tov, eds. *"Shaʿarei Talmon": Studies in the Bible, Qumran, and the Ancient Near East Presented to Shemaryahu Talmon.* Winona Lake: Eisenbrauns, 1992.

Focant, Camille, and André Wénin. "L'alliance ancienne et nouvelle," *NRTh* 110 (1988) 850–66.

Forbes, A. Dean: see Andersen, Francis I.

Freedman, David Noel. "Patterns in Psalms 25 and 34," in Eugene Ulrich et al., eds., *Priests, Prophets and Scribes: Essays on the Formation and Heritage of Second Temple Judaism in Honour of Joseph Blenkinsopp.* JSOT.SS 149. Sheffield: JSOT Press, 1992.

Frevel, Christian. "Die gespaltene Einheit des Gottesvolkes. Volk Gottes als biblische Kategorie im Kontext des christlich-jüdischen Gesprächs," *BiLi* 66 (1993) 80–97.

Füglister, Notker. "Die Verwendung und das Verständnis der Psalmen und des Psalters um die Zeitenwende," in Josef Schreiner, ed., *Beiträge zu Psalmenforschung: Psalm 2 und 22.* fzb 60. Würzburg: Echter, 1988, 319–84.

Fuhs, Hans F. "Heiliges Volk Gottes," in Josef Schreiner, ed., *Unterwegs zur Kirche: Alttestamentliche Konzeptionen.* QD 110. Freiburg: Herder, 1987, 143–67.

García López, Felix. "תּוֹרָה," *ThWAT* 8 [in press].

Gerstenberger, Erhard S. *Psalms: Part I with an Introduction to Cultic Poetry.* FOTL 14. Grand Rapids: Eerdmans, 1988.

_____. "Der Psalter als Buch and als Sammlung," in Klaus Seybold and Erich Zenger, eds., *Neue Wege der Psalmenforschung: Für Walter Beyerlin.* HBS 1. Freiburg: Herder, 1994, 3–13.

Gese, Hartmut. "Die Entstehung der Büchereinteilung des Psalters," in Josef Schreiner, ed., *Wort, Lied und Gottesspruch, II: Beiträge zu Psalmen und Propheten. Festschrift für Joseph Ziegler.* fzb 2. Würzburg: Echter, 1972, 57–64; reprinted in idem, *Vom Sinai zum Zion,* 159–64.

_____. *Vom Sinai zum Zion. Alttestamentliche Beiträge zur biblischen Theologie.* BEvTh 64. Munich: Kaiser, 1974.

_____. *Zur biblischen Theologie: Alttestamentliche Vorträge.* BEvTh 78. Munich: Kaiser, 1977.

Gese, Hartmut, and Hans Peter Rüger, eds. *Wort und Geschichte: Festschrift für Karl Elliger zum 70. Geburtstag.* AOAT 18. Kevelaer: Butzon & Bercker; Neukirchen-Vluyn: Neukirchener Verlag, 1973.

Girard, Marc. *Les psaumes: Analyse structurelle et interprétation: 1–50.* Recherches, NS 2. Montreal: Editions Bellarmin; Paris: Cerf, 1984.

Goldingay, John. *Songs from a Strange Land. Psalms 42–51.* The Bible Speaks Today. Downers Grove, Ill.: InterVarsity, 1978.

Görg, Manfred. *Mythos, Glaube und Geschichte. Die Bilder des christlichen Credo und ihre Wurzeln im alten Ägypten.* Düsseldorf: Patmos, 1992.

Görg, Manfred, and Augustin R. Müller, eds. *Die Väter Israels. Beiträge zur Theologie der Patriarchenüberlieferungen im Alten Testament. Festschrift für Josef Scharbert zum 70. Geburtstag.* Stuttgart: Katholisches Bibelwerk, 1989.

Görg, Manfred, and Bernhard Lang, eds. *Neues Bibellexikon: Band I: A–G.* Zürich: Benziger, 1991.

Gosse, Bernard. "Le Psaume 2 et l'usage rédactionnel des Oracles contre les Nations à l'époque post-exilique," *BN* 62 (1992) 18–24.

_____. "Le Psaume 83, Isaïe 62,6-7 et la tradition des Oracles contre les Nations des livres d'Isaïe et d'Ezéchiel," *BN* 70 (1993) 9–12.

_____. "Les introductions des Psaumes 93–94 et Isaïe 59,15b-20," *ZAW* 106 (1994) 303–306.

_____. "Le Psaume CXLIX et la reinterprétation post-exilique de la tradition prophétique," *VT* 54 (1994) 259–63.

Goulder, Michael D. "The Fourth Book of the Psalter," *JTS* 26 (1975) 269–89.

_____. *The Psalms of the Sons of Korah.* JSOT.SS 20. Sheffield: JSOT Press, 1982.

Graetz, Heinrich. *Kritischer Commentar zu den Psalmen nebst Text und Uebersetzung.* 2 vols. Breslau: Schottlaender, 1882–1883.

Grieshammer, Reinhard, "Zum 'Sitz im Leben' des negativen Schuldbekenntnisses," in Wolfgang Voigt, ed., *XVIII. Deutscher Orientalistentag vom 1. bis 5. Oktober 1972 in Lübeck: Vorträge.* ZDMG.Suppl 2. Wiesbaden: Steiner, 1974, 19–25.

Groß, Walter. "YHWH und die Religionen der Nicht-Israeliten," *ThQ* 169 (1989) 34–44.

_____. "Wer soll YHWH verehren? Der Streit um die Aufgabe und die Identität Israels in der Spannung zwischen Abgrenzung und Öffnung," in Hermann J. Vogt, ed., *Kirche in der Zeit: Walter Kasper zur Bischofsweihe: Gabe der Katholisch-Theologischen Fakultät Tübingen.* Munich: Wewel, 1990, 11–32.

_____. "Israel und die Völker: Die Krise des YHWH-Volk-Konzepts im Jesajabuch," in Erich Zenger, ed., *Der Neue Bund im Alten* (1993) 149–67.

Groß, Walter, Hubert Irsigler, and Theodor Seidel, eds. *Text, Methode und Grammatik: Wolfgang Richter zum 65. Geburtstag.* St. Ottilien: EOS, 1991.

Groß, Walter, and Karl-Josef Kuschel. *"Ich schaffe Finsternis und Unheil!" Ist Gott verantwortlich für das Übel?* Mainz: Matthias Grünewald, 1992.

Gunkel, Hermann. *Die Psalmen.* HK 2,2. Göttingen: Vandenhoeck & Ruprecht, 1926.

_____. *Einleitung in die Psalmen: Die Gattungen der religiösen Lyrik Israels.* Completed by Joachim Begrich. 1st ed. HK II. Ergänzungsband Göttingen: Vandenhoeck & Ruprecht, 1933; 3rd ed. 1975. English: *Introduction to Psalms. The Genres of the Religious Lyric of Israel.* Completed by Joachim Begrich. Translated by James D. Nogalski. Mercer Library of Biblical Studies. Macon, Ga.: Mercer University Press, 1998.

Gunneweg, Antonius H. J. *Biblische Theologie des Alten Testaments. Eine Religionsgeschichte Israels in biblisch-theologischer Sicht.* Stuttgart: Kohlhammer, 1993.

Haag, Ernst. "'Gesegnet sei mein Volk Ägypten' (Jes 19,25): Ein Zeugnis alttestamentlicher Eschatologie," in Martina Minas and Jürgen Zeidler, eds., *Aspekte spätägyptischer Kultur: Festschrift für Erich Winter zum 65. Geburtstag.* Aegyptiaca Treverensia 7. Mainz: Verlag Philipp von Zabern, 1994, 139–47.

Haag, Ernst, and Frank-Lothar Hossfeld, eds. *Freude an der Weisung des Herrn: Beiträge zur Theologie der Psalmen: Festgabe zum 70. Geburtstag von Heinrich Groß.* Stuttgart: Katholisches Bibelwerk, 1986.

Hahn, Ferdinand, et al., eds. *Zion—Ort der Begegnung: Festschrift für Laurentius Klein zur Vollendung des 65. Lebensjahres.* BBB 90. Bodenheim: Athenäum Hain Hanstein Verlagsgesellschaft, 1993.

Hempel, Johannes, and Leonhard Rost, eds. *Von Ugarit nach Qumran. FS Otto Eissfeldt.* BZAW 77. Berlin: de Gruyter, 1958.

Hermisson, Hans-Jürgen. "Voreiliger Abschied von den Gottesknechtsliedern," *ThR* 49 (1984) 209–22.

Hillers, Delbert R. "Bᵉrit ʿām: 'Emancipation of the People,'" *JBL* 97 (1978) 175–82.

Hirsch, Rabbi Samson Raphael. *The Psalms.* Jerusalem and New York: Feldheim Publishers, 1978 (first published in German in 1882).

Holladay, William L. "A Proposal for Reflections in the Book of Jeremiah of the Seven-Year Recitation of the Law in Deuteronomy (Deut 30,10-13)," in Norbert Lohfink, ed., *Deuteronomium: Entstehung, Gestalt und Botschaft.* BEThL 68. Louvain: University Press/Peeters, 1985, 326–28.

_____. *Jeremiah 2: A Commentary on the Book of the Prophet Jeremiah Chapters 26–52.* Hermeneia. Minneapolis: Fortress, 1989.

Hossfeld, Frank-Lothar. "Ps 50 und die Verkündigung des Gottesrechts," in Friedrich V. Reiterer, ed., *Ein Gott, eine Offenbarung: Beiträge zur biblischen Exegese, Theologie und Spiritualität: Festschrift für Notker Füglister OSB zum 60. Geburtstag.* Würzburg: Echter, 1991, 83–101.

_____. "Bund und Tora in den Psalmen," in Helmut Merklein et al., eds., *Bibel in jüdischer und christlicher Tradition: Festschrift für Johann Maier zum 60. Geburtstag.* BBB 88. Frankfurt: Hain, 1993.

_____. "Psalm 95: Gattungsgeschichtliche, kompositionskritische und bibeltheologische Anfragen," in Klaus Seybold and Erich Zenger, eds., *Neue Wege der Psalmenforschung* (1994) 29–44.

Hossfeld, Frank-Lothar, and Erich Zenger. "'Selig, wer auf die Armen achtet' (Ps 41,2): Beobachtungen zur Gottesvolk-Theologie des ersten Davidpsalters," *JBTh* 7 (1992) 21–50.

_____. *Die Psalmen I: Psalm 1–50.* NEB 29. Würzburg: Echter, 1993.

_____. "'Wer darf hinaufziehn zum Berg JHWHs?': Zur Redaktionsgeschichte und Theologie der Psalmengruppe 15–24," in Georg Braulik, Walter Groß, and Sean McEvenue, eds., *Biblische Theologie und gesellschaftlicher Wandel* (1993) 166–82.

_____. "'Von seinem Thronsitz schaut er nieder auf alle Bewohner der Erde' (Ps 33,14): Redaktionsgeschichte und Kompositionskritik der Psalmengruppe 25–34," in Ingo Kottsieper et al., eds., *"Wer ist wie du, Herr, unter den Göttern?": Studien zur Theologie und Religionsgeschichte Israels für Otto Kaiser zum 70. Geburtstag.* Göttingen: Vandenhoeck & Ruprecht, 1994, 375–88.

Howard, David M. *The Structure of Psalms 93–100.* Ann Arbor: University Microfilms, 1986.

_____. "Editorial Activity in the Psalter: A State-of-the-Field Survey," in J. Clinton McCann, ed., *The Shape and Shaping of the Psalter.* JSOT.SS 159. Sheffield: JSOT Press, 1993, 52–70.

_____. "A Contextual Reading of Psalms 90–94," in idem, 108–23.

Hupfeld, Hermann. *Die Psalmen.* 4 vols. 2nd ed. by Eduard Riehm. Gotha: Perthes, 1867–1871.

Illmann, Karl-Johan. *Thema und Tradition in den Asaf-Psalmen.* Publications of the Research Institute of the Abo Akademi Foundation 13. Abo: Research Institute of the AAF, 1976.

Irsigler, Hubert. "Thronbesteigung in Psalm 93? Der Textverlauf als Prozeß syntaktischer und semantischer Interpretation," in Walter Groß, ed., *Text, Methode und Grammatik* (1991) 151–90.

Janowski, Bernd. *Rettungsgewißheit und Epiphanie des Heils: Das Motiv der Hilfe Gottes "am Morgen" im Alten Orient und im Alten Testament. I: Alter Orient.* WMANT 59. Neukirchen-Vluyn: Neukirchener Verlag, 1989.

_____. "Das Königtum Gottes in den Psalmen. Bemerkungen zu einem neuen Gesamtentwurf," *ZThK* 86 (1989) 389–454. Reprinted in idem, *Gottes Gegenwart,* 148–213.

_____. *Gottes Gegenwart in Israel. Beiträge zur Theologie des Alten Testaments.* Neukirchen-Vluyn: Neukirchener Verlag, 1993.

Janowski, Bernd, ed. *Weisheit außerhalb der kanonischen Weisheitsschriften.* Veröffentlichungen der Wissenschaftlichen Gesellschaft für Theologie 10 (Gütersloh: Kaiser/Gütersloher Verlagshaus, 1996).

Jensen, Joseph. *The Use of the Word tôrā by Isaiah: His Debate with the Wisdom Tradition.* CBQ.MS 3. Washington, D.C.: Catholic Biblical Association, 1973.

Jeremias, Jörg. *Das Königtum Gottes in den Psalmen. Israels Begegnung mit dem kanaanäischen Mythos in den Jahwe-König-Psalmen.* FRLANT 141. Göttingen: Vandenhoeck & Ruprecht, 1987.

Kaiser, Otto. *Das Buch des Propheten Jesaja Kapitel 1–12.* ATD 17. 5th, completely revised ed. Göttingen: Vandenhoeck & Ruprecht, 1981.

Kannengiesser, Charles, and Yves Marchasson, eds. *Humanisme et foi chrétienne: Mélanges scientifiques du centenaire de l'Institut Catholique de Paris.* Paris: Beauchesne, 1976.

Keel, Othmar. *Die Welt der altorientalischen Bildsymbolik und das Alte Testament. Am Beispiel der Psalmen.* 4th ed. Neukirchen-Vluyn: Neukirchener Verlag; Zürich: Benziger, 1984.

_____. "Fern von Jerusalem. Frühe Jerusalemer Kulttraditionen und ihre Träger und Trägerinnen," in Ferdinand Hahn et al., eds., *Zion—Ort der Begegnung* (1993) 439–502.

Keel, Othmar, and Uehlinger, Christoph. *Göttinnen, Götter und Gottessymbole: Neue Erkenntnisse zur Religionsgeschichte Kanaans und Israels aufgrund bislang unerschlossener ikonographischer Quellen.* QD 134. Freiburg: Herder, 1992.

Kelly, Sidney. *The Zion-Victory Songs: Psalms 46, 48 and 76. A Critical Study of Modern Methods of Psalmic Interpretation.* Dissertation Vanderbilt, 1968.

Kirchberg, Julie. *Theo-logie in der Anrede als Weg zur Verständigung zwischen Juden und Christen.* Innsbrucker Theologische Studien 31. Innsbruck and Vienna: Herder, 1991.

Kittel, Rudolf. *Die Psalmen, übersetzt und erklärt.* KAT XIII. 5th–6th ed. Leipzig: Deichert-Scholl, 1929.

Klappert, Bertold, Hans-Joachim Kraus, Friedrich-Wilhelm Marquardt, and Martin Stöhr. *Jesusbekenntnis und Christusnachfolge.* Munich: Kaiser, 1992.

Klappert, Bertold. "Eine Christologie der Völkerwallfahrt zum Zion," in idem, et al., *Jesusbekenntnis,* 65–93.

Knapp, Dietrich. *Deuteronomium 4: Literarische Analyse und theologische Interpretation.* Göttinger Theologische Arbeiten 35. Göttingen: Vandenhoeck & Ruprecht, 1987.

Koch, Klaus. "Wort und Einheit des Schöpfergottes in Memphis und Jerusalem," *ZThK* 62 (1965) 251–93. Reprinted (with additions and corrections) in idem, *Studien zur alttestamentlichen und altorientalischen Religionsgeschichte,* 61–105.

_____. "כון, *kūn,*" *ThWAT* 4 (1984) 95–107 [= *TDOT* 7 (1995) 89–101].

_____. *Studien zur alttestamentlichen und altorientalischen Religionsgeschichte.* Göttingen: Vandenhoeck & Ruprecht, 1988.

_____. "Der Psalter und seine Redaktionsgeschichte," in Klaus Seybold and Erich Zenger, eds., *Neue Wege der Psalmenforschung* (1994) 243–77.

Koehler, Ludwig. "Psalm 23," *ZAW* 68 (1956) 227–34.

Kottsieper, Ingo, et al., eds. *"Wer ist wie du, Herr, unter den Göttern?": Studien zur Theologie und Religionsgeschichte Israels für Otto Kaiser zum 70. Geburtstag.* Göttingen: Vandenhoeck & Ruprecht, 1994.

Kratz, Reinhard G. *Kyros im Deuterojesaja-Buch: Redaktionsgeschichtliche Untersuchungen zu Entstehung und Theologie von Jes 40–55.* FAT 1. Tübingen: Mohr, 1991.

Kraus, Hans-Joachim. *Psalmen.* 2 vols. BK 15/1, 15/2. 5th fully revised and rewritten ed. Neukirchen-Vluyn: Neukirchener Verlag, 1978.

Kraus, Hans-Joachim: see Klappert, Bertold.

Küchler, Max, and Christoph Uehlinger, eds. *Jerusalem. Texte – Bilder – Steine. Zum 100. Geburtstag von Hildi und Othmar Keel-Leu.* NTOA 6. Fribourg: Universitätsverlag; Göttingen: Vandenhoeck & Ruprecht, 1987.

Kuschel, Karl-Josef. *Streit um Abraham. Was Juden, Christen und Muslime trennt —und was sie eint.* Munich: Piper, 1994.

Kuschel, Karl-Josef: see Groß, Walter.

Kutsch, Ernst. *Verheißung und Gesetz: Untersuchungen zum sogenannten "Bund" im Alten Testament.* BZAW 131. Berlin: de Gruyter, 1973.

_____. "פרר," *THAT* 2 (1976) 486–88.

_____. *Neues Testament—Neuer Bund? Eine Fehlübersetzung wird korrigiert.* Neukirchen-Vluyn: Neukirchener Verlag, 1978.

LaCocque, André. *But As For Me: The Question of Election in the Life of God's People Today.* Atlanta: John Knox, 1979.

Langer, Birgit. *Gott als "Licht" in Israel und Mesopotamien.* ÖBS 7. Klosterneuburg: Österreichisches Katholisches Bibelwerk, 1989.

Lauha, Aare. "'Der Bund des Volkes': Ein Aspekt der deuterojesajanischen Missionstheologie," in Herbert Donner, Robert Hanhart, and Rudolf Smend, eds., *Beiträge zur alttestamentlichen Theologie* (1977) 257–61.

LeRoux, J. H. "A Holy Nation Was Elected (The Election Theology of Exodus 19.5-6," in Wouter C. van Wyk, ed., *The Exilic Period: Aspects of Apocalypticism.* OTWSA 25 [1982] and 26 [1983]. Pretoria: University of Pretoria, 1984.

Levin, Christoph. "Das Gebetbuch der Gerechten. Literargeschichtliche Beobachtungen am Psalter," *ZThK* 90 (1993) 355–81.

Lohfink, Norbert. "Der Bundesschluß im Land Moab: Redaktionsgeschichtliches zu Dt 28, 69–32,47," *BZ* 6 (1962) 32–56. Reprinted in idem, *Studien zum Deuteronomium,* 1:53–82.

_____. *Das Hauptgebot: Eine Untersuchung literarischer Einleitungsfragen zu Dtn 5–11.* AnBib 20. Rome: Pontificium Institutum Biblicum, 1963.

_____. "Über die Irrtumslosigkeit und die Einheit der Schrift," *StZt* 174 (1964) 161–81. Reprinted in idem, *Studien zur biblischen Theologie,* 13–39.

_____. *Höre, Israel! Auslegung von Texten aus dem Buch Deuteronomium.* WB 18. Düsseldorf: Patmos, 1965.

_____. *Die Landverheißung als Eid: Eine Studie zu Gn 15.* SBS 28. Stuttgart: Katholisches Bibelwerk, 1967.

_____. "Dt 26, 17-19 und die 'Bundesformel,'" *ZKTh* 91 (1969) 517–53. Reprinted in idem, *Studien zum Deuteronomium,* 1:211–61.

_____. "Beobachtungen zur Geschichte des Ausdrucks עם יהוה," in Hans Walter Wolff, ed., *Probleme biblischer Theologie: Gerhard von Rad zum 70. Geburtstag.* Munich: Kaiser, 1971, 275–305. Reprinted in idem, *Studien zur biblischen Theologie,* 99–132.

_____. "'Israel' in Jes 49,3," in Josef Schreiner, ed., *Wort, Lied und Gottesspruch, II* (1972) 217–29.

_____. "Die Abänderung der Theologie des priesterlichen Geschichtswerks im Segen des Heiligkeitsgesetzes: Zu Lev. 26,9.11-13," in Hartmut Gese and Hans Peter Rüger, eds., *Wort und Geschichte* (1973) 129–36. Reprinted in idem, *Studien zum Pentateuch,* 157–68.

_____. *Great Themes from the Old Testament.* Translated by Ronald Walls. Edinburgh: T & T Clark, 1982. Original: *Unsere großen Wörter: Das Alte Testament zu Themen dieser Jahre.* Freiburg: Herder, 1977.

_____. "Theology as the Answer to Plausibility Crises in Emergent Pluralistic Situations, Taking the Deuteronomic Law as the Basis for Discussion," in idem, *Great Themes from the Old Testament,* 17–37. Original: "Theologie als Antwort auf Plausibilitätskrisen in aufkommenden pluralistischen Situationen, erörtert am Beispiel des deuteronomischen Gesetzes," *Unsere großen Wörter,* 24–43.

_____. "'I am Yahweh, your Physician' (Exodus 15:26). God, Society and Human Health in a Postexilic Revision of the Pentateuch (Exod. 15:2b, 26)," in Norbert Lohfink, *Theology of the Pentateuch. Themes of the Priestly Narrative and Deuteronomy.* Translated by Linda M. Maloney. Minneapolis: Fortress; Edinburgh: T & T Clark, 1994, 35–95. Original: "'Ich bin Jahwe, dein Arzt' (Ex 15,26): Gott, Gesellschaft und menschliche Gesundheit in einer nachexilischen Pentateuchbearbeitung (Ex 15,25b.26)," in Norbert Lohfink, et al., eds., *"Ich will euer Gott werden,"* 11–73. Reprinted in idem, *Studien zum Pentateuch,* 91–155.

_____. "יָרַשׁ, *yāraš,*" *ThWAT* 3 (1982) 953–85 [= *TDOT* 6 (n.d.) 368–96].

_____. *Das Jüdische am Christentum: Die verlorene Dimension.* Freiburg: Herder, 1987.

_____. *Studien zum Pentateuch.* SBAB 4. Stuttgart: Katholisches Bibelwerk, 1988.

_____. *The Covenant Never Revoked. Biblical Reflections on Christian-Jewish Dialogue.* Translated by John J. Scullion. New York and Mahwah, N.J.: Paulist, 1991. Original: *Der niemals gekündigte Bund: Exegetische Gedanken zum christlich-jüdischen Dialog.* Freiburg: Herder, 1989.

_____. "'Der den Kriegen einen Sabbat bereitet.' Psalm 46—ein Beispiel alttestamentlicher Friedenslyrik," *BiKi* 44 (1989) 148–53.

_____. "Das Deuteronomium: Jahwegesetz oder Mosegesetz? Die Subjektzuordnung bei Wörtern für 'Gesetz' im Dtn und in der dtr Literatur," *ThPh* 65 (1990) 387–91.

_____. *Studien zum Deuteronomium und zur deuteronomistischen Literatur I.* SBAB 8. Stuttgart: Katholisches Bibelwerk, 1990.

_____. "Bundestheologie im Alten Testament: Zum gleichnamigen Buch von Lothar Perlitt," in idem, *Studien zum Deuteronomium,* 1:325–61.

_____. "Gibt es eine deuteronomistische Bearbeitung im Bundesbuch?" in Christian Brekelmans and Johan Lust, eds., *Pentateuchal and Deuteronomistic Studies,* 91–113.

_____. "Die Universalisierung der 'Bundesformel' in Ps 100,3," *ThPh* 65 (1990) 172–83.

_____. *Lobgesänge der Armen: Studien zum Magnifikat, den Hodajot von Qumran und einigen späten Psalmen.* SBS 143. Stuttgart: Katholisches Bibelwerk, 1990.

_____. "Covenant, Torah and Pilgrimage of the Nations to Mount Zion," *SIDIC* 24/2–3, English ed. (1991) 3–15.

_____. "Der neue Bund und die Völker," *Kirche und Israel* 6 (1991) 115–33.

_____. "Der Begriff 'Bund' in der biblischen Theologie," *ThPh* 66 (1991) 161–76.

_____. "Einige Beobachtungen zu Psalm 26," in Friedrich V. Reiterer, ed., *Ein Gott, eine Offenbarung* (1991) 189–204.

_____. "Lexeme und Lexemgruppen in Ps 25: Ein Beitrag zur Technik der Gattungsbestimmung und der Feststellung literarischer Abhängigkeiten," in Walter Groß, et al., eds., *Text, Methode und Grammatik* (1991) 271–95.

_____. "Bund," in Manfred Görg and Bernhard Lang, eds., *Neues Bibellexikon* 1:343–48.

_____. "Der weiße Fleck in *Dei Verbum,* Artikel 12," *TThZ* 101 (1992) 20–35.

_____. "Psalmengebet und Psalterredaktion," *ALW* 34 (1992) 1–22.

_____. "Deuteronomy 6:24: לְחַיֹּתֵנוּ 'to maintain us,'" in Michael Fishbane and Emanuel Tov, eds., *"Shaʿarei Talmon"* (1992) 111–19.

_____. *Studien zur biblischen Theologie.* SBAB 16. Stuttgart: Katholisches Bibelwerk, 1993.

_____. "Die Lieder in der Kindheitsgeschichte bei Lukas," in Cornelius Mayer, et al., eds., *Nach den Anfängen fragen. Gerhard Dautzenberg zum 60. Geburtstag* (1994) 383–404.

_____. "Psalmen im Neuen Testament: Die Lieder in der Kindheitsgeschichte bei Lukas," in Klaus Seybold and Erich Zenger, eds., *Neue Wege der Psalmenforschung* (1994) 105–25.

_____. "Bund als Vertrag im Deuteronomium," *ZAW* 107 (1995) 215–39.

Lohfink, Norbert, ed. *Deuteronomium: Entstehung, Gestalt und Botschaft.* BEThL 68. Louvain: University Press/Peeters, 1985.

Lohfink, Norbert, et al. *"Ich will euer Gott werden": Beispiele biblischen Redens von Gott.* SBS 100. Stuttgart: Katholisches Bibelwerk, 1981.

Lohfink, Norbert: see also Fischer, Georg.

Lutz-Bachmann, Matthias, ed. *Und dennoch ist von Gott zu reden. Festschrift für Herbert Vorgrimler.* Feriburg: Herder, 1994.

Marböck, Johannes. "Die 'Geschichte Israels' als 'Bundesgeschichte' nach dem Sirachbuch," in Erich Zenger, ed., *Der Neue Bund im Alten* (1993) 177–97.

Marcus, Marcel, et al., eds. *Israel und Kirche heute: Beiträge zum christlich-jüdischen Dialog: Für Ernst Ludwig Ehrlich.* Freiburg: Herder, 1991.

Marquardt, Friedrich-Wilhelm. "Entwurf zu einer christlichen Theologie des Bundes, in Martin Stöhr, ed., *Lernen in Jerusalem—Lernen mit Jerusalem* (1993) 93–109.

Marquardt, Friedrich-Wilhelm: see Klappert, Bertold.

Matheus, Frank. *Singt dem Herrn ein neues Lied: Die Hymnen Deuterojesajas.* SBS 141. Stuttgart: Katholisches Bibelwerk, 1990.

Mathys, Hans-Peter. *Dichter und Beter. Theologen aus spätalttestamentlicher Zeit.* OBO 132. Fribourg: Universitätsverlag; Göttingen: Vandenhoeck & Ruprecht, 1994.

Mayer, Cornelius, Karlheinz Müller, and Gerhard Schmalenberg, eds. *Nach den Anfängen fragen. Gerhard Dautzenberg zum 60. Geburtstag.* Gießener Schriften zur Theologie und Religionspädagogik 8. Gießen: Selbstverlag des Fachbereichs Evangelische Theologie und Katholische Theologie, 1994.

Mays, James L. *Psalms.* Interpretation. A Bible Commentary for Preaching and Teaching. Louisville: John Knox, 1994.

_____. "Worship, World and Power: An Interpretation of Psalm 100," *Int* 23 (1969) 315–30.

McCann, J. Clinton. *A Theological Introduction to the Book of Psalms. The Psalms as Torah.* Nashville: Abingdon, 1993.

McCann, J. Clinton, ed. *The Shape and Shaping of the Psalter.* JSOT.SS 159. Sheffield: JSOT Press, 1993.

McCarthy, Dennis J. *Treaty and Covenant: A Study in Form in the Ancient Oriental Documents and in the Old Testament.* AnBib 21A. Rome: Biblical Institute Press, 1963; 2nd, completely rewritten ed. 1978.

Mélanges bibliques rédigés en l'honneur de André Robert. TICP 4. Paris: Bloud & Gay, 1957.

Merklein, Helmut, et al., eds. *Bibel in jüdischer und christlicher Tradition: Festschrift für Johann Maier zum 60. Geburtstag.* BBB 88. Frankfurt: Hain, 1993.

Mettinger, Tryggve N. D. "Die Ebed-Jahwe-Lieder, ein fragwürdiges Axiom," *ASThI* 11 (1977/78) 68–76.

_____. *A Farewell to the Servant Songs: A Critical Examination of an Exegetical Axiom.* Scripta Minora Regiae Societatis Humaniorum Litterarum Lundensis, 1982/83, 3. Lund: Gleerup, 1983.

Millard, Matthias. *Die Komposition des Psalters. Ein formgeschichtlicher Ansatz.* FAT 9. Tübingen: Mohr, 1994.

Miller, Patrick D. *Interpreting the Psalms.* Philadelphia: Fortress, 1986.

_____. *They Cried to the Lord: The Form and Theology of Biblical Prayer.* Minneapolis: Fortress, 1994.

_____. "Kingship, Torah Obedience, and Prayer: The Theology of Psalms 15–24," in Klaus Seybold and Erich Zenger, eds., *Neue Wege der Psalmenforschung* (1994) 127–42.

Minas, Martina, and Jürgen Zeidler, eds. *Aspekte spätägyptischer Kultur: Festschrift für Erich Winter zum 65. Geburtstag.* Aegyptiaca Treverensia 7. Mainz: Verlag Philipp von Zabern, 1994.

Möller, Hans. "Strophenbau der Psalmen," *ZAW* 50 (1932) 240–56.

Mosis, Rudolf. "Ex 19,5b.6a: Syntaktischer Aufbau und lexikalische Semantik," *BZ* 22 (1978) 1–25.

_____. "'Ströme erheben, Jahwe, ihr Tosen . . .' Beobachtungen zu Ps 93," in Friedrich V. Reiterer, ed., *Ein Gott, eine Offenbarung* (1991) 223–55.

Müller, Hans-Peter. "Der 90. Psalm. Ein Paradigma exegetischer Aufgaben," *ZThK* 81 (1984) 265–85.

_____. "Theodizee? Anschlußerörterungen zum Buch Hiob," *ZThK* 89 (1992) 249–79.

Muñoz Leon, Domingo. "Un reino de sacerdotes y una nación santa (Ex 91,6)," *ExtB* 37 (1978) 149–212.

Nasuti, Harry P. *Tradition History and the Psalms of Asaph.* SBL.DS 88. Atlanta: Scholars, 1988.

Niccacci, Alviero. *Un profeta tra oppressori e oppressi: Analisi exegetica del capitulo 2 di Michea nel piano generale del libro.* SBFA 27. Jerusalem: Franciscan Printing Press, 1989.

Nicholson, Ernest W. *God and His People: Covenant and Theology in the Old Testament.* Oxford: Clarendon, 1986.

Nötscher, Friedrich. *Das Buch der Psalmen.* EB 4. Würzburg: Echter, 1959.

Nowack, Petrus. "Psalm 83 in der Feier der Liturgie," *Dienender Glaube* 68 (1992) 53–55.

Odendall, D. H. "Covenant—the Centre of the Old Testament," *NGIT* 30 (1989) 143–51.

Oorschot, Jürgen van. "Nachkultische Psalmen und spätbiblische Rollendichtung," *ZAW* 106 (1994) 69–86.

Otto, Eckart. "Kultus und Ethos in Jerusalemer Theologie: Ein Beitrag zur theologischen Begründung der Ethik im Alten Testament," *ZAW* 98 (1986) 161–79.

_____. "Mythos und Geschichte im Alten Testament. Zur Diskussion einer neuen Arbeit von J. Jeremias," *BN* 42 (1988) 93–102.

_____. "צִיּוֹן, *ṣijjôn,*" *ThWAT* 6 (1989) 994–1028.

_____. "Techniken der Rechtssatzredaktion israelitischer Rechtsbücher in der Redaktion des Prophetenbuches Micha," *SJOT* (1991,2) 119–50.

Panikkar, Raimon, and Walter Strolz, eds. *Die Verantwortung des Menschen für eine bewohnbare Welt.* Freiburg: Herder, 1985.

Pannenberg, Wolfhart. *Systematische Theologie* 3. Göttingen: Vandenhoeck & Ruprecht, 1993.

Perlitt, Lothar. *Bundestheologie im Alten Testament.* WMANT 36. Neukirchen-Vluyn: Neukirchener Verlag, 1969.

Perrot, Charles, ed. *Etudes sur la première lettre de Pierre: Congrès de l'ACFEB.* LeDiv 102. Paris: Cerf, 1979.

Petersen, Claus. *Mythos im Alten Testament: Bestimmung des Mythosbegriffs und Untersuchung der mythischen Elemente in den Psalmen.* BZAW 157. Berlin: de Gruyter, 1982.

Pfeiffer, E. "Eine Inversion in Psalm xxiii 1bα?" *VT* 8 (1958) 219–20.

Podella, Thomas. "Der 'Chaoskampfmythos' im Alten Testament. Eine Problemanzeige," in Manfried Dietrich and Oswald Loretz, eds., *Mesopotamica—Ugaritica—Biblica* (1993) 283–329.

Pury, Albert de, ed. *Le Pentateuque en question: Les origines et la composition des cinq premiers livres de la Bible à la lumière des recherches récentes.* Le monde de la Bible. Geneva: Labor et fides, 1989.

Ravasi, Gianfranco. *Il libro dei Salmi: Commento e attualizzazione.* 3 vols. Bologna: Edizioni Dehoniane, 1986.

Reindl, Joseph. "Weisheitliche Bearbeitung von Psalmen. Ein Beitrag zum Verständnis des Psalters," *VTS* 32 (1981) 333–56.

Reiterer, Friedrich V., ed. *Ein Gott, eine Offenbarung: Beiträge zur biblischen Exegese, Theologie und Spiritualität: Festschrift für Notker Füglister* OSB *zum 60. Geburtstag.* Würzburg: Echter, 1991.

Renaud, Bernard. *La théophanie du Sinaï Ex 19–24: Exégèse et théologie.* CRB 30. Paris: Gabalda, 1991.

Rendtorff, Rolf. *Das Alte Testament: Eine Einführung.* Neukirchen-Vluyn: Neukirchener Verlag, 1983.

_____. "'Covenant' as a Structuring Concept in Genesis and Exodus," *JBL* 108 (1989) 385–93.

_____. *Hat denn Gott sein Volk verstoßen? Die evangelische Kirche und das Judentum seit 1945. Ein Kommentar.* Munich: Kaiser, 1989.

Rendtorff, Rolf, and Hans Hermann Henrix, eds. *Die Kirchen und das Judentum: Dokumente von 1945 bis 1985.* 2nd ed. Paderborn: Bonifatius-Druckerei; Munich: Kaiser, 1989.

Reventlow, Henning Graf. *Hauptprobleme der alttestamentlichen Theologie im 20. Jahrhundert.* EdF 173. Darmstadt: Wissenschaftliche Buchgesellschaft, 1982.

_____. *Gebet im Alten Testament.* Stuttgart: Kohlhammer, 1986.

Ridderbos, Nicholaas H. *Die Psalmen: Stilistische Verfahren und Aufbau: Mit besonderer Berücksichtigung von Ps 1–41.* BZAW 117. Berlin: de Gruyter, 1972.

Rosenmüller, Ernst F. C. *Psalmi annotatione perpetua illustrati.* 3 vols. Scholia in Vetus Testamentum IV/1–3. Leipzig: Barth, 1821–23.

Rudolph, Wilhelm. *Micha—Nahum—Habakuk—Zephanja.* KAT 13,3. Gütersloh: Mohn, 1975.

Ruppert, Lothar. "Psalm 25 und die Grenze kultorientierter Psalmenexegese," *ZAW* 84 (1972) 576–82.

_____. "פרר," *ThWAT* 6 (1989) 773–80.

_____. "Das Heil der Völker (Heilsuniversalismus) in Deutero- und 'Trito'-Jesaja," *MThZ* 45 (1994) 137–59.

Sandevoir, P. "Un royaume de prêtres," in Charles Perrot, ed., *Etudes sur la première lettre de Pierre* (1979) 219–29.

Schäfer-Lichtenberger, Christa. "Vom Nebensatz zum Idealtypus: Zur Vorgeschichte des 'Antiken Judentums' von Max Weber," in Erhard Blum, ed., *Die hebräische Bibel und ihre zweifache Nachgeschichte* (1990) 419–33.

Schelling, Pieter. *De Asafpsalmen. Hun Samenhang en Achtergrond.* Dissertationes Neerlandicae: Series Theologica. Kampen: Kok, 1985.

Schmidt, Werner H. "'Der du die Menschen lässest sterben!' Exegetische Anmerkungen zu Ps 90," in Frank Crüsemann, et al., eds., *Was ist der Mensch . . . ?* 115–30.

Schmuttermayr, Georg. "Um Psalm 87(86),5," *BZ* 7 (1963) 104–10.

Schreiner, Josef, ed. *Wort, Lied und Gottesspruch, II: Beiträge zu Psalmen und Propheten. Festschrift für Joseph Ziegler.* fzb 2. Würzburg: Echter, 1972.

_____, ed. *Unterwegs zur Kirche: Alttestamentliche Konzeptionen.* QD 110. Freiburg: Herder, 1987.

_____, ed. *Beiträge zur Psalmenforschung: Psalm 2 und 22.* fzb 60. Würzburg: Echter, 1988.

Schröer, Siegfried, ed. *Christen und Juden. Voraussetzungen für ein erneuertes Verhältnis. Mit Beiträgen von Edna Brocke, Peter Fiedler, Hubert Frankemölle, Klemens Richter, Herbert Vorgrimler, Erich Zenger.* Altenberge: Oros, 1992.

Schröten, Jutta. *Lobt JHWH. Ja, gut ist Er! Psalm 118 im Kontext des Hallel. Untersuchungen zu seiner Entstehung, Komposition und Wirkungsgeschichte.* Dissertation Münster, 1993. Published as *Entstehung, Komposition und Wirkungsgeschichte des 118. Psalms.* BBB 95. Weinheim: Beltz Athenäum, 1995.

Schweitzer, Wolfgang. *Der Jude Jesus und die Völker der Welt. Ein Gespräch mit Paul M. Van Buren. Mit Beiträgen von Paul M. Van Buren, Bertolt Klappert und Michael Wyschogrod.* VIKJ 19. Berlin: Institut Kirche und Judentum, 1993.

Schwienhorst-Schönberger, Ludger. "Zion—Ort der Tora: Überlegungen zu Mi 4,103," in Ferdinand Hahn, et al., eds., *Zion—Ort der Begegnung* (1993) 107–25.

Scoralick, Ruth. *Trishagion und Gottesherrschaft. Psalm 99 als Neuinterpretation von Tora und Propheten.* SBS 138. Stuttgart: Katholisches Bibelwerk, 1989.

Seebaß, Horst. "בחר, *bāchar,*" *ThWAT* 1 (1973) 592–608 [= *TDOT* 2 (1977) 73–87].

Segal, Alan F. *The Other Judaisms of Late Antiquity.* Brown Judaic Studies 127. Atlanta: Scholars, 1987.

_____. "Covenant in Rabbinic Writings," in idem, *Other Judaisms,* 147–65.

Seybold, Klaus. *Das Gebet des Kranken im Alten Testament.* BWANT 5,19. Stuttgart: Kohlhammer, 1973.

_____. *Die Psalmen. Eine Einführung.* Urban-Taschenbücher 382. Stuttgart: Kohlhammer, 1986.

_____. "Das 'Wir' in den Asaph-Psalmen. Spezifische Probleme einer Psalmgruppe," in Klaus Seybold and Erich Zenger, eds., *Neue Wege der Psalmenforschung* (1994) 143–55.

Seybold, Klaus, and Erich Zenger, eds. *Neue Wege der Psalmenforschung: Für Walter Beyerlin.* HBS 1. Freiburg: Herder, 1994.

Ska, Jean L. "Ex 19,3-8 et les parénèses deutéronomiques," in Georg Braulik, et al., eds., *Biblische Theologie und gesellschaftlicher Wandel* (1993) 307–14.

Smart, James D. "The Eschatological Interpretation of Psalm 24," *JBL* 52 (1933) 175–80.

Smith, Mark S. "*Beᵉrit ʿam / bᵉrit ôlām:* A New Proposal for the Crux of Isa 42:6," *JBL* 100 (1981) 241–43.

_____. "The Structure of Psalm LXXXVII," *VT* 38 (1988) 357–58.

_____. *The Early History of God: Yahweh and the Other Deities in Ancient Israel.* San Francisco: Harper & Row, 1990.

Smith, P. L. "The Use of the Word תורה in Isaiah, Chapters 1–39," *AJSL* 46 (1929) 1–21.

Sorg, Rembert. *Ecumenic Psalm 87. Original Form and Two Rereadings.* With an Appendix of Ps 110,3. Fifield, Wis.: King of Martyrs Priory, 1969.

Sperling, Uwe. *Das theophanische Jahwe-Überlegenheitslied. Forschungsbericht und gattungskritische Untersuchung der sogenannten Zionlieder.* EHS XXIII. 426. Frankfurt: Peter Lang, 1993.

Spieckermann, Hermann. *Heilsgegenwart: Eine Theologie der Psalmen.* FRLANT 148. Göttingen: Vandenhoeck & Ruprecht, 1989.

_____. "'Barmherzig und gnädig ist der Herr . . . ,'" *ZAW* 102 (1990) 1–18.

_____. "'Die ganze Erde ist seiner Herrlichkeit voll': Pantheismus im Alten Testament?" *ZThK* 87 (1990) 415–36.

_____. "Stadtgott und Gottesstadt. Beobachtungen im Alten Orient und im Alten Testament," *Bib* 73 (1992) 1–31.

_____. "Rede Gottes und Wort Gottes in den Psalmen," in Klaus Seybold and Erich Zenger, eds., *Neue Wege der Psalmenforschung* (1994) 157–73.

Stadelmann, Andreas. "Psalm 87 (86)—Theologischer Gehalt und gesellschaftliche Wirkung," in Friedrich V. Reiterer, ed., *Ein Gott, eine Offenbarung* (1991) 333–56.

Stamm, Johann J. "Berît ʿam bei Deuterojesaja," in Hans Walter Wolff, ed., *Probleme biblischer Theologie* (1971) 510–24.

Steck, Odil Hannes. "Zion als Gelände und Gestalt. Überlegungen zur Wahrnehmung Jerusalems als Stadt und Frau im Alten Testament," *ZThK* 86 (1989) 261–82. Reprinted in idem, *Gottesknecht und Zion* (1992) 126–45.

_____. "Zu Eigenart und Herkunft von Ps 102," *ZAW* 102 (1990) 357–72.

_____. *Der Abschluß der Prophetie im Alten Testament. Ein Versuch zur Frage der Vorgeschichte des Kanons.* BThSt 17. Neukirchen-Vluyn: Neukirchener Verlag, 1991.

_____. *Gottesknecht und Zion. Gesammelte Aufsätze zu Deuterojesaja.* FAT 4. Tübingen: Mohr, 1992.

_____. "Gottesvolk und Gottesknecht in Jes 40–66," *JBTh* 7 (1992) 51–75.

_____. "Der Gottesknecht als 'Bund' und 'Licht': Beobachtungen im Zweiten Jesaja," *ZThK* 90 (1993) 117–34.

Steingrimsson, Sigurdur Ö. *Tor der Gerechtigkeit: Eine literaturwissenschaftliche Untersuchung der sogenannten Einzugsliturgien im AT: Ps 15; 24,3-5 und Jes 33,14-16.* ATSAT 22. St. Ottilien: EOS, 1984.

Steins, Georg. *Die Chronik als kanonisches Abschlußphänomen: Studien zur Entstehung und Theologie von 1/2 Chr.* BBB 93. Frankfurt: Hain, 1994.

Stemberger, Günter, and Ingo Baldermann, eds. *Zum Problem des biblischen Kanons.* JBTh 3. Neukirchen-Vluyn: Neukirchener Verlag, 1988.

Steymans, Hans Ulrich. *Deuteronomium 28 und die Adê zur Thronnachfolgeregelung Asarhaddons: Segen und Fluch im Alten Orient und in Israel.* OBO 145. Fribourg: Universitätsverlag; Göttingen: Vandenhoeck & Ruprecht, 1995.

Stöhr, Martin, ed. *Lernen in Jerusalem—Lernen mit Jerusalem. Anstöße zur Erneuerung in Theologie und Kirche.* VIKL 20. Berlin: Institut Kirche und Judentum, 1993.

Stöhr, Martin: see Klappert, Bertold.

Stolz, Fritz. *Strukturen und Figuren im Kult von Jerusalem.* BZAW 118. Berlin: de Gruyter, 1970.

_____. *Psalmen im nachkultischen Raum.* ThSt 129. Zürich: Theologischer Verlag, 1983.

Strolz, Walter: see Panikkar, Raimon.

Tate, Marvin E. *Psalms 51–100.* WBC 20. Dallas: Word, 1990.

Taylor, J. Glen. *Yahweh and the Sun: Biblical and Archaeological Evidence for Sun Worship in Ancient Israel.* JSOT.SS 111. Sheffield: JSOT Press, 1993.

Thiel, Winfried. *Die deuteronomistische Redaktion von Jeremia 26–45: Mit einer Gesamtbeurteilung der deuteronomistischen Redaktion des Buches Jeremia.* WMANT 52. Neukirchen-Vluyn: Neukirchener Verlag, 1981.

Thoma, Clemens. *Das Messiasprojekt. Theologie Jüdisch-christlicher Begegnung.* Würzburg: Pattloch, 1994.

Tromp, Nicholas. "Jacob in Psalm 24: Apposition, Aphaereses or Apostrophe?" in W. C. Delsman, et al., eds., *Von Kanaan bis Kerala* (1982) 271–82.

Trublet, Jacques, and Jean-Noël Aletti. *Approche poétique et théologique des Psaumes: Analyses et Méthodes.* Initiations. Paris: Cerf, 1983.

Uehlinger, Christoph. "'Zeichne eine Stadt . . . und belagere sie!' Bild und Wort in einer Zeichenhandlung Ezechiels gegen Jerusalem (Ez 4f)," in Max Küchler and Christoph Uehlinger, eds., *Jerusalem. Texte – Bilder – Steine* (1987) 111–200.

Uehlinger, Christoph: see Keel, Othmar.

Ulrich, Eugene, et al., eds. *Priests, Prophets and Scribes: Essays on the Formation and Heritage of Second Temple Judaism in Honour of Joseph Blenkinsopp.* JSOT.SS 149. Sheffield: JSOT Press, 1992.

Van Winkle, D. W. "The Relationship of the Nations to Yahweh and to Israel in Isaiah XL–LV," *VT* 35 (1985) 446–58.

Vanoni, Gottfried. "Der Geist und der Buchstabe: Überlegungen zum Verhältnis der Testamente und Beobachtungen zu Dtn 30,1-10," *BN* 14 (1981) 65–98.

Vejola, Timo. *Verheißung in der Krise. Studien zur Literatur und Theologie der Exilszeit anhand des 89. Psalms.* AASF B 220. Helsinki: Academia Scientiarum Fennica, 1982.

Vermes, Geza. "'The Torah Is Light,'" *VT* 8 (1958) 536–38.

Vermeylen, Jacques. *The Book of Isaiah: Les oracles et leur relectures, unité et complexité de l'ouvrage.* BEThL 81. Louvain: University Press/Peeters, 1989.

Vincent, Jean M. "Recherches exégétiques sur le psaume xxxiii," *VT* 28 (1978) 442–54.

Vogt, Hermann J., ed. *Kirche in der Zeit: Walter Kasper zur Bischofsweihe: Gabe der Katholisch-Theologischen Fakultät Tübingen.* Munich: Wewel, 1990.

Voigt, Wolfgang, ed. *XVIII. Deutscher Orientalistentag vom 1. bis 5. Oktober 1972 in Lübeck: Vorträge.* ZDMG.Suppl. 2. Wiesbaden: Steiner, 1974.

Vorgrimler, Herbert. "Israel und Kirche vor dem gemeinsamen Bundesgott," in Siegfried Schröer, ed., *Christen und Juden* (1992) 104–26.

Vriezen, Theodorus C. "Einige Notizen zur Übersetzung des Bindewortes *kī*," in Johannes Hempel and Leonhard Rost, eds., *Von Ugarit nach Qumran* (1958) 266–75.

Wanke, Gunther. *Die Zionstheologie der Korachiten in ihrem traditionsgeschichtlichen Zusammenhang.* BZAW 97. Berlin: de Gruyter, 1966.

Weinberg, Joel P. "Demographische Notizen zur Geschichte der nachexilischen Gemeinde in Juda," *Klio* 54 (1972) 45–49.

_____. "Das Beit ʾAbot im 6.–4. Jahrhundert v.u.Z.," *VT* 23 (1973) 400–14.

_____. "Die Agrarverhältnisse in der Bürger-Tempel-Gemeinde der Achämenidenzeit," *AAH* 22 (1974) 473–86.

Weippert, Manfred. "Die 'Konfessionen' Deuterojesajas," in Rainer Albertz, et al., eds., *Schöpfung und Befreiung* (1989) 104–15.

Weiser, Artur. *Die Psalmen. Zweiter Teil: Psalm 61–150.* ATD 15. Göttingen: Vandenhoeck & Ruprecht, 1950; 10th ed. 1987.

Wellhausen, Julius. *Die kleinen Propheten, übersetzt und erklärt.* 3rd ed. Berlin: Reimer, 1898.

Wénin, André: see Focant, Camille.

Werbick, Jürgen. *Kirche. Ein ekklesiologischer Entwurf für Studium und Praxis.* Freiburg: Herder, 1994.

Westermann, Claus. "Die Begriffe für Fragen und Suchen im Alten Testament," *KuD* 6 (1960) 2–30. Reprinted in idem, *Gesammelte Studien II*, 162–90.

_____. *Forschung am Alten Testament: Gesammelte Studien II: Zu seinem 65. Geburtstag am 7. Oktober 1974.* Edited by Rainer Albertz and Eberhard Ruprecht. ThB 55. Munich: Kaiser, 1974.

Wifall, Walter. "The Foreign Nations. Israel's 'Nine Bows,'" *Bulletin of Egyptological Seminar* 3 (1981) 113–24.

Wilson, Gerald H. *The Editing of the Hebrew Psalter.* SBL.DS 76. Chico: Scholars, 1985.

_____. "Shaping the Psalter: A Consideration of Editorial Linkage in the Book of Psalms," in J. Clinton McCann, ed. *The Shape and Shaping of the Psalter* (1993) 72–82.

Wolff, Hans Walter. *Dodekapropheton 4: Micha.* BK 14,4. Neukirchen-Vluyn: Neukirchener Verlag, 1982.

_____. "Schwerter zu Pflugscharen—Mißbrauch eines Prophetenwortes? Praktische Fragen und exegetische Klärungen zu Joël 4,9-12, Jes 2,2-5 und Mi 4,1-5," *EvTh* 44 (1984) 280–92. Reprinted in idem, *Studien zur Prophetie* (1987) 93–108.

_____. *Studien zur Prophetie: Probleme und Erträge.* ThB 76. Munich: Kaiser, 1987.

Wolff, Hans Walter, ed. *Probleme biblischer Theologie: Gerhard von Rad zum 70. Geburtstag.* Munich: Kaiser, 1971.

Wyk, Wouter C. van., ed. *The Exilic Period: Aspects of Apocalypticism.* OTWSA 25 [1982] and 26 [1983]. Pretoria: University of Pretoria, 1984.

Zenger, Erich. "Ps 87,6 und die Tafeln vom Sinai," in Josef Schreiner, ed., *Wort, Lied und Gottesspruch, II* (1972) 97–103.

_____. "'Dem vergänglichen Werk unserer Hände gib Du Bestand!' Ein theologisches Gespräch mit dem 90. Psalm," in Raimon Panikkar and Walter Strolz, eds., *Die Verantwortung des Menschen für eine bewohnbare Welt* (1985) 11–36.

_____. "Der Gott Abrahams und die Völker. Beobachtungen zu Psalm 47," in Manfred Görg and Augustin R. Müller, eds., *Die Väter Israels* (1989) 413–30.

_____. "Israel und Kirche im einen Gottesbund? Auf der Suche nach einer für beide akzeptablen Verhältnisbestimmung," *KuI* 6 (1991) 99–114.

_____. "Israel und Kirche im gemeinsamen Gottesbund: Beobachtungen zum theologischen Programm des 4. Psalmenbuchs (Ps 90–106)," in Marcel Marcus, et al., eds., *Israel und Kirche heute* (1991) 236–54.

_____. "Asaf/Asafiten," *LThK* 1 (1993) 1052–53.

_____. "Die Bundestheologie—ein derzeit vernachlässigtes Thema der Bibelwissenschaft und ein wichtiges Thema für das Verhältnis Israel–Kirche," in idem, ed., *Der Neue Bund im Alten* (1993) 13–49.

_____. "'So betete David für seinen Sohn Salomo und für den König Messias.' Überlegungen zur holistischen und kanonischen Lektüre des 72. Psalms," *JBTh* 8 (1993) 57–72.

_____. "Der Psalter als Wegweiser und Wegbegleiter: Ps 1–2 als Proömium des Psalmenbuchs," in Arnold Angenendt and Herbert Vorgrimler, eds., *Sie wandern von Kraft zu Kraft* (1993) 29–47.

_____. "Zur redaktionsgeschichtlichen Bedeutung der Korachpsalmen," in Klaus Seybold and Erich Zenger, eds., *Neue Wege der Psalmenforschung* (1994) 175–98.

_____. "Die Gotteszeugenschaft des 83. Psalms. Anmerkungen zur pseudo-theologischen Ablehnung der sogenannten Fluchpsalmen," in Matthias Lutz-Bachmann, ed., *Und dennoch ist von Gott zu reden* (1994) 11–37.

_____. "Juden und Christen doch nicht im gemeinsamen Gottesbund? Antwort auf Frank Crüsemann," *KuI* 9 (1994) 39–52.

_____. *Das Erste Testament. Die jüdische Bibel und die Christen.* 4th ed. Düsseldorf: Patmos, 1994.

Zenger, Erich, ed. *Der Neue Bund im Alten: Studien zur Bundestheologie der beiden Testamente.* QD 146. Freiburg: Herder, 1993.

_____, ed. *Die Tora als Kanon für Juden und Christen.* HBS 10. Freiburg: Herder, 1996.

Zenger, Erich: see also Hossfeld, Frank-Lothar.

Zimmerli, Walther. *Erkenntnis Gottes nach dem Buch Ezechiel. Eine theologische Studie.* AThANT 27. Zürich: Theologischer Verlag, 1954. Reprinted in idem, *Gottes Offenbarung* (1963) 41–119.

_____. "Sinaibund und Abrahambund: Ein Beitrag zum Verständnis der Priesterschrift," *ThZ* 16 (1960) 268–80. Reprinted in idem, *Gottes Offenbarung* (1963) 205–16.

_____. "Das Wort des göttlichen Selbsterweises (Erweiswort), eine prophetische Gattung," in idem, *Gottes Offenbarung* (1963) 120–32.

_____. *Gottes Offenbarung: Gesammelte Aufsätze zum Alten Testament.* ThB 19. Munich: Kaiser, 1963.

_____. "Zwillingspsalmen," in Josef Schreiner, ed., *Wort, Lied und Gottesspruch, II* (1972) 105–13.

Zmijewski, Josef, ed. *Die alttestamentliche Botschaft als Wegweisung: Festschrift für Heinz Reinelt.* Stuttgart: Katholisches Bibelwerk, 1990.

Zyl, Albertus H. van. "Psalm 23," in *Studies on the Psalms: Papers Read at 6th Meeting of Die Ou Testamenties Wergemeeskap in Suid-Afrika Held at the Potchefstroom University for C.H.E., 29–31 January, 1963.* Potchefstroom: OTWSA, 1963, 64–83.

General Index

Selective Index of Biblical Citations